Controversies in Digital Ethics

Controversies in Digital Ethics

Edited by
Amber Davisson and Paul Booth

Bloomsbury Academic
An imprint of Bloomsbury Publishing Inc

B L O O M S B U R Y
NEW YORK · LONDON · OXFORD · NEW DELHI · SYDNEY

Bloomsbury Academic
An imprint of Bloomsbury Publishing Inc

1385 Broadway   50 Bedford Square
New York   London
NY 10018   WC1B 3DP
USA   UK

www.bloomsbury.com

BLOOMSBURY and the Diana logo are trademarks of Bloomsbury Publishing Plc

First published 2016

Library of Congress Cataloging-in-Publication Data
Controversies in digital ethics / edited by Amber Davisson and Paul Booth.
pages cm
Includes bibliographical references and index.
ISBN 978-1-5013-1056-0 (hardback : alk. paper) 1. Mass media—Moral and ethical aspects.
2. Digital media—Moral and ethical aspects. I. Davisson, Amber L., editor. II. Booth, Paul,
1981–editor.
P94.C77 2016
175—dc23
2015028754

ISBN: HB: 9781501310560
ePDF: 9781501310539
ePub: 9781501310546

Typeset by Deanta Global Publishing Services, Chennai, India
Printed and bound in the United States of America

Contents

List of Illustrations

Acknowledgments

Editing a book about ethics makes acknowledgments a thorny issue: ethically, we should probably thank every person who has helped us over the past year. But since that would fill more than a hundred times the pages you hold in your hands, we shall have to resort to the simpler—but no less heartfelt—thank you to you all. You know who you are, and we appreciate it.

Our sincerest thanks to all our contributors. We couldn't be happier with the incredible work ethic, interest, scholarship, and engaged discussions demonstrated by all of you. We are so grateful for your continued work, even when you thought the final draft was actually going to be a final draft. We are especially grateful to Charles Ess, who not only helped introduce the field of digital ethics to us, but also very graciously offered to write our afterword.

Paul would like to acknowledge his colleagues in Communication at DePaul University, who continually remind him that being ethical is a way of a life. He would also like to thank Katie Booth, with whom every day is better than the one before, and his loving colleagues Slinky, Rosie, Gizmo, and Black Kitty Booth.

Amber would like to acknowledge her academic colleagues who reside at other universities, and who are constantly using digital technology to reach out and offer support. A particular debt of gratitude is owed to Angela Leone, Shira Chess, and Hillary Ann Jones, whose encouragement provides the motivation to see projects like this through to the end. She would also like to thank Christopher Wood, who is always available with a listening ear and kind words, and her constant work companion Macey Allen Davisson.

Introduction to *Controversies in Digital Ethics*

Amber Davisson and Paul Booth

While the study of ethics in communication and philosophy has a long history, interest in media ethics in terms of technology in particular has increased since the 1980s (German and Drushel 2011; Ess 2013; Patterson and Wilkins 2013; Wilkins and Christians 2009). Scholars have addressed the fact that changing media formats raise ethical questions for communication professionals working in a variety of fields—including journalism, advertising, public relations, politics, and media entertainment. While much of the conversation in media ethics has focused on the need to equip communication professionals with the necessary tools to make moral decisions, a parallel discussion has developed in the field of media literacy surrounding the need to train media consumers. Media literacy does not focus on ethics *per se*, but in the process of teaching people to evaluate and analyze messages, it deals with many of the same ethical challenges and promises as those within professional communication. Digital technology blurs the line between producer and consumer in a way that calls for an approach to media ethics that deals with the two roles simultaneously.

This edited collection offers consumers and producers, teachers and students, and scholars and readers an overview of ethical thinking in the digital age through specific case studies about contemporary ethical situations, as well as suggestions for dealing with the ethical issues they encounter using digital technology. Ethical issues arise as digital communication technology has created an overlap between the categories of media consumers and producers, and individuals not employed as communication professionals routinely take to the internet to distribute user-generated content, participate in acts of citizen journalism, provide free advertising, or take part in cooperative communities that design and code software. Conversely, communication professionals often face ethical questions as their content circulates through the same media formats as content created by individuals they previously thought of as audience members. This collection seeks to understand some of the ways digital technology alters conversations about ethics by highlighting these shifts in media production and consumption.

Of key ethical concern for many media producers in the digital age is the ever-increasing power of consumer participation. As the availability and growing popularity of digital technology and social media reveals, new interactions with the media herald changing conceptions of media presence and participatory culture. In their edited collection about participatory cultures, Delwiche and Henderson (2012) discuss the growing trend of "people of all ages and backgrounds . . . [becoming] increasingly active and engaged" in the creation and development of digital technology (3). They argue that "our world is being transformed by participatory knowledge," and scholarship of participatory culture has extended our understanding of the key tools and audiences of this transformation. Since the mid-1980s, Delwiche and Henderson argue, academic studies of participatory cultures have developed in four different phases (3–4): Emergence, Web Studies, Push-button Publishing, and Ubiquitous Connections. But as researchers we need to be cautious to not ignore the growing need for discussions of ethics in participatory cultures as well. For new media researchers like Henry Jenkins, et al. (2009), participation in the media environment is a meaningful step in the development of children's education, but such a step comes with what they call "the ethics challenge": Any participatory turn in media education cannot assume that "children, on their own, can develop the ethical norms needed to cope with a complex and diverse social environment online" (15). Indeed, they argue, any attempt to "provide meaningful media education in the age of participatory culture must begin" by addressing ethics (along with issues in participation and transparency, 16). The issue is one of education. In professional contexts, as the chapters throughout this book illustrate, "professional organizations [can be] the watchdog[s] of ethical norms" (Jenkins et al. 2009, 25). But,

> in a world in which the line between consumers and producers is blurring, young people are finding themselves in situations that no one would have anticipated a decade or two ago. Their writing is much more open to the public and can have more far-reaching consequences. Young people are creating new modes of expression that are poorly understood by adults, and as a result they receive little to no guidance or supervision. The ethical implications of these emerging practices are fuzzy and ill-defined. (25)

It is crucial for researchers and scholars in participatory cultures, as well as practitioners and professionals within media corporations and contexts, to understand and develop ethical frameworks to define the future of media interaction. If participatory cultures studies (Delwiche and Henderson 2012, 4) is going to develop a fifth phase, we would argue that ethics should be central to this contemporary era.

As the title indicates, the collection is directed toward controversies. The term *controversy* points toward ongoing disputes and heated conversations. As such, many of the essays in the collection do not seek to provide standard guidelines or direct answers to ethical questions. Instead, these essays point to the places where digital technology users are struggling to deal with innovations that make possible behaviors we had not previously worried about. For the ethics researcher, concrete answers are rarely easy, but through the discussion such issues generate, ethical considerations can be reflected. For instance, in a pre-digital world, violations of privacy largely involved human actors who surreptitiously observed their subjects. Digital technology makes it possible to engage not only in mass surveillance, but also to process the data from that surveillance in a way that no human actor previously could. Privacy violations by nonhuman actors, and on such a large scale, necessarily require a rethinking of the approach we take to the ethical issues surrounding surveillance.

Digital technology has expanded the human capacity to communicate in ways that raise previously unforeseen ethical quandaries. With that said, many of the authors in this collection draw their response to these controversies from well-established ethical frameworks. Philosophical conversations surrounding normative and deontological ethics, descriptive ethics, virtue ethics, humanism, and identity politics all provide frameworks for evaluating the issues that have emerged with digital media. The issue that is raised by this collection as a whole is not whether or not we need a new system for evaluating the way we use media. Instead, the controversies in this collection invite us to consider the issues that arise from our increased capacity to create, distribute, store, and process media. As technology extends our reach, we must continually evaluate and reevaluate the things we are reaching for.

Outline of the book

Our volume explores controversies in digital ethics in four parts. We begin, in Section 1, with a series of chapters dealing with privacy and digital surveillance. J. J. Sylvia's essay addresses the use of big data for advertising purposes, tracing the roots of modern surveillance back to the commodification of television audiences in a pre-digital age. The ability of companies to collect information that may be valuable for advertising purposes is increased by the ease with which multiple sources of data can now be combined. A company does not merely take information from Facebook and use it to advertise on the social networking site. They collect information from social networking sites like Facebook, from mobile phone apps, from third-party advertising companies using cookies to track behavior, and a variety of other sources. All that information is combined to create a complete picture of the consumer, and consumers can then be packaged and sold based on purchasing demographics. Sylvia's essay provides an overview of the massive scope of surveillance that has been undertaken in the name of digital marketing and advertising. Along the way, the essay raises serious questions about the ethical obligations of consumers to protect their data and the ethical practices of marketing firms who possess and collect the data.

Awareness of digital surveillance among internet users has increased greatly in recent years. In the 1980s and 1990s, scholars like Sherry Turkle (1984, 1995) touted the awesome power of anonymity online. In more recent years, major internet companies like Google and Facebook have actively pushed to associate internet users' offline identities with their online activities. Anonymity online has become increasingly difficult. Two essays in this collection deal directly with the consequences of this decrease in anonymity. In an essay on surveillance and digital journalism, authors Mary Grace Antony and Ryan J. Thomas discuss the impact of digital surveillance on professors in the classroom. The ubiquity of cell phone cameras has made it easy to record events as they happen and post them online as news events. Antony and Thomas discuss the responses of professors after two prominent incidents of this form of surveillance in the college classroom. While many professors tout the importance of the activities of citizens, there is a reasonable fear that these kinds of behaviors will lead to self-censorship in the classroom. Amber Davisson, in her essay on Reddit users' distribution of images of women without their permission, discusses the impact of digital surveillance on the day-to-day lives of female internet users. Communities have developed on Reddit that collect and share sexually provocative images of women, such as creepshots. These pictures are taken on the street, collected from sites like Facebook, and even illegally obtained by hacking computers and cell phones. The result is an overall message to women, even those who have not had their images taken or distributed, that there is no safe place for the expression of sexuality. Constant digital surveillance by average netizens leads to the belief that individuals need to censor themselves continually or face potential public humiliation.

Digital surveillance practices are not limited to tracking the behaviors of average internet users. The power to collect and distribute seemingly private data has been used to play watchdog over government and corporate behaviors as well. Ryan Gillespie's essay deals with one prominent incident of this form of surveillance involving Julian Assange and Wikileaks. Julian Assange and his associates collected and distributed sensitive information about the US government. As Gillespie points out, the incident was easily identifiable as a national security threat, but it also took the form of the established American tradition of investigative journalism. The news industry has long dealt with ethical conflicts over the need to inform the public about government behavior and the awareness that some information needs to be withheld in the interest of public safety. What makes this incident all the more interesting is Assange's role as a citizen journalist, as opposed to someone working for a more traditional journalistic outlet.

Section 2 of the collection focuses on participatory culture. Participatory culture often involves the volunteer labor of large networks of individuals. Coordinating collaboration outside of official channels requires participants to develop both informal agreements and official codes of ethics to guide their behavior. Several chapters in this section consider the process by which these communities settle on moral and ethical guidelines. We begin this section with an essay from Brett Lunceford, which explores the way that hackers, who necessarily operate outside the law, develop codes of ethics to guide their participation in international politics. Lunceford's essay focuses on the work of two activists groups that responded to the World Trade Organization (WTO) through digital hacktivism. He invites us to consider how communities acting outside the mainstream deliberate about the values that guide their actions. Along these same lines, an essay by Tom Bivins and Matthew Pittman explores a group of volunteer programmers online who have worked collaboratively to create the game *Defense of the Ancients* (*DotA*). There is much debate about the ethics of game programmers. Bivins and Pittman discuss how those ethics are negotiated by a community of volunteer programmers. Furthermore, they address the implications the game design has for the development of virtue ethics among players. While the essay does not argue for an overarching code of ethics, it points strongly to the way that digital ethics is developed among communities in the process of making things. Conversely, Lucy Bennett, Bertha Chin, and Bethan Jones discuss the need for a more established code of ethics among members of digital fan communities. Their work points to conflicts between fan communities and the mainstream media industry.

The work of internet users can have an impact on the perception of the texts that those users borrow from and contribute to. This can be seen in Michelle Amazeen and Susan O'Sullivan-Gavin's essay on rogue advertising. Rogue advertisements are generally sensationalized, fake advertisements that are generated for real products and most commonly produced by established members of the advertising industry. In digital spaces, these advertisements are often circulated in a way that implies they were created in cooperation with or endorsed by the company whose product they are advertising. Amazeen and O'Sullivan-Gavin argue that making these advertisements, created in the name of self-promotion, violates the advertising industries' ethical obligations to clients. Journalism is another industry that has experienced problems with fakes. Shane Tilton discusses the ethical implications of fake news reports created by citizen journalists posting their work under the banner of official news outlets like CNN. Much as with the advertising industry, these news reports reflect on the credibility of an established brand. Because the reports are found on the CNN site, they seem to be endorsed by the news outlet. In both cases, user-generated content has a direct impact on mainstream media outlets.

Section 3 of the book deals with the impact of digital technology on ethics in professional communication. We begin with an essay from Sam Ford dealing with the development of ethical guidelines in the marketing and communication industry. Ford points out that much of early focus in these industries has been on the possibilities of new technology. Professional development organizations have focused their attention on workshops and conferences that provide information for industry leaders about capitalizing on new developments. The focus often comes with a lack of conversation about the ethical implications of those new developments. Ford points to several places where this very narrow view of technological progress in the industry has had negative consequences, and he calls for the development of professional guidelines to deal with the persistent emergence of new communication technology.

With that call to arms in mind, we have a series of chapters that explores the implications of these new technologies for political strategists, journalists, and video game designers. Luis Hestres invites us to consider the ethical issues facing political strategists adopting digital technology for campaign purposes. Strategists use social networking sites like Facebook and simple mailing list to collect information about voters and target specific voting populations. What is seldom discussed are the ethical obligations these strategists have when a campaign ends and they move on to their next endeavor. Who owns the information collected by a campaign? Is it right to transport that data to the next campaign? Beyond protecting data, Hestres considers the way that strategists shape the digital public sphere. As more individuals move their political action online, we must consider the role the campaigns play in dictating what constitutes meaningful participation in the public sphere.

Digital technology has led to numerous changes in the economic infrastructure that supports journalism and the day-to-day practices of journalists. Joe Cutbirth, in his essay on nonprofit news sites, outlines the ethical concerns behind the question of who funds journalism online. Sites like *ProPublica* and the *Texas Tribune* have moved away from subscriptions and ad sales as primary sources of revenue. Instead, these news organizations work as nonprofits—receiving grants from major contributors and donations from site visitors. Journalism has a long history of working to create boundaries between those who report the news and those who fund news organizations. The focus is on creating unbiased news sources. Cutbirth details the way these new funding sources challenge those historical efforts.

While funding mechanisms for journalism are changing, the practice of being a journalist also appears to be undergoing some changes. Increasingly, digital news sources have fewer gatekeepers monitoring stories and more of a rush to report what is happening. The constant push to get the scoop can lead to a relaxation of standards surrounding reporting on a variety of minority groups. Susan Wildermuth discusses recent controversies surrounding news media coverage of members of the transgender community. Specifically, she focuses on the ethics of outing the physical sex organs of the subject of a news story. At its heart, the sensationalism of outing stories gets at the ethical tension between generating page views and deciding what is truly newsworthy. Sensationalism often drives internet traffic, but it does so at the expense of members of an already subjugated community. Wildermuth offers guidelines for how reporters should deal with media coverage of transgender subjects.

Many of the chapters in this section turn our attention to the way that professional practices are altered by digital technology. Ryan Rogers redirects our focus to those individuals designing digital technology. The impact of violent video games on minors has long been debated. Recent Supreme Court rulings offer guidelines and restrictions for the making and marketing of these games. Rogers's essay sorts through those rulings to discern what they mean for the ethical obligations of professionals within the video game industry to both consumers and to society at large.

Section 4 of the collection looks at the ethical issues involved with the development of identity in relationship to digital technology. David Gunkel begins the conversation with a discussion of the identity of the technology itself. Online, users increasingly find themselves interacting with a variety of forms of artificial intelligence and social robots. These "bots" shape the way we understand the information we consume and the human beings with which we interact. Gunkel invites the reader to reconsider traditional ethical approaches to digital technology by first rethinking the status of that technology as a tool. Instead, we should consider it an entity with which we interact.

The many social networking sites that make up digital spaces offer a variety of opportunities for individuals to interact, mobilize, and distribute information. Some of the positive potential of this space can be seen in Erin Watley's writing on the YouTube series *The Mis-Adventures of Awkward Black Girl*. Watley details the narrow image of Black women portrayed in mass media television shows. The YouTube series provides an image that is counter to many of the ones seen in mainstream media. More than that though, the YouTube platform serves as an important place for the audience to discuss the portrayal in the web series. Watley argues that the positive ethical potential of digital content is found not just in the new ideas that are spread but in the ways discussion is generated around those ideas.

Where Watley's essay provides a view of the positive potential of digital technology, the essays by Scott Stroud and by Molly Bandois and Paul Booth demonstrate some of the destructive potential of online spaces. In his essay on bullying on Twitter, Stroud discusses online groups that mobilize to out pedophiles on social networking sites. While arguably engaging in important acts of digital community policing, these groups also create a climate of violence online. The mob mentality of citizen policing groups has very few safeguards to keep it in check. For individuals who are misidentified as pedophiles, there is little they can do to protect their identity from the mob. Stroud's essay points to some of the dangers of digital organizing. In Bandonis and Booth's essay, they argue that the platforms where conversations take place may have their own ethical issues. In particular, their essay discusses ostensibly feminist conversations taking place on the Gawker Media site *Jezebel*. The comments section on the articles is designed to promote popular comments that will draw in more site readers. In their analysis, they argue that the elements that make a comment popular—humor or even trolling—are not conducive to the type of feminist discussion the site hopes to promote.

Historically, the primary users of technology have been thought of and portrayed, rightly or wrongly, as mostly male. That is particularly true in the video game industry, where the stereotypical vision of the market has been men under the age of thirty. In Shira Chess's essay, she addresses changes in the gamer demographic, and the failure of the industry to recognize that in their advertising practices. The past ten years have seen a shift, and for the first time the number of adult women gamers exceeds the number of teenage boy gamers in industry reports. Increasingly, the industry is seeing mothers who take up gaming, not just to play with their kids, but to fill up their leisure time. This essay compares an advertisement from the 1980s, which portrayed moms as fearful of video games, to advertisements from the 2000s that also feature mothers. Chess finds that, while the demographic of gamers shows more mothers gaming, advertisements from the gaming industry portray an even more hostile relationship between moms and video games than they did thirty years ago. Where the previous chapters in this section discuss the potential for dealing with identity issues through digital technology, Chess's essay indicates that our understanding of that technology is still firmly tied to larger issues in identity politics. We conclude with an afterword by renowned ethicist Charles Ess, focusing on the state of ethics in the digital age.

Individually, the essays in this collection offer a jumping off point for rich discussion on the variety of ways that digital technology has complicated our understanding of the ethical issues surrounding privacy, participatory culture, professional communication, and identity politics. Seen as a whole, the collection speaks to the way digital technology blurs the line between consumer and producer, and in the process, forces us to rethink our perspective on a variety of issues. We encourage instructors in ethics to frame each chapter with their students' own unique experiences, but never to ignore the larger ethical paradigms shaping our understanding of media and technology. While the ethical frameworks we use to make decisions remain largely unchanged, the controversies outlined in this collection indicate that the role of technology complicates those decisions in ways we are only beginning to understand.

Section One

Seeking Privacy in the Age of Digital Surveillance

1

Little Brother: How Big Data Necessitates an Ethical Shift from Privacy to Power

J. J. Sylvia IV

As our world increasingly becomes more and more datafied, we must understand how data is collected, who owns this data, how people make money from this data, and how all these changes affect our traditional understanding of privacy. Much of the data now being generated is related to individuals on a personal level. It can range from something basic, like what books he or she buys online and which websites he or she has visited, to the more advanced biometric data of the kind collected by those involved with self-tracking movements such as the quantified self, which is often collected using proprietary hardware and software that stores data on the cloud, thus clearly putting such data in the hands of businesses and their big databases. Traditionally these issues have been understood through ethical frameworks associated with notions of commodification and privacy. For example, one might hold a particular individual ethically responsible for willingly trading his or her data for access to websites. Alternatively, laws could be passed that allowed companies to only collect and/or use customer-generated data in very specific ways.

The ability of both people and organizations to leverage big data in new ways has rendered the traditional ethical frameworks for dealing with these issues ineffective and archaic. The leveraging of such data raises concerns beyond the questions of commodification and privacy to questions of power generated for businesses through the big data divide—the gap separating those who have access to big data and those who do not. Using big data undoubtedly does encroach on the privacy of consumers. However, because big data also offers so many benefits, it is difficult to craft any regulation that can uphold both consumer privacy and the beneficial outcomes of big data such as medical insights or breakthroughs. Traditional legal protections such as anonymization and notice and consent are rendered ineffective by big data. It also becomes difficult to hold an individual ethically responsible for trading his or her data for access, as this trade is necessary if one is going to participate in the contemporary technologically driven world. Although these ethical issues have historical roots in commodification, a new ethical framework is needed for the age of big data. Rather than focusing on privacy issues, big data can be better understood through the issue of power discrepancies created by the gap between those who have access to big data and those who do not. I argue that one ethical aspect of this shift is seeking more emancipatory and affirmative uses of big data.

Historical roots of commodification

The development of the commodification of big data can be traced to the emergence of the media audience as a product. Dallas W. Smythe (2012) helped usher in a view of the audience as a commodity that does labor, departing from traditional Marxist analyses that lump all press and their advertisements together with other superstructure organizations such as education. Advertisers are buying "the services of audiences with predictable specifications which will pay attention in predictable numbers and at particular times to particular means of communication (television, radio, newspapers, magazines, billboards, and third-class mail) in particular market areas" (188). Although not every audience member will be paying attention to every advertisement, the sheer volume of advertisements assures that, probabilistically, a large number of viewers will see each one. While on the surface it seems like audiences are simply trading their unpaid work time for program material and advertisements, a deeper examination reveals that the audience members are also paying for the ability to play these programs and advertisements through purchasing the viewing equipment, such as a television, in addition to a monthly cable fee. Smythe estimates that audience members in the United States paid three times more to watch programs and advertisements than the advertisers paid to place the ads (191–92).

What work is it that the audience is doing while watching advertisements? They are learning to buy goods! The audience, then, ends up paying for the privilege of doing work rather than being themselves remunerated. Smythe (2012) argues that through this understanding, every minute of one's life is commodified and used for work, be it in the traditional sense, or through restorative work such as eating and sleeping which prepares one for work the next day, or through one's labor time being sold as an audience commodity (197–200). Yet, this work being done as an audience does in some ways overlaps with the needs that arise in one's life. We all need to buy some type of soap to keep us clean, for instance. But what kind of soap should we buy? What scent? What brand? Multiply these questions by the hundreds of products a typical household will purchase in a month and it quickly becomes impossible to rationally research which decisions are best in all cases. Ultimately, this understanding of the audience doing work eliminates the clear distinction between Marxist understandings of base and superstructure. Media scholars (Andrejevic 2006, 2009; Cohen 2008; Terranova 2000; van Dijck 2009) have extended this notion of commodification to popular social media websites, going so far as to show how Google's targeted advertising system is able to commodify users at an individual, rather than an aggregate level. I will analyze how websites such as these utilize big data in this process of commodification, as well as its implications and challenges for traditional ethical frameworks.

Becoming big data

Smythe's (2012) understanding of the audience as a commodity can be extended to the modern use of big data in two distinct ways: first, through a richer commodification of data generated during "free" time; second, as a way to further extend audience segmentation in the service of driving impulse purchasing. Though Smythe is correct in pointing to the ways that all leisure time was commodified through the creation of audience and preparation for future work, the link was in many ways still relatively small. Through commodification of data related to daily experience, it is now possible to trace a direct link. To fully appreciate the power of big data, and the full extent to which it has been commodified, I will consider some concrete examples: (1) the way that Facebook has leveraged demographic, web browsing, and screen movement data for its advertising platform, (2) Verizon Wireless' usage of multi-device browsing and cell phone location data aggregation, and (3) BlueKai's use and aggregation of multiple big data sources for micro-targeted advertisements. These three cases will highlight the way that power discrepancies arise through these organizations' ability to collect and use large amounts of data that generates insight about how to induce action of viewers. Individuals typically do not have access to this data, and, further, do not know in exactly what ways such data is being used to manipulate action.

To start, there are many similarities between Smythe's (2012) analysis of the cost of advertising and the cost to consumers to maintain the devices on which the advertising is done. Users access Facebook through computers using traditional internet connections or via mobile smartphones or tablets. In many cases, the Facebook audience seamlessly switches the mode of access between these devices depending on their location. In such a case, they pay for computer and cell phone devices, as well as internet connections and mobile data plans. Although the service of Facebook itself is free, there are typically substantial costs incurred in the process of accessing the platform. Once able to access the platform, users still do the work of reading ads in Facebook. Further, the distinction between personal status updates and sponsored posts is precariously subtle. With traditional mass media, one might trade their viewing of advertisements for the entertainment of the content. With a site such as Facebook, the users are actually laboring further to create that entertaining content themselves.

Once a user creates a Facebook account, the system automatically begins to collect and commodify a large amount of data. The latest financial filings show that the average revenue per user in the United States and Canada is $5.85 (Petronzio 2014). Facebook generates this revenue by selling information to advertisers. First, there is the information that users willingly and knowingly input into their accounts: age, gender, hometown, etc. Additionally, by connecting with other people, one tells Facebook with whom they are friends. Each status update provides insight into his or her interests and behaviors. However, this information is only the beginning. Facebook offers its login system for use to other websites and applications via a standard software development kit (SDK). This allows Facebook users to easily log in, interact with, and comment on a wide variety of sites and applications without creating separate login credentials for each of them. This added benefit to the user comes at the cost of allowing Facebook knowledge of one's visits to each of these sites, effectively giving Facebook the ability to understand one's internet browsing habits over a wide variety of websites. Even if a user is not currently logged in to Facebook, or does not use the Facebook log-in function on other websites, Facebook, like most major sites, places tracking software in the form of cookies on the user's computer to collect data. Even a user who does not have a Facebook account, but visits a partner site associated with Facebook, will generate a cookie that will collect anonymous aggregated data (Facebook Help Center 2014).

Facebook uses this type of personal information to help sell advertisements by segmenting audiences, often through connecting with other large datasets.

A few examples given on the Facebook advertising page help explain how this process works. First, and most obviously, advertisers could use information you have already provided them to market to you, for example, a store might show ads to users who are already subscribed to their newsletter (Facebook 2014). Additionally, Facebook allows marketers to use other information they have on consumers to direct advertisements at them. Two examples highlight just how complex this process can be. First, it might allow companies to display ads to users who have previously visited their websites. Additionally, the advertisements may also be based on real-world shopping habits as well, as in a grocery store using rewards card information to promote a sale to all of its customers on Facebook who regularly purchase orange juice (Facebook 2014). In these ways, Facebook makes it quick and easy to sell advertisements to very specific audiences, based not just on information one has intentionally entered into the site, but based on other activities such as websites that have been visited and purchases that have been made at stores.

On top of this, Facebook takes advantage of big data to extend its mastery of impulse buying or—perhaps more accurately in this case—impulse clicking. The social networking site is able to track and record all of the actions users take on its website, including things as detailed as how long the mouse hovers in a certain position and which part of a website is visible on the screen. This information can be used for a wide range of purposes, but has been specifically leveraged to develop targeted advertising (Rosenbush 2014).

This type of tracking extends traditional A/B and multivariate testing of websites to much greater on-page analytic capabilities. A/B and multivariate testing makes it possible for a website to create two or more versions (A and B, etc.) of a particular web page and test the effect of the differences between them on a desired outcome. For example, a store might test which version of a web page leads to more completed sales or a greater number of newsletter subscriptions. Generally only one element of each page is changed in A/B testing, for example, the color of a link, while multiple components are changed in a multivariate test. Each of these little bits of data adds up to a bigger picture of user behavior. Leveraging big data analytics to understand this behavior and its correlation to desirable behaviors such as ad clicking allows for Facebook to fine-tune the way its pages are displayed, certainly overall but even on a user-by-user basis. Not only is the consumer directly generating all of the content that draws other users to Facebook, but also his or her movements on the site are being datafied and sold to advertisers. Consumer labor is more robustly than ever a source of profit

(Andrejevic 2002). Facebook uses this data collection and tracking primarily so that it can sell advertising that is used to manipulate consumers into taking some action, ranging from following another Facebook page to purchasing items on a third-party site.

Verizon wireless creates an interesting question of privacy, as it extends the issue across multiple devices. If Verizon Wireless customers use a computer to access their Verizon account, the website automatically, and without consent or notice, installs a tracking cookie that tracks all of the user's web browsing—web browsing done on devices that do not use even Verizon's service (Lazarus 2014). This data can then be sold to marketers and used across platforms and devices: "So, by way of example, let's say you enjoy watching videos on the Victoria's Secret website on your personal computer in the privacy of your home. You shouldn't be surprised if ads for women's undergarments start appearing on your Verizon Wireless mobile device" (Lazarus 2014).

Though this type of data collection for commodification is similar to that of Facebook, Verizon is able to add an additional level of information that includes a consumer's location. Verizon's Precision Marketing Insights division has successfully partnered with the National Basketball Association team the Phoenix Suns in order to use location data for marketing:

> Verizon uses that granular location data to keep track of which Verizon Wireless-enabled devices were in a sports arena, or near it, or at a particular fast food restaurant or car dealership. Though Verizon holds on to that device-identifiable data, it provides a more general view to its clients after "hashing" or anonymizing the data. Clients like the Suns end up with aggregated data on the types of people who visited a venue and later visited a sponsor's place of business. Verizon layers on Experian profile data to segment consumers demographically. For example, it can report which percentage of an audience segment who attended a game then visited a sponsor's burger joint at a particular time on a given day afterwards. (Kaye 2013)

In this example, Verizon is able to determine how many people were exposed to an advertisement in one location, and then physically visited a location related to the advertising. The physical movement associated with the leisure activities of watching a basketball game and having dinner are now directly commodified. Facebook is currently in the process of rolling out its own platform to allow for location-based advertising (Constine 2014). These location-based tracking systems extend the range of activities that companies can commodify, moving past indirectly commodifying leisure activities as preparation for work to the direct commodification of one's physical location in space, blending the personalization of online and physical locations in ways that echo the often-referenced ads in Steven Spielberg's film *Minority Report* (2002). Yet, the true potential of big data is only realized when multiple datasets are combined: "Corporations can exploit information precisely because they can aggregate it—because the information gains in value when it is placed within a larger information environment that individuals cannot access" (Andrejevic 2002, 258). It is no longer difficult to imagine the Phoenix Suns determining which advertisements to display at each night's game based on an aggregated browsing history of the fans in the stands on that particular night.

Big data management organizations such as BlueKai and Exelate, as well, work to aggregate and sell this data as part of marketing strategies. On its website, BlueKai explains its partnership with thirty sources of big data and how each dataset can help customize micro-targeted advertising (BlueKai 2014). One of its partners, MasterCard Advisors, "analyzes the spending patterns across billions of anonymous transactions to segment like-spending patterns into anonymous groups called micro-segments" (61). Experian Marketing Services' "TrueTouch segmentation system offers 11 Touch-points to define the motivational messages that appeal to various audiences. Understanding Touch-points makes it possible for advertisers to align offers with the values and attitudes of the consumers they wish to reach, using language proven to resonate" (41). Acxiom offers demographic information (occupation, gender, education), real property data (home type, home value, length of residence), age, date of birth, income, net worth, and buying activity categorized by type based on purchase history information (7). Combining just these three datasets with information from Facebook would allow one to create a highly micro-targeted ad to someone who is known to buy a particular type of product, and provide the advertiser with language to which the consumer is particularly drawn.

What about combining the data of Facebook, Verizon, and BlueKai? BlueKai offers just such an example with their whitepaper, "A Top Wireless Telco Creates 6x Lift in Facebook Ad Performance & Reduces 3rd Party Data Costs 50%" (BlueKai 2013). The ability to leverage such vast amounts of information fundamentally alters the way we need to think about privacy and power. It represents what Andrejevic (2013) describes as an undemocratic shift in knowledge practices that creates a big data divide (21). Large national and transnational corporations are able to collect and/or purchase information that allows them to derive insights about the way individuals act and make decisions, which ultimately allows the corporations to tailor messages that are most likely to affect the decision-making process. Individuals do not have and cannot afford access to such data, and therefore to such knowledge. This data/knowledge gap forces us to rethink traditional notions of privacy. Companies are able to use information about individuals to craft persuasive messages that can be customized to a single individual. The ability to draw on such massive amount of information and create custom messages gives companies the ability to create manipulative messages on the individual level, all without the individuals being able to tell that the message and design has been customized or whether and what information about them has been used in crafting such a message.

The waning efficacy of privacy protection

Digital technology's datafication of society has long been characterized as a threat to privacy. President Barack Obama (2014) recently called for an overview of big data and surveillance in light of Edward Snowden's revelations regarding the National Security Agency's use of data for spying, casting the debate in just such a way: "The challenges to our privacy do not come from government alone. Corporations of all shapes and sizes track what you buy, store and analyze our data, and use it for commercial purposes." The discussion about the death of privacy is merely a red herring that masks a much larger argument about the changing character of the risks stemming from the power differential created by corporate control of information (Andrejevic 2002, 2004; Mayer-Schönberger and Cukier 2013). The nature of privacy has undergone a fundamental shift in the age of big data, and this shift requires a new way of thinking about how we access and control such information.

Historically, concern about data has been focused on its primary use, which occurs when an individual's data is used to make a decision specifically about that person. A traditional example of this is the way credit ratings are used to make lending decisions. When a bank is determining whether or not to lend money to someone, they will consider that person's individual, personal credit history. Insurance companies, on the other hand, tend to rely more on secondary uses of information. If statistics show that young males tend to get in to accidents most frequently, then the insurance company might charge higher rates to all young males, regardless of individual driving histories. Big data's most innovative insights tend to greatly extend these secondary uses of data, often by discovering unintuitive correlations. To take a hypothetic example: perhaps a mortgage company buys access to information about the web browsing habits of consumers and determines that shoppers who most often abandon their carts without completing a purchase are actually more likely to make mortgage payments on time. This information could then potentially be used to offer lower loan interest rates for certain consumers. In this example, information collected in one context is being used in an entirely new context—a context that might not have been imagined when the data was collected.

This shift from primary to secondary uses of data represents both the best and worst possibilities opened up by big data. Much of the popular reporting on big data tends to focus on privacy violation issues. Following our hypothetical example, one might argue that personal web browsing habits are private and should not be a factor in determining interest rates on loans. However, big data offers many opportunities for insights from secondary uses of data that can undoubtedly benefit society, such as predicting flu outbreaks, preventing fires in New York City, fraud prevention, and medical research (Mayer-Schönberger and Cukier 2013; Cate and Mayer-Schönberger 2013). Preventing secondary use in order to protect privacy would also eliminate the many beneficial uses of secondary data analysis. Additionally, traditional privacy laws that focus on the anonymization of data and the enforcement of notice and consent cannot prevent the negative uses of secondary data analysis.

One of the surprises of big data has been the ease with which it is possible to de-anonymize data. Mayer-Schönberger and Cukier (2013) offer two such examples involving anonymized data from Netflix movie ratings and from old America Online (AOL) search history. Anonymous Netflix ratings cross-referenced with named users on the IMDB.com website allowed for the Netflix user to be identified with only a few obscure ratings. Perhaps even more surprising was the ability of the *New York Times* to use AOL's anonymized search data to identify a particular person. They "cobbled together searches like '60 single men' and 'tea for good health' and 'landscapers in Lilburn, Ga' to successfully identify user number 4417749 as Thelma Arnold, a 62-year-old widow from Lilburn, Georgia" (Mayer-Schönberger and Cukier 2013, 154). Demonstrations such as these help us understand that as the amount of data increases, the ability to effectively anonymize the data decreases.

Notice and consent offers another strategy that has been complicated by the change in the quality of the risk wrought by big data. Rules related to notice and consent are largely based off resolutions created in 1980 by the Organization for

Economic Co-operation and Development (OECD) Privacy Guidelines. These guidelines offered the now standard model that requires users to be notified, usually during the sign-up process for a service or website, about what data will be collected and how it will be used. Yet, these guidelines have given rise to a proliferation of extremely long and technical privacy policies and notices, that by one account would take seventy-six working days for the average person to read all of those which applied to their activities (McGeveran 2014, 68–69). In 2012, Microsoft hosted a summit that brought together leaders across industries and disciplines to discuss the new challenges to privacy laws and possible ways to update the original OECD guidelines. The efficacy of notice and consent in the face of big data was challenged, argue Cate and Mayer-Schönberger (2013), primarily because in the context of the way big data is used, its value is not clear at the time it is collected, when notice and consent is normally required. Going back and getting consent from past users would be both costly and cumbersome, potentially preventing important benefits to both individuals and society that may stem from future uses of such data. Finally, they note that data is collected so often that it would be a burden to users to ask them to consent so frequently (76–78).

Notice and consent practices greatly hinder the secondary uses of data and the benefits that these uses offer. Big data is valuable precisely because it can combine data in new ways that were not known at the time of collection. Giving a robust notice that effectively explains all of the ways in which a website will use collected data is actually quite challenging.

Most major websites use third-party analytics software and/or advertising systems, which call for some exchange of user information if these tools are able to function at all. In light of these additional flows of data, truly informed notice and consent becomes even more improbable:

> To make an informed choice, users must fathom: (1) Which actors have access (which is not at all obvious); (2) What information they have access to (which varies significantly across actors); (3) What they do or may do with this information; (4) Whether the information remains with the publisher or is directly or indirectly conveyed to third parties; and (5) What privacy policies apply to the publisher as compared to the all the third parties, assuming these are even known to the users. (Barocas and Nissenbaum 2009, 5)

The flow of data facilitated by modern advertising platforms alone complicates the notion of notice and consent to such a degree that it is rendered nearly, if not completely, ineffective. For example, Barocas and Nissenbaum (2009) discovered that the *New York Times* website shared data with at least fourteen other organizations as part of their web service platform. Participants in the Microsoft summit were unable to determine any clear changes to the privacy guidelines that would allow for these secondary uses but still provide an effective protection to a traditional understanding of privacy. What are some possible protections that have been suggested?

In his earlier book *Delete*, Viktor Mayer-Schönberger (2009), in discussing the importance of forgetting, suggested that data should be created in such a way that it automatically deletes itself at some point in the future. This may be part of the initial notice and consent process between a consumer and service, but it could also be built explicitly into all files. For instance, when saving any file on one's own computer, a user could be prompted to enter an expiration date—a date that the file will automatically delete itself.

Though this proposal offers an interesting and creative solution, it is not ultimately effective. As Mayer-Schönberger (2009) himself suggests, the power divide between users and companies would likely nullify the effectiveness of such a change. Even now, most notice and consent operations have turned into a binary choice: either consent to these terms and conditions or do not use the service at all. Without inducement through legal structures, companies could easily extend the deletion period of data to such a length that it ultimately defeats the original purpose of the deletion. If Facebook, for example, sets a deletion period of 100 years, then most of the data uploaded would likely outlive its source. Yet, even if laws were changed to mandate shorter deletion periods of five, ten, or even twenty years, this process of deletion would negatively affect the many potential benefits of big data in much the same way as requiring companies to obtain consent for all future uses of data. Medical records being collected today could potentially be the data that allow for a cure to cancer to be developed thirty years down the road. The point is that we simply cannot know ahead of time exactly which data will be important and relevant.

In Mayer-Schönberger's more recent book *Big Data* (2013), this notion of deletion is no longer present. Instead, he and his coauthor Cukier suggest that we shift away from notions of protecting privacy to instead legislating responsible use of data. This shift in perspective also mirrored proposed changes to the OECD Privacy Guidelines that were discussed at the Microsoft summit (Cate and Mayer-Schönberger 2013). In the first guideline, the limits on data collection, as well as the requirement for notice and consent of the subject are removed. This shift is also in the third guideline, in which the specification of the purposes for which data is collected is removed, instead requiring that the purposes be lawful and available to users should they choose to look them up. In the fourth guideline, the uses of data are expanded nearly infinitely, so long as they are not harmful or inappropriate, as deemed by "society." In no case can consumers actually take action regarding the uses of their own data.

These shifts reflect exactly the change argued for by Andrejevic (2013)—a change from the framework of privacy to the framework of power. Rather than truly being guidelines for protecting the privacy of consumers, they instead more closely resemble guidelines for managing the power wielded by corporations. Interestingly, these guidelines are still framed in the context of privacy. Though these suggestions certainly move the conversation about updating the guidelines in a helpful direction, they are, on at least one level, still not very realistically useful. Much of the data storage and processing is now done in the cloud, meaning through distributed computing. Big data projects are especially likely to be done this way because individual computers are often not powerful enough to process such large amounts of information, giving rise to services such as Apache's Hadoop, which offers just such distributed computing. Cloud computing, in combination with website services being distributed to so many third-party organizations, means that data flows are frequently crossing many different borders spanning organizations, nations, and most importantly, legal frameworks. Even if the United States were to create strong laws as a dissuasion to using data, it seems likely that data-reliant organizations would find a welcoming home in other countries with less strict laws. This process might, for instance, mirror those transformations in online gambling. Though illegal in the United States, the servers are hosted in other countries, and still relatively accessible by US citizens.

Perhaps the most practical suggestion for how to deal with these changes is the one that simply gives up on notions of privacy protection altogether. Adam Thierer (2014) suggests that education efforts related to digital citizenship should model themselves after the awareness for online child protection efforts including "the importance of media literacy, awareness building efforts, public service announcements, targeted intervention techniques, and better mentoring and parenting strategies" (114). Thierer admits that these educational outreaches would simply help develop coping mechanisms and usher in new social norms. Rather than attempting to rescue privacy, this strategy helps make the public more aware of how data is being used, which is doubtless a laudable goal. These discussions make it clear that traditional ethical frameworks related to privacy are no longer effective due to the extended uses of big data. It becomes important to move away from an ethical framework related to privacy and instead focus on the issues related to power.

The ethics of the growing power gap

Despite events such as Microsoft's Privacy Summit and Stanford Law School's Big Data and Privacy Workshop, no true privacy protections have emerged that also leave room for the beneficial uses of big data. Our traditional notions of privacy seem archaic from this perspective. While there will likely remain a place for laws to protect the most egregious privacy violations, notions of what we consider private are undergoing significant change. What we are left with instead is the difference in power between those who have access to data and those who do not. Who has access?

> Big data sensors and big data pools are predominantly in the hands of powerful intermediary institutions, not ordinary people. Seeming to learn from Arab Spring organizers, the Syrian regime feigned the removal of restrictions on its citizens' Facebook, Twitter, and YouTube usage only to secretly profile, track, and round up dissidents. (Richards and King 2014)

Here the apparently open and liberating tools were used instead as a means of surveillance. Yet, the use of social media by protestors is a continually evolving battle. More recently in Kiev, cell phones were used as means to identify protestors in a specific geographic region and send an ominous warning. Rather than the hoped-for chilling effect of this message, it seemed instead to further fuel the embodied protests.

How might this struggle play out down the road? Andrejevic (2013) offers an example of a potential worst-case use for big data:

> At its most dystopian, the resulting information landscape is one in which those with access to the database can derive practical, if probabilistic ("post-comprehension"), knowledge about how best to influence populations while members of these population are left with an outmoded set of critical tools that, in practice, can be pitted against one another's worldview, but which have little purchase on the forms of knowledge turned back upon them by database-driven apparatuses of influence. In somewhat more concrete terms, this dystopia would be one in which political parties, for example, might use giant databases to exert influence in the affective register (by determining which

appeals result in triggering desired voting behavior), overleaping the tangle of "reality-based" policy analysis, verification, and so on. This asymmetry would free up politicians to engage in "infoglut" strategies in the discursive register (promulgating reports that contradict themselves endlessly, pitting "expert" analysts against one another in an indeterminate struggle that does little more than fill air time, or perhaps reinforce preconceptions) while simultaneously developing new strategies for influence in the affective register. Fact-checkers would continue to struggle to hold politicians accountable based on detailed investigations of their claims, arguments, and evidence, while politicians would use data-mining algorithms to develop impulse- or anxiety-triggering messages with defined probabilities of success. (154)

Andrejevic imagines a future where big data-driven decision-making is able to sway easily the population at large without their having realized it. The growing power gap is potentially of much larger concern than lost privacy. Behind the scenes, politicians would be pulling the strings that actually drive actions, while the public sphere as we might understand it today would be filled with talking heads that serve only to further confuse the true state of things. One might just as easily imagine corporations using big data in the same way—finding the best ways to sell new products by commodifying data collected from consumers. Practices such as these are already happening today, but the data gap is one that continues to grow larger. How can we deal with this power discrepancy?

The ethical framework arising out of this shift will need to wrestle with complex questions such as who gets access to data and how to differentiate between good and bad uses of that data. Some of these cases will be clear. Predicting the spread of the flu in order to better allocate flu vaccines is clearly a good use, while altering Facebook feeds to sway an election is clearly a problematic use. I am arguing that examining the more nuanced cases will be made easier if they are viewed through the ethical framework of power rather than privacy.

Conclusion

This chapter has examined how an understanding of the commodification of consumers grew from television through the rise of big data. Both Facebook and Verizon Wireless' use of big data commodifies a great amount of information collected from different areas of users' lives, including friendships, physical attendance of sporting events, and leisure-related internet browsing activities. Considering the activity through the perspective of political economy, which remains quite relevant, bolsters this understanding of commodification. New digital tools make it easier than ever for advertisers to collect and make use of this information, not only in selling advertisements, but in manipulating the advertisements themselves in ways that make its viewers all the more likely to impulsively click and purchase.

While it is true that large corporations and governments currently have more access to and ownership of big data repositories, framing the discussion in such all-or-nothing dystopian language seems unnecessarily pessimistic. Instead we might embrace the Deleuzian notion that "a technology is always part of an assemblage that contains the possibility of both emancipation and capture" (Savat 2009, 8) and seek ways to use big data that are emancipating. Many sources of big data are either actually or potentially available to individuals. Corporations often use social networking sites such as Twitter and Facebook as a source of big data that can be used for projects such as sentiment analysis. Moderate programming skills and a small investment in Amazon Web Hosting services can enable this sentiment analysis to be completed by any individual. In theory, these skills and services are open to anyone willing to take the time to learn to do such analysis. Such skills could be part of the media literacy education advocated by Thierer (2014), as an understanding of how such analyses works can lead to a stronger awareness of how one's own data is being used by others.

Endeavors such as citizen science projects also open up the possibility of both creating and analyzing data sets to individuals. Although citizen science projects have so far been primarily propagated by research departments at universities, such as the Your Wild Life project at North Carolina State University, there is no significant barrier that would prevent an individual from creating a project. These projects rely on participants from around the world to collect, submit, and/or analyze data, and can often generate extremely large datasets. Lea Shell, digital media curator for the Your Wild Life Team and the Rob R. Dunn Lab at North Carolina State University, explained this impact to me in a conversation on April 29, 2014: "We can do in one week through social media what used to take a scientist an entire lifetime of traveling and collecting data." Projects such as these invariably take time and dedication to launch, but the point is that they are doable.

Rather than dwelling too long on the problems of privacy and power, it may ultimately be more beneficial to simply be creative and productive. One can ask:

how can I, as an individual, leverage data in ways that will improve the world or the lives of others? How can the internet facilitate new and creative ways to think about and interact with the world? Such actions will not restore privacy or entirely eliminate the power of corporations and governments, but in the long run, they just might help reduce the data gap and related power gains.

2

"The classroom is NOT a sacred space": Revisiting Citizen Journalism and Surveillance in the Digital Classroom

Mary Grace Antony and Ryan J. Thomas

In September 2013, a Michigan State University creative writing professor achieved instant notoriety when a cell phone video depicting him ranting against Republicans in class surfaced online. William Penn was unaware that he was being recorded by one of his students when he described Republicans as "closet racists" who had "already raped this country and gotten everything out of it they possibly could" (DeSantis 2013a). Although initially suspended from teaching, Penn was later reinstated and assigned courses for the spring semester. This incident has prompted increased attention to faculty responsibilities and the impact of social media on teaching and learning (DeSantis 2013b). Six months later in February 2014, eighteen-year-old Kyle Brooks, a student of the University of Wisconsin–Whitewater secretly recorded Eyon Biddle, Sr., a guest lecturer in his general education class ("Individual and Society"), as he attributed the results of the contentious 2010 congressional elections to "white rage." Biddle argued that this Republican victory was predicated on "white people having to pay for health care for blacks and browns and gays" (Schmidt 2014).

Both videos were uploaded and promoted by Campus Reform, a self-described "watchdog to the nation's higher education system . . . [that] exposes bias and abuse on the nation's college campuses" (Campus Reform 2014). Campus Reform is a project of the Leadership Institute, a "non-partisan educational organization college news source." This conservative organization envisions itself as an agent of social change and aspires to the journalistic ideal of a watchdog press. However, Campus Reform and similar organizations have been criticized for pursuing an ideological "social media blitzkrieg" (Kuykendall and Nails 2013, 9) against academics, chilling free speech and academic freedom. Given this, do the self-assumed labels of a "news source" and "watchdog"—as Campus Reform touts itself—necessarily imply that such actions constitute citizen journalism?

Clearly, access to smartphone technology has empowered audiences to record and share images and videos on matters of self-evident public interest, as perhaps best evidenced by vigilant citizens utilizing their cell phone cameras and the video-sharing website YouTube to expose police brutality in the death of the unarmed Oscar Grant in Oakland, California (Antony and Thomas 2010). Citizens have also provided footage of atrocities from war zones (Wedeman 2014) and of teachers and school officials physically abusing young students (LiveLeak 2014). Such user-generated content (UGC) is refashioning the relationship between the journalist and their audience in some fundamental ways (Rosen 2008). We take the normative perspective that function, not form, ought to be the criterion by which journalism is defined. Some of the rhetoric around citizen journalism—such as the notion that "we're all journalists now," to quote a recent author (Gant 2007)—emphasizes the *citizen* to the detriment of *journalism*. It remains important to ascertain how audiences interpret UGC and the criteria by which they ascribe journalistic categorization to such content.

Scholars have illuminated the perspectives of those who create UGC (Robinson and DeShano 2011; see, e.g., Holton, Coddington, and Gil de Zúñiga 2013) and those of traditional journalists in response (see, e.g., Canter 2013; Hermida and Thurman 2008). However, there is little literature to date on the extent to which audiences regard UGC as journalistic, as well as the antecedents to these interpretations. Examining audience perspectives is a valuable tool for scholars interested in the meaning-making processes by which publics interpret the world around them and engage with issues relevant to their particular communities.

Some may deem Campus Reform's videos unlikely exemplars of citizen journalism. After all, popular instances of citizen journalism are indelibly linked with political scandals, civic abuse, police brutality, and war crimes. Yet we argue that these particular incidents warrant critical attention precisely because they reflect the increasing prevalence and ubiquity of the citizen "journalist" in mundane everyday contexts, such as university classrooms. Accordingly, we analyze audience responses to the cases highlighted above to delineate how *particular* audiences on *particular* forums ascribe *particular* interpretations to UGC. Specifically, can an act of digital surveillance be construed as citizen journalism? In a technology-saturated environment where the boundaries of what constitutes journalism are seemingly difficult to draw, what are the conditions by which audiences recognize "citizen journalism" as "journalism," and how do these connect with normative conceptions of journalism's role in a democracy?

Roles and responsibilities of journalism

Journalism emerges out of a prevailing social system and therefore inevitably takes on the character of that social system (Baker 2002; Siebert, Peterson, and Schramm 1963). Much has been written about the functions of journalism in a democracy. Indeed, the multitude of functions that are associated with journalism can be attributed to the simple fact that there is no single, linear definition of democracy itself (Baker 2002; Allen and Hindman 2014). Consequently, journalism serves plural functions, meeting different democratic needs in various ways. As a result of this close relationship between journalism and democracy, the aggregate of these functions ultimately serves to ensure the ongoing vitality and viability of self-governance (McChesney 2012).

Though scholars differ on the precise number of normative functions that journalism serves, some common ground has nonetheless emerged. Craft and Davis (2013) point to five key functions of journalism in a democracy. First, it *informs*. This is where journalism provides "information of all kinds about current and recent events, plus warnings about future developments" (Christians et al. 2009, 125). Second, it *investigates*, exposing acts of wrongdoing through journalistic endeavor. This function casts journalism as "a relentless adversary of the powerful" (Ettema and Glasser 1998, 64). Third, it *creates a public conversation* by providing the conditions that allow for a robust public sphere where citizens can engage with the major issues of the day. Fourth, it helps *generate social empathy* by connecting citizens to one another and illuminating aspects of our society to which we would not otherwise be exposed. Finally, journalism *encourages accountability*. This is akin to the classic notion of journalism as a "Fourth Estate" working to safeguard and ensure the honesty of other institutions. Journalism thus provides the "checking value" against powerful interests that society needs (Blasi 1977).

The extent to which journalism has been able (or, indeed, willing) to fulfill these functions remains a matter of academic contention and debate. However, it is clear that journalism as an institution has long held a monopoly over its terrain, reserving and upholding these functions for itself alone. Recent technological innovations, occurring within a turbulent economic context, have disrupted that monopoly. This begs the question of how audiences interpret definitions of journalism—and, correspondingly, journalism ethics—in a changing media environment.

Interpretations of citizen journalism

Recent innovations in communication hardware and software, and their accessibility, have made it possible for ordinary citizens to create, edit, and share their own media, or, to use the academic parlance, their "user-generated content" (see, e.g., Holton, Coddington, and Gil de Zúñiga 2013). The tools that were once wielded exclusively by journalists and assorted other media professionals are now broadly available to everyday citizens, moving from a "technology for a privileged few, to essentially a mainstream technology" (Castells et al. 2004, 5). Audiences now have the capacity to create their own journalism, and journalistic merit is increasingly determined by the extent to which content invigorates the public sphere. This is the essence of "citizen journalism," defined by Bowman and Willis (2003) as

> the act of a citizen, or a group of citizens, playing an active role in the process of collecting, reporting, analyzing and disseminating news and information . . . [in order to] provide independent, reliable, accurate, wide-ranging and relevant information that a democracy requires. (9)

Similarly, Carpenter (2010) defines a citizen journalist as "an individual who intends to publish information online meant to benefit a community" (1064). These definitions are born out of normative assumptions over what journalism consists of, which are held to be applicable regardless of the individual behind it and which reinforce arguments made by organizations like the Electronic Frontier Foundation (in the context of media shield laws) that we ought to focus on defining *journalism* and not *journalists* (see, e.g., Weiland 2013).

The process of drawing dividing lines is deceptively simple, yet laden with "serious ethical, legal, and craft ramifications" (Black 2010, 103). The traditional definition, where journalists were those individuals employed by news organizations, has been thrown into jeopardy by the ability of ordinary citizens to create and share their own news and subvert the "we write, you read" model of traditional journalism (Deuze 2003, 220). At the same time as this technological shift, scholars have expressed caution in allowing the boundaries of the field—or, at least, its definitional boundaries—to become too diffuse and thus eroded of meaning. Indeed, some argue that journalism ought to be defined on normative, rather than technological, grounds (Craft and Davis 2013; Black 2010; Meyers et al. 2012). In other words, journalism—regardless of who practices it—ought to comprise content that corresponds to long-standing journalistic norms while fulfilling its democratic prerogative to serve as "the eyes and ears of the people" (Hindman 1997, 3).

However, how scholars and journalists draw dividing lines between journalist/non-journalist and journalism/not-journalism is wholly separate from how audiences demarcate this terrain. On what grounds do publics, possessing varying degrees of media literacy (see, e.g., Potter 2004), identify and ascribe meaning to journalistic functions? And to what extent is journalism, by extension, expected to embody and uphold an ethical imperative to inform, stimulate public debate, promote social empathy, and encourage civic accountability? Elucidating these perceptions is an important aspect of understanding how audiences interpret media content and discern it as journalistic or non-journalistic. Furthermore, it directly addresses the definitional issues alluded to above; what if (as problematic as such a notion may seem), for all the scholarly and trade narrative around definitions, ultimately journalism exists in the eye of the beholder? Somewhat surprisingly, there is still very little literature on this topic, meaning that we know comparatively little about how audiences assign meaning to media content in a pluralized, diverse, and increasingly chaotic public sphere.

There are some exceptions to this prominent gap in the literature. Wahl-Jorgensen, Williams, and Wardle (2010) compared focus group findings of audience members to interviews with BBC producers and journalists. The study found audiences saw journalistic merit in news-based UGC (such as eyewitness accounts and live footage) but scorned opinion-based UGC. Similarly, Antony and Thomas' (2010) analysis of audience reactions to YouTube footage of police officer Johannes Mehserle's 2009 killing of unarmed African-American Oscar Grant found that audiences considered these cell phone videos journalistic, despite relatively trivial objections about the video quality. In doing so, they connected citizen journalism to the watchdog function of the press. How might other audiences connect normative functions of journalism to UGC, or alternatively reject the "journalism" of UGC as a result of its failure to adhere to these normative functions? Amid the tumultuous upheaval to traditional journalistic models, it increasingly falls upon the consumers of news content to determine and avow the journalistic validity of a citizen reporter. In other words, the audience affirms and situates particular acts as citizen journalism by ascribing particular motives to the "journalist," as well as assessing the contextual relevance and utility of the provided information. The "journalism" in citizen journalism may therefore be determined on the basis of its conformation with key journalistic functions.

Research goal and method

This research examines audience responses to Campus Reform's exposés of William Penn and Eyon Biddle, Sr. in an attempt to understand the extent to which these videos are perceived as citizen journalism. Specifically, we are interested in how the segment of the public sphere directly implicated through these videos responds to this event, and (in particular) the self-assumed watchdog imperative of the concealed cameraperson. To this end, we performed a qualitative textual analysis of audience comments, in the vein of prior research (Antony and Thomas 2010). These comments are an ideal data source to examine audience responses for two reasons. First, they are the product of an engaged media user, someone who is motivated to respond beyond passive media consumption. Second, as documented virtual interaction between digital users, online forums provide a particularly rich record of discussion within the public sphere as new users encounter and respond to other users' comments—sometimes over several days.

We gathered audience responses to news articles about both incidents from *The Chronicle of Higher Education* (hereafter, *The Chronicle*). This website published three related articles about the Michigan State University incident: two of these appeared in response to Penn's apology following the video's release online (DeSantis 2013a; Huckabee 2013), and a third was published two months later when Penn was reinstated as an instructor (DeSantis 2013b). Similarly, audience responses to the University of Wisconsin incident were collected from the news report published on *The Chronicle* (Schmidt 2014). These online discussion forums allow readers to post their responses to news events and also interact with one another. A total of 416 comments were posted to the three related articles about William Penn (319 comments, 90 comments, and 7 comments, respectively), and 139 comments were posted to news article about the University of Wisconsin incident. Any effort at generalization is limited by the self-selected readership of this relatively niche publication. Nonetheless, such an analysis provides valuable insight into how participating members responded to an issue of direct concern to their community and interacted with one another to make sense of: (a) the incidents themselves, as well as (b) the self-proclaimed citizen journalists who recorded and framed these incidents as instances of "bias and abuse on the nation's college campuses" (Campus Reform 2014).

In order to determine how this particular audience responded to the cell phone videos, we conducted a qualitative interpretive thematic analysis. This process involved the constant comparative approach (Glaser and Strauss 1967), and entailed multiple iterative readings of the comments in their entirety to establish context and the overall tone of the discourse. We then implemented open coding to identify dominant response categories among *The Chronicle's* users, looking for the ways in which these readers discerned or decried the journalistic utility of the videos. The next stage involved axial coding, during which we compared our results from the preceding stage, while looking for areas of overlap, intersection, and contrast within the data (Lindlof and Taylor 2002). This facilitated the emergence of distinct categories, as themes coalesced and developed around specific foci of interest. For instance, some comments criticized the camerapersons for using intimidation tactics to forward their agenda, whereas others accused them of bias and the selective presentation of information. Considered together, however, both these subcategories essentially dismiss the videos as faulty evidence and thus diminish the audience's interpretation of the journalistic validity of these Campus Reform reporters. In this manner, we were able to identify the broader themes that characterized responses to these videos among the academic community. Eventually, a careful third reading accomplished the dual task of ensuring that the identified final categories were mutually distinct, while simultaneously confirming that these themes were representative of all available viewer responses to *The Chronicle's* news reports on the concealed video footage.

Our analysis revealed that responses to Campus Reform's cell phone recordings—that depicted classroom instructors engaging in tirades against the Republican Party—resolved into two broad categories. First, several users critiqued the videos, claiming that they were the product of a biased and unethical journalistic agenda. Second, others applauded this footage that exposed power abuse within higher education. The following sections explore these dominant themes in more detail, while supplementing them with data excerpts where relevant. In an effort to protect the identity of these contributors, all usernames have been replaced with pseudonyms.

Unfair and unbalanced reporting

Within the first category, *The Chronicle's* users attacked Campus Reform for their surreptitious tactics, accusing them of bias, selective editing, and a failure to provide adequate context in both situations. For example, defending Penn, user *ken30298* argued that "the university should not cave in to external pressures such as biased videos." *WesDunham4u* accused Campus Reform of deceit: "You guys do know how to twist the truth. Is YAF.ORG running workshops on Spin/Distortion/Purge these days?" Similarly, in another response to a comment that accused Democrats of waging a "war on women," this same user said, "Wow! Talk about YAF.ORG distortion of the facts." Campus Reform was also accused of pandering to their political agenda, and defenders of Penn critiqued Campus Reform for their "blitzing style," accusing them of being "neo-Brown Shirts" and trying to "force their opponents to speak with [Campus Reform's] voice." Another user, *atari434ever*, criticized the hidden cameraperson for lacking in integrity, saying the cameraperson should have debated Penn in the classroom instead of seeking to "expose" Penn by other means: "I would have rather seen the 'video recorder' have a debate with the professor—this is what college is for. Rather he tattled on him. These are apparently the values that are rewarded in our society." Other users, such as *whereisheaven*, pointed fingers at Campus Reform's selective editing that did not provide sufficient context for Penn's remarks within the classroom: "I suspect that if we watched a video of the rest of the class period instead of the scalped version put out by yet another group of mendacious righties, it would be clear what he was doing." For this user, the video needed to be understood in a broader context of political conflict, where "righties" did not police the boundaries of academic speech. Furthermore, by referring to the video as "scalped," this user alludes to the unethical foundations of the artifact (and we can infer, therefore, the journalist himself), thus directly confronting the ethical standards of this "journalistic" act. Penn, for this user and others, had been the victim of hypocritical and selective editing. *2837ioudy*, for example, asked: "Would Campus Reform have been as upset with this professor had he been similarly critical of liberals? Would they have applauded his punishment then?" This particular comment encapsulates the contributor's prerogative to protect the university classroom as a subsidiary of the public sphere, wherein opposing perspectives may engage one another in lively and spontaneous intellectual debate.

Similar concerns were evident in the University of Wisconsin incident, in which another Campus Reform representative captured a guest lecturer's unexpected tirade against the Republican Party on his cell phone. User *not1ofthem* criticized the fact that both this lecturer and the course instructor were unaware that the video was being created at the time, as well as that it was eventually utilized for "partisan purposes," concluding that "the fact that it was recorded surreptitiously suggests to me something less than an honorable intention." Voicing agreement, another user *kalis37th* noted that guest lecturers are seldom bound by the academic policies that apply to university employees, and therefore "guest lecturers should never be recorded without their explicit knowledge and permission." These commentators and others who shared this opinion (users *kwuc5283* and *nwl9739*) thus concur that the Campus Reform reporter should not have made the recording without the prior awareness and approval of the speaker. In doing so, the selective presentation of information devoid of context suggests underhanded and less-than-noble motives. Some users argued that the cameraperson demonstrated impulsive and immature behavior by surreptitiously recording the lecture, rather than approaching the guest lecturer, instructor, or even university administration to express his sentiments. *Galathon* claimed that if the student had indeed "got legitimately offended by something a speaker said," the appropriate channels could have addressed this issue. Instead, "releasing a snippet of such a video online with no warning and no attempt to redress his issues in an appropriate venue" ultimately made it more difficult for all parties involved to engage in productive dialogue in its aftermath.

Interestingly, some commentators who watched Campus Reform's cell phone video recording concluded that the content itself appeared to be relevant to the course. However, the act of recording this speaker *without his apparent awareness* demonstrated "that it's very easy for such recordings to be taken out of context and used to attack discussions which are entirely appropriate to a classroom" (user *jw9203pi*). In this sense, the video's existence was evidence that "the kid who leaked the video had an agenda and I am guessing it was to raise ire because he was hearing something he didn't agree with" (user *rpaincor*). This user by using the term "kid" seemed to be implying implies that the reporter is inexperienced and immature.

This category of responses thus demonstrates how those who critiqued the Campus Reform videos pointed to the lack of context, believing that the additional information would have been useful in ascertaining the veracity of recorded events. In so doing, these users implicitly chided Campus Reform for their selective editing that denied audiences with the information necessary to make an informed opinion about both instructors' conduct. For these users then, the fact that these young reporters resorted to producing concealed camera footage rather than in-class discussion and dialogue implied that they were motivated by an unethical partisan agenda. We therefore see that audiences may reject or decry journalistic content that seemingly withholds vital information in the interest of promoting an unethical agenda. Such actions interfere with the journalistic merit of this content, while simultaneously implying that the journalist is motivated by a biased personal agenda that compromises his integrity as a reporter. However, these opinions were not indiscriminately shared by all contributors, and other commentators had radically different responses to the videos. The next section explores this second theme.

Surveillance as evidence

A second contrasting theme situated the videos—and by extension, the citizen journalists—as sources that expose and reveal power abuse within higher education. Here, comments generally indicate that both instructors were engaging in behavior that was inappropriate for the classroom, and that their tirades were well beyond their respective areas of expertise. Campus Reform's prerogative to capture and publish the incident for wider circulation is thus lauded and commended by these members of the academic community.

With regard to the Michigan State University incident, *Q&AGuy* observed that Penn may have avoided his tirade against the GOP, save for some private assurance that this manner of behavior would not be penalized, concluding that "it may well be he's had rants like this in the past, it could be he'd managed to get a good bit of ideological reinforcement from his peers in the faculty lounge." The implication here is that Penn's behavior constitutes a regular pattern of power abuse, one that is endorsed by other faculty. Campus Reform's hidden "journalist" has thus provided evidence to help break this cycle of inappropriate conduct by a professor. This perspective is shared by *ke$$erle* who wrote, "He is no different than 95% of professors; he just got caught. Democrats own the media, Hollywood and education. They have become very successful at indoctrination while doing everything possible to prevent education and critical thought." The conspiratorial tone of this comment suggests an agenda at work by mainstream media and higher education to undermine the true goals of education: rational argument and critical thought. The phrase "he just got caught" underscores this particular video's significance with regard to confronting and disrupting the conspiracy. Through their actions, the cameraperson has thus defended higher education's primary imperative.

In response to comments from other users who defended Penn's right to broach controversial topics and create vibrant debate in the classroom, *398472abc* claimed, "Nothing he said had anything to do with the actual class. An argument could be made that he, and by extension the university, was defrauding the students and tax payers of monies by not providing the service promised." This comment suggests that academia operates along a corporate model, providing services to a customer commensurate with payment. Therefore, Penn's outburst constitutes a breach of contract between the university and its students, and this video is thus crucial in protecting the rights of the customer (student) and ensuring that the vendor (university) fulfills its end of the bargain.

Indeed, some users applauded the video and called for greater video surveillance within the classroom to expose similar instances of academic impropriety, as in the case of *YesMan28*, "There needs to be more of this. Students who are forced to endure partisan hackery masquerading as education should make use of modern technology and record what goes on." *YesMan28* celebrates students' agency to monitor and police their instructors within the classroom, and clearly endorses new media technology as a valuable tool to democratize existing power (im)balances. Similarly, *DrEthos2* applauds the fact that this video directly challenges traditional media gatekeepers: "But ain't that beautiful? If there's one positive trajectory this country is headed on, it's the fact that the media is no longer the gatekeeper for stories like this. The internet sheds the light of day on this kind of malfeasance, and the NYT can't easily shovel a load of manure over it to hide it." Here, we witness a heartfelt appreciation for the value of the watchdog citizen journalist, and specifically the capacity to represent alternative perspectives that are ignored by mainstream news media. *DrEthos2* attributes this positive development directly to new technologies that "shed the light of day" on issues that were conveniently disregarded or overlooked in the past. For these users, the implied vast media conspiracy to protect those in power is seemingly overturned by the courageous citizen journalist.

Nevertheless, based on this incident, other academics cautioned colleagues to monitor their conduct in classrooms—"Must remember they [students) can and do record EVERYTHING" (*MeMo38s*). *ChemBioRulz* also warned against the selective presentation of evidence out of context to incriminate unsuspecting instructors:

Professors watch out. Cameras are ubiquitous. We have to cover ourselves from the soundbite culture that can take what is said out of context and put us front and center in scandals that are unfounded. The classroom is NOT a sacred space as it once was understood.

An inescapable consequence of cell phones in the classroom is that instructors must now devote diligent attention to appropriate pedagogical behavior, because any perceived misconduct can be swiftly and speedily recorded and distributed.

Similar sentiments were evident in users' responses to the University of Wisconsin incident, with some applauding Campus Reform's exposé of power abuse. User *carsimmon5* observed, "We're talking about someone using a position of power to influence others to a particular point of view. That's not teaching, it's the spread of propaganda. And it deserves to be exposed every time it's done." For *carsimmon5*, the guest speaker was exploiting the power of the classroom podium by attempting to vilify the GOP and thus coerce his "captive audience." Another user concurs, claiming that because "all too often people say things they believe away from news cameras they won't say in front of them" (user *b39dim*), and he did not realize that a journalist was embedded in the midst of the students. The Campus Reform reporter, in this view, thus foiled this attempt at exploitation by revealing the guest speaker's behavior "away from news cameras." The guest speaker's lapse apparently befuddled those who recognized the pervasiveness of smartphones on university campuses, such as user *kalis37th*: "Considering the availability of unobtrusive recording devices and the pervasive use of social media, I don't understand how anyone could ever contemplate that what they say in a public setting will not be instantly recorded and disseminated." For *kalis37th*, therefore, vigilance is already warranted by those in public spaces, including those in higher education. Others argued that video recording would not be required so long as "instructors and their invited speakers are incendiary in a meaningful way" (user *owijn3*). The implication is thus that this was an instance of irrelevant and provocative instigation that the guest speaker would have done better to avoid.

Interestingly, however, one commentator noted that video recordings could function as evidence for all parties involved, including instructors and administrators, and even be used to demonstrate an instructor's apparent "innocence." *VictoryOrNot* referred to an incident

where a student claimed that a prof was saying inappropriate things in the classroom, while the classroom recording saved the prof a bunch of grief since very early in the investigation the recordings were reviewed and the student was proven to be lying (the report said "mistaken").

Videos can thus function as objective and reliable recordings of actual events as they transpired in the classroom. Notably, however, *VictoryOrNot* specified that this was a university-sanctioned video recording, where "essentially all classes are recorded by a central service and available to students enrolled in the class as a study aid." There is thus no opportunity to selectively record and/or edit or tamper with this content as it is an automated process. Mandated classroom recordings may therefore ultimately confront the perceived journalistic value of Campus Reform's videos because they are objective and reliable representations of classroom events, and as such are untouched by bias and editorializing.

Within this category, we therefore witness multiple reactions to the videos. While many laud Campus Reform's videos as evidence that exposes and implicates errant and misguided instructors, others advise that mandated recordings might ultimately be more useful while subverting the agendas of unethical journalists. Therefore, while audiences may applaud and appreciate the temerity of citizen journalists who aim to expose and disrupt institutionalized power hierarchies, the selective presentation of incriminating evidence can subvert and taint perceptions of this very content and (by extension) the journalist. In such circumstances, the journalist's ethical prerogative is called into question, prompting support for other seemingly less biased measures (such as mandated recordings) that will function as more accurate indicators of systemic corruption. We now turn to the implications of these findings with regard to the ever-evolving role of the citizen journalist and surveillance devices in the classroom.

Conclusion

Campus Reform's videos may initially seem to be unlikely case studies of citizen journalism. After all, they do not fit the traditional contexts that one might associate with other citizen journalism exemplars: political and sport scandals, police brutality, war crimes, and so forth. However, this is precisely why these particular incidents merit critical media attention. Herein lies the opportunity to gage the burgeoning popularity and ubiquity of the citizen "journalist" in mundane everyday contexts, such as university classrooms. Indeed, it is precisely in "gray areas" such as this—where the journalistic merit is not necessarily self-evident—that scholarly attention needs to be focused.

Our findings demonstrate a range of polarized responses on both sides of this debate, with voices alternately commending and condemning the value of these videos. Campus Reform's self-avowed "watchdog journalism" was resoundingly rejected by users, who focused on the organization's bias, selective editing, and failure to provide context. This demonstrates, to some extent, that journalistic value exists in the eye of the beholder, and that merely proclaiming oneself a watchdog press does not necessarily imply that one's audience shares this perception. Audiences, of course, wield a degree of interpretive agency.

However, other audience members embraced the videos as evidence that exposed power abuse and corruption in higher education, lauding Campus Reform's potential to disrupt vague media and liberal political conspiracies. It may therefore be that those who perceive themselves as marginalized or oppressed members within particular social institutions are particularly receptive to acts of citizen journalism that reflect and resonate with their experiences. In this case, those who perceived higher education as the arena of liberal Democrats were thrilled to encounter hard evidence that validated their suspicions. Then again, others who felt victimized by this conservative attack on free speech within the academic arena argued that the *lack* of evidence was tantamount to a witch hunt against liberal academics.

Our findings are limited and tentative in scope; to be sure, we do not claim our findings to be generalizable to all situations and contexts. Users of *The Chronicle* undoubtedly filter their interpretations of these instructors' conduct and Campus Reform's actions through the lens of their experiences in higher education, as well as individual preferences and biases. The viewer comments may therefore be indicative of these users' individual ontological assumptions about the nature of higher education, as well as the instructor's role within contemporary university classrooms. Nevertheless, acknowledging the active role that audiences play in the construction of meaning behooves us to closely examine the particulars of message reception, and how particular audiences accept, contest, or otherwise engage with UGC.

Research on citizen journalism and UGC must examine these phenomena as part of a circuit. As noted earlier, scholarship generally tends to examine UGC either from a production- or content-based perspective. Our study adds to a small body of work focusing on the ways in which UGC is received among *audiences*. We encourage others to examine the intricacies of this relatively overlooked area of media studies, specifically *how UGC is used*. What do audiences do with this content? What meanings do they ascribe to it? How do these meanings contrast or challenge the meanings inscribed by producers? In what contexts, and according to what antecedents, do audience ascribe journalistic functions or attributes to UGC? Scholars have much to do to as they continue to map this terrain.

3

Passing Around Women's Bodies Online: Identity, Privacy, and Free Speech on Reddit

Amber Davisson

In September of 2012, the website Jezebel broke a story about Christopher Bailey, a thirty-five-year-old substitute teacher at East Coweta High School (Ryan 2012). Bailey was part of a Reddit group called Creepshots, which features images of women that have been taken in public places, for instance, while walking down the street, without their permission. The images are typically of women who are perceived as attractive or dressed provocatively, and the pictures posted tend to be accompanied by commentary about the subject's appearance. Bailey's pictures were newsworthy because they featured female students from the high school where he worked. The teacher had posted pictures with captions like "Hot senior girl in one of my classes" or "Girl in my class bending over" (Baker 2012; Walsh 2012). It is worth noting that, though the images Bailey posts violated site standards on Reddit, they were technically legal. The images were meant to sexualize underage girls, but the girls featured in the pictures were not nude and the photos were taken in a public place. This is just one of many prominent incidents— the fappening was another such incident—that has garnered media attention in recent years and in which provocative images of women have been distributed online without the permission of the photos' subjects. Often times, as was the case when Bailey posted the pictures on Reddit, there are very few legal remedies available to the women featured in these photos. Additionally, as will be detailed later in this chapter, the subjects of these photos may experience extreme harassment and find both their online and offline identity compromised. At stake in these incidents is a long-running conflict between the right to free speech claimed by those who distribute the images and the right to privacy claimed by the subjects of those images. While free speech is a critical value in the development of the digital public sphere, it cannot be considered an absolute right, above questioning or restriction, when its use makes the Web an unsafe place for a large population of would-be internet users.

Privacy and free speech

At the core of the conversation about spreading images of others without their consent lies a conflict between two individual rights: freedom of speech and privacy. Freedom of speech is often cited as a founding principle of America's practice of democracy, and the defense of the value has taken on a prominent role in the push for a neoliberal democracy online (Godwin 2003; Anthony Lewis 2007; Nelson 2005). Mike Godwin (2003) points to free speech as a critical component of the development of a healthy web ecology. He argues for free speech as an absolute right, meaning that when balanced against other rights, free speech should always take precedence, as when individuals are allowed free and open expression "it's far more likely that they'll do good than otherwise. This is because freedom of speech is itself a good. The framers of the Constitution were right to give it special protection, because societies in which people can speak freely are better off than societies in which they can't" (Godwin 2003, 23). Free and unrestricted speech is regarded as a necessity for the development of a truly democratic web. When discussing limitations to free speech, philosophers tend to focus on the harm principle, as articulated by John Stuart Mill (1863): "The only purpose for which power can be rightfully exercised over any member of a civilized community, against his will, is to prevent harm to others" (23). Over time, society has ruled that a variety of behaviors—such as slander, copyright violations, child pornography, and hate speech—can result in sufficient harm to others to warrant a restriction on one's right to free speech. Traditionally, privacy has been thought of as an individual right that complements, not conflicts, with the exercise of free speech (Solove 2011). Individuals who feel safe from privacy violations by government entities are more likely to feel comfortable exercising their right to free speech. Civilian surveillance activities online have altered the symbiotic relationship between the two rights.

Understanding the relationship between privacy and identity allows us to reflect on the relationship between freedom of speech and privacy. Privacy is frequently discussed in terms of the ability to release or not release information about oneself. However, Helen Nissenbaum (2010) and Daniel Solove (2004, 2007, 2008) have argued that privacy is less about the absolute release of information, and more about the ability to control how much information is revealed within a given social context. Individuals reveal and guard private information differently depending on whether they are interacting with an intimate partner, a close friend, a casual acquaintance, or a coworker. Regulating the amount of information revealed gives a person some control over how they are seen and a way of managing identity within different contexts. danah boyd (2014), in her work on youth attitudes toward digital privacy, talks about the concept of contextual collapse. The collapse happens when multiple parts of one's life converge in the same place. It may be easy to realize that appropriate behavior at work is not the same as appropriate behavior at a bar with friends. What is harder to navigate is running into colleagues from work while at the bar with friends. That is the moment of contextual collapse. Siva Vaidhyanathan (2011) points out that digital environments are very much like that moment in the bar: "The online environments in which we work and play have broken down the barriers that separate the different social contexts in which we move. . . . Most online environments are intentionally engineered to serve our professional, educational, and personal desires simultaneously" (95). Vaidhyanathan (2011) goes on to explain that this privacy problem is compounded by services online that collect and organize information. A Google search does not distinguish between our private and professional selves. Individuals use privacy to maintain their identity, but once information is released online, it can become difficult, at times even impossible, to control one's identity. This essay looks at three case studies from the website Reddit where the right to privacy and the right to free speech are in direct conflict. In each case, the conflict exists because one person's right to free speech infringes on the privacy of the person who is the subject of the speech.

Reddit, a social networking site launched in 2005, touts itself as the "Front Page of the Internet." The site is designed as a bulletin board where users can post entries and other users can comment on and promote those entries. Entries are often grouped into subreddits based on topics or interests. These subreddits are governed by moderators who both organize and police the conversation. Reddit users can subscribe to specific subreddits that appeal to their personal interest. In October 2014, Reddit reported more than three million registered users from 186 countries around the globe. The site is opened to non-registered users as well, and in September 2014 it had 174,088,361 unique visitors. While the site draws in a broad audience, Reddit estimates that 59 percent of its users are males aged 18–29. On the whole, the site has some pretty basic rules: don't post personal information, child pornography, sexually suggestive content featuring minors, or spam. Also don't break the site. Beyond these basics, individual subreddits may have more expanded rules. In many ways, the site is a libertarian "wild west," hosting all manners of free speech and defending the importance of minimal regulation. Often the sentiment on Reddit is that people who do not want to see certain content should avoid those subreddits as opposed to policing the site (Alfonso 2011). The official Reddit moderators have argued that being a free speech site means protecting speech they find offensive, but what these arguments may not acknowledge is just how much site owners profit from protecting that speech (Alfonso 2011). Based on the high level of traffic to the site, it is estimated that Reddit generates more than a million dollars a day in revenue, and the projected site worth is more than $ 5 billion.

In this chapter, I consider three types of subreddits that distribute provocative or pornographic images of women without their permission. The first is /creepshot subreddits, which are dedicated to photos taken of women in public places.[1] The second is a series of subreddits devoted to the fappening, which was the release of thousands of private images of celebrity women without their permission. Finally, there are a series of subreddits under the heading of Facebookcleavage. These subreddits trade provocative images of women that have been posted to social networking sites. Each of these case studies presents a different set of issues for thinking through the relationship between privacy and free speech.

Creepshots: Privacy in public

Traditionally, privacy has been a matter of protecting clearly demarcated physical boundaries. Coming into a house without the owner's permission is trespassing, and as such "the expectation of privacy in what is reasonably understood to be 'private' spaces remains unchallenged" (Lessig 2006, 201). What constitutes infringements on privacy in public spaces is much harder to articulate and, as a result, those infringements are easier to justify. To understand the issues involved with creepshots, we need to move past the traditional public/private dichotomy. As Siva Vaidhyanathan (2011) explains,

> Privacy is not just about personal choices, or some group of traits or behaviors we call "private" things. Nor are privacy concerns the same for every context in which we live and move. Privacy is an unfortunate term, because it carries with it no sense of its own customizability and contingency. When we complain about infringements of privacy, what we really demand is some measure of control

over our reputations. Who should have the power to collect, cross-reference, publicize, or share information about us?" (93)

The conversation about creepshots and expectations of privacy in public spaces is, at its core, a conversation about power. In particular, it is about the power women exert over their identity when they occupy public spaces.

Creepshots are a form of what is known as *verité voyeurism*, where the target does not know they are being viewed (Calvert and Brown 2000). The main creepshots subreddit describes the photos it archives as candid, stating that a "creepshot captures the natural, raw sexiness of the subject without their vain attempts at putting on a show for the camera. That is the essence of the creepshot, that is what makes a true creepshot worth the effort and that is why this subreddit exists." The subreddit has a couple of basic rules: No upskirt shots, no shots in or around schools, no shots of anyone who is underage, no shots of anyone in a position or place where they might reasonably expect privacy (e.g., sleeping or in the bathroom). The site has been designed to focus on images of women taken in public places. Clay Calvert and Justin Brown (2000) have raised questions about the way that hidden camera laws could be used to stop these types of voyeuristic behaviors in public, but the fear is that going after people who take photos like the ones on creepshots could also have implications for law enforcement and journalists who use hidden cameras. In response to questions of privacy, the official creepshots description stated that: "When you are in public, you do not have a reasonable expectation of privacy. We kindly ask women to respect our right to admire your bodies and stop complaining." Often the "right to admire" was defended with appeals to free speech in two ways. First, the taking of the images was cited as a form of free expression. The photographers were pointed to as artists who had a right to document life. Second, the act of posting the images was articulated as an exercise in free speech. Preventing distribution, especially since the images violated no laws, was pointed to as a form of censorship.

In 2012, after a series of journalistic outlets began reporting on the forum, Reddit said they would not ban the /creepshot subreddit or other similar forums, citing their long-held rule of only stepping in to moderate if content is illegal (Herman 2012). While the subreddit had rules that arguably could have kept it from violating the law, posts that violated these rules were often ignored by moderators. As a result, in October 2013, Reddit reversed their decision and the /creepshot subreddit was officially banned from the site (Golgowski 2012). At that point, it had over 12,000 subscribers (Alfonso 2014a). Fernando Alfonso (2014a) writes that persistent journalistic coverage got /Creepshot banned, and the follow-up coverage worked to police new subreddits that continued the/Creepshot legacy with new names. As Alfonso (2014a) points out, this is where the profitability of the Reddit site becomes a problem. The creepshot forums are hugely successful and big moneymakers for Reddit. Without outside attention, there was an incentive for administrators to simply overlook legal violations on the original site or attempts to create new sites that hosted the same material.

The ban of Creepshots on Reddit caused serious debates about the site's overall policy regarding free speech. Some thought that these kinds of bans were indicative of the larger direction of Reddit. As one redditor commented: "The end of this site has already come. It's become accountable to the public at large because of the sheer number of people who use it: they can't risk *any* bad publicity because they run for profit." Another site member chimed in by saying: "Future historians will consider the mass banning of the creepshots subs to be the True and Final Holocaust, and over-eager social justice advocates will denounce jewish use of the term, considering it to be a bourgeois appropriation of this truer horror" [all *sic*]. Several redditors were quick to point out that, while they found the activities on the subreddit offensive, free speech was the most important issue. As one member put it: "Whatever it is, it's not illegal. You may wish it were, but it's not currently. It does anger me, but so do a lot of ways people choose to use their personal liberty and I have no authority or grounds to stop them; and neither do you." Some redditors went after the journalistic outlets that reported the story and blamed them for the ban. The feeling was that the reporting damaged the free speech environment of the site: "Regulating speech is extremely difficult and tricky for both governments and private entities. Personally, I have no qualms with saying 'fuck the people who ran Creepshots, fuck the people who read it and made it popular, fuck the society that enabled those people to have those views . . . but also fuck Gawker and SRS for making their point in the most aggressive and damaging possible way.'" Posts like this one get at a tricky issue when it comes to free speech: the free speech of some can harm the free speech of others. Arguably, both the journalists reporting the story and the subreddit members were exercising a right to free speech. However, valuing free speech does not simply mean *allowing* all speech to continue unfettered, it means recognizing that some speech acts can create an environment where others feel afraid to exercise their freedom of expression. The reporting on the event brought scrutiny to the subreddit that made some individuals afraid to continue to participate. In legal terms, when a law that is passed does not directly restrict individual rights but does make it uncomfortable for people to exercise their rights, that law is said to have a chilling effect. The argument from participants on Reddit is that journalistic attention created a hostile environment for free expression. One reporter responded to the complaints from redditors by noting, "Women's bodies are not public domain, and demanding control over our images isn't 'ruining anyone's fun.' It's asking to be treated like a goddamn person" (Ryan 2012). This quote harkens back to the harm principle. The reporter is saying that she has a right to exert power over others, in terms of creating a hostile environment, to restrict someone's ability to exercise free speech because that speech is harming the rights of others.

For at least one member of creepshots, the conflict on the site spilled over into real life. Journalist Adrien Chen of Gawker tracked down and unmasked the moderator behind creepshots: Michael Brutsch, a forty-nine-year-old computer programmer. Brutsch had previously run a subreddit called "Jailbait," a forum which hosted sexualized images of underage girls (Chen 2012b). For several years he had specifically been interested in testing the limits of free speech on Reddit with forums like: Chokeabitch, Niggerjailbait, and Jewmerica. Brutsch had not launched creepshots, but he was made the moderator when the forum started receiving media attention (Chen 2012b). Interestingly, when Brutsch pleaded with Adrien Chen to not out him, he appealed to his right to privacy—to keep parts of his life separate and distinct. Many of the arguments he made were about his ability to keep his work life, home life, and internet life separate, a right his online activities had denied many women. After Chen revealed Brutsch's identity, Brutsch was fired from his job. A year later, in an interview on Anderson Cooper, he apologized for his behavior, and argued that it was motivated largely by ranking systems on the site that rewarded him for posting the most offensive things he could find (Alfonso 2012). In the wake of the revelation of Brutsch's identity, many of the moderators of Reddit forums blocked links to articles from the Gawker site (Kiss 2012). Site users expressed fear that Gawker's doxxing—revealing the real-life identity associated with a screen name—of site participants would hurt the free speech environment of the site. They considered some level of anonymity, or privacy, critical to free speech.

The fappening

In late August of 2014, a member of the online community 4Chan hacked over 100 celebrity iCloud accounts, stole a variety of nude and seminude photos from the accounts, and posted the images online (Goldstein 2014). The photo dump included photos of Jennifer Lawrence, Kate Upton, McKayla Maroney, Victoria Justice, Ariana Grande, Kirsten Dunst, Mary Elizabeth Winstead, Krysten Ritter, Yvonne Strahovski, Rihanna, Kim Kardashian, Cara Delevingne, and Teresa Palmer (Klausner 2014; Mendelson 2014; Selby 2014). While some sites took the initiative to delete links to all images from the photo dump, a subreddit forum called "The Fappening" became a place for people to post both links and the images themselves (Price 2014). The word fappening combines "fap," which is internet slang for masturbation, and the word happening. Reddit's official policy was to only delete links from the forum if they involved the images of McKayla Maroney, an Olympic gymnast, because the images were taken before she turned eighteen and were legally classified as child pornography (Klausner 2014). The subreddit drew in over 130,000 subscribers and a number of other lurkers (Price 2014). Originally Reddit refused to take down the subreddit under the argument that while the photos were morally questionable, the content was legal and constituted free speech. That statement was made before celebrity lawyers began hitting the site with hundreds of Digital Millennium Copyright Act (DMCA) take down orders.[2] The site managers could not keep up and, almost a full week after the photos were released, the subreddit was shut down (Butterly 2014).

Much of the coverage surrounding the photo dump, and the rights of various sites hosting the images, focused on a question of who was to blame for the images being distributed. One side of the discussion placed the blame on hackers who illegally obtained photos and the ethically suspect individuals who helped to keep the private images circulating through the Web. On the other side of the discussion were those who questioned the choice of these female celebrities to take the photos to begin with. Actress Mary Elizabeth Winstead, one of the celebrities whose photos were leaked, used Twitter to respond to the incident. She wrote: "To those of you looking at photos I took with my husband years ago in the privacy of our home, hope you feel great about yourselves," and later, "knowing those photos were deleted long ago, I can only imagine the creepy effort that went into this. Feeling for everyone who got hacked" (as quoted in Heller 2014). One of the prominent celebrities who had her photos released was *Hunger Games* star Jennifer Lawrence. In response to articles questioning the actresses' judgment, one reporter wrote that "vital to this victim-blaming is the claim that, because Lawrence is a celebrity, she's not allowed to have any photos of herself without sharing them with us. And underneath that is this more sinister, omnipresent insistence that women's bodies are there for the viewing, for the judging, for the taking. That men who desire an all-access pass to the woman of their choosing should be able to acquire one, whether or not she consents" (Goldstein 2014). In an interview with *Vanity Fair* a month after the event, Lawrence described her reaction to the posting of her private nude photos. She defended taking the pictures by pointing out that the photos had been taken for a boyfriend she dated for four years. They were meant to be part of an intimate relationship. In response to the people who accessed her photos online, the actress said: "Anybody who looked at those pictures, you're perpetuating a sexual offense. You should cower with shame. . . . I didn't tell you that you could look at my naked body" (Kashner 2014).

The issues raised by the fappening are not exclusive to this event or the celebrities who were involved; these issues have become particularly prominent in media literacy education targeted at teenage girls. Amy Hasinoff (2012) points out that educational campaigns designed to keep girls safe online often stress the responsibility not to post anything provocative. Media depictions of girls who post provocative images of themselves often portray these teens as out of control, wild, and disinhibited (Thiel-Stern 2009). The message is that good girls do not sexualize themselves. Hasinoff (2012), in her work on teen sexting, has argued that the critical component often left out of conversations about the sexualization of minors is consent. While teen girls report feeling empowered by the voluntary or consensual distribution of images, they are often emotionally traumatized by the unauthorized distribution of these same images. It appears, for the girls involved, that the issue is not the taking or sharing of the images. The issue is having the choice to share removed from your control. This argument echoes Jennifer Lawrence's response to having her photos leaked, and larger conversations about why one needs privacy to manage identity. Brett Lunceford (2011), in writing about teenage girls expressing sexuality online, has said that "women are caught in a paradox, required to perform both the innocent virgin and the sexually knowing wanton" (107). Both boys and girls who share images of themselves are caught between the desire to develop their own sexuality and the very real threat of having that sexuality made public and shameful (Burton 2012; Calvert 2009). Digital technology creates a double bind: "We live today within a culture that embraces exhibitionism" and punishes women who comply (Calvert 2009, 17).

The mainstream media and media literacy educators have focused much of their conversation surrounding privacy on stories of individuals embarrassed, or even ruined, by information found online. As Scott Stroud (2014) points out in his writing on revenge porn, the "victims are harmed precisely because they lose their anonymity—they are raised out of the anonymous masses and connected to specific nude pictures that will forever surface in Internet searches involving their name" (174). Conversations surrounding incidents such as the fappening send the message that women who use their right to privacy to express their sexuality put themselves in danger. The answer to the problem seems simple: women should not take provocative images of themselves. Ever. Unless, of course, they are ready and willing to share those images with every person in their life, and possibly a host of strangers online. Hasinoff (2012) argues that in a society that largely marginalizes teenage girls, these messages reinforce shame for girls and women who attempt to explore, take charge of, and express their sexuality. In the long run, arguments about privacy can make it difficult for women and girls to learn to voice their sexuality and their desires. For Hasinoff (2012), the production of provocative media can be an important form of expression for girls learning to communicate about their bodies. When that form of expression is cast as both dangerous and out of control, it can have a long-term impact on how women and girls understand their sexuality more generally. Thinking beyond teenage girls, it is dangerous in a broader sense to communicate to women that any articulation of sexuality, even seemingly private ones, opens one up, deservingly, to having their lives ruined. The ability to express sexuality and develop a sexual identity is a key example of the way the right to privacy can enable the right to free speech. Violations of privacy in this area create a hostile environment for girls and women attempting to express free speech.

Facebookcleavage

In March of 2014, several articles began showing up online about a subreddit called Facebookcleavage (Alfonso 2014b; Bahadur 2014; Faircloth 2014; Sanghani 2014). The subreddit was created for members to post provocative pictures of attractive women they were friends with on Facebook. Most the images on the subreddit were what one would expect: selfies taken at seemingly drunken parties and girls in bikinis on spring break. Site moderators laid down some basic rules, which included a ban on posting pictures of underage girls (they threatened to ban those who posted such pictures), and asked posters to avoid using the real names of the women in the pictures. Journalists investigating the site argued that a decent number of the images were screenshots, which included names and other Facebook profile information that could be used to identify the photo's subject (Bahadur 2014; Faircloth 2014). Additionally, as journalist Fernando Alfonso (2014b) pointed out, many of the women on the site could be identified by running a reverse image search on Google or using identifying information in the image, such as the name of a university written on a hoodie. So, even in cases where names have not been included, there is very little protection of the subject's anonymity. In some instances, multiple pictures of the same woman were posted, making it possible for viewers to piece together a lot of information. One site users went so far as to create a photo album with 500 pictures of the same woman (Alfonso 2014b).

Where cases like creepshots and the fappening may be easily understood as privacy infringements, sites like Facebookcleavage occupy a more complicated place in the conversation about privacy and free speech. The images being shared on the site were ostensibly freely distributed by the subjects on their Facebook profiles, and as long as the girls are clothed and of age, no laws have been violated. One wonders how much privacy an individual should expect when she is the one posting the pictures. Not surprisingly, Reddit moderators were unwilling to take down the subreddit, even though they acknowledged the activities taking place on the site were unsavory. Much like in the case of creepshots, the distribution of images was articulated as an act of expression, protected as free speech. The potential issue, as Nina Bahadur (2014), a contributor to the *Huffington Post*, put it is that "sharing images of yourself to a carefully curated audience of friends is one thing—being plastered all over the Internet for the enjoyment of predatory, anonymous users is another." On Facebook, users can modify privacy settings to decide who sees their profile and who in their network is able to view a particular image. Additionally, they can untag themselves from pictures posted by other users, making it possible to regulate what images are associated with their identity. Once the images are taken from Facebook, the user loses all control of them. Furthermore, journalist Radhika Sanghani (2014) explains that the comment thread on Reddit is part of the overall issue with the subreddit. On Facebook, image posters can block a person or delete a comment if they feel the comment crosses a line. On the subreddit, there is no way for the person who posted the picture on Facebook to deal with the lecherous comments or conversations of site users. Whereas on Facebook they are participants in a discussion, on Reddit the subject of the photo is made purely an object for discussion.

One might argue that this subreddit is a microcosm of some of the larger issues surrounding images of women online. Sarah Neely (2012) argues that the lack of physical embodiment in cyberspace does not lead to increased anonymity; instead this makes human bodies a fetish and an object of desire. There is a need to see bodies and to know the people who occupy them. That desire has been focused primarily on women. Situated within the extreme pornification of mainstream culture, women online are often encouraged to represent themselves in pornographic ways (Neely 2012). This may explain why, as Scott Stroud (2014) notes, a portion of the images on revenge porn sites are actually submitted by women looking for the approval and temporary fame that comes with exhibiting their bodies online. The sheer number of images of female bodies online, and the fetishism that surrounds those bodies, impacts the way women are seen as participants in these forums. Sarah Neely (2012) observes that "when compared to the active (male) techno-geek the presence of the woman in online spaces is more likely to be marked by her body, or what she looks like, rather than what she does" (101). That marking becomes more pronounced in forums like Facebookcleavage, where women lose control of images they might have otherwise freely distributed. When the photos are distributed by the original subject on Facebook, they may be seen as an expression of sexuality by that subject. They are, to some extent, a speech act by the subject. On Reddit, the redistribution of the images transforms them into the speech act of someone else. That transformation changes the role of the subject in the overall conversation.

Possibly because the operators of Reddit were unwilling to step in, after several articles were written about the subreddit, some Reddit users managed to take over the moderator roles on the subreddit and proceeded to vandalize the site until it was no longer functional. At the time of its destruction, the subreddit had close to 17,000 subscribers. Facebookcleavage lives on at the site Imgur. One group of internet vigilantes sought to shut down all the versions of this site throughout the internet. They inundated Facebookcleavage sites on Imgur, Reddit, and Tumblr with images from anime pornography depicting women with very large penises. What happened in this case is an important example of how free speech concerns are sometimes dealt with in a diverse society. The site users had the right to free speech, and legally there was no recourse for the women whose privacy had been removed through the posting of their pictures. However, just as the subreddit users had a right to free speech, so did those who found the forum offensive. Those who were bothered by the forum used their skills and their voices to drown out the original participants. When free speech is a recognized right for all, there is always a risk that public conversations deteriorate into screaming matches.

Conclusion

While the example of yelling fire in a crowded theater may seem trite, it does draw attention to the fact that speech can have real, physical consequences. The right to free speech is not absolute, and is regulated in many instances—laws on libel and slander are examples of this—where society has recognized the ability of words to cause harm. In the cases discussed in this chapter, the types of physical harm may vary, but they are no less real. Teenage girls who are photographed and have their images distributed without their permission by those wishing to sexualize them or castigate them for their sexuality can experience extreme emotional distress. That distress impacts their ability to perform in school and develop social relationships during a period in their life where those activities are vital. Prominent stories circulate on a regular basis of teen girls committing suicide after their nude images or sexts are circulated among peers (Burleigh 2013; Kaye 2010; Zetter 2009). This is in addition to research that indicates that teen girls who may not go to such extremes are highly likely to engage in other forms of self-harm as a result of the sexual harassment that results from the circulation of these images (Ramirez 2011). Brett Lunceford (2011) argues that harm—both to the individual and to society—must be the core consideration when discussing the ethics of adolescents taking images of themselves and distributing them. For female celebrities, their income is often related to both their public image and their willingness to share their bodies with the world. When that public image is ruined, or the ability to negotiate the sharing of the body is taken away, the financial losses can run to millions of dollars. Beyond this, we should consider the impact public conversations about these incidents have on the female population as a whole. The threat of having images taken from Facebook, stolen from a personal phone, or even snapped while the subject is unaware, sends a message that any expression of sexuality makes the female body a public domain for ridicule and erotic fantasy. This speaks to women's ability to engage in freedom of expression as it relates to expressing sexuality.

While the internet is a well-established medium, in terms of the discussion of civil rights, it is in many ways still in its infancy. Stan Cohen (2007) writes that, in the face of current conversations, "the whole project of protecting the individual right to self-expression must look quite anachronistic in the Internet world. The sheer amount of people, money, technology and global networks that are needed to create an interface of millions of messages exchanged each minute can hardly be grasped, let alone controlled by the liberal model of civil liberties" (Cohen 2007, 112). Protecting liberties such as free speech, privacy, and the right to create and express oneself is a project so big it requires the participation of everyone involved. It cannot be the sole responsibility of women to constantly police themselves to avoid harassment. All involved must push for the regulation of digital platforms, the policing of virtual spaces to make them safe, and must constantly make the individual choice to not engage in the viewing, publicizing, and distribution of images that were not intended for broad public consumption.

Notes

1 Note that while creepshot and upskirt images are often hosted on the same sites or forums, the two photo genres are considered separate.
2 The DMCA, passed in 1996, makes it illegal to distribute content without the copyright holders' permission (Cobia 2009). The safe harbor provision of the law says that websites are not punished when users violate copyright by posting copyrighted material, so long as the site responds to a copyright holders' takedown notice in a timely manner.

4

Freedom, Democracy, Power, Irony: The Ethics of Information and the Networked Fourth Estate

Ryan Gillespie

Upon learning that the United States' National Security Agency (NSA) was listening to her personal mobile phone, German Chancellor Angela Merkel reportedly told President Obama: "This is like the Stasi" (Traynor and Lewis 2013). Merkel grew up in East Germany under communist rule with that repressive, state-run surveillance secret police. The comparison of the NSA to the Stasi is meant to shock, as the former is part of a regime that prides itself on being the ambassadors of human rights and liberal democracy throughout the globe, whereas the other was a known oppressive regime dubbed "worse than the Gestapo."[1] But the extent of the NSA's surveillance and intrusion into domestic and foreign peoples' lives, national allies and national enemies alike, was unclear until the leak of classified documents in 2013. This classified leak was one in a series of significant leaks since 2010.

The three names associated with the series of leaks of classified information— Private Chelsea (formerly Bradley) Manning, Julian Assange, and Edward Snowden—and their actions have sparked public debate about the ethics of information in the contemporary era. Assange and his outfit WikiLeaks obtained thousands of classified US documents from Manning,[2] and collaborated with major international newspapers in their publication. The contents of these leaks were: a video, "Collateral Murder," which featured two US Apache helicopters knowingly firing on Iraqi civilians and the calloused dialogue of the gunman, field war logs from Afghanistan, field reports from Iraq, and most strikingly, embassy cables revealing US intelligence persons' candid assessments of countries and world leaders. Snowden also obtained thousands of classified US documents and made them available to journalists, the major thrust of these leaks being the extent, and perhaps illegality,[3] of the NSA's information collection programs and the potential lies government officials told about it.[4] What are we to make of both the content of the information that has since been released, and of the debate about the ethics of information in a democratic society that the release of this information has generated?

The debate has been heated, and the stakes are high. Some extreme calls, such as those from former presidential hopefuls Mike Huckabee and Sarah Palin, are for Assange's execution (Siddique and Weaver 2010; Beckford 2010). *The New York Times'* Thomas Friedman (2010) declares that the two biggest threats to the "world system" are China and mass individual networks like WikiLeaks. On the other hand, legal scholars like Yochai Benkler (2011a) and Geoffrey Stone (2012) and journalists like Glenn Greenwald (2014), with whom Snowden partnered, consider, for the most part, these leaks on par with investigative journalistic practices, protected by the First Amendment, and serving the necessary democratic watchdog functions against abuses of power.[5]

For nearly all parties involved, the debate about the ethics of information, then, is intimately tied to anxieties about the future of democracy: Do such leaks, as a networked fourth estate, contribute to the improvement and refinement of democratic practices of freedom and stability, or are they the very things that undermine democratic practices of freedom and stability? That is perhaps the key overarching question in discussions of contemporary information ethics.

Rather than attempt to answer the normative ethical questions directly, the goal of this chapter is to clarify the—often very different—ends on which the deployment of normative language in conversation turns. Usage of normative terms commits speakers to certain positions and ends (Cuneo 2014; Gillespie forthcoming), and utilizing the notion that normative speech is about inducing interlocutor acceptance of our aims (Gibbard 2008) and ends which are often implicit in the discourse (Finlay 2014), I seek to make the political and ethical ends in this debate more explicit en route to collective deliberative judgment on the ethics of information and the networked fourth estate.

The focus here is on two major issues in debates about information and media technologies, corresponding to the two major subsections of this chapter: (1) the tension between the ends of national security and the principles of transparent, open governance in a democracy, and (2) the emergence of a networked public sphere as a fourth estate check on abuses of power. Overall, this chapter highlights: (a) just what the competing ends and meanings in discussions of freedom, democracy, and power, are, especially as seen in the Information Wants To Be Free trope, and, in conclusion, (b) the ironies throughout the discourse of information ethics, democratic futures, and human freedoms.

National security, the public interest, and principles of democracy

A central concern in information ethics, from the perspective of a national citizenry, is striking the right balance between secrecy and transparency. There is a need for secrecy in the name of national security, on the one hand, and an informed public able to maintain democratic practices of checks and balances in curbing abuses of power, on the other.

There are clearly instances of the necessity of state secrecy under a geopolitical regime. In the words of First Amendment scholar Geoffrey Stone (2012), "Examples traditionally offered include the sailing dates of transports or the precise location of combat troops in wartime. The publication of such information would instantly make American troops vulnerable to enemy attack and thwart battle plans already underway" (490). The statement from Justice Stewart in the Pentagon Papers Supreme Court case sets the bar, prohibiting the publication of materials that would "surely result in direct, immediate, and irreparable damage to our Nation or its people" (*New York Times Co.* 403 U.S. 1971, 730).[6] The general idea is that speech that poses immediate grave harm to the nation is unprotected, and thus prosecutable. Part of statecraft is promoting the welfare of citizens and providing for their essential safety, and in a democratic state, this requires mutual trust between citizen and elected leaders.

There are equally clear imperatives for a free press to disseminate sensitive information, as speech is not just a right of expression under the First Amendment but also a key part of promoting and maintaining a free flow of information essential to a thriving democratic society. In the words of Justice Black (1971), "Only a free and unrestrained press can effectively expose deception in government" (*New York Times Co.* 1971, 717). For Justice Brandeis (1917), law should never interfere with free speech without an "emergency justifying it" (*Whitney v. California* 274 U.S. 1927, 357). James Madison ([1822] 2000) famously says, "A popular Government, without popular information, or the means of acquiring it, is but a Prologue to a Farce or a Tragedy; or, perhaps both."

Thomas Jefferson ([1787] 2000) quips that "were it left to me to decide whether we should have a government without newspapers, or newspapers without a government, I should not hesitate a moment to prefer the latter." In these statements, a free press is thus singled out as serving a fundamental democratic function. The general trend over the last several decades in the United States is to err on the side of permissibility of information dissemination, as underscored by the Freedom of Information Act (FOIA) adopted in 1966 and the Supreme Court ruling on the Pentagon Papers.

The challenge is to identify what counts as posing grave harm and unnecessarily undermining public trust and what counts as essential public information, even if uncomfortable and unflattering to the nation and its leaders. The landmark case of the *New York Times Co. v. United States*, based on Daniel Ellsberg's possession of classified documents (the Pentagon Papers) and their subsequent publication in newspapers, clearly illustrates the matter. The Supreme Court ruled in favor of protecting the right of a press (*The New York Times* and *Washington Post* in this case) to publish the materials in the name of public interest, as the revelations included systematic deception surrounding military engagements and involvement in the Vietnam War. Though classified, the Court ruled that the information was essential to enlightening the public about its government's operations, and that an enlightened public represents a key check and balance function in healthy democracies. In Justice Stewart's (1971) words, "Without an informed and free press, there cannot be an enlightened people" (*New York Times Co.* 1971, 728). In this judgment, one sees the protection that is afforded to the press, under the First Amendment, to disseminate crucial, sensitive information to a deliberating, voting populace.

One of the confusing elements in the debate is that activist cryptographers (hacktivists) who gain access to the sensitive information are hardly unified in their political or ethical ends. While the general trope "information wants to be free"—that is, uncontrolled by corporations, governments, etc.—unites most,[7] the governances and political economies associated with that notion vary significantly. For example, a prominent version of hacktivism is the promotion of liberal democracy. The basic idea is to use the tools of cryptography and networking technologies to establish fairer and more just societies along typical liberal democratic theory lines: public accountability, equality of opportunity and legal standing for all citizens, ending abuses of power, protecting those who cannot protect themselves, protection of civil liberties, and governance via democratic deliberation.

Snowden and Manning see themselves as following this path of democracy and justice. Snowden said that as he tried to raise concerns internally, he was told that "this isn't your job" and "you don't have enough information to make those kind of judgments," and that "this was when [he] really started seeing how easy it is to divorce power from accountability, and how the higher the levels of power, the less oversight and accountability there was" (Greenwald 2014, 18, 42). Similarly, in a statement read by her lawyers after her conviction, Manning said that she acted "out of a love for [her] country and a sense of duty." She further said that if her plea for pardon was not granted, she would "gladly pay the price" of prison "if it means that we could have a country that is truly conceived in liberty and dedicated to the proposition that all women and men are created equal" (Courson and Smith 2013).

Andy Greenberg (2012) notes another shared goal of hacktivists: destroying "institutional secrets."

> The ideological arrow I see from Ellsberg to Assange and beyond [is] a revolutionary protest movement bent not on stealing information, but on building a tool that inexorably coaxes it out, a technology that slips inside of institutions and levels their defenses against the free flow of data like a Trojan horse of cryptographic software and silicon. (7–8)

For Snowden, the purpose of leaks and cryptography seems to be to right the ship of liberal democracy. He seems less interested in destroying all institutional secrets *per se* than he is in, based on a knowledge-is-power assumption, redrawing certain boundaries between what is national security classifiable in the public interest and what a voting democratic public needs to know. After all, in his manifesto, Snowden writes, "My sole motive is to inform the public as to that which is done in their name and that which is done against them," and elsewhere has said that he "selected these documents based on what's in the public interest" (Greenwald 2014, 23, 53). Furthermore, one of his early pseudonyms, Cincinnatus, is a reference to the civic republican tradition of the Romans, virtue aimed at the common good.[8]

Other hacktivists fall outside the ethical and political dimensions of liberal democracy, such as cypherpunks, techno-libertarians, and crypto-anarchists.[9] On the one hand, people like Assange write about WikiLeaks freeing the world's information and being an activity for cypherpunks—"bright people [to] form an engine for justice" (Greenberg 2012, 97).On the other hand, crypto-anarchists desire to free the world's information with the purpose of destroying all forms of government, everywhere, with alternative social arrangements ranging from libertarian utopias *à la* Galt's Gulch (a reference to Ayn Rand's *Atlas Shrugged*) to cold, dark societies run via "Assassination Politics."[10] Anonymous, a cypherpunk collective, aims to free the world's information based not necessarily on civic republican virtues of the public interest and common good nor on libertarian ethos of individual privacy and antigovernance, but rather (or also) on (collective) personal grievances.[11]

My purpose here is not to weigh in on the normative ethics of who—from among leakers, cypherphunks, crypto-anarchists, and those working in the official interest of national security—has the better or more ethical approach. Rather, I hope to have explicated the primary tension between national security requiring some degree of secrecy and hacktivists and whistleblowers who, for varying reasons, seek to eradicate the secrecy.

The salient metaethical point is that different actors have different motives for their actions based on differing political ends. What the discussion in this section amounts to so far is this: *freedom*, both internet and human, means one thing to the entrenched liberal democratic establishment of government officials and another thing to the leakers and hacktivists who aim to improve upon the methods and practices in the name of that same ideal, and yet another to the crypto-anarchists and techno-libertarians who use the same terminology.

The debate about information ethics is then inexorably tied to political ends, as best understood via the word freedom, and is thus, following Aristotle, entirely a debate about substantive moral commitments, given that "questions of freedom are essentially moral in character."[12] Debates about the meaning of "Information Wants To Be Free"—free to what, free from what, freedom for whom?—are as plagued by discursive and philosophical disagreements as by ethical debates about the meaning of freedom. Advocates rest their arguments on clashing and incompatible notions of *freedom* and *moral obligation* (cf. Miller 1983)— for example, freedom as requiring certain collective governance practices as opposed to freedom as meaning a complete lack of governance. In a sense, one can think of certain leakers as upholding the same liberal democratic principles and desiring a similar sense of justice in society as officials in the Congress or the Central Intelligence Agency (CIA), and other leakers and hacktivists as seeking to subvert those very principles in order to achieve political ends and regimes that are incompatible with a liberal democracy.

The networked fourth estate: The ethics of citizenship and ideas of a public sphere

Underwriting some of the tensions between safety and surveillance is the second ethical issue to be worked out in debates on information ethics in the era of hacktivism and whistleblowing: the relationship between national and global citizenship under the networked fourth estate. As a global citizen, duties to one's nation and duties to humanity writ large conflict more substantively under the social, political, and economic processes of globalization in this era than in any other.

The idea of a global citizenry has Enlightenment roots and finds a clear manifestation in the United Nation's 1948 Declaration, the opening lines of which announce that the "recognition of the inherent dignity and of the equal and inalienable rights of all members of the human family is the foundation of freedom, justice and peace in the world" ("Universal Declaration on Human Rights" 2014). The development of this notion further, accelerated by media technologies, has led some scholars to claim the existence of a global civil society (e.g., Kaldor 2003). And there are empirical exigencies in addition to the ethical underpinnings of a global citizenry, namely, that in a globalized world, problems are typically global problems—think of climate change or the financial crisis beginning in 2007. And global problems require global solutions. Ideas of democracy in conjunction with universal human rights, then, make something like a global public sphere—a space for rational democratic deliberation—necessary.[13] Communication technologies enable at least the possibility of such a space, especially as information sharing between citizens of repressed regimes might strengthen internal bonds and facilitate coordination, as well as, perhaps most importantly, the possibility for global dissemination of abuses. As the saying goes, the whole world is watching.[14]

The idea of using communication technologies and the free flow of information to promote ethical ideals of human freedom is one that the U.S. State Department has officially endorsed. In her landmark speech on Internet freedom, Secretary of State Hilary Clinton (2010) declared, "The spread of information networks is forming a new nervous system for our planet. When something happens in Haiti or Hunan, the rest of us learn about it in real time—from real people. And we can respond in real time as well"; the problem, she said, was that there were "threats to the free flow of information"—and then she named China, Tunisia, Uzbekistan, Vietnam, and Egypt.

But what are we to make of such promotions of the free flow of information as being vital to protecting and achieving human freedoms against the secrecy and power abuses of elites and dictators when it is the United States that wants to impede that very same free flow of information based on the need for secrecy in the name of national security? (cf. Cramer 2013). The free flow of information is essential in China, the United States says, because its people are unaware of all that the government does; if they were aware, they'd do something about it. But this, recall, is Snowden's rationale for distributing his NSA leaks: "My sole motive is to inform the public"—for example, US citizens—"as to that which is done in their name and that which is done against them." While I will discuss these sorts of ironies more in the conclusion, the point is not to claim that domestic, nationalistic ties are antiquated; after all, not all regimes are equally committed to promoting prosperous, peaceful, and just societies. The system, rather, is meant to be one of checks and balances with different offices serving the democratic society, from the official capacities of state departments to the essentiality of the information dissemination and public opinion-forming process of the press—the fourth estate.

In the contemporary era, the fourth estate—and all of its functions and protections—must extend to the internet and other communication technologies. Benkler (2011a) puts it this way:

> What is being protected by this refusal to privilege the *New York Times* over WikiLeaks [and other online outlets for whistleblowing and investigative reporting] is the continued access of the public to a steady flow of truthful, relevant information about its government's inner workings. (362)

Benkler continues, placing the importance of First Amendment protections for watchdog press functions precisely in terms of a public sphere:

> As the networked public sphere develops, as a more diverse set of actors . . . come to play an ever larger role in the construction of a public sphere, the functional importance of divorcing the constitutional protection from the degree to which the actor is a familiar part of the twentieth century model of mass media increases. (362)

Whether a networked public sphere can become a global public sphere is unknown, as is whether as much would be truly desirable. The ethics of information, from the perspective of a networked fourth estate, turns on questions of *which* information, *whose* information, and *for whom* the information is created and shared, and the tensions that can arise between national and global citizen duties. The concerns of protecting human dignity and promoting human freedom are liberal democratic values already in place in countries like the United States, and so many leakers, like Snowden, claim to act as whistleblowers, not traitors, holding their government to account for its failures of such protections and promotions. But that is not every country, and that is not every leaker.

Freedom and irony in information ethics

In addition to explicating the differing political ends implicit in the normative language of information ethic agents, this chapter aimed to make clear two essential ethical dimensions to information and its flows: the relationship between secrecy and transparency in the promotion of human freedom and internet freedom, and the relationship between being a national citizen and a global citizen to a networked fourth estate. The key to understanding discussions of information ethics is that the common terms of freedom, democracy, and power are always tied to *ends*.

In conclusion, the ethical question is: with what motives and toward what ethical and political goals do information disseminators act? The ends matter in assessing the morality of actions and events. What the ends are—negative liberty, positive liberty, international stability, economic advantage, anarchy, personal ego, embarrassment, imperialism, domination, destruction, reform, ending Western hegemony, destroying trust, repairing trust, etc.—conditions how we ought to think through the normative ethical judgments in cases of information sharing and flows. At a minimum, I hope to have made clear how discussions of the freedom of information depend on differing understandings of internet and human freedom, and that the debate about information ethics is inescapably tied to discussions of political ends and substantive moral commitments, as glimpsed in the discursive deployment of normative concepts like freedom and democracy.

But ironies permeate discussions of and action around the ethics of information. First, there is the fact that the freedom of information advocates Julian Assange and Edward Snowden are being legally protected by the governments of Ecuador and Russia, respectively, and neither country has a strong reputation for protecting freedom of speech or promoting a free press.[15]

Furthermore, Snowden chose to release his leaks from within Hong Kong, a decision made partly because Hong Kong's tenuous relationship with the United

States made the former more likely to "resist U.S. pressure" on extradition (Greenwald 2014, 49). The involvement of Russia, Ecuador, and Hong Kong with issues of internet freedom and freedom of speech and the press seems to reflect not stronger commitments to those ideals than the United States but rather another irony: the participation in the practice of the very kinds of nation-state geopolitics that much internet freedom and human rights rhetoric seeks to abolish.

Secondly, as discussed briefly above in relation to Clinton's remarks on internet freedom, the United States continues to pursue figures like Snowden and Assange for deploying classified information—even if this was done in the name of checking government abuses—and at the same time celebrates internet freedoms and scolds governments in countries like China and Egypt for suppressing information. As Micah Sifry (2014) puts it, "If we promote the use of the Internet to overturn repressive regimes around the world, then we have to either accept the fact that these same methods may be used against our own regime—or make sure our own policies are beyond reproach" (10).

Thirdly, Chancellor Merkel, who compared the NSA spying program to the Stasi, also then used the fact of the leak of this information—the NSA spying on foreign leaders like herself—as proof that US intelligence gathering is untrustworthy because its information is unsecure. So the problem, it seems, was that the United States was acting unethically by spying on allies, but also that it couldn't keep this ally-spying a secret; as the joke goes, the food in this restaurant is terrible, and such small portions![16]

Fourthly, a resounding theme in the chorus against leakers and hacktivists is that these new media types fail to have the maturity of judgment and professional discretion of traditional, established media. A study of major US newspaper editorial discourse found a sharp contrast between "traditional journalism's emphasis on discretion, responsibility, and good judgment and WikiLeaks' aggressive, devil-may-care approach to the mass communication of information."[17] Snowden, to some degree, follows this theme as well.[18] And in general, this is likely a meaningful distinction; the training, experience, and resources of a journalist at a top-tier international outlet will trump the typical journalist, let alone the typical blogger or hacktivist.

But the irony is that, when it comes to the WikiLeaks story itself being correctly reported, traditional journalism fell down, with many outlets claiming that WikiLeaks dumped 250,000 classified documents, unredacted, on its website. But that was not the case. Recall that WikiLeaks only made the documents available privately to *New York Times, Der Spiegel, El País, Le Monde,* and *The Guardian,* and that those outlets in turn published redacted versions and accompanying stories. Benkler (2011a, 327) notes that "over 60% of print news reports at the time explicitly stated that WikiLeaks had released thousands of documents (usually over 250,000), and another 20% implied that it did so. In fact, over the course of the first month and more, the site released a few hundred documents, limited almost exclusively to those published and redacted by other organizations."[19] The point is that the accuracy and essentiality of the information is what matters, not the technological medium.

Perhaps the most central irony is that the Information Wants to Be Free trope has a positive liberty connotation (freedom to) and a negative liberty connotation (freedom from), often forming a contradiction in the promotion of transparency and freedom for some people's information but privacy and secrecy for other people's information. That is, most adherents claim that information wants to be free, as opposed to corporately controlled, or government controlled. But it is also many of these same adherents who struggle to maintain their privacy, to shroud her identity and preserve her anonymity.

A clear example is WikiLeaks and Julian Assange. Bill Keller, editor of the WikiLeaks' reporting for the *New York Times,* calls WikiLeaks "a secretive cadre of antisecrecy vigilantes" (Keller 2011). Andrew O'Hagan (2014), the author commissioned to ghostwrite Assange's autobiography, notes how guarded Assange often was about his personal life and information, and even asked O'Hagan to sign a confidentiality agreement.

The "core argument," in Benkler's (2011b) words, is that "privacy is at risk when there are powerful observers and vulnerable subjects. Transparency, by contrast, involves disclosure of information about powerful parties that weaker parties can use to check that power or its abuse" (33). The idea, then, isn't ironic, it is claimed, but rather about a correction in power asymmetries: "they" know everything about you, and you know nothing about them, and the matter needs to be reversed.

A potential problem with the reversal of communicative asymmetries of information, though, is that, in addition to flipping the asymmetry in the other direction and seemingly moving power from one small group (of elite government officials, corporate heads) to another small group (of hacktivists), distrust and cynicism in society is further perpetuated. Disempowering the *surveillance state* by withdrawing into deeper secrecy and personal privacy reflects a destabilization of civic virtues and social connection. The digital *panopticon* threatens not only to internalize its disciplinary mechanism (the watchful eye of power), but also to breed mistrust among all peoples.[20] The anarchist or techno-libertarian solution imagines a bleak society of isolation and cynicism, a society devoid of mutual trust and collaborative deliberation.

The contemporary situation, of mass surveillance and power exercised through secrecy and information asymmetries, is hardly ideal either. The shortcomings in information ethics in the United States of both the George W. Bush administration, with its establishment of the warrantless wiretapping and surveillance programs in 2001–07,[21] and the Obama administration, with its continuation and extension of many of those programs, are known, and understood, for better or worse, via the leaks of WikiLeaks and Edward Snowden. These leaks mark the era in a way that the Pentagon Papers marked theirs—if not even more so.[22] The, if not outright lie,[23] then at least mismatch between what, say, President Obama told the United States—"What I can say unequivocally is that, if you are a U.S. person, the N.S.A. cannot listen to your telephone calls, and the N.S.A. cannot target your e-mails" (Davidson 2013)—and the revealed surveillance practices of the NSA[24] can inspire recoil and retreat from public life and civic participation, or it can inspire reinvigorated checks and balances of power and democratic functioning. Michael Lynch (2014) advocates democratic renewal of citizenship and reformed governance:

> A government that sees its citizens' private information as subject to tracking and collection has implicitly adopted a stance toward those citizens inconsistent with the respect due to their inherent dignity as autonomous individuals. It has begun to see them not as persons, but as something to be understood and controlled. That is an attitude that is inconsistent with the demands of democracy itself.

In the least, the ironies in discussions of both information freedom and human freedom mean that there is room, through critical reflection and deliberative practices, to more carefully articulate ethical ends and political practices. It is becoming harder to espouse democratic political values and inherent human dignity and to remain silent on the antidemocratic and antihumanitarian effects of regimes, both so-called liberal democratic and otherwise. Reformers seek to use media technologies to free (certain) information so as to make nations and leaders more accountable and less cruel. The techno-anarchists seek to free the world's information so as to make nations moot and render the possibility of leaders taking power in the first place impossible.

Conclusion

The contrast between the vision of citizenship in Cincinnatus and theories of civic virtue, of the public interest, connected humanity, and the common good that Snowden aims to embody, and the vision of John Galt and neoliberalism, with the retreating, leave-me-alone ethos that certain hacktivist libertarians embody, could not be starker. In either strategy, though, the centrality of media and communications technology is clear, and so as we try to promote human flourishing, we must continue to think through the ethical implications of information technologies, and the ethical ends at which we aim in our discourses of freedom and democracy.

Notes

1 "The Stasi was much, much worse than the Gestapo, if you consider only the oppression of its own people," says Simon Wiesenthal. The Stasi had "more spies than had any other totalitarian government in recent history" (Koehler 1999, 8–9). Cf. Angwin (2014).

2 Private Manning was convicted of being the source of WikiLeaks' leak, providing over 700,000 documents, and was sentenced to thirty-five years in prison in August 2013 (Savage and Huetteman 2013).

3 Snowden's files revealed several surveillance programs such as Boundless Informant, PRISM, and XKeyscore. The notion that these programs are illegal depends upon a specific reading of what is meant by purposeful collection of data, understandings of the FISA Court, and the Fourth Amendment. A lawsuit (*ACLU v. Clapper.* No. 13-3994. S.D.N.Y. 2013. https://www.aclu.org/national-security/aclu-v-clapper-legal-documents) was brought against James Clapper, as the director of National Intelligence, for illegally collecting the (meta)data. A lower court ruled in 2013 that the collection was consistent with the Fourth Amendment, and the ruling is being appealed.

4 These include statements made by President Obama and James Clapper, discussed more in the conclusion to this chapter.

5 The United States has filed charges against Snowden under the Espionage Act. As the only official government employee, and a member of the military, in this mix, Manning's case is legally different than other leakers' cases.

6 The roots of speech unprotected by the First Amendment stem from the "bad tendency" phrase of *Masses* to the famous "clear and present danger" test

introduced by Justice Holmes in 1919. See *Masses Publishing Co. v. Patten*, 244 F.
535 (S.D.N.Y 1917); *Schenck v. United States* 249 U.S. 47 (1919); cf. Balkin (2014).

7　Following Wagner (2003): "The trope 'information wants to be free' is a well-
known techie-activist rallying cry, typically invoked against any efforts to limit
access or charge money for information. . . . Though it has clearly taken on a life of
its own, most people attribute the origins of the phrase to Stewart Brand" (999).

8　Lucius Quinctius, called Cincinnatus, was a fifth-century B.C. Roman farmer
who, after being appointed dictator of Rome to expel the Aquians, successfully
defended Rome and then immediately resigned from his dictatorship and retired
back to farming. Dante invokes him as a storied figure of civic virtue (contrasted
with 13th c. Florentines) in *The Paradiso* Canto XV ("A Cornelia or Cincinnatus
would amaze/a modern Florentine . . ."; cf. Canto VI, lines 46–48). The civic
republican tradition of civic virtues in the Roman tradition contrasts with the
neoliberal frameworks of the contemporary era. See Dante Alighieri (2003, 725).

9　*Cypherpunk* seems to be another broad term for a style of (libertarian-tinged?)
hacktivism, given that the "Crypto-Anarchist Manifesto," the "Cypherpunk's
Manifesto," and "Assassination Politics" all appeared via the Cypherpunk Mailing
List. I borrow these labels and understanding of this material from Greenberg
(2012, esp. 49–134).

10　The influence of libertarian ethos and Rand in particular is discussed in
Greenberg (2012, 58–70, 117–25). "Assassination Politics" was a James Bell essay
that imagines a world in which gamblers bet on the time, day, and place that a
certain person will die. With enough money pooling around a certain person
and time-space, in effect a bounty would be created, and hitmen—or anyone
else—would have significant incentive to perform the murder, and then collect
untraceable digital cash. If such a notion makes cypherpunks immediately
dismissible, Greenberg notes that the pieces "inflamed the Cypherpunk Mailing
List" too (Greenberg 2012, 121).

11　Their slogan, often appending their cyberattacks, runs: "Knowledge is free. We
are Anonymous. We are Legion. We do not forgive. We do not forget. Expect us"
(Greenberg 2012, 185).

12　As seen in Aristotle (1984, 1729–867). The quote is from Clapp (1943, 85), whom
I follow in making the connection between morality and freedom.

13　A sampling of works on global public sphere, democracy, and global networks:
Benkler (2006, esp. 212–72), Bohman (2004), Castells (2008).

14　The role of communication technologies in revolutions, especially in the so-called
Arab Spring, is starting to be explored. See Lotan et al. (2011). A skeptical take on
technology's impact on regime change is Evgeny Morozov (2011), who quips, "If
an authoritarian regime can crumble under the pressure of a Facebook group . . .

its not much of an authoritarian regime" (198). The phrase *the whole world is watching* was popularized as a chant during the protests at the 1968 Democratic Convention and serves as the title of a touchstone book in academic studies of journalism (Gitlin 1980). President Obama also invoked the phrase during citizen protests in Iran: "The Iranian government must understand that the world is watching" ("Obama to Iran: 'The Whole World is Watching,'" 2009).

15   Organizations devoted to investigating and memorializing the unexplained deaths and abuses of journalists (e.g., the Committee to Protect Journalists) maintain extensive lists from Russia, with a recent report being of Russian journalists attacked while doing an investigating piece tied to Russian military and the Ukraine (Gorst 2014). Ecuador has a record of being unfriendly to the press, with current president Rafael Correa going after writers, according to Human Rights Watch ("World Report 2013").

16   Merkel: "The NSA clearly couldn't be trusted with private information, because they let Snowden clean them out" (Traynor and Lewis 2013). The joke is often attributed to Grouch Marx, as popularized by Woody Allen in *Annie Hall* (1977).

17   Furthermore, "In drawing such a contrast, the editorials positioned old media as the true stewards of the public interest . . . [and WikiLeaks] as lacking the values and ethics necessary to belonging in the journalistic community" (Hindman and Thomas 2014, 546).

18   "I selected these documents based on what's in the public interest, but I'm relying on you to use your journalistic judgment to only publish those documents that the public should see and that can be revealed without harm to innocent people. . . . If I wanted the documents just put on the Internet en masse, I could have done that myself" (Greenwald 2014, 53).

19   However, Greenberg (2012, 305–09) claims that all the documents and the cypher key were eventually published online, thus accessible to anyone with cryptographic sophistication.

20   In Foucault's (1980) words: "In the Panopticon each person, depending on his place, is watched by all or certain others. You have an apparatus of total and circulating mistrust, because there is no absolute point. The perfected form of surveillance consists in a summation of *malveillance*" (157).

21   A brief overview: "Bush Administration's Warrantless Wiretapping Program," 2008.

22   Leigh and Harding (2011) call WikiLeaks' exposures "the biggest leak in the history of the world" (2). The absence of a high-profile case so far, *à la* the Pentagon Papers, make this less likely to be true. Occurring after the writing of their book, it seems the Snowden leaks have had a larger impact, at least in the United States.

23 James Clapper told Congress in 2012 that the NSA didn't collect data on Americans. Snowden's files seem to reveal the contrary. The Department of Justice is reviewing the case (Reilly 2014).

24 The NSA leaks revealed indiscriminate collect-it-all data on Americans and non-Americans alike, in the form of internet and personal information, and if the PRISM program was operational, then e-mails were indeed targeted. Wiggle room exists for telephones, where metadata was collected. *Metadata* is word that sometimes connotes that no personal details are rendered. But through metadata one can piece together phone numbers with phone owners, time, place, and length of call. So, for example, while the content of my phone call to the pizza shop would be unknown without a warrant, that I called the pizza shop every Friday and spoke with them for a few minutes would be known. Replace pizza shop with suspected terrorist, or pastor, or suicide hotline, extend it out over a period of time, combine it with emails and contacts, and a fairly detailed picture can form. As Edward Felten, director of Princeton's Center for Information Technology Policy, testified in *ACLU v. Clapper* (2013): "Metadata is often a proxy for content."

Section Two

Participatory Culture

5

Programs or People? Participation and the Ethics of Hacktivism

Brett Lunceford

The widespread diffusion of internet access and new media technologies have opened new opportunities for social movements and protest actions. Protestors are no longer limited to acting in the physical spaces in which they reside, as protest can take place online. Moreover, as police have become increasingly militarized, potential protestors must consider whether they wish to place their physical bodies on the line and/or if they can afford to be arrested for their cause. Protesting through a virtual presence can be a powerful tool toward mitigating perceived dangers of physical protest because, as Thomas (2002) notes, "the virtual presence of the hacker is not enough to constitute a crime—what is always needed is a body, a real body, a live body" (182). In this chapter I will consider one form of digital activism: hacktivism, or politically motivated computer hacking.

Hacktivism is often referred to as "electronic civil disobedience" (ECD), but although *hacktivism* is *activism*, it does not enjoy the same protection under the First Amendment as traditional protest methods. Indeed, this chapter makes no argument concerning the legal aspects of hacktivism—hacktivism is clearly a criminal act—but rather, my focus is on its ethical dimensions. Elsewhere I have argued that scholars must consider hacktivism not merely as a criminal act, but as a rhetorical act (Lunceford 2012). Actions that are legal are not always ethical, ethical acts are not always legal, and protestors may find themselves in disagreement concerning specific tactics, even if they agree with the goals of the protest itself.

This chapter examines the arguments between two hacker groups concerning the ethical dimensions of actions that took place during the 1999 protests of the World Trade Organization (WTO) meetings in Seattle, Washington. One group, the electrohippies collective, engaged in a distributed denial-of-service attack in order to take down the WTO's website. In a distributed denial-of-service attack, a large group of computers overloads the server of the targeted website and shuts down access to the website. Distinguishing this tactic from other forms of denial-of-service attacks, which do not require a large group of participants, is an important strategy for the electrohippies, who argued that because the denial-of-service attack required the participation of many individuals to work it was inherently democratic and, thus, ethical. Another group, the Cult of the Dead Cow (cDc), argued that the protest was unethical because it violated the principle of freedom of speech. This argument illustrates how the changing media landscape challenges the ethical principles readily accepted in traditional protest and how different groups can come to very different conclusions when employing traditional ethics.

What is hacktivism?

Wray (1999) explicitly connects the tactics of hacktivism with those of traditional protest: "The same principles of traditional civil disobedience, such as trespass and blockage, will be applied, but more and more these acts will take place in electronic or digital form: The primary site for ECD will be in cyberspace" (108). Hacktivism has become an important component in many protest activities as the internet becomes increasingly integrated into our lives. For example, the antiglobalization and the environmental movements have been particularly web-savvy in their protests (DeLuca and Peeples 2002; Juris 2005; Kahn and Kellner 2004; Van Aelst and Walgrave 2002). In some ways, social movements have had to enter the digital realm to remain relevant; McKenzie (1999) argues that "long-entrenched practices of political activism—street protests, strikes, sit-ins, boycotts—are becoming less and less effective and in their place have arisen practices of 'electronic civil disobedience' and 'hacktivism'" (¶32).

Like traditional protest actions, there are many forms in which hacktivism can take place. The two most common incarnations of hacktivism are website defacements and denial-of-service attacks. Website defacement is pretty much what it sounds like. The hacker takes control of a website and replaces the original content with a message from the hacker. In order to do this, hackers run scripts to find potential security holes, allowing the hackers to automate this aspect of hacking. As such, hackers can deface many sites in a short period of time (Lunceford 2012). In these cases, the website itself may be inconsequential, serving only as a means of reaching potential viewers. However, these hacks can also be targeted to specific entities against whom the hackers have some grievance; for example, an antifur activist hacks the website of a furrier. In each case, the goal is to disseminate one's message.

Denial-of-service attacks, alternatively, attempt to silence the message of the target rather than replace it: "At its most basic, a denial-of-service attack is overloading a server through the use of a zombie network or a script" (Lunceford 2009b, 243). Some have compared this attack to a virtual sit-in because the principles are similar (Lane 2003; Wray 1999). Bandwidth is not infinite and a server can only handle a certain amount of traffic. When the requests for the website exceed the allotted bandwidth, others cannot access the site. The bandwidth is consumed entirely by the protestors. There are two forms of denial-of-service attacks: denial-of-service (DoS), which involves a single attacker or group, and distributed denial-of-service attacks (DDoS), which involves multiple sources of attack (Chowriwar et al. 2014; Ghazali and Hassan 2011).

It may be tempting to directly map digital strategies onto traditional protest actions. As Schwartau (2000) put it, "Graffiti on billboards, graffiti on web sites, same difference, different medium" (25). But hacktivism is more than the same tactic in a digital sphere; one cannot change the medium without changing the nature of the act in some way (see McLuhan 1994). As Postman (1993) explains, "A new technology does not add or subtract something. It changes everything" (18). One must come to new tactics like hacktivism with a fresh outlook, considering them on their own terms.

Jordan (2002) argues that "hacktivists are not so much bending, twisting and reshaping information flows as creating alternative infrastructures to enable new types of flow" (135). Hacktivism has the potential to give voice to those who would otherwise be drowned out in a flood of mass-mediated messages. McChesney (1997, 1999) and others (Aufderheide et al. 1997; Sussman 1997) have pointed out that as the mass media have consolidated, the available messages have likewise become consolidated, leaving less room for alternative voices. In this environment, it is difficult to voice dissenting opinions and present alternate viewpoints. Moreover, as the costs of participating in the public sphere become higher, fewer citizens will have a chance to participate in the deliberations that will have an impact upon their lives. Hacktivism has changed the nature of protest and some groups have created tools that allow non-hackers to participate in acts of electronic civil disobedience. For example, Electronic Disturbance Theater created a program called Zapatista FloodNet that automated denial-of-service attacks (Lane 2003). One needed only to type the URL of the website he or she wished to attack and the program would do the rest. As Martin (2000) explains, "Electronic protesting these days is a simple matter of downloading easy-to-use software from the Web, or of visiting a protest site where you can set your browser to bombard a target site with requests for information. Anyone can be a hacktivist" (6). By allowing for the automation of political action, hacktivism allows those who may have the desire, but not the time, to participate.

The digital battle of Seattle: A tale of two ethics

Contrary to media accounts of hacking, hackers have long been political actors (Jordan and Taylor 2004; Lunceford 2009a). One hacker group in particular that has fully embraced hacktivism (even claiming that one of their members coined the term) is Cult of the Dead Cow (cDc) (see Ruffin 2004). In 1999, they formed "Hacktivismo" to emphasize this focus. The Hacktivismo Declaration (2001) draws on the United Nations Universal Declaration of Human Rights and states:

> We are convinced that the international hacking community has a moral imperative to act, and we declare:
>
> That full respect for human rights and fundamental freedoms includes the liberty of fair and reasonable access to information, whether by shortwave radio, air mail, simple telephony, the global internet or other media.
>
> That we recognize the right of governments to forbid the publication of properly categorized state secrets, child pornography, and matters related to personal privacy and privilege, among other accepted restrictions. But we oppose the use of state power to control access to the works of critics, intellectuals, artists, or religious figures.
>
> That state sponsored censorship of the Internet erodes peaceful and civilized coexistence, affects the exercise of democracy, and endangers the socioeconomic development of nations.
>
> That state-sponsored censorship of the Internet is a serious form of organized and systematic violence against citizens, is intended to generate confusion and xenophobia, and is a reprehensible violation of trust.
>
> That we will study ways and means of circumventing state-sponsored censorship of the Internet and will implement technologies to challenge information rights violations.

These words portray an extreme depiction of the hacker motto, "information wants to be free." For cDc, censorship of the internet is equivalent to "systematic violence." There are some paradoxes within this declaration, many of them dependent upon definition. For example, they recognize the right to "forbid the publication of properly categorized state secrets, child pornography, and matters related to personal privacy and privilege," but what constitutes a "properly categorized state secret?" From this perspective, all that must be done to enable wholesale censorship and remain within the bounds of this declaration is to simply declare the censored material a "state secret," a tactic that has been used to great effect in squelching the release of information even in the United States (see "Government Secrecy" 2005).

Perhaps the most problematic aspect of the Hacktivismo Declaration is the conclusion: "We will study ways and means of circumventing state-sponsored censorship of the Internet and will implement technologies to challenge information rights violations." What, exactly, is an information rights violation? Hacktivismo's argument seems to be based mainly on the consumption of information, but the production of information is likewise essential. In the Hacktivismo FAQ, they state: "We are also interested in keeping the Internet free of state-sponsored censorship and corporate chicanery so all opinions can be heard" (Ruffin, Warren, and Marie 2000–01). This underlying focus on information access and consumption at times paints them into an ideological corner. Even as they proclaim the importance of information access and decry the use of censorship, they still grant governments the ability to decide what should be censored. "Accepted restrictions" may, even in the United States, apply to critics who wish to see the government overthrown, so the kinds of critics and the types of criticism matter.

The writers of the declaration refuse to become bogged down in the details of what information should be available and what kinds of actions should be censored (besides obvious ones like child pornography), leaving this open to interpretation by the state. Hacktivismo likewise recognizes the difficulty of prescribing specific guidelines in light of varying levels of legality in different jurisdictions:

> The term "lawfully published" is full of landmines. Lawful to whom? What is lawful in the United States can get you a bullet in the head in China. At the end of the day we recognize that some information needs to be controlled. But that control falls far short of censoring material that is critical of governments, intellectual and artistic opinion, information relating to women's issues or

sexual preference, and religious opinions. That's another way of saying that most information wants to be free; the rest needs a little privacy, even non-existence in the case of things like kiddie porn. Everyone will have to sort the parameters of this one out for themselves. (Ruffin, Warren, and Marie 2000–01)

As one could expect, other hacker groups have come to different conclusions as to how these parameters should be sorted out. One such group that came to different conclusions is the electrohippies collective, a hacktivist group in the United Kingdom.

Within hacktivist collectives, an age-old question arises: do the ends justify the means? And, more precisely, which means justify desired ends? This is an argument that plays out in the white paper published by the electrohippies, titled "Client-side Distributed Denial-of-Service: Valid Campaign Tactic or Terrorist Act?" and the response to this action by cDc. In their white paper, the electrohippies defend the use of client-side denial-of-service attacks and reveal their anticapitalist leanings from the very beginning:

> As Jesus ransacked the temple in Jerusalem because it had become a house of merchandise, so the recent attacks on ecommerce web sites are a protest against the manner of its recent development. But, do we label Jesus as a terrorist? Those involved probably have a reverential view of the 'Net. The public space that the 'Net represents is being promoted as a marketplace for large corporate interests, and many of those who use the 'Net for other purposes are dissatisfied with this. (DJNZ and Collective 2001, 1)

The electrohippies clearly place the internet within the realm of the public sphere and decry the commercial nature of the internet and the associated concentration of power by corporate interests, comparing the internet to the den of thieves that Jesus Christ cast out of the temple (Mk 11:17). Like cDc/ Hacktivismo, the electrohippies have a penchant for placing their causes in epic terms and share a commitment to hacking as a form of social change, but there are many differences between the two groups; these points of disagreement illuminate ideological schisms within the hacker community concerning appropriate means for enacting hacktivism.

The first difference between the groups concerns how each views the legitimacy of denial-of-service attacks. The electrohippies argue that client-side denial-of-service attacks have greater legitimacy as a protest action because of their distributed nature. "Client-side distributed actions require the efforts of real people, taking part in their thousands simultaneously, to make the action effective. If there are not enough people supporting [the] action it doesn't work. The fact that service on the WTO's servers was interrupted on the 30th November [and] 1st of December, and significantly slowed on the 2nd and 3rd of December, demonstrated that there was significant support for the electrohippies action" (DJNZ and Collective 2001, 3). They contrast this form of denial-of-service attack with server-side denial-of-service attacks that can be done with only a few individuals and a legion of zombie computers. The fact that the electrohippies use client-side attacks gives them what they call a "democratic guarantee."

cDc rejects this premise, arguing that

> Denial of Service, is Denial of Service, is Denial of Service, period. The only difference between a program like Stacheldraht [a DDoS application written by The Mixter] and the client side javascript program written by the Electrohippies is the difference between blowing something up and being pecked to death by a duck. And if numbers lend legitimacy—as the Electrohippies propose—then the lone bomber who tried to assassinate Hitler in his bunker was wrong and the millions who supported the dictator were right. (Ruffin 2000)

Ignoring for a moment the resort to Hitler in this statement, this illustrates a fundamental disagreement on the nature of online democratic practice. In essence, the electrohippies seem to subscribe to the great hope of democracy—that the majority of the people will support that which is just and good the majority of the time.

If cDc does not believe that numbers grant legitimacy, then what does? In their appeal to the First Amendment, it is difficult to ascertain whether cDc appeals to a transcendent ideal of freedom of speech or an appeal to the First Amendment as rule of law. Either of these possibilities are ethically problematic. If they are appealing to a transcendent ideal of freedom of speech, they do so unilaterally and with little authority. If they base their appeals on the First Amendment, they gloss over the fact that the internet is a global entity and that the United States Constitution is not the standard by which all other nations should be judged (Lunceford 2013). Each group is committed to the idea of free exchange of information, although they differ in what information should be available to whom and by whom. The main concern of cDc is government censorship of information. The right to access information belongs to the individual, so cutting off any information is undesirable, even if it comes from a controversial entity. In other words, the information flows toward the individual. The electrohippies, on

the other hand, see the flow of information going in the other direction—toward
the organization from the individual. Silencing the WTO's website is less an act
of censorship and more an act of compelling the organization to listen to the
protestors. Each seeks to perpetuate the "I-Thou" relationship prescribed by
Buber (1958), but differ in who deserves to be "I."

This raises an ethical question however, as Buber (1958) would likely
wonder at the wisdom of ascribing either I or Thou to such institutions as
the WTO, remarking that "the separated *It* of institutions is an animated clod
without a soul" (53). In short, who deserves to speak, and are individuals
ethically obligated to listen to an organization, especially a nongovernmental
organization like the WTO? For cDc, this seems an irrelevant question, as they
seem driven by a sense of duty toward the principle of freedom of speech for
everyone. In this regard, they seem to follow Kant's ([1785]1959) categorical
imperative: "Act only according to that maxim by which you can at the same
time will that it should become a universal law" (39). In other words, if it is
unacceptable to squelch speech for one person, one must accept free speech
for all. As such, they are placed in the position of defending the WTO's right
to expression, regardless of what they say. The electrohippies recognize that
by engaging in denial-of-service attacks they prevent free speech, but they
justify their actions under two conditions: the target must be reprehensible
to a majority of the people, and the attack should be limited to a specific,
politically salient occasion. They point out that their actions against the WTO
only took place during the conference in Seattle, which not only provided the
opportunity to raise consciousness concerning the actions of the WTO, but
also allowed those who opposed the WTO to voice their arguments (DJNZ and
Collective 2001, 7–8). Although this may work in theory, it may not be very
effective in practice. In the case of the WTO protests, where the actions of the
electrohippies were likely to generate news coverage in addition to that already
generated by the disruptions taking place in the physical space of Seattle, this
would likely be an effective use of denial-of-service attacks. Still, the question
remains whether it did anything to actually raise consciousness concerning the
WTO. One can only speculate on how effective this act of hacktivism would be
with little action taking place in physical space; indeed it seems unlikely that
the electrohippies would engage in such actions because they would be less
likely to bear a stamp of legitimacy (the organization must be reprehensible to a
majority of the people and the widespread protests seemed to serve as evidence
of this fact).

In contrast to the cDc's Kantian leanings, the electrohippies seem more aligned with the utilitarian school of ethics, which considers the outcomes of one's actions. Their defense of the action against the WTO call to mind Bentham's (1823) argument that "it is the greatest happiness of the greatest number that is the measure of right and wrong" (vi). If one group (the WTO) must be silenced to provide a space in which the many (the protestors) can be heard, the net result in happiness is positive. As such, the two groups are fundamentally at odds concerning what constitutes the greatest good. The electrohippes are willing to accept some collateral damage in free speech if it makes more people happy, while cDc is unwilling to budge on squelching freedom of speech out of a sense of duty.

Another fundamental difference between the two groups concerns the ontological nature of cyberspace compared to physical space. The electrohippies argue that "as another part of society's public space the Internet will be used by groups and individuals as a means of protests. There is no practical difference between cyberspace and the street in terms of how people use the 'Net" (DJNZ and Collective 2001, 2). The electrohippies suggest that tactics that work in the offline world will work in the online world, which is demonstrated in their comparison between online and offline protest actions. "Distributed clientside DoS action is only effective if it has mass support, and hence a democratic mandate from a large number of people on the Net to permit the action to take place. These type[s] of actions are directly analogous to the type of demonstrations that take place across the world. One or two people do not make a valid demonstration—100,000 people do" (DJNZ and Collective 2001, 5). The electrohippies view the internet as a public space rather than a private space, so they reject arguments of virtual trespassing. Once again, we see the principle of greatest happiness at work in the electrohippies' reasoning. The website may belong to the WTO, but the internet belongs to everyone and no one person or entity has any special right to be heard over the masses. If the website is publicly accessible and a mass of people want to enter the website repeatedly in order to hinder access to the site, this should be their right. The electrohippies argue that the strategies of the digital world and the strategies of the physical world are equally valid, and this is demonstrated by means of electronic protest. They are borrowing strategies that have worked in the past (sit-ins, demonstrations) and adapting them to the digital world. Only the location has changed.

cDc acknowledges that for street protests, larger numbers suggest greater legitimacy—cDc member Oxblood Ruffin (2000) notes that he has participated in such protests—but they dismiss the core assumption that there is little difference between cyberspace and physical space: "Where a large physical mass is the currency of protest on the street, or at the ballot box, it is an irrelevancy on the Internet. Or more correctly, it is not always necessary. . . . But to think that it takes a lot of people to execute an act of civil disobedience on the Internet is naive. Programs make a difference, not people." The desired end of shutting down a website can be done with an efficient program much more effectively than hoping that enough individuals take part in the action. But although cDc is correct that the nature of the internet allows for different modes of protest that are impossible in traditional protest (e.g., using only a few hackers to create a digital sit-in that would otherwise take thousands), to say that a mass of people is an irrelevancy is an overstatement. As Jordan (2002) observes, a large mass of people makes it a "popular protest"; "A mass event needs the masses. Hacktivists producing denial-of-service actions choose a technically inefficient means to serve politically efficient ends" (125). Even as cDc recognizes that the online environment changes the nature of legitimacy, they overlook how this may affect their own standards of legitimacy. cDc seem to draw their legitimacy from transcendent values (e.g., freedom of speech), but there is no reason why those values must function the same way in both online and offline environments. Both the electrohippies and cDc seem to place greater importance on the values of the offline world.

cDc argues that programs are what matter in cyberspace, the electrohippies argue that people are what matter, and both have written programs for use in protest activities. But the question of whether people or programs matter more in cyberspace depends more on one's ethical stance than on what is technologically possible. Both the electrohippies and cDc are technologically savvy enough to create programs that would take full advantage of the medium of cyberspace, so this must be a conscious choice. For the electrohippies, the means are precisely what justify the ends. They are ethically justified in silencing the WTO because a large number support this action. For the cDc, the desired ends are morally suspect and thus would be indefensible by any means.

This argument between the electrohippies and the cDc illuminates some of the basic issues surrounding the ethics of hacktivism and illustrates how two groups with similar aims (social justice) can disagree on the means to that end. With the electrohippies invested in the "greatest happiness" principle (Mill 1907, 9–10) and cDc duty-bound to the principle of freedom of speech, they cannot help but arrive not only at different conclusions, but at different means to those ends. If the goal is to fight censorship and ensure free speech for all, without exception, then a technological solution may be the most effective means of doing so. On the other hand, if one's ethics require both qualitative judgments and quantitative validation, then creating a structure that facilitates a large number of participants in the protest action would be desirable. But because each considers their respective stances to be axiomatic truths—cDc argues that denial-of-service attacks violate First Amendment rights and the electrohippies believe that the more people involved, the more democratic—the electrohippies and the cDc talk past each other.

Despite these differences, both parties have valid concerns and flaws in their arguments. Do we take for granted that the First Amendment is always good? Is this an appeal to the law or an appeal to the idea that free speech is an inalienable human right? If so, to whom does that right belong—to citizens, corporations, political parties? Although the courts have ruled that commercial speech is not protected by the First Amendment, a recent Supreme Court decision equates financial political contributions with protected speech, opening the door for corporate entities to enjoy even more protections (for more on the problematic legal nature of corporate entities, see Aljalian 1999; Edwards and Valencia 2002; Manning 1984; Rafalko 1989; Wilson 1994). But corporate entities do not enjoy all of the same rights as citizens, so the argument that cDc makes about suppressing a company's First Amendment right is problematic, especially when upholding the website owner's freedom of speech by squelching that of the hacktivists denies the hacktivists' equally valid (in terms of the First Amendment) right to peaceably assemble. The electrohippies seem to believe that to have thousands of people on your side is to have justice on your side. Although numbers do grant at least a veneer of legitimacy—despite cDc's claims—the amount of people it takes to shut down a website is a very small percentage of the population. Even if one takes at face value the electrohippies' assertion that around 450,000 people around the world took part in the action against the WTO (believing for the moment that these were separate individuals, which would be difficult to verify), then considering a world population of six billion people, roughly 0.0075 percent of the world's population participated. Their argument that "tens of thousands (if not hundreds of thousands) of people" provide a "democratic guarantee," then, is not really accurate (DJNZ and Collective 2001, 7).

The disagreement between the electrohippies and the cDc is a continuation of familiar arguments concerning protest rhetoric: Do the ends justify the means? What is the difference between terrorism and activism? Where does one draw the moral and ethical lines for protest behavior; are extralegal means of protest still ethical? These questions are not inconsequential, and the answers to each one by different groups are bound to differ depending on the fundamental assumptions held by each group. If an organization has a fundamental assumption, for example, that the legal system is irreparably corrupt and broken, then such an ideology would invite extralegal means of protest.

One fundamental assumption of the electrohippies is that they are not simply silencing the WTO—they are opening a space in which the voices of others, which are drowned out when the WTO is granted the opportunity to continually speak, can be heard. In considering the restriction of protest activities in white residential neighborhoods during the civil rights movement, Haiman (1967) asks:

> The question, I think, is what price a society is willing to pay to insure that the messages of minority groups are not screened out of the consciences of those to whom they are addressed. For once the principle is invoked that listeners may be granted some immunity from messages they think they would rather not hear, or which cause them annoyance, a Pandora's box of circumstances is opened in which the right of free speech could be effectively nullified. (106)

Similar arguments can be made concerning the WTO protests. Hacktivists can easily post web pages arguing against WTO policies, just as Black marchers could have easily marched in their own neighborhoods during the civil rights era. The point of the marches was to take the message to those whom the protestors believed needed to hear it. The electrohippies' stated goal was to "substitute the deficit of speech by one group by encouraging debate with others" (DJNZ and Collective 2001, 7). The cDc would argue that this is still wrong, but the electrohippies may see no other way to place their message on a relatively level-playing field with the WTO, which has the backing of the establishment. As Barnlund and Haiman (1960) explain:

> When one person or a few people in a group or society possess all the guns, muscles, or money, and the others are relatively weak and helpless, optimum conditions do not exist for discussion, mutual influence, and democracy. Discussion in such circumstances occurs only at the sufferance of the powerful; and generous as these persons may sometimes be, they are not likely voluntarily to abdicate their power when vital interests are at stake. (12)

Ethical considerations of hacktivism must also consider its lack of permanence. Unlike the physical world, the medium of the internet is a constantly shifting, evolving space. One cannot simply re-upload a building that has been burned down, but one can replace a defaced website with a backup. In other words, "hackers are not defacing property so much as they are defacing a presentation of self that can quickly be reclaimed" (Lunceford 2012, 44). Of course this creates problems when attempting to quantify the damages to the organization that has been defaced. It is difficult to know how to compensate an organization for a brief loss of image. After all, most hackers do not attempt to represent the organization—although this has happened in protest actions (Yes Men 2004)—because they want the defacement to be obvious. Therefore it is unlikely that visitors to the defaced site will mistake the defaced site for an authentic version of the website. Denial-of-service attacks are likewise transitory; the electrohippies limited their actions to the dates in which the WTO meetings were taking place. Even if they wished to continue the attack, the WTO would be able to counter by addressing the technical flaw in the server or by increasing available bandwidth. In short, any attack that takes place in the digital domain will be temporary at best. When considering the ethics of hacktivism, this fact must be taken into account—the destruction of a virtual presence is not equal to the destruction of a physical presence.

Conclusion

The debate between the cDc and the electrohippies illustrates the perils of mapping the ethics of the industrial age onto the internet. The cDc's assertion that programs, not people, matter in the digital realm is a profound refutation of most social movement strategies in which the goal is to mobilize resources—most importantly people. Perhaps the electrohippies cling to the notion that a large enough mass of bodies will somehow grant legitimacy to one's cause because this is how causes have often been evaluated in the past. But hacktivism need not adhere to old notions of legitimacy any more than it need slavishly ape old protest tactics. Hacktivism allows for new forms of protest much as the internet allows for new ways of constructing citizenship, governments, and society (see Jordan 1999, 2002). Indeed, Bodó (2014) explains that hacktivism itself is undergoing a kind of evolution, moving away from the model championed by the electrohippies in which the nonspecialist can be a hacktivist and toward "a much more potent form of hacktivism, which relies on insiders to expose the ways power operates and create a more transparent society" (8).

As the world becomes more globalized, protest activities likewise become more globalized because the effects of organizations and legislation may be experienced beyond national borders. Moreover, because there is no longer a need to physically assemble, the risks inherent in assembly are dissipated as well. One no longer need risk bodily harm by engaging in protest activity. Law enforcement officials are highly skilled in crowd control, but in the virtual domain, the playing field is slanted toward the activists. But more importantly, one no longer need even be somewhere at all. As the cDc notes, one can simply automate protest. This leads to another ethical consideration; one should exercise caution when one press of a button can reproduce the actions of millions.

Still, hacktivism has a long way to go before it can yield the same effects of traditional protest, and traditional means of protest seem to be alive and well. Marches in Washington, D.C. are still rather common. Letter-writing campaigns are also in heavy use. Lobbyists still wield significant power. It seems that there are many for whom protest occurs outside of the digital realm. One limitation of hacktivism is its relative invisibility. The first order of business for any protest action is to gain the attention of the media (Oliver and Myers 1999). Physical demonstrations of protest are often covered in the media, but the electrohippies' actions have been largely forgotten. Hackers stand little chance against impressive displays of black bloc anarchists and smashed windows in the battle for gaining mindshare (see DeLuca and Peeples 2002).

Hacktivism seems to be a double-edged sword. There are ethical dilemmas concerning the silencing of other voices, but there is also the increased possibility for more individuals to engage in activism in previously impossible ways. Hacktivism takes advantage of the networked society in ways that traditional means of protest cannot. However, these hacktions are unlikely to stand alone successfully—they are best understood within the context of movements and actions that take place in the physical world. We are far from the science fiction fantasy of leaving the body behind as our minds traverse the vast expanse of cyberspace. As such, we cannot completely abandon the physical world and the material considerations with which most social movements are concerned.

6

Just War Craft: Virtue Ethics and *DotA*

Matthew Pittman and Tom Bivins

Traditionally, edited volumes on media ethics deal with less playful issues of ethical behavior in mass media. Journalism, public relations, violent content, advertising, privacy, censorship, and media ownership have been covered in great depth and certainly create necessary dialogue for sound moral reasoning in a flourishing democracy. So what makes a video game like *Defense of the Ancients* (*DotA*) a worthy addition to the existing scope of research under the broad label of "media ethics"?

For one thing, *DotA* embodies what has become known as "participatory culture." Attributed primarily to Henry Jenkins et al. (2009), this is the relatively recent phenomena wherein the confluence of technological accessibility and creative capacity gives individuals the ability to actively create, modify, and participate in the culture of which they were previously just passive consumers. Common examples would be *Star Wars* fan fiction or The *Harry Potter* Alliance, a real-life fan activist group inspired by the J. K. Rowling novels. *DotA* is a game created by fans of Blizzard's highly popular *Warcraft* series; its democratized and ongoing development, maintenance, and community consist entirely of the individuals who play it.

Additionally, these individuals inhabit the dual roles of media makers and community participants. This makes *DotA* a prime candidate for exploring the ethical challenge that comes along with participatory culture: there is a "breakdown of traditional forms of professional training and socialization that might prepare young people for their increasingly public roles as media makers and community participants" (Jenkins et al. 2009, xiii). Traditional game development consists primarily of a one-way flow of information from producers to consumers. A two-way flow of communication between those playing the game and those producing it (and those making the gradual changes over time) makes for a more social, integrated, and truly participatory game culture.

Finally, an integrated system of game and game culture necessarily requires an integrated system of ethics to understand how exactly it might produce successful, mature, enlightened gamers. This is why Virtue Ethics—a framework that strives to cultivate wholly integrated individuals, not just assist with one difficult decision—is a useful approach to understanding a complex and evolving media platform like *DotA*. This chapter will argue that using Virtue Ethics as a lens to explore *DotA* highlights the potential of both to cultivate character.

Ethics and/of/in video games

Aside from being the highest form of art[1] (or not[2]), video games have become big business. In 2013 the video game industry raked in over $93 billion in revenue, and in 2014 it crossed the $100 billion mark ("Global" 2014). By comparison, in 2013 Starbucks made just shy of $15 billion (*Starbucks* 2013), and Warner Bros., Disney, and Universal (the top three grossing studios) *together* made $13.4 billion globally ("Studio" 2013). The enormous popularity and profitability of video games has led to—or perhaps resulted from—its rise as a serious cultural medium. It is increasingly common for an upcoming game to have big-budget commercials (with recognizable celebrities), tie-ins with films or sporting events, or similar fanfare.

Additionally, video games matter—particularly for ethical exploration—because more people are playing them. The stereotype of the thirteen-year-old boy camped out for hours in his living room (while his parents coax him to "go play outside") is long gone. According to the Entertainment Software Association's most recent statistics ("2014 Sales" 2014), 50 percent of Americans play video games. The average gamer is thirty-one years old and has been playing video games for fourteen years. Interestingly, 48 percent of all gamers are female and over half of all American adults play video games (Lenhart, Jones, and MacGill 2008). In terms of social gaming, 77 percent of all gamers spend at least one hour per week playing with others: 42 percent play with friends, 32 percent with family members, 18 percent with parents, and 14 percent with their spouse or significant other. Over half of parents believe that video games are actually a positive part of their child's life.

A final factor that makes video games ideal media sites for examining ethical behavior: advances in mobile, console, and computer technologies have given many personal devices the potential to run games. We play games while watching television, while falling asleep, alone or with friends, while waiting in lines, and yes, 73 percent of us play mobile games while going to the bathroom (Edmonds 2013).

Not only are we playing more games on more devices in more places, but those games are increasingly integrated with our "real" lives. We use our Facebook accounts to log into a new mobile gaming site or our PayPal account to purchase a software update on our computer. We accumulate a community of friends or followers through the games we frequently play. Or, as the previous statistics indicate, we simply play games with people we know in real life.

Video games are excellent phenomena through which we can examine ethical behavior. Games usually have some element of fantasy or escapism, but the principles and skills required for success within the game typically mirror those found in real life. Miguel Sicart (2011), a scholar who studies video games and ethics, puts it like this: "Computer games are complex cultural objects: they have rules guiding behavior, they create game worlds with values at play, and they relate to players who like to explore morals and actions forbidden to society" (4). This chapter will attempt to unpack an admittedly complex video game, *DotA 2*, in the hopes that we might learn something about how video games have the potential to cultivate virtuous behavior.

In some sense, games can be viewed as morality experiments—a chance to behave in ways we would not dream of in the real world. Sid Meier, creator of the enormously successful *Civilization* games, said that a game is merely a "series of interesting choices."[3] The *Civilization* series of games can be addictive, but because they are turn-based it makes it *somewhat* easier to save one's game and walk away. They are morality experiments on a grand scale: what if you play as the Egyptians and develop iron instead of building the Pyramids? What if you play as India and convince your allies (say, China and Mongolia) to attack Japan only to turn around and stab them in the back? When ethical questions are posed to video games, the series of choices quickly teaches the gamer about the power of choice and consequence. Unlike real life, however, most video games afford players a chance to replay situations, experiment with different choices until the desired result is achieved.

These examples may begin to demonstrate why some ethical frameworks might fall short when it comes to game studies. It is possible to apply to video games consequential ethics, developed by John Stuart Mill, and deontological (rule-based) ethics, developed primarily by Immanuel Kant, in an attempt to identify ethical or unethical behavior. Simplifying somewhat, consequentialism assumes that the ends justify the means as long as the greatest good is achieved. So, if a player wins, it doesn't matter how she achieved victory, only that she achieved it. Similarly, in deontological ethics, as long as the player adhered to her duty or obligation, she would be in the right. In video games, the obligation is usually to win, so the result is similar to consequentialism. However, both approaches risk reducing the game and gamer to ethical egoism.

On the other hand, Virtue Ethics (as originally developed by Aristotle) is a system that transcends merely achieving goals or adhering to duties. Virtue Ethics encourage the development of virtuous qualities leading to consistently moral behavior in the actual person. Instead of asking the question, "Is it OK if I do this or that?" it seeks to answer the question, "What kind of person should I be?" Applying Virtue Ethics to video game scholarship reveals that consistent goodwill in video game play will help contribute to the internal good of media culture.

Not everyone would agree that Virtue Ethics are best suited for video games. Some scholars have even used them to argue that a responsible person would never play a violent game because it would lead to violent tendencies in real life (McCormick 2001). Therefore it should be noted that as we make our case in this chapter, we are assuming the reader has moved past the moral panic of previous eras, and like us attributes a fair amount of autonomous self-awareness to today's digital natives (Palfrey and Gasser 2008). Many people have enjoyed the *Halo* series of games, and to our knowledge, none have subsequently confused their own life with that of a futuristic space marine. For those who seek to explore Virtue Ethics through the lens of video games, the potential is great.

Virtue Ethics

Overview

In the Western world, Virtue (or character) Ethics arose in ancient Greece. The idea in the most common Aristotelian form is to construct a personal character that can deal successfully with, and contribute positively to, the world we inhabit. Virtue Ethics combines moral education with lived experience in order to reach a level of "moral maturity" from which a person is capable of making ethical decisions based on character development. Thus, a morally mature character will tend to make morally correct choices.

Virtue Ethics concentrates neither on the action itself nor the consequences of that action. Rather, it focuses on the actor and the characteristics that make that person capable of making a right decision. Virtue can be defined as strength of character—a disposition to act consistently in a certain way, in both feeling and action. Character, in turn, can be defined as the accumulation of virtues, which ultimately leads to "moral maturity"—an integration of both intellectual and practical experience. This integrated character will, according to Aristotle, be best able to make moral judgments. Virtue Ethics are also community centered; they contribute to the betterment of society, not just the individual. The goal of Virtue Ethics is not just a life lived well, but a life lived within a society of others to which we contribute both on our behalf and theirs.

Virtue Ethics may seem to the uninitiated to be arbitrary—no rules, no "greater good" argument, etc. However, it is intuitively logical in that it proposes that a good person is the sum of her learned experience, both educational and practical. That person will have developed a good character and thus be consistent in her actions, no matter how different each situation is. Virtue Ethics puts the onus of morality squarely on the character of the individual. Ultimately, actions taken by the morally mature person must contribute to the well-being of the society in which she lives. Ideally, even in a virtual world, our actions would not tend to debase our character or the character of the community in which we operate. As Hickok (1849) noted, "In the society of the virtuous, there is a reverential respect for all" (664).

Digital virtue

If we believe life transcends the objective (real) and that the objective and the virtual are inextricably bound, what do we lose by allowing our darker urges to have free reign as long as their expression is outside of reality? What real person is being hurt if we murder in virtual reality? The answer for Virtue Ethics, of course, is that what happens in a virtual world, even if it doesn't affect others, affects the self by debasing character. As Lajoie (1996) noted, "Objects in virtual reality differ from material objects to the extent that they exist only by virtue of human intention" (161).

Virtue Ethics tells us that who you are, as a person inhabiting the "real" world, cannot be jettisoned simply because you choose to inhabit another "virtual" world. One of the hallmarks of a virtuous character is consistency, which would seem to suggest that if we ignore our painstakingly built character, based on virtue, when we visit other layers of our lives, we are not virtuous at all. We have separated our character into segments suited to our various roles within our partitioned worlds. The problem is, when we consciously divide our lives, we divide our character, which negates the entire concept of virtue and a virtuous character.

Who you are as a person inhabiting the "real" world should impact who you are in the virtual world of gaming. Although the constraints faced in each world may differ, the fact that we can construct existences beyond and outside the objective, embodied world in which we ultimately live speaks to the necessity of realizing the importance of the link we must maintain among them. Those constraints are born of the real world. However, we must carry with us those constraints, to some degree, in order to prevent an ethical schizophrenia that, like its real-world counterpart, can only result in moral confusion.

Contemporary philosopher Alasdair MacIntyre's (1984) attempt to revitalize Virtue Ethics has resulted in conceptualizing the proper context of virtue, the places in which it is most likely to thrive. He points out that any area of human endeavor in which standards of excellence guide the production of societal goods is an "appropriate locus for the exercise of the virtues, and the virtues are those qualities that allow practitioners to excel in their roles" (Levy 2004, 109). Any community involved in a common experience and a common goal might be viewed as a "practice," even a virtual one. According to MacIntyre (1984, 198), a practice is a unique environment in which people may apply their virtues to their work, and by so doing, help establish and further standards of excellence within that practice. The community may define what constitutes excellence but it also has the onus of encouraging virtuous behavior in order to achieve it.

Any enterprise, be it real or virtual, that supports and encourages virtuous behavior, might be understood as a MacIntyrian (1984) practice. The goal of a MacIntyrian practice is to produce internal goods benefiting the whole of the community in which the practice exists. "External goods," by contrast, are those such as money, power, and fame, the acquisition of which by an individual or a practice is self-serving, and often runs counter or even interferes with the production of internal goods. According to MacInryre (1984), then, virtue is "an acquired human quality the possession and exercise of which tends to enable us to achieve those goods which are internal to practices and the lack of which effectively prevents us from achieving any such goods" (194). In short, those "goods" produced with the cooperation and to the benefit of the community are the virtuous results of virtuous action by a virtuous person—no matter what world they inhabit.

If we choose to participate in a virtual community, we have no choice but to take with us the character we have developed in the real world and the communities and practices we have inhabited there. Gee (2007) posits that, in addition to virtual and/or real-world identities, a third "projective" identity is at stake in video games, wherein the player projects his or her real-life desires and values onto the virtual character (55). In this way, real-world virtue can be tested virtually. Thus, the character we have developed in the real world must not be ignored as we explore virtual worlds. If we abandon who we *really* are, how can we reconcile our own character? Our character is an integrated whole that we may not and cannot alter in order to adapt to any given situation. To the extent that we may alter it, we must ask ourselves if the referent (real-world) character is either not what we thought it was, or was itself altered by our virtual choices.

It is our moral maturity that allows us to adapt, and that maturity is unalterably based on character and acquired virtues. The entire concept of Virtue Ethics is based on the acquisition of a good and consistent character, one that can transcend our own reality and function fully in any reality in which we find ourselves. Our intellectual and practical selves form the basis of who we are. If we have strived to become the best person we can become, how then can we abandon that person to the whims of any other world that we might come in contact with? You have the choice, even in games that may feature non-virtuous characters, to contribute positively to the community in which you find yourself.

DotA 2

Overview

DotA stands for Defense of the Ancients, a multiplayer (5 vs. 5) online battle game. Players attempt to destroy the opposing team's "ancient," a structure that lies in the center of a heavily fortified base at the opposite end of the map. After choosing a hero (there are currently over 100 available and each one has four unique skills), a player works with four teammates to battle the opposing team. There are friendly AI-controlled units (creeps) and enemy AI-controlled creeps which automatically spawn and battle in three lanes of activity. Neutral creeps appear in fixed locations in the woods, between the lanes, but are more powerful and generally fought later in the game. Heroes battle alongside their creeps to gradually "push" their lane to the next enemy tower, and upon its destruction they are one step closer to killing the enemy ancient.

Like persistent, virtual world games (*Skyrim*, *World of Warcraft*), *DotA* heroes gain experience and gold to level up and earn attributes (strength, agility, and intelligence), skills, and powerful weapons. Unlike persistent games, *DotA* games are discrete—once a team defeats the opponent's ancient, the game is over. Games typically take anywhere from thirty minutes to an hour. *DotA* is a modification of characters from Blizzard's *Warcraft III: Reign of Chaos* (and its expansion, *Warcraft III: The Frozen Throne*) and a map from another Blizzard game, *Starcraft*.

Several individual developers created and maintained early versions of *DotA*. The most prominent early developer was an anonymous coder known only as "IceFrog," and when Valve Corporation acquired the game to create its sequel, *DotA 2*, they kept IceFrog as the lead designer. *DotA 2* is technically a sequel but is essentially just a better-looking, less-lag-filled, more streamlined version of *DotA*. It remains free to play through Valve's *Steam* platform. It makes money from sales of cosmetic items: "outfits" for heroes, different voice announcer packs, and similarly aesthetic perks that don't directly affect gameplay.

Approximately eight million individuals play *DotA 2* per month. At the most recent global tournament, The International 2014, a prize pool worth nearly $11 million was handed out, with over $5 million going to the winning team, "Newbee." Over 20 million viewers tuned in on their Xbox, through the Steam platform, or even on ESPN2 to watch the nineteen teams from ten countries battle it out. *DotA 2* is enormously complex—a fan on Reddit calculated the number of different possible team matchups to be 1,764,707,365,859,256. Because of this complexity and the teamwork required, *DotA 2* currently has more prize money than any other video game in the world. *DotA*'s popularity demonstrates that a complex, democratized game that reinforces ethical behavior (internal goods) can also be profitable (external goods). So what are the components of *DotA* that allow it to cultivate consistent virtuous character?

Game design, community, and players

DotA 2 demonstrates Virtue Ethics as the community ethos it embraces also encourages individual development. It exemplifies a true MacIntyrian practice that attempts to produce internal goods—fun, well-played games—while external goods like a gamer's real-life bank account are irrelevant (for the average player who does not compete), and there is no fee to subscribe, stream content or play with others. Media ethicist Charles Ess (2013) notes the importance of this distinction: "If we subordinate our cultivation of excellence as ethical and political beings to any other activity—e.g., the pursuit of wealth or power—we thereby put our capacity for reason and ethical judgment at risk" (209). *DotA 2* deals in a currency of internal goods: at the very least, it does not *restrict* the ethical development of its players, but at best it actively facilitates virtuous character that gamers can bring back into reality.

Miguel Sicart (2011) has previously applied Virtue Ethics to computer games, with three areas of analysis—the game system that conditions player capacities, the player's individual reasoning and skill, and the community to which the player belongs (116). We shall follow this outline regarding the ways in which *DotA 2*'s design, individuals, and community all reflect Virtue Ethics.

Game design

If we take as a definition that a "game" is merely a formalized set of rules that constitute an environment in which one experiences play (Salen and Zimmerman 2003), then it matters who sets the rules of the environment, and why. Who is best equipped to design a game? Accountants? Marketing departments? The first *DotA* designers were simply the players who created the game. Unlike *World of Warcraft*, *Call of Duty*, or other mainstream games, it was never meant to be commercially successful, only fun.

There are five qualities of participatory culture—the first being relatively low barriers to artistic expression and the second being strong support for creating and sharing with others (Jenkins et al. 2009, 5–6). We have already discussed the first criterion: how the low barrier to creativity (world-editing software bundled with the original *Warcraft III* game) allowed for fans to make the first *DotA* map. It was a noncommercial entity created at and from the fringes of a commercial product, but it resonated with gaming communities in a way that earned a small but loyal following in its infancy.

The third quality of participatory culture is some type of mentorship where knowledge is passed from experienced players to novices; we discuss this in the community section. The fourth is that members believe their contributions matter, and the fifth quality is that members feel some degree of social connection or accountability with one another. As Jenkins et al. (2009) put it, "Not every member must contribute, but all must believe they are free to contribute when ready and that what they contribute will be appropriately valued" (6). The second criterion for participatory culture—strong support for creating and sharing with others—is what helped *DotA* grow in those first few years. Because the developers played the game with other regular players (not just each other) they got constant feedback on the game by being privy to ongoing conversations on bugs, glitches, cheaters, or opportunities for improvement. They fostered a democratic environment where suggestions were not only tolerated, but welcomed—player IceFrog put his or her personal e-mail on early loading screens!

Because a complex game such as *DotA* required a minute or two to sync up ten individual computers with the internet server, a loading screen with a static image would be displayed on each computer screen. Loading screens would usually display recent fixes to bugs (errors in the game), new game or hero options, and any changes to gameplay. A new loading screen occurred with each new version of *DotA*, which might be released every few days, weeks, or months, depending on how popular and/or efficient the last release was.

The loading screen is an example of how *DotA* designers embedded the second criterion for participatory culture: strong support for creating and sharing with others. It would frequently feature artwork created by a fan of the game, with credit being given to the artist. It would also give credit to fans who made suggestions that ended up being coded into the game: a new item that allows for a hero to temporarily store a power-up instead of using it immediately (a bottle), a new hero who has a pirate-captain MO, complete with a spell that calls a ghost ship into battle ("Kunkka"), or a game mode that randomly assigns heroes instead of letting players choose them ("all-random" mode).

The different modes of the gameplay also give players the chance to work on specific aspects of their overall skillset. Two tenets of Virtue Ethics are intent and consistency, and being open to different modes of gameplay lets an individual be intentional (or not) about their desire to become consistently adept with the breadth of heroes. If a gamer wants to get better at using a specific hero, there is an all-pick mode. If a gamer wants to improve on her teamwork, there is a captain's mode, where the "captain" chooses the five heroes for her team, and then the players choose among themselves who plays which hero. If a gamer wants to truly test her skill, there is an all-random mode, where any one of over a hundred heroes might be assigned to them. This mode has the most social capital among *DotA* players; respect is given to the well-rounded players who can succeed with any hero.

These kinds of details being built into the system are not inconsequential. There is a massive difference—and one that gamers certainly notice—between a for-profit product that developers only fix when they *have* to (because everyone is complaining), and a community-owned product that developers keep upgrading (before anyone ever complains) out of passionate fervor and too many valid ideas pouring in. Miguel Sicart (2005) addresses the interplay of game design and ethical responsibility:

> A computer game is a designed system of rules that creates a game world. These rules and that game world can have embedded ethical values: the behaviors they create, and how those are communicated to players, constitute the ethics of computer game design. The creators of games are then ethically responsible for the design of the rules and world, while players are responsible for their experience of the game—the ways they interpret and enact the embedded ethical values of a computer game. (13–18)

The developers of *DotA 2* have designed a game that repurposes existing video game conventions—hero pools, loading screens, strategy guides, and fan contributions—in a way that reinforces positive engagement. The environment communicates a clear vision of excellence that lets individual gamers aspire to greatness even if they are still a "n00b." In Jesper Juul's (2011) *Half-Real*, he discusses how computers have exponentially expanded upon the possibilities presented by traditional games, opening up new degrees of autonomy, interactivity, and scope of (occasionally non) fictional worlds. If it is true that computers took gaming to the next level, then it is also true that the internet took computer games to the next level. New kinds of gameplay and community are now possible, and *DotA* is engineered to take advantage of both.

Individual players

DotA 2 also encourages virtuous player development on an individual level, although with so many dozens of heroes, all with varying capabilities and usefulness, there has always been a steep learning curve. Beginners either had to learn quickly, or they would get harassed, booted from games, or just generally fail to have fun. Unsure players would pick the comfortable, safe, popular heroes with whom it was easy to win a game. Generally speaking, it was the hard-hitting agility heroes (like "Drow Ranger," a high-damage hero whose attack slowed opponents, or "Riki," an assassin hero with permanent invisibility) or the cheesy intelligence heroes (like "Zeus," whose ultimate ability damages every enemy hero on the map, regardless of where they are) who were chosen for every game. Games became stale and prohibitive for anyone who tried different approaches that didn't immediately work. Imagine a chessboard where every piece is a queen, or a football team where every player wants to be quarterback.

Thus when *DotA 2* was designed, developers came up with ways to encourage the use of more difficult heroes. One such addition to the game was the implementation of tutorial levels that had to be completed (using various heroes) before a player could participate in multiplayer games. Essentially like the driving test teenagers must pass before they get a license, it made sure people knew what they were doing before they went public. Even after the player beat these introductory levels, a new "bot mode" was available at any time, where a player could practice using a certain hero against all-AI opponents before he or she tried using them in a real online multiplayer match.

This kind of practice is not only good for the individual, but the other gamers he or she will play with and against. MacIntyre and Carus (1999) discuss how improvement is not just for one's self: "A good human being is one who benefits her or himself and others . . . both *qua* human being and also characteristically *qua* the exemplary discharge of particular roles or functions within the context of particular kinds of practice" (61). It might sound a bit strange to talk about being a "good" video game player. Isn't a good player just one who wins a lot? Perhaps, but the beauty of Virtue Ethics is that it neither ignores nor glorifies one's skill as a gamer. Rather, it places skill alongside other virtues. Aristotle's list of intellectual virtues included skill, knowledge, common sense, intuition, wisdom, resourcefulness, understanding, judgment, and cleverness. What does it mean to possess skills *and* the wisdom, understanding, and judgment to know how and when to use them? The first-person shooter genre is enormously popular, and success in those games (*Modern Warfare, Call of Duty*) requires quick reflexes. In addition to quick reflexes, elite *DotA* players need knowledge (of heroes, items, map locations, etc.), wisdom and experience (knowing how to combine all those factors), patience (farming neutral creeps to get to necessary levels, or waiting for opportune moments), selflessness (if playing a support hero), and more. In short, games like *DotA* cultivate a multitude of qualities that are also useful in reality.

In addition to the offline practice feature, when making *DotA 2*, developers encouraged the dynamic, diverse teams that can engage in the visually epic battles for which *DotA* is famous. This means that not everyone gets to be a "carry" hero, or the one who carries the team to victory on his or her back by single-handedly demolishing the opposition. Instead, *DotA 2* makes it clear which heroes are adept at playing which roles based on their attributes, skills, or commonly-obtained items. Certain heroes are labeled by their common role: carry, initiator (good at starting fights), disabler (have spells that can stun or silence enemies), lane support (good at pushing a lane), nuker (hard and fast damage output), support, and more. According to the definition of "Role" (2014) on the *DotA 2* wiki, a support hero can "focus less on amassing gold and items, and more on using their abilities to gain an advantage for the team."

Choosing to play selflessly as a support is not the natural inclination of most gamers. Most video games give people a chance to be the center of the action. Yet *DotA* gives players every opportunity to learn, practice, and even watch others who excel in playing a variety of roles. In addition to the practice mode, the game has a guide for each hero. Even while in a multiplayer game, a single click on the corner of the screen pulls up strategy guide for how to play each hero. Players can use the one provided, upload their own, or search for other guides online. These guides are made to be flexible. For example, if you have a carry hero on a team with one or two other carries, someone is going to have to change their role. *DotA 2* in-game guides have strategies for if you are winning, losing, playing support, playing aggressive, etc. to allow for maximum flexibility in one's approach to any given game. Thus a player can grow not only in skill but other virtues as well, facilitating the development of mature character. The point of the in-game strategy guides isn't just to help you flourish with this hero on a single occasion, but to help your team flourish with *any* hero *every* time.

Of course, the best players neither gloat when they flourish nor make excuses when they fail. They respect other players because they respect the game, understanding that sometimes a team might be unlucky, unprepared, or just outmatched. In addition to this basic sportsmanship, "possible strategies, and an awareness of both our own and our opponent's strengths and weaknesses, playing the game further requires us to exercise an Aristotelian sort of *phronesis* or judgment about how to respond best to specific choices in specific situations" (Ess 2013, 156). Over time, players tend to develop the perspective that comes with knowledge and experience.

Along these same lines, *DotA* also has a "coaching" option where experienced players can sit in on a game, see everything one team sees, and help instruct them in real time. Informal mentorship like strategy guides and coaching is an instance of the third criterion of participatory culture: that there exists some type of mentorship where knowledge is passed from experienced players to novices. When veterans help out rookies, both benefit and the internal good of the community is strengthened.

Furthermore, when one plays different roles—coach and mentor, carry and support—it contributes to Aristotle's "golden mean" that Virtue Ethics promotes. The golden mean of a character trait is a balance between excess and deficiency. For example, an excess of courage is recklessness, but its deficiency is cowardice. Neither is useful in *DotA 2*: a reckless hero would die too often, giving the other team valuable experience and gold, but a cowardly hero would fail to help in team battles, also putting his own team at a disadvantage.

A virtuous individual hero in *DotA* knows her strengths and weaknesses, communicates with the team, and is courageous enough to play her role in fights. The side with the best teamwork usually wins battles in *DotA*, carefully coordinating the timing of multiple heroes, spells, and attacks to achieve victory. Yet this sort of efficiency is not easy to achieve. It takes weeks, months, and even years to achieve "1337" ('leet, short for elite) status.

Community

In earlier incarnations of *DotA*, the community was occasionally hostile. Games were hosted by individual players who could exclude anyone from the game, the aforementioned kicking and map-hack programs were rampant, and the random nature of game assignments meant there was no structure to who played whom. Five elite friends could team up and destroy five random beginners. While the idea of the Seattle Seahawks playing against a middle-school football team sounds entertaining on some level, it would not necessarily be good for the sporting community at large.

The designers of *DotA 2* knew they had to fix these inadequacies. Games are now hosted on the Steam server (where hacking programs are easier to police) but the biggest development was the option to play ranked games. Players can still join random games, but there is a ranked game option that pits players only against others with similar experiences. When games are played with others of similar skill, they are more evenly balanced, which results in greater learning and growth for both sides. This balance is possible because *DotA 2* now keeps track of every detail of a player's experience: hours played, wins, losses, games abandoned, level and battle points, and each hero played. Keeping a record of a player's activity is a good first step toward accountability that promotes the good and consistent character toward which Virtue Ethics is directed.

Another step toward accountability is allowing players to give feedback on each other's performance. In the original *DotA* this took the form of the dreaded "banlist." Usually players were added for leaving (prematurely quitting games), but "flaming" (using profanity or slurs in the in-game chat), "feeding" (deliberately dying over and over), and using hacks also warranted addition to the banlist. However, the banlist was too easy to abuse. Players could add each other to the list simply out of spite or disagreement. Differing banlists claimed to be the legitimate one. Banlists failed because they relied on negative reinforcement. Banning other players was a currency that became inflated to the point of collapse.

Thus for *DotA 2* a new system of accountability was needed that would foster a genuine sense of community and positively reinforce virtuous behavior in its members. So the system of commendation was implemented. After or during a game, one player can commend another for being friendly, forgiving, teaching, and/ or leadership. *DotA 2* records these honors (as they do all statistics), and the first thing you see when clicking on a player's profile is the commendation track record.

Negative reinforcement still exists—leaving a game prematurely puts you in the "low-priority" game pool, where games are scarcer—but the new positive reinforcement of commending each other is what really incentivizes the community to strive toward moral virtue. Good teams want good players, and the best way to quickly scout a new player (in addition to looking at their win/loss record) is to check out their commendations. Are they friendly? Do they give good instruction? These sorts of questions help talented, fun-loving, excellence-seeking players find each other.

The ability to commend fellow players for positive characteristics meets the final two criteria for participatory culture: members believe their contribution matter, and members feel some degree of social connection with one another. *DotA 2* keeps a record of who commended whom for what, on which day, and even what heroes they were playing. Because standards of excellence guide the production of *DotA 2*'s internal goods (a player's win percentage and commendations), the MacIntyrian definition of virtues as "those qualities that allow practitioners to excel in their roles" crystallizes in a specific way: a virtuous *DotA 2* player is one with enough character, maturity, and experience to successfully play any role (caster, support, carry) his or her team needs in that game.

Conclusion

To what extent will virtuous development in the digital realm transfer over into a player's real-life persona? This will be different for everyone. The cultivation of virtuous behavior in *DotA 2* is one example of how video games can contribute to a consistency of character. As technology continues to make gaming more realistic and integrated with everyday life, the kind of games we play, as well as how we play them, will increasingly engage our imaginations and shape us as individuals. Digital culture records every transaction, comment, photograph, and web page view; it behooves us, then, to become the kind of people online we feel we ought to be offline.

Virtue Ethics promotes consistent character that will make our individual lives easier and contribute to the internal good of every community to which we belong. Whether attempting to be a successful gamer or a successful human being, one skill is constant: "becoming adept at gaining and matching skills with different aspects of the environment to use them as affordances to accomplish important goals" (Zagal 2011, 136). Hopefully, more games and platforms will, like *DotA 2*, evolve to the point of cultivating skill *and* consistently virtuous character—a character that informs every world we visit.

Notes

1 http://www.gameinformer.com/blogs/members/b/eternalquiet_blog/
   archive/2009/11/04/video-games-might-be-the-highest-form-of-art.aspx.
2 http://www.rogerebert.com/rogers-journal/video-games-can-never-be-art.
3 Game Development Conference, 1989. http://www.gdcvault.com/play/1015756/
   Interesting.

7

Between Ethics, Privacy, Fandom, and Social Media: New Trajectories that Challenge Media Producer/Fan Relations

Lucy Bennett, Bertha Chin, and Bethan Jones

In November 2013, the British Film Institute held a special screening for "The Empty Hearse," the highly anticipated third series premiere episode of BBC's *Sherlock*. The global success of the show, as well as star Benedict Cumberbatch's popularity in coveted international markets such as the United States, China, and Japan, ensured that the screening attracted much fan and public interest. As an added bonus to the event, BBC invited author and *The Times* columnist Caitlin Moran to moderate a Q&A session with the show's main cast (Cumberbatch and Martin Freeman) and producers (cocreators Mark Gatiss and Steven Moffatt, as well as producer Sue Vertue). Before the event was over, however, word began to spread among fans on Twitter and Tumblr of a controversial incident that occurred during the Q&A.

As reported by many popular mainstream media such as *The Telegraph* and *The Daily Dot*,[1] Moran had printed out a piece of slash[2] fan fiction (hereafter fanfic), and forced Cumberbatch and Freeman (despite their reluctance) to read in front of the crowded room an excerpt featuring an erotic scene between their respective characters. Fans in the audience quickly reported on the actors' discomfort, as well as the humiliation fans were made to feel as Moran went on to mock the fanfic as well as its author, whose work, fans argued, she had taken, outed, and appropriated without the author's express permission. Moran was criticized for humiliating and mocking fans, with those in *Sherlock* fandom attesting that Moran was no stranger to shaming fans in her tweets, writings, and interviews.[3]

More importantly, Moran's actions prompted a discussion about ethics in fandom, suggesting that this is an issue that necessitates more engagement for those interested in studying fan culture. It was clear that this was not an issue endemic to *Sherlock* fandom. Neither was Moran the only media personality to have appropriated fanworks for public entertainment at the expense of fans— British talk show host Graham Norton regularly surprises guests, especially popular actors, on his television program with risqué fan transformative works as a comedic stunt to see how the actors react. As fan and acafan[4] discussions about "Morangate," as the incident became known, took shape across blogs, LiveJournals, Tumblrs, and Twitter posts, it became evident that this was a conversation—a debate—that was timely and overdue.

Much has been argued in fandom about the risk fans take when they post their fanfic and fan art on publicly accessible websites such as Fanfic.net, Archive of Our Own (hereafter AO3), DeviantArt, Tumblr, and the like. Fans who are themselves critical of creative fanworks argue that unless the stories and art are not published in any form, fanfic authors and fan artists cannot stop these works from being appropriated, and thus judged, by those who come across it. However, does that mean that fans are giving up their right to a notion of privacy (to not be outed in public)? Does it mean that fans who do post publically are giving up their right to not have their creative works taken and appropriated without express permission (particularly if their work is being appropriated for entertainment value that would potentially cause humiliation and shame)? For that matter, what does an ethic of privacy mean in the age of social media? While fans and fan studies scholars alike can, and have, criticized Moran's actions for being callous and irresponsible, the fanfic she had obtained was published on AO3, a public site. Likewise, fan discussions and fan postings of transformative works on sites where these works are not locked up (i.e., do not require a password to access) are considered public, even if fans work on the assumption that "the space where they create their artworks [is] closed" (Busse and Hellekson 2012, 38) and the media and public are not interested in the works fans produce.[5]

Of course, as is becoming increasingly evident, both the media and the public *are* interested in the work that fans produce. This interest has repercussions not only for fan communities, as we will discuss in this chapter, but for privacy online more broadly. Alan Westin (1967) defines privacy as "the claim of individuals, groups, or institutions to *determine for themselves* when, how, and to what extent information about them is communicated to others" (7, emphasis added). By posting online, in public (or semipublic) forums, individuals are determining where, how, and how much information is shared. As soon as that information is removed from its context, however, and shared by media producers or news organizations, that power is removed from the individual. Privacy has been breached. Of course, as Helen Nissenbaum (2010) asks, "Has a person who intentionally posts photographs of himself [/herself] to a Web site such as Flickr lost privacy?" (71). Can fans who write fanfic and post it to websites such as AO3, really complain when it is used elsewhere?

In this chapter, we explore, through the context of fan studies, how fans conceptualize their privacy. We examine how media appropriation of fanworks, and how directing the attention of actors and media producers to fanworks, is considered an ethical breach to the fannish code of conduct. We consider how social media sites have changed the ways in which fans interact with producers (and vice versa) and question the ways in which fan studies methodologies could provide media industry insiders with ethical ways to approach fans and fanworks. In examining these issues in relation to a small, in some ways powerless, group such as fans we suggest that their application can also be applied to larger groups of individuals. Ultimately, we argue that respect, which we define as due regard and consideration for the rights and wishes of others, is an essential value that should be embraced by fans and media producers when engaging with each other. In addition, the power wielded by the media industry and the use of fanworks by the media industry needs to be balanced with the idea of respect, as defined here. As we will show, different social, racial, and cultural contexts are always at work when fans are interacting with one another (as well as with media producers) and it is critical to remember that there is not just one reading or use of a text, but many. Thus, we argue that there needs to be a sense of respect placed at the forefront of interactions between fans and media producers, especially surrounding fanworks and copyright, which, as we will now move on to show, is an ethical issue that has been fraught with complex tensions and power negotiations.

Copyright and power: Why fans have the right to be outraged

In *Textual Poachers* Henry Jenkins (1992) positions fans as active consumers of media products. He challenges stereotypes of fans as "cultural dupes, social misfits, and mindless consumers" (23), arguing that fans "actively assert their mastery over the mass-produced texts which provide the raw materials for their own cultural productions" (23–24). Jenkins terms fans poachers who "transform the experience of watching television into a rich and complex participatory culture" (23), but he also acknowledges the tentative hold that fans have on their objects of fandom. Fanworks often exist on the margins of the text, and many producers adopt a negative approach to them. Anne Rice, for example, states on her website:

> I do not allow fan fiction. The characters are copyrighted. It upsets me terribly to even think about fan fiction with my characters. I advise my readers to write your own original stories with your own characters. (Quoted in Pugh 2005, 13)

Rice's invoking of copyright law makes it clear that she believes fanfic writers who use her characters are stealing from her, although as Sheenagh Pugh (2005) points out, fanfic writers go to great lengths to call attention to the fact that the characters they write are not their property and they are not profiting from their use by including disclaimers at the beginning of their works. Aaron Schwabach (2011) rebuts this, however, in an important way. We have already noted that fans utilize work which does not belong to them—a point which many outside of fandom regard as negating fans' concerns about their own work being used in a similar way. Schwabach suggests that fans' disclaimers are meaningless for copyright purposes (74). Referring to Annie Proulx's position on *Brokeback Mountain* fanfic, he says,

> Her suggestion that the fanfic authors are violating her copyright is only partly right: the characters may be (and in this case probably are) her intellectual property, but her copyright in the characters does not mean that no one else can use them; they are protected but not untouchable. (7)

Schwabach goes on to note the different ways in which copyrighted works may be utilized by others and argues that, as fan works are often transformative, they are "more likely to be protected as fair use, even if they make use of copyrighted characters or other content" (69). Fans' use of copyrighted work is thus very different to the media's use of fanworks.

The issue of fair use and transformative works is highly contested among media producers, however, and the continuing issuing of cease-and-desist letters to fans by film studios further consolidates this view of fanfic as a quasi-criminal activity: Warner Bros. attempted to intimidate *Harry Potter* fans into removing their work from the internet and Lucasfilm attempted to prevent the circulation of slash set in the *Star Wars* universe (Jenkins 2006). Will Brooker (2002) notes that Lucasfilm's threat of legal action against websites circulating *Star Wars* fanfic was enough to convince administrators to quash the fanfic groups themselves. But he also notes that Lucasfilm's 2000 decision to offer fans web space in the "virtual backyard" of its official site "suggests a new strategy toward fan activity of all kinds" (168). As R. M. Milner (2009) notes, as active audiences become more prevalent, media producers recognize the value of courting them, and Mark Andrejevic (2008) suggests that "fan culture is at long last being deliberately and openly embraced by producers" (26). Tensions, however, continue to exist between fans and producers in relation to fan contributions. Andrejevic acknowledges that some fans have expressed concern that fan sites may be reduced to just another marketing strategy, and the more cynical note that "there is a certain amount of public relations value to be gained from suggesting that online fans influence the production process" (37). Jenkins (2006) explains the delicate relationship between the producer and productive consumer as it stands in the age of the active audience:

> The media industry is increasingly dependent on active and committed consumers to spread the word about valued properties in an overcrowded media marketplace, and in some cases they are seeking ways to channel the creative output of media fans to lower their production costs. At the same time, they are terrified of what happens if this consumer power gets out of control. (138)

Producer response to fan labor is often somewhere between suppression and supervision: as Jenkins (2006) writes, "fan productivity . . . can no longer be ignored by the media industries, but it can not be fully contained or channeled by them, either" (134). Fans, then, are no longer operating from the same position of social weakness as they were in the early 1990s, though they may still be disciplined and subordinated in a range of ways (Johnson 2007b).

If fans are less subordinated, then, why are we concerned with affording them ethical privileges that are not granted to, for example, bloggers or authors? Fans appropriate and decontextualize the work of others without their permission; why are they outraged when the same thing happens to them? The key issue here, we suggest, is that of power. Fans may not be in the same position of (perceived?) cultural weakness as they were in 1992, but they are still far less powerful than media producers. Those producers have access to money, legal advice and networks that fans simply do not have and the balance of power thus remains with them. Nissenbaum (2010) writes:

> Extrinsic losses of freedom occur when people curtail outward behaviors that might be unpopular, unusual, or unconventional because they fear tangible and intangible reprisals, such as ridicule, loss of a job, or denial of benefits. Intrinsic

losses of freedom are the result of internal censorship caused by awareness that one's every action is being noted and recorded. (76)

Fan practices are often still framed as strange or taboo in media discourse, despite the shifting attitude toward fans since the early 1990s. To use or mock the work of someone in a less powerful position impacts upon that person in ways which are potentially damaging, not least because it may prevent them from engaging with their community in the future. Perhaps one way to construct an ethical framework for these challenges is through the adoption of Michael Walzer's (1984) concept of "spheres of justice." Walzer contends that there are distinct social spheres (healthcare, education, marketplace) which are defined by distinctive social goods (money, commodities, teaching positions) containing specific meanings in those spheres, which are distributed within the spheres according to distinctive sets of principles (competitive free market, social security, academic achievement). Social justice therefore occurs when "social goods in a particular sphere [are] distributed in accordance with the principles of distribution that are appropriate to the meaning of those social goods within that sphere" (Nissenbaum 2010, 167). Jeroen van den Hoven (2001) builds on this to argue that information belonging in one sphere should not be allowed to migrate into another or others because if it does, informational injustice will have been perpetrated (cf. Nissenbaum 2010, 80). One example van den Hoven gives of this is a job candidate's medical history or religious affiliation finding its way into the files of a company considering him for employment. If we consider fannish spheres separate from media or journalistic spheres (or academic spheres, as we describe later), the same argument can hold: fanworks should not find their way into another sphere *without permission,* as the harm to the fan may far outweigh the benefit to the journalist or researcher.

As we have noted, Jenkins (1992) argues that fans are poaching from copyrighted properties when creating fanworks, but despite the illegality that the term implies, fandom often functions according to an unspoken code of conduct. This code of conduct stresses the protection of the fan identity, as Kristina Busse and Karen Hellekson (2012) remind that the outing of a fan identity to the public has "real-world repercussions . . . [and that is] a fan's forced withdrawal from a community important to her [/him]" (41). Violation of this code equates to a violation of fandom's code of ethics, which was precisely why Moran's actions drew much criticism from fans. As Busse and Hellekson (2012) argue, "fans perceive the space where they create their artworks as closed" (38).

Matt Hills (2012), additionally, asserts that fandom operates around a "fannish code of secrecy" (cf. Larsen and Zubernis 2012, 6), their identities, practices, and culture closely guarded against those they deem outsiders who may put the community at risk of exposure, and its inherent consequences. This kind of distrust is not just imposed on media personalities, like Moran, or the press. American actor, producer, and activist Orlando Jones, for example, who caught the attention of the media, fans, and acafans alike when he started engaging in conversations with fans and acafans on Twitter,[6] has remarked on the distrust he is often confronted with by fans who doubt his sincerity in engaging with fandom (Bennett and Chin 2014). Likewise, when the actress Celina Jade of the TV show *Arrow* (CW, 2012-present) discovered fanfic and began tweeting about her discovery to fellow cast members, some fans commented on their embarrassment at being discovered, preferring to be left alone, hidden from the media industry's view. This appears in contrast to the media industry's attempts at actively courting fans and co-opting them into promotional and marketing strategies (cf. Murray 2004), which has become increasingly common such as with MTV's *Teen Wolf* official community that invites fans to upload and share their fan art and poetry (Gonzalez 2014) and Amazon's Kindle Worlds, where fans are invited to publish their fanfic of licensed properties on the platform.[7] However, as we will now move to show, these emerging interactions can raise ethical complexities, most specifically surrounding the consent and use of fanworks.

Copyright in reverse: Authorial consent and use of fanworks

Jenkins (2006), Johnson (2007b), Jenkins, Ford, and Green (2013), and other works have explored this ongoing change within the industry. As viewing habits become increasingly fragmented, industry insiders are looking to retain engaged and loyal audiences for their media properties. In the passion of celebrating this shift, it is easy to forget that some fans view their practices as independent of the media industry, despite utilizing media properties in their fiction and artworks. With the media industry's attention and interest now even more on fandom, as public interest and curiosity heightens and fans adopt social media platforms like Twitter and Tumblr to perform their fan identity, there is a greater need to think about the notion of ethics in fandom and how fans conceptualize their privacy.

In the first marked difference between Tumblr and other sites of fandom, community boundaries (if there are communities at all) are less clear-cut. Conversations are followed through hashtags, and participation requires the user to reblog a post in order to add to the "conversation" rather than responding directly to it. In addition, Tumblr's image-friendly stance has likely opened up global fandom—especially non-English speaking fandom—to a new range of audiences. What Tumblr has offered, as Lori Morimoto (2014a) showcases in her reflection on the phenomena, is access to fans and fan transformative works on a global scale. However, with this "globalization of fandom" also come complications. Morimoto (2014b) alludes to the complexity of asking for permission to use fan art because "there are different producer/fan and fan/academic relations (real and perceived), as well as fan ethics, to contend with." These issues, coupled with fans' rising public profiles, and the media industry's constant attempts to find ways to monetize fandom, can result in fans feeling threatened and unsafe in seemingly private platforms where their practices (and identities) are assumed to be removed from the public eye, where preservation of their fan identity and fanworks are of the utmost importance. In their chapter on "Identity, Ethics and Fan Privacy," Busse and Hellekson (2012) declare that the worst fannish sin is to reveal the real-life identity of a fellow fan, which may result in real-world repercussions where the fan has to withdraw from his or her fannish life. For personal and often professional reasons, fans' identities are often masked behind pseudonyms, especially if they produce transformative work that may potentially jeopardize their career and personal lives. As Busse and Hellekson (2012) reflect:

> Although many fans believe that they ought not hide and that fictional (homo) erotic fantasies ought not be shameful, most are well aware that exposing fannish activities in real-world situations can be a difficult situation for some fans; it may negatively affect their family or work life. (41)

This outing does not necessarily have to be performed by a fellow fan. Increasingly, fanworks are found and presented by media industry insiders, often as objects of ridicule, as Moran did at the *Sherlock* premiere. Much of the debate in fandom after the *Sherlock* premiere incident centered on the ethics of Moran's actions, with criticism aimed at Moran for mocking and shaming the fanfic author, and by extension, fans in general, as "fans themselves [already] often feel a strong sense of shame" (Zubernis and Larsen 2012, 44) for their fan activities. Many female fans of *Sherlock* felt that Moran was a "safe" choice for moderator as she had long positioned herself as a Sherlock/Cumberbatch "fangirl" and for a lot of white female fans she seemed like "one of us" (Bethan Jones 2014). The sense of betrayal felt by these fans then was at least in part because Moran had seemed to sell them out in the same way other journalists had—simply to get a cheap laugh at their expense. While the fan's real-life identity was not outed in any way, her fan activity of writing slash fanfic based on her favorite television show—an activity many others in the room are likely to have been doing as well—was used as a comedic punchline for the public's entertainment. "Fans are still derided in the media even as they are being embraced by media producers," Lynn Zubernis and Katherine Larsen (2012) remind us (44). The ethical implications of this, as we have touched on previously in this chapter, are many. Mocking (female) fans for producing homoerotic work functions to reinforce the gendered way in which women are treated in media culture (as well as culture more generally). Perhaps more pertinent for this discussion, however, is the way in which the mocking of fans by the media reinforce power relationships between the mass media and consumers.

The ethical dynamics of media producer/ fan relations on social media

The embracing of fans by media producers provokes a multitude of ethical and moral concerns. Although the use of social media by media producers is delivering many valued and positive examples of communication and participation between these individuals and their fans (e.g. the production team of NBC's *Community* welcomed feedback from fans via Twitter surrounding the narrative and engaged them in some creative processes of the show), these practices can also give prominence to ethical challenges and concerns for both parties (Bennett and Chin 2014). Given this, in this section we will identify and consider several key ethical implications and demands that revolve around these seemingly reciprocal interactions, and the problems that they can unfold surrounding our contemporary uses and contemplations of digital and social media. These include the ethical currency of the follow and pursuance of recognition, and the negotiation of hate online.

How media producers and their fans negotiate each other on social media platforms is a significant area for consideration that can raise problematic ethical issues, most prominently hinged around value placement on "the follow" and securing replies or comments. For instance, as social media use becomes more widespread, with more individuals and public figures using the platforms, fans can become situated as one among millions of others, yet perhaps expect, or anticipate, a personal response. When this situation occurs, how a reciprocal connection can fully be maintained is put into question. The ethical charge of this question, then, rests on both parties. First, media producers/celebrities have the dynamics of the platform to grapple with: which fans to follow, selecting some over others, and how to deal with those who tweet unfavorable, or controversial messages. In an interview (Bennett and Chin 2014) conducted with Orlando Jones, we asked him how he leveraged which fans to follow on Twitter, and how to negotiate these requests. Jones stated: "I've certainly had fans who are persistent in their attempts to get me to follow, but I try to encourage them to provide a legitimate reason why I should follow them instead of just because." In this case, just being a fan is not enough to secure a follow, since there are so many of them demanding Jones's attention on the platform; instead, he fosters a moral consideration and treats the fans as respected individuals, rather than numbers to accumulate.[8]

In alignment with these prospects, fans also have to negotiate the demands of the platform—for example, how to react when they are not replied to while others are, and how to respond to other fans who engage in attempts at emotional blackmail and persistent tactics (such as repeatedly tweeting the individual) to receive a follow and attention from the actor/producer. Ultimately however, fan policing has long been an element of fan cultures, whereby some fans act as regulators over others to ensure morally correct behavior (Bennett 2011), and on Twitter these behavioral processes continue to be very much evident.

Fan policing is not limited to fans policing other fans, however. Another ethically challenging aspect of social media use is exposure to outpourings of hate online, and the question of how to negotiate and respond to these challenging messages. As outlined earlier, fans and media producers can sometimes engage in a conflictive and morally charged relationship, most especially when some fans foresee the text is heading in a direction they do not approve of, and construct hate campaigns to make themselves heard. As Derek Johnson (2007a) states, "Fans attack and criticize media producers whom they feel threaten their meta-textual interests" (298). When this "fan-tagonism" occurs, media producers can be vilified, as the case with *Buffy the Vampire Slayer*'s Marti Noxon, who received a barrage of hateful postings on the *Buffy* online message boards and websites (Johnson 2007a). However, contemporary behavior in this vein has a difference: vilification and posting tinged with hate are not just posted on bounded online communities, but tweeted directly to the object of disdain (Bennett forthcoming; Chin forthcoming). How media producers handle this is a morally charged debate, with no clear answer. Whereas Noxon claimed at the time that these messages indicated she was "doing a good job" (Johnson 2007a), in today's climate, where messages could be posted more directly to her, her response may have been different. In this sense, how actors and media producers respond to online hate differs between individuals: whereas some endeavor to highlight the ugliness of the hate through retweets, such as Orlando Jones, others, as Bertha Chin (forthcoming) has demonstrated in her study of Michelle Borth from *Hawaii Five-0*, have responded in the same hate-tinged manner, challenging these fans, with equally unfavorable results. Ultimately, the moral tension within these interactions remain—while fans have a right to have their voices, and dissatisfactions about a text be heard and listened to, vilification is a problematic, and morally dubious practice. However, at the same time, media producers and actors also have a responsibility to negotiate these messages in ways that do not escalate matters further, or do not appear to reduce the value and power of their fan base.

Thus, although social media use delivers media producers and their fans increased opportunities to interact and converse with each other that are valued and pleasurable, it also raises some ethical problems and complications for both, which may intensify as social media use develops further. Essentially, these moral considerations pose no clear-cut solutions, other than a commitment to the expression of mutual respect between both parties.

Adopting academic approaches

The expression of mutual respect is one which academic approaches to fans from within the field of fan studies have endeavored to adopt. In an essay explaining the rationale behind the permissions policy in the journal *Transformative Works and Cultures*, Kristina Busse and Karen Hellekson (2009) note that it is up to fans to protect their own identities: "The burden of what we share in public is on us. If we don't publicly connect fan and real-life names, readers won't make that connection either" (n.p.). Social media sites, however, tend to cross the fannish/ non-fannish divide. In that respect it is difficult to disconnect fannish and real-life names and identities. As Busse (2009) notes elsewhere, "simple dichotomies of private and public spaces seem to fall short of the more complicated realities of current social media experiences" (n.p.). That is, a site can be both private and public at the same time, with users regarding their posts as semipublic even while recognizing that the site itself is a public one. As Angus Johnston (2014) writes:

> The reality is that the boundary between private acts and public acts is blurry, and always has been. People do private stuff in public all the time, and while we often have a legal right to violate the privacy of those moments, mostly we don't, because it's understood that we shouldn't. It's understood that it's a jerky thing to do. (n.p.)

Fans have an expectation that the content they share online is limited to a certain number of people, and given the number of fanworks posted online compared to the relatively small number of fanworks shared by media industry insiders, this expectation appears to be a valid one. But as long as fan activities remain a fascination for the media, the issue of preventing media personalities like Moran from accessing and appropriating fanworks for entertainment value will remain complex. It is here that approaches made to studying fans by fan studies scholars may provide the industry with an ethical framework through which to consider using fanworks already shared in the public domain. Busse and Hellekson (2012) acknowledge that "industrial fan interpellation is continuing, if not increasing" (51) despite some fans' reluctance and insistence that their activities remain grassroots and counter-cultural. The approach taken by *Transformative Works and Cultures*, which shows respect to fans and puts them first, might be one solution. Busse and Hellekson (2009) write,

> we (as in Karen and Kristina, but also the entire TWC staff, as well as the OTW supporting us) consider ourselves fans first. We don't think we're academic interlopers who think it's neat to add to the *Lord of the Rings* debate by looking at those crazy women slashing the hobbits. We are fans, we create fan works, and we participate in the community—a community that makes art which is worthy of study. We'd rather fandom and its works be studied not by some random outsider, but by people who know fandom's nuances—who know that fandom is always more complex and more complicated than we may believe or see. We are very, very concerned to ensure the privacy and security of fans. (n.p.)

The potential problems with this approach, which Busse and Hellekson acknowledge, is that engaging the fan might actually scare the fan off. Informing fans that their work is worthy of study could result in the discussions the researcher is interested in being taken offline in an effort to shut down the project, thus jeopardizing the acafan's research. With understandable reasons—the "Morangate" incident being one—fans are incredibly protective of how their communities and fandoms are portrayed. When engaging with fans on Twitter, for example, Orlando Jones has encountered resistance from fans, whereby he was pointedly told by a fan that if he was to identify as "one of us," then some things (in this case, the less positive side of fandom)[9] should not be publicized (see Figures 7.1 and 7.2).

The other problem, however, lies with much deeper cultural understandings of fans and fandoms. Academic researchers working in the field of fan studies

Figures 7.1 and 7.2 Tweets to Orlando Jones, November 2013.

are in many cases fans themselves and, as Busse and Hellekson point out, do not want to write in a way that continues the pathologization of fandom. In contrast, many in the media industry, while relying on fans to spread the word about their projects and engage with them commercially, do not truly understand fandom. Fans, up to a point, are useful, but beyond that it becomes easier to pathologize and denigrate them than to engage with them on social media.

Conclusion

In this chapter we have explored how fans conceptualize and understand their privacy, and how media appropriation of their fanworks and actively directing the attention of actors and media producers to fanworks can be considered as an ethical breach to the fannish code of conduct. We demonstrated the ways in which media producers and fans interact on social media and the complicated ethical and moral considerations that underpin these new avenues for communication. Examining privacy in the age of social media is not an easy task, and discussions around fan outrage are often polarized. On the one hand, journalists should not be mining fan communities for the next embarrassing story about internet culture; on the other, fans posted in a public forum so what do they expect? Nissenbaum (2010), writing about privacy, notes that "In almost all situations in which people must choose between privacy and just about any other good, they choose the other good. . . . People choose the options that offer convenience, speedy passage, financial savings, connectivity, and safety rather than those that offer privacy" (105). For fans, and indeed for many people, the internet offers far more positives than negatives, and gives the formerly secluded nature of fan communities the expectation that the likelihood of their fanworks being discovered is small. To that end, some fans choose the much larger benefit of engaging with other likeminded individuals over the relatively small chance of their work being discovered. With media interest in fandom increasing, however, changes are needed in the ways in which fanworks are adopted and used.

　　As we have shown, there are many ways in which fan studies methodologies could provide media industry insiders with ethical ways to approach fanworks. In essence, we argue that in order to make progress within challenging areas, the essential value that should be embraced by fans and media producers when engaging with each other is that of respect. In other words, with some situations being fraught by ethical and moral complexities, such as those concerning fanworks and privacy, and others surrounding fan/producer interactions on Twitter, and revealing no clear-cut solutions, it is mutual respect that should be at the forefront of these occurrences, for both parties.

Notes

1   Some of the mainstream and popular press coverage can be found in Brown (2013), Magnanti (2013), and Romano (2013).

2   Fanwork (art, fiction, video mash-ups) featuring the romantic/sexual relationship of two (or more) characters of the same gender. Slash is more commonly used for male pairings (with femslash the preferred term for female pairings). Some scholars have written extensively about the practice being dominated by heterosexual women as a creative outlet for exploring their sexuality (cf. Jenkins 1992; Green, Jenkins, and Jenkins 1998).

3   Some have been documented by fans in Conigliaro (2013) and Rodes (2013).

4   Much has been debated about the term "acafan" (popularized by Hills 2002) and the term's adequacy for those in fan studies scholarship. The lengthy debates for and against the term are beyond the scope of this chapter, but for more see Stein (2011), Jenkins (2011), and Hills (2012). We have also opted to continue using the term interchangeably with fan studies scholars for the sake of familiarity and convenience.

5   It should be noted here that media use of fanfic is not illegal—if the works are posted online and attribution is given to the author, there can be no accusation of copyright theft (which is often the argument levied against fanfic). What we suggest, however, is that media use of fanfic could be unethical, particularly when used in the ways outlined in this chapter.

6   Jones is one of the main cast members of *Sleepy Hollow* (FOX, 2013-present) and a self-proclaimed fan. He frequently comments on other TV series, engaging in conversations not just with other cast members from those shows but also with fans. He live-tweets episodes, engages in conversation with fan studies scholars like Henry Jenkins and, as a result, has been invited to speak at various university classes on fandom and academic conferences on his embracing fandom and fan studies.

7   See, for example, Fanlore.org's write-up on the discussion and controversy surrounding Kindle Worlds (Fanlore 2014).

8   We should note that there may also be something self-serving in this as well— Jones' attitude of "tell me why you're special and I will follow you" hierarchizes fans and forces fans into particular niches, as well as potentially fostering divisions within fandom.

9   In identifying as a fan of *Supernatural* and then going on to publicly comment
    about the relationship of a popular slash pairing, Jones began to receive a number
    of hate tweets from supporters of another popular slash pairing, who admonished
    him for openly taking sides and inciting (further) hate and antagonism between
    the two factions in the *Supernatural* fandom. Some fans, like the one pictured,
    protested to his publicizing the antagonism. While antagonism between the
    two factions is well known within *Supernatural* fandom, it is likely not common
    knowledge outside of the fandom, and it is indicated that by engaging with the
    hate and with one section of a vocal fandom, Jones appears to have violated an
    unspoken code of conduct here. Figure 7.1: Tweets to Orlando Jones, November
    2013.

8

"Rogue" Advertising in the Digital Age: Creative Reputation Building or Industry Irresponsibility?

Michelle A. Amazeen and Susan A. O'Sullivan-Gavin

A genre of advertising that previously remained behind closed doors, known as "rogue" advertising, is currently gaining mainstream media attention. Surprisingly, it includes some of the leading US companies, such as Ford Motor Company, Coca-Cola, McDonald's, Gap Inc., and Yum Brand's Pizza Hut. Even more surprising is that in many cases these leading advertisers either had no knowledge of the advertisements or did not realize what the advertisements would entail. Rather, they are victims of ads crafted by freelancers or agency creatives (people tasked with conceptually developing an ad) who seek to push acceptable advertising limits in return for industry recognition and awards. Typically, these are controversial ads created without client permission. For instance, an ad for the Ford Figo depicts former Italian Prime Minister Silvio Berlusconi smiling from the front seat of the car while gagged and bound women are in the trunk. This ad had reportedly been created by JWT India—without Ford's knowledge—and was entered into an advertising award competition ("Scam ads" 2013).[1] While the creation of unsanctioned ads is not a new phenomenon in the advertising industry, changes in technology have removed many of the gates that once shielded consumers from material not meant for public consumption. The rise of social media and the digital evolution of business have brought global attention to unsanctioned advertising. Moreover, many in the ad industry are increasingly under pressure to win awards for their work in order to promote or even maintain their careers (Wentz 2013a). This chapter explores the practice of rogue advertising from consequentialist and duty-based perspectives on ethics. By considering the consequences of rogue advertising as well as the codes of conduct by which ad practitioners are bound, we argue that this practice is detrimental to brands, the ad industry itself and society as a whole.

This chapter first explores the ethical foundations upon which our analysis is grounded. We then define rogue advertising and offer a typology of its complexities. Various examples of rogue ads are articulated with a focus on the case of the Ford Figo ad scandal in the spring of 2013. Our experimental research into the effects of rogue ads on consumer attitudes toward advertising and brands provides empirical support for our arguments. We next outline the industry debate over rogue advertising issues and also address the legal considerations of these types of ads in addition to corporate social responsibility implications. Finally, we offer recommendations about how professional advertisers can protect themselves; these recommendations include reviewing retainer contracts, monitoring award competition websites as well as monitoring social media. While the phenomenon of rogue advertising may be representative of our era of profound distrust, and signals a tolerance toward the spread of ethically problematic practices perpetuated by digital media, we close with evidence that public backlash is demanding greater accountability.

Ethical perspectives

The study of ethics allows individuals or professions to distinguish good from bad, or, in other words, to distinguish behaviors that are considered right from those that are considered wrong. Philosophical ethics in particular are normative (or prescriptive), recommending the type of behavior that ought to be practiced. Two influential branches of normative ethics involve teleology and deontology. Teleological ethics (also known as consequentialist ethics) are based upon the consequences of an action or behavior, whereas deontological ethics depend upon the underlying principle driving a behavior (James, Pratt, and Smith 1994). Studies have found that advertising practitioners tend to follow the standard of consequentialism, where decisions are made based upon the perceived best outcomes (or those that are least problematic) for the immediate parties involved (James, Pratt, and Smith 1994; Rotzoll and Christians 1980).

Instead of consequentialist-based ethics, a more appropriate framework within which to consider advertising is deontological, or duty-based ethics (Christians 2007; James, Pratt, and Smith 1994). One exemplification of duty-based ethics is the codes of conduct adopted by many self-regulatory groups (James, Pratt, and

Smith 1994). While the Federal Trade Commission (FTC) provides oversight of the US advertising industry to prevent practices that are anticompetitive to other businesses or deceptive/unfair to consumers, ethical issues remain in the realm of self-regulation. Industry trade groups such as the American Association of Advertising Agencies (4A's) and the American Advertising Federation (AAF) have codes of conduct to which their members must commit. At the outset of its Standards of Practice, the 4A's states, "We hold that a responsibility of advertising agencies is to be a constructive force in business." Moreover, according to its Creative Code, members are prohibited from creating advertising that contains "false or misleading statements or exaggerations, visual or verbal" ("Standards of Practice" 2011, ¶7). Similarly, the AAF in collaboration with the Reynolds Journalism Institute at the University of Missouri has developed "Principles and Practices for Advertising Ethics." Among the eight principles, we are advised that advertising professionals "have an obligation to exercise the highest personal ethics in the creation and dissemination of commercial information to consumers" ("Principles and Practices" 2011, ¶13). An explanation of rogue advertising and the extent to which it is ethically defensible is considered next.

Defining "Rogue" advertising

Characterizations of rogue ads are variable, with fine distinctions between the different types. Even the name for this phenomenon is inconsistent. In Brazil, they are called "truchos"; in India "scam" ads. In other places they are varyingly called fake, ghost, unsanctioned, speculative, or chip shop ads. For our purposes, we refer to these ads as rogue ads. In every case, rogue advertising involves the submission of an ad to an advertising industry award competition. In most cases, the submission is under false pretenses. For example, in order to qualify for competition, ads are supposed to be client-approved and should have already aired or run in a legitimate broadcast, electronic or print media schedule. Often, however, client companies are unaware of these ads. Essentially, we find that rogue ads can be characterized by one of five categories: (1) ads that were *neither* approved by a client *nor* ran/aired; (2) ads that were *not* approved by a client but ran/aired *anyway*; (3) ads that *were* approved by a client but *never* ran/aired; (4) ads that *were* approved by a client and ran on a limited scale at *client* expense; and (5) ads that may or may not have been client-approved but ran on a limited scale at an *agency's* own expense (O'Sullivan-Gavin and Amazeen 2016; Wentz 2001).

To explore this phenomenon from an ethical perspective, we first need to understand what advertisements are supposed to do. Fundamentally, the purpose of advertising is to benefit its sponsoring client by persuading consumers that the product or service merits purchase. According to Donald Johnston, former president of JWT Group, the essence of an advertising agency is to effectively service its clients (Mattelart 1991). Moreover, the industry's leading trade publication, *Advertising Age*, suggests the job of a creative person tasked with developing an ad is to help companies sell their products (Wheaton 2013). Indeed, each of the varying advertising hierarchy of effects models ultimately includes contributions to a client's market share, sales, and/or profit (Lavidge and Steiner 1961; McGuire 1976; Ray and Webb 1974; Rossiter and Percy 1985). Thus, advertising is supposed to be advantageous to its client.

Rogue advertising, in contrast, is often detrimental to the client (and as we will show, to others, as well). Because the agency or freelance creatives who develop these ads are primarily concerned with winning awards for their work, they frequently push acceptable boundaries with provocative material linked to familiar brand names. Often the content is offensive, discriminatory, sexual, and/or socially or culturally inflammatory. When the interest of the ad creator takes primacy over the interests of the brand, the resulting ad campaign can be problematic.

The following are examples of different types of rogue ads as viewed through the lens of teleological and deontological ethics. In 2007, for instance, three ads for Hanes brand underwear featured antigay slurs and racist words in an English-language Indian daily newspaper (Bagri 2013a). A sexually suggestive ad for Unilever's Kibon ice cream depicted spoons chasing a ball of ice cream, similar to sperm fertilizing an ovule (Wentz 2001). In a Suzuki Motorcycles ad, a crowd looks at a crashed motorcycle and ignores the injured rider (Wentz 2001). A 2013 ad for Flora margarine depicted a bullet shooting toward a heart-shaped butter dish with the words, "Uhh, Dad I'm gay," as if coming out as gay was like a bullet to a father's heart (Stampler 2013). Another 2013 ad for Hyundai Motor Co. depicted a man unsuccessfully attempting to commit suicide inside a new Hyundai model (Krashinsky 2013). In all of these examples, the ads were never authorized by the client, so the creative has violated his or her duty to the client. In addition, the ads were strategically unaligned with the brands' positioning, likely tarnishing the brand, company and agency reputations and, in turn, hurting sales.

An experiment we conducted confirmed that an advertiser who is the victim of rogue ads can suffer in multiple ways. First, consumer attitudes are less favorable toward scam ads than toward client-authorized ads. Second, once a client is linked to a scam ad, the client appears to suffer damage to its reputation. We found that an advertiser attains significantly less favorable brand attitudes when its trademark is associated with a scam ad. Finally, we live in an era where ads spread virally and exist on in perpetuity on the internet. Thus, advertisers may suffer from being victimized not only by rogue creatives, but also by prolonged public exposure to ads in a manner that may not align with their brand objectives (O'Sullivan-Gavin and Amazeen 2016). And as noted by *Advertising Age's* Ken Wheaton (2013, ¶3), "Neither consumers nor general-market media care to distinguish between a scam ad and a real ad."

These unfortunate consequences were seen during the Ford Figo ad scandal as well. A Google Trends search identified a spike in web inquiries during March and April 2013 soon after the rogue ads were revealed. This spike in web traffic was accompanied by a significant amount of media coverage in trade journals as well as in domestic and international mainstream news media. In the United States, the Ford Figo scandal attracted coverage in various news outlets, which included the *New York Times, The Wall Street Journal, The Economic Times, USA Today*, the Associated Press, *Huffington Post*, NPR, and CNN. Internationally, the scandal attracted coverage in news media articles in India, Wales, Ireland, Scotland, New Zealand, China, Singapore, and South Africa. There was coverage of the scandal in many year-end reviews as well. For instance, Ford achieved Ad Gully's 2013 "oops! moment in advertising" ("13 Events" 2013) and took the top prize in *Business Insider's* list of the "top 10 most outrageous ads companies were forced to apologize for in 2013" (Taube 2013). Even today, a Google search of the keywords "Ford Figo" still associates the brand with the scandal. To the casual observer, Ford is responsible for the offensive campaign—the information identifying the campaign as a scam is unattached to some of the images floating around the internet.

Thus, from a consequentialist perspective, rogue advertising is ethically indefensible when it presents material offensive to society that is strategically unaligned with a brand's positioning. Rather than benefitting the brand, this type of rogue advertising tarnishes its reputation and draws unfavorable media attention that spreads virally on the internet through social media. Moreover, it is often the client that must issue an apology to the world—Ford, Hanes, and Unilever are among those companies that have offered apologies—despite having never authorized the offending advertisement (Taube 2013).

Offensiveness, however, may not be the only problematic issue with rogue advertising. A deontological lens may be a more useful perspective through which to examine the typically (although not always) less offensive types of rogue ads of which clients are aware. Awareness, however, does not necessarily correspond with approval for the ads to be used for anything other than the client's benefit at the client's direction. Ads expressly rejected by the client have been submitted for industry awards without client authorization—an example of this was the ad for Taronga Zoo in Australia. In this case, it was later discovered that the Zoo did not retain the agency, did not approve the ad, and did not approve the submission to the Cannes competition (Krashinsky 2013). The ad was created for the Zoo's consideration, rejected, and the subsequent submission was clearly without client authorization—solely for the creatives' benefit. Another type of rogue ad includes "director's cuts" in which the advertising or production agency submits for award consideration a version of the ad that is different from the version that ran—for example, a longer version of what the client chose as the final ad. While these ads may not necessarily be offensive to society, they circumvent the award contest entry rules, according to which submissions must be client-authorized and must have run in a legitimate media schedule.

There are also rogue ads that *are* created with the client's authorization but are aired or published on a limited scale so as to qualify for industry award consideration. Not only do these rogue ads violate contest entry rules, but they also create an uneven playing field between creatives who are simply vying for industry recognition and those with client-authorized ads that ran in a legitimate media schedule for the purpose of selling a product or service. The Electrolux vacuum ad is one example of this form of a rogue ad. The ad, which implied that the vacuum was strong enough to suck a turtle out of its shell, aired only once, with client approval, and thus qualified for industry award consideration (Wentz 2001). With such a limited media run, this ad clearly could not have had much, if any, influence on the target audience and thus could not have benefited the brand. Furthermore, this example also illustrates a case where the ad agency itself, rather than the client, paid to run the ad. In another example of an approved ad, the World Wildlife Foundation ran an ad once in a small Sao Paulo, Brazil newspaper in 2009 in order to become award eligible. The ad caused an uproar due to the fact that it depicted numerous airplanes attacking New York City and its Twin Towers, thus evoking the September 11, 2001, terrorist attacks (Wentz

2009). In these cases, the ads were approved and were not inconsistent with each brand's previous positioning efforts. What makes these ads ethically problematic is the legitimacy of each brand's media schedule for the ads in question.

Whether or not an ad had legitimate media placement is an important factor in determining whether it qualifies as rogue. Sometimes the airdate for an authorized ad may be delayed due to client postponements, yet an agency submits the ad to an award competition anyway. Other ads are run once in a little-known media vehicle or aired during a time in which the audience is scant in order to make the ad eligible for award consideration. In essence, these types of rogue ads are not intended to sell the product or service or gain advertising exposure for the client. The sole intent of the ad is to win an award—this subverts the rules of the competition, undermines the intent of the contest, and pits legitimate, client-approved ads against single-run/limited-schedule ads. According to Ian Thubron, CEO of M&C Saatchi, Hong Kong, "Even if an ad legitimately runs on TV and therefore meets the strict criteria, if it is a washing machine ad running once on a children's channel at 4 a.m. with a 0.000001 rating, then clearly it's a scam" (Wentz 2001, ¶27).

Apart from client approval, the question remains as to whether or not ads were legitimately designed to promote a product or if they were created simply to become eligible for submission for award consideration. "Sometimes an ad may have run in one medium on a very limited scale and it doesn't necessarily mean it's not a scam ad," said Romain Hatchuel, the Cannes Festival's CEO. He continued, "A media invoice is not enough if the letter but not the spirit of the rule is complied with" (Wentz 2001, ¶6). In these cases, the issue is less about problematic content and more about compliance with award contest rules and the true purpose of the advertisements. In an effort to eliminate speculative creative work and maintain a level-playing field among entrants, the more prestigious award shows generally require legitimate media schedules demonstrating the ads were a part of the normal course of business.

Thus, rogue ads are ethically indefensible because they lack client authorization, legitimate public exposure, and/or were created solely for the purpose of entering award contests. Because of the offensive/questionable nature of the material in some rogue ads, a brand's managers may be kept unaware that the ad has been produced, disseminated to the public, and submitted to an ad competition. When this material is inconsistent with a brand's positioning, its reputation may become tarnished and its sales negatively impacted. These types of ads are ethically problematic not only because of their negative consequences for the client (and arguably for society), but because they falsely represent a brand message—a violation of industry trade-group standards to ethically create and disseminate truthful commercial information to consumers. While some of these ads may not have been placed in any media (a violation of contest-entry rules), should an ad win an award, it will surely draw media attention. Furthermore, award entries are often submitted electronically or wind up being posted to the internet somewhere. Once digitally uploaded, there is little to stop an ad from spreading virally, particularly when the material is controversial in nature and associated with a familiar brand name. Despite the ethically dubious nature of rogue advertising, the practice continues virtually unabated in the industry.

Industry debate

It used to be that some practitioners considered rogue advertising "not so terrible" because "no one is getting hurt" (Hatfield 2001, ¶6). However, over the last decade, the increasing use of the internet and social media has made it nearly impossible to keep mis- and dis-information—like rogue ads—from the public. At the same time, many in the ad industry are increasingly under pressure to win awards for their work in order to promote or even maintain their careers (Wentz 2013a). As a result, the practice of rogue advertising has become a simmering ethical issue with both detractors and advocates.

Advertising award shows have become part and parcel of the profession. There are many advertising industry award shows with the ADDY Awards, the Cannes Lions International Festival, the CLIO Awards, D&AD, the Effie Awards, and the One Show as some of the more prestigious competitions. Estimates suggest that there are over 500 award shows around the world annually (Polonsky and Waller 1995). These competitions are a means for agencies to gain recognition for their work, encourage creativity among individual staff members, allow agencies or creatives to increase their prestige within the industry, and facilitate new business leads (Schweitzer and Hester 1992). While multiple industry-sponsored studies suggest award-winning ads do increase client sales (Hall 2010; Hatfield 2001), independent academic research suggests the link between awards and an agency's financial performance is tenuous at best (Polonsky and Waller 1995). Nonetheless, the pressure to win awards has become analogous to an arms race both between creatives and between competing agencies. Furthermore, with a holding-company-of-the-year award introduced a few years ago at the Cannes Festival, the stakes have become even higher (Wentz 2013b).

While the award shows are purported to promote creativity and draw attention to meritorious talent, criticisms do exist. First, ads are generally judged on the subjective construct of "creativity," which is hard to measure and fails to take into consideration the effectiveness of the ad for the client (the Effie Awards notwithstanding). Second, the award shows are also generally judged by individuals within the profession (rather than by independent critics who have no proverbial horse in the race) lowering their credibility. Third, most award shows are a profit-generating enterprise. Thus, the incentive is to maximize the number of entrants for the greatest profitability. This benefits larger agencies and penalizes small shops which may not be able to afford the high entry fees. Finally, and quite likely as a result of all of these criticisms, many of the participating ads are purportedly fake (Raszl 2009; Wentz 2001). Because the shows want to maximize profits, there is little incentive to penalize agencies for fake entries, particularly if the submission of rogue ads is pervasive.

There appears to be a clear division among advertising professionals regarding rogue ads: those who believe the rogue ads are "harmless" and those who believe there is no place or rationale in the industry for this type of practice. Many of the professionals who believe they are "harmless" wink and turn a blind eye toward rogue ads. Others excuse or even promote the use of rogue ads as creative and essential for career recognition and future success (Wentz 2013b). Some professionals excuse rogue ads created for non-existing clients, or those created with approval from clients, simply as "proactive" creativity (Priyanka Mehra 2013).

With the controversy at the professional level as to whether or not the issue of rogue ads is being addressed appropriately, the industry award organizations receive mixed messages. In response to the public expressions of disgust and outrage toward several of the recent rogue ads, many award organizations that already required verification of client approval letters have strengthened their positions on and rules regarding rogue advertisements. For example, in 2009 the One Show competition instituted a five-year ban against creatives and their agencies for submission of an ad that was unauthorized and only ran once in off hours. That same year, the Cannes Lions International Advertising Festival and the Art Directors Club released policies to deal with "scam ads," defined as "work that did not have client approval or that only ran once in paid media" (Patel 2009, ¶2). The Cannes Festival instituted a ban against creatives who submitted scam ads, but not their agencies. The 2011 Kia Motors Brazil case was the first time that creatives were banned from the following year's competition due to the submission of a rogue ad (Wentz and Penteado 2011). At some award shows, however, the practice has become pervasive enough that new competitive categories have been established to accommodate rogue ads. The national awards show in Chile, for example, added a "free expression" category in December 2000 just for fake ads (Wentz 2001). Not only have some award shows added specific categories for these fake ads, but entire competitions have emerged dedicated to this genre. Further reinforcing the practice of rogue ads, industry professionals from respected agencies have served as judges for just such an award competition: the Chip Shop Awards (Parekh 2013).

The Chip Shop Awards competition is specifically designed for rogue ads. Originating in 2003 (Thomson 2014), this competition emerged from creatives who provided free work to a client in order to get their advertising business up and running. Far from its roots of free ads created by struggling creatives, the Chip Shop Awards currently welcomes any type of ad—sanctioned or unsanctioned—eligible for award consideration. "So rather than have anyone bend or break the rules of more exacting awards schemes," says its website, "we decided the industry needed a platform where anything and everything was allowed." Entries pertaining to "unspeakable" news stories, those that are in "bad taste," or those that are beyond the budget of a client are specifically encouraged. Winning campaigns as well as nominees are publically accessible, even those that are "in bad taste" and "plagiarize" the intellectual property of established brands ("The Chip Shop Awards" 2014).[2]

Those in the industry who believe there is no place for this type of practice recognize the damages sustained by trademarked brands and even the creatives themselves. For example, the 2013 Ford Figo series of rogue ads led to several firings. Not only did multiple creatives who worked on the ads lose their jobs, so did the creative director as well as the chief creative officer/managing partner of JWT India (Choudhury and Bennett 2013). In the Hanes case of anti gay rogue ads, the ad agency lost the Hanes account in India (Bagri 2013b). Nancy Hill, president-CEO of the 4A's, stated, "Creative directors have to take responsibility... and ask 'WWCT: What would the client think?'" (Wentz 2013b, ¶3). Colvyn Harris, a juror at the 2014 Cannes Festival believes, "Companies do not scam [sic], and do not believe in scam. The integrity and purpose of a company shouldn't be put up for speculation, when people are the ones who created that scam and they are chasing their own ambitions, fame and glory" (Mehra 2014, ¶9).

John Boiler, president of the advertising agency 72andSunny, stated, "I can't think of a punishment too severe for agencies that promote scam ads and pollute shows with them. It's the most disgusting manifestation of ego in our industry, [and it] hurts clients and agencies reputation" (Diaz 2013, ¶3). Boiler recommends firing the creators of the unsanctioned ads and having award competitions adopt a "zero-tolerance" policy that would "permanently ban any agency responsible for one bona fide and probable offense" (Diaz 2013, ¶5). Susan Creadle from the Leo Burnett agency suggests that what might be needed is an ad industry type of Hippocratic oath reminding us of the great responsibility that comes with public communication. She further notes, "A scam ad might collect a shiny object or two. A scam ad might ignorantly be celebrated in our insular community. A scam ad might make a portfolio stand out. But a scam ad will not sell a product, build a brand or, if we aim incredibly high, change the world" (Diaz 2013, ¶8).

Cultural issues such as discrimination and sexism must also be addressed in the case of rogue ads. Shockingly, the Ford Figo ads were entered in the 2013 Goafest Abby awards competition even after the global outrage in response to several brutal rapes and subsequent deaths of women in India. The ads were withdrawn, but appeared to be entered with proof of having run along with a client approval letter. Because the approval letter was general, however, it is not clear that the client (Ford India) was aware of the ads' content (Wentz 2013a). Whereas the majority of social media and press coverage condemned the Figo Berlusconi ad as offensive to Indian women specifically and all women generally, there are those who continue to defend the ad as funny within the context of how Indians view politicians as villains, classifying the outrage as "overreaction" and ignoring the brutality promoted in the ad (Vishal Mehra 2013). Others defend the practice as based upon lack of knowledge of cultural implications such as one anonymous creative director who claimed, "In India, 'we lack the knowledge about international icons. We don't know where to draw the line—here you'll see people wearing Hitler T-shirts'" (Bagri 2013b, ¶10). Clearly, the Ford Figo ads breached global ethical norms on many levels, and the defense of same is both egregious and insulting to the general public.

Legal considerations

Beyond ethics, there are also legal ramifications to rogue advertising. Unsanctioned ads raise legal questions relative to intellectual property (copyright and trademark infringements), contracts, and harm to clients' reputations. Because many of the rogue ads are initiated outside of the United States, they give rise to similar international issues. It is particularly important to recognize that in the United States, rogue ads are not considered parody, content utilized in a fair use manner, or deceptive advertising regulated by the FTC (O'Sullivan-Gavin and Amazeen 2016). Nor are we discussing the work of students practicing their craft. This is the intentional action of professionals who steal a brand's intellectual property for personal gain. Not only are brand names mentioned in these types of ads, but actual logos, trademarks, taglines, and corporate identities are also being assumed (Parekh 2013). Whereas it is always the responsibility of a property owner, including the owners of intellectual property rights, to guard their legal rights, rogue ads strike at the heart of the advertising business relationship. Clients who enter into business relationships with agencies and creatives do not expect their intellectual property to be used without permission by creatives seeking individual gain. Rogue ads violate concepts of trust, breach contractual duties and, in many cases, involve outright theft of a client's intellectual property. Thus, advertisers must take steps to guard their intellectual property rights, brand reputations, and overall corporate reputation.

Advertisers can protect themselves from unauthorized rogue ads by taking several steps at the beginning of any relationship with an advertising agency. Initially, the contract between the client and the agency must be reviewed for strict language specifying exactly what the agency is being retained to create and all acceptable media outlets (such as television, radio, print, and online) in which the end product will appear. Clients can and should clarify in agency retainer contracts that any and all products produced by the agency must be reviewed by the client and cannot be released for any purpose, including award contests, without client approval. In addition, advertisers should reserve the right to review all award competition submissions and require that competition letters accurately specify the ad that was submitted and how and when it aired/ran (O'Sullivan-Gavin and Amazeen 2016). Companies such as Mazda North American, Coca-Cola, and Adidas International all require award competition entries to be reviewed prior to submission (Wentz 2013b). Clients should include in their retainer contracts language that clearly states the ad agency will be liable for civil damages for breach of contract, unauthorized use of intellectual property, and for harm to client name and brand reputation if the agency uses the client name and brand without authorization. In addition, the retainer contract should make it explicitly clear that any unauthorized use of the client's intellectual property to create unsanctioned ads will result in the right of the client to immediately terminate the contract (O'Sullivan-Gavin and Amazeen 2016). Advertisers should also monitor social media to ensure their brand name(s) is/are being utilized properly. In addition, award competitions should be monitored for both unauthorized submissions using a client's name and brands, and for authorized submissions that might have been altered from the originally authorized ad. Given the explosive growth of new communication media and vehicles for advertising on the internet, advertisers should also continue to monitor relevant outlets for unauthorized and altered ads posted to the various award competition websites (O'Sullivan-Gavin and Amazeen 2016).

Conclusion

Whereas advertising is premised upon the basic norm of trust (Pollay 1986), rogue advertising is associated with breaches of trust, particularly when unsanctioned. From a client/advertiser standpoint, unauthorized rogue ads threaten the trust that clients have with their advertising agency and/or with relationships to other ad industry professionals and may also damage a brand's reputation among consumers. Among ad practitioners, rogue advertising violates industry codes of conduct, may breach legal contracts, and creates an unequal playing field between those who compete for recognition of their work playing by the rules and those who do not. From the consumer perspective, these types of commercial messages are not what they appear to be because they are generally not intended by the client/advertiser and are not meant for our consumption. With the emergence of the internet, the gates that once shielded us from these ads have disappeared. Consequently, rogue ads have proliferated via social media and mainstream media, are archived forever, and are often taken out of context.

There are various remedies for rogue advertising that the advertising industry can implement. First, while there are hundreds of award competitions worldwide, the most prestigious must set the standard by establishing competitive best practices and consistently enforcing a zero-tolerance policy toward rogue advertising. Second, the industry may be spared embarrassment and loss of credibility by following its own established codes of ethics and responsibly rejecting agencies or individuals from membership for violating those codes.

Third, as Bugeja (2007) observes, the goal of ethical accountability is to make something that was damaged whole again. Therefore, to be ethically accountable and to attempt to repair any damage by rogue advertising, the industry must apologize to both advertisers and consumers for rogue infractions, state how the oversight took place, and indicate what measures are being taken to avoid a similar situation in the future. Finally, the industry must "name and shame" serial agency or individual producers of rogue ads. This form of deterrent might cause clients to think twice about hiring an agency that has repeatedly practiced rogue advertising; agencies might think twice about hiring a creative who has a history of rogue ads. From this perspective, it is thus interesting to note that the chief creative officer/managing partner of WPP Group's JWT India agency, who was fired because of the Ford Figo scandal, was hired just two months later by Publicis Worldwide as their chief creative officer for South Asia. The executive chairman of Publicis stated that the hiring demonstrates his firm's commitment to "invest in top talent" (Wentz 2013c, ¶9).

From a broader vantage point, rogue advertising may be part of a larger societal trend signaling a troubling tolerance toward the spread of questionable ethics perpetuated by digital media/technological advances. For example, with the growth of the internet, a "crisis" in online advertising has emerged with fake web traffic generated by robots, fraudulent click activity, and a lack of transparency as to on which websites advertisers' ads appear. A *Wall Street Journal* report estimated that over one-third of website traffic is fake, unethically driving up the price of online ads for advertisers (Vranica 2014). In other instances, editorial decisions about newsworthiness are increasingly being made based upon algorithms from Google and Facebook (O'Donovan 2014) with no regard for the authenticity or accuracy of the information being shared (Kranish 2014). Similarly, "content farms" produce thousands of articles and videos a day, written by thousands of freelancers to help fill the pages of digital newspapers and magazines with articles that have the primary purpose of appealing to individuals that advertisers want to reach. Perhaps the sheer volume of information available on the internet, as well as the current tolerance of rogue ads has brought about a national tolerance for exaggerations, distortions, and downright falsehoods (Skornia 1965). As a society, we are in an era of profound distrust, particularly of persuasive messages (Pollay 1986). Rogue ads, when discovered by the public, reinforce the belief that the advertising industry cannot be believed or trusted.

Fortunately, although perhaps not quickly enough, there have been emergent cottage industries striving for accountability. The enterprise of political fact-checking, for instance, has served as a bulwark against inaccurate claims made in political advertisements and other public forums (Amazeen 2013). Elsewhere, the practice of forensic auditing has emerged and been applied to digital media by companies such as White Ops and Telemetry to detect and protect against ad fraud and other digital security issues (Vranica 2014). The general public, through grassroots movements such as viral sharing, digital complaints and internet-led boycotts, has also begun to demand transparency and accountability while applying pressure for industry action after a rogue ad is revealed. Along the same lines as these efforts at accountability, there apparently is a new business opportunity within the advertising industry: policing award shows for rogue ads. Whether or not an entity or entities will actually enforce public calls for this type of oversight is unknown. The advertising industry must respond to the global awareness and condemnation of rogue ads. Rogue ads can no longer be tolerated, ignored or considered humorous by an industry that relies upon client and public trust in the messages created and presented to the world.

Notes

1 The Ford Figo scandal was actually a series of three ads varying on the theme of the car's spacious trunk. The Berlusconi ad seemed to draw the most attention and is thus the focus of our critique. The ad can be viewed at: http://www. businessinsider.com.au/ford-wpp-apologizes-for-offensive-car-ad-2013-3.
2 These types of rogue ads can be viewed at http://www.chipshopawards.com/.

9

"Steve Jobs is Dead": iReport and the Ethos of Citizen Journalism

Shane Tilton

Citizen journalism and its relationship to traditional media and journalistic institutions are modern constructions. The convergence of the tools of media production, the opening of wider bandwidth for distribution, and a more media-literate international populace have placed this mode of reporting in the spotlight. One of the traditional roles of journalism is to unite communities by presenting an honest representation of those communities through a diversity of voices (Carpenter 2008). Citizen journalists represent a projection of the "voice of the voiceless" ethos found in classic journalistic traditions. This mantra can be extended to online citizen journalism, as an online citizen journalist can be described "as an individual who intends to publish information online meant to benefit a community" (Carpenter 2010). Any benefit to a community (whether those communities are traditional geographic communities, shared interest communities, or communities in the ritual sense of the term) is only delivered if the reporting meets some standards of ethics accepted by the given community.

Ethical standards, while rarely formalized, have some precedent in citizen journalism. It is fair to argue that blogs are a foundational platform for citizen journalism, and in 2002, Rebecca Blood attempted to formalize some form of blogging ethics by giving six tenets of ethical blogging:

1. Publish as fact only that which you believe to be true. If your statement is speculation, say so.
2. If the material exists online, link to it when you reference it. Linking to referenced material allows readers to judge for themselves the accuracy and insightfulness of your statements.
3. Publicly correct any misinformation.

4. Write each entry as if it could not be changed; add to, but do not rewrite or delete, any entry.
5. Disclose any conflict of interest.
6. Note questionable and biased sources.

Blogs are one tool of the online citizen journalist, and also the beginning point of the "produsage" of journalism (Bruns 2008). Produsage, a word formed by combing "production" and "usage," is defined as content developed via open participation channels and communal evaluation of the materials presented. In addition, produsage reveals some form of organization of the work via a meritocratic system. Finally, produsage stems from universal access to the works of user-generated content. Individual content producers are rewarded based on the norms of the community (Ibid). The common good of the citizen journalism community becomes the ethical foundation for these produsage aspects when those creators follow the standards and practices of their community.

An examination of the principles of citizen journalism and the ethos of the mediated environment becomes a keystone in the research as citizen journalism often has less authority when compared to other media sources. Most media organizations have a standard code of ethics. The implementation of the code of ethics allows those organizations to survive during times of dishonest reporting. A single violation of ethical norms does not bring down the whole of journalism. Examples of past unethical behavior in the business fill journalism ethics textbooks, and the profession still exists mostly intact today (Groshek and Conway 2012). An individual citizen journalist that fails to report honestly, however, does threaten the progress made by other citizen journalists. Citizen journalists who do break the ethos created by former citizen journalistic content force the entire effort of citizen journalism into the larger rabble of non-journalistic UGC. The authenticity of editorial content is called into question when the more important practice of citizen journalism breaks the sense of ethos created between the journalists, the networks of distribution, and the audience at-large (Singer and Ashman 2009). The audience at large no longer accepts the truth, in all of its forms and manners, if citizen journalism is showed to have a history of "bad faith" reporting. A discussion about the ethics of citizen journalism should take place with this in mind.

The case of false iReport story on Steve Jobs in 2008 is a representation of the formal breakdown of ethics in citizen journalism. In this chapter, I first assess the effects of this incident, specifically looking at how this false story impacted the credibility of citizen journalism and traditional journalistic institutions. I then consider the ethical issues related to this event and future "breaking news" conditions. Finally, I examine the term "citizen journalist" as it was used in the CNN case, and will trace how multiple entities have defined the citizen journalist in the years since. Citizen journalist ethics is the focal point because the controversy stemmed from the breakdown of citizen and traditional journalism ethics.

The iReport case

Around 4 a.m. on October 3, 2008, a CNN iReport "citizen reporter" named Johntw pitched the followed story to the site:

> Steve Jobs was rushed to the ER just a few hours ago after suffering a major heart attack. I have an insider who tells me that paramedics were called after Steve claimed to be suffering from severe chest pains and shortness of breath. My source has opted to remain anonymous, but he is quite reliable. I haven't seen anything about this anywhere else yet, and as of right now, I have no further information, so I thought this would be a good place to start. If anyone else has more information, please share it. (Allan and Thorsen 2009, 2)

For two hours following this posting, the internet began to generate multiple stories and links that derived from this original post. Some of the stories extended this premise to conclude that Steve Jobs had died. Silicon Alley Insider (SAI), a sub-page of Business Insider's website, posted a story at approximately 9:25 a.m. on October 3, 2008, under the headline "Apple's Steve Jobs Rushed To ER After Heart Attack, Says CNN Citizen Journalist."

There was no confirmation of the story by mainstream media sources. Thirty minutes after SAI published the write-up, the organization called Apple's VP of Worldwide Communications, Katie Cotton, to inquire about the accuracy of the reported heart attack. She denied the report (Perez 2008). Twenty minutes after SAI published a retraction to the story and reported the falsehood of the original iReport, CNN took down user Johntw's post. CNN responded to this event with a press release stating:

> iReport.com is an entirely user-generated site where the content is determined by the community. Content that does not comply with Community Guidelines

will be removed. After the content in question was uploaded to iReport.com, the community brought it to our attention. Based on our Terms of Use that govern user behavior on iReport.com, the fraudulent content was removed from the site and the user's account was disabled. (Diaz 2008)

This story followed an erroneous August obituary published by Bloomberg (Perez 2008). In September 2008, Apple gave a keynote address about their newest iPod. Jobs stood in front of the crowd and displayed the infamous Mark Twain quote, "The reports of my death are greatly exaggerated" on the screen behind him. The tech community consistently called Steve Jobs' health into question as he continued to battle pancreatic cancer, and the stock market moved on news related to Jobs' health for most of 2008 (Koch, Fenili, and Cebula 2011).

Following the discovery that the CNN iReport was false, other media sources looked at the potential motivations for producing the release. Several of the news organizations investigated the economic initiatives for causing this panic. David Scheer (2008) published a series of stories in Bloomberg describing the US Securities and Exchange Commission's examination of CNN's response and role in the distribution. In these stories, Scheer questioned whether Johntw would face felony charges. One of the key elements that led to this focus was the fact that Apple's stock dropped 2 percent on October 3, leading to the theory that Johntw was an investor that sold Apple stock at the higher price without owning the stock. Hypothetically, Johntw could have intended for the story to lead to a drop in the stock price. The drop would enable that person to buy back the stock at a lower price, thus "shorting" the company.

There was a general handwringing from the other mainstream news outlets as CNN was judged poorly for allowing a "non-journalist" use of the CNN brand to mislead the public. Sarah Perez (2008) summarized the viewpoint of the mainstream media by stating, "The problem here stems from the fact that because CNN has obviously decided not to police or edit the iReport section of their web site, the section is left wide open to 'reporters' who want to wreak a little havoc." Bob Sullivan, who writes for MSNBC.com, wrote, "It was just a blogger writing something that was 100 percent false. But because it was under the CNN brand, it carried a lot more weight than any anonymous blogger would" (National Press Club 2008).

CNN was indicted by the public and media outlets for allowing a story with no credible sources on its website. Although the story never "crossed over" onto CNN's television networks, and CNN's on-air talent, reporters, & other various journalistic staff members never reported the heart attack in their publications, the newsgroup was tarnished by a lack of moderation on its social network.

The theory of citizen journalism

The Jobs controversy reveals how "citizen journalism" lies in relation to traditional journalism. There are a few factors that have thrust citizen journalism into the forefront even though it is not any newer than the established traditional sources of information. Low-cost tools of production have allowed more people to tell their stories in ways that resemble the style and tone of more professional journalistic pieces. Accessible modes of distribution have given those individual journalists a wider audience and allowed stories that would not be told on traditional media platforms a chance to be heard and seen (Allan and Thorsen 2009). In addition, the social nature of modern citizen journalism means that this content can be shared and commented on in ways that a decade before would have been impossible. The public sphere can be inspired to react to stories as long as content creators are savvy enough to understand how the social networks respond to any given topic or event, how the audience responds to a given message, and how the traditional media system distributes those stories to larger mediated audiences (Goode 2009).

Outing (2005) claims that the first level, or the most fundamental form, of citizen journalism originates with the opening up of online news stories to public comments. He argues that extending this "letters to the editor" function of journalism enhances original news content because "readers routinely use such comments to bring up some point that was missed by the writer, or add new information that the reporter didn't know about. Such readers can make the original story better." The next level is called "the citizen add-on reporter," wherein the citizen journalist adds on contributions for stories written by professional journalists. In this level of engagement, citizens select stories, solicit information and experiences from members of the public, and add them to the main story for the purpose of enriching the content by adding complexity and avenues of debate. The argument for citizen add-on reporting is that such participation offers the community better and deeper coverage than is possible with lone journalistic endeavors. These two models make the citizen auxiliary to the reporters and the reporting.

A by-product of this connection is that it forces the organization to become more social and respond to the issues present in the community. One of the larger complaints regarding the professional journalistic organization use of social and new media is the idea of "shovelware," or the process of "tweeting the same headline used in the print edition" (Boyle and Zuegner 2012). Citizen journalists using the channels of social media can shape the dialogue and focus of the story better than the preprogrammed feed of information that comes from reprocessing the news stories from an organization's central website or channel of communication.

One of the major issues associated with this form of interaction is the lack of agency of the citizen journalist. Those producing content under the banner of a professional news organization often give their content freely without necessarily being rewarded or even acknowledged for their work (Deuze, Bruns, and Neuberger 2007). In this type of citizen journalism organization, the citizen journalist's work is profitable without the citizen journalist making money from the work.

Arguably, CNN's iReport system represents a version of the stand-alone citizen journalism site. Frequently, an organization will create a separate service that allows community members to sign up and become an amateur journalist for that site. CNN considers the iReport a different element from their primary site (www.cnn.com), and it is, therefore, considered separate from their core news brand. The majority of the contributions to the site come from the community at large whereas community moderators manage the rest of the site content. The structure and flow of the site is a hybrid between an online social network (OSN) and a traditional journalist site. This hybridization represents one of the key issues pertaining to the Jobs heart attack controversy. Because the process of signing up with iReport uses an interface similar to that of an OSN instead of a journalistic site, a few observers questioned the credibility of a semi-anonymous author involved in an established journalistic organization (Sandoval 2008).

The stand-alone citizen journalism site with limited editorial control like iReport works if the citizen journalist community itself maintains some control against "bad postings" (e.g., inappropriate content, false information, and inflammatory speech) with the help of the superstructure supporting the site itself (i.e., the community managers hired by CNN to run the site). The network (with its superstructure) acts as "commons-based peer production" platform in that content creators own their posting and must act as the protectors of the common space to ensure its continuous survival (Benkler and Nissenbaum

2006). Outing (2006) points to the "Report Misconduct" buttons as a way of dealing with these bad postings by stating:

> Users click these when they spot something inappropriate, and a message is sent to site editors so someone can take a look, and take action if necessary. Also worth considering is having a script written that automatically takes down an item when, say, at least three people click the misconduct button—a safeguard that will come in handy in the middle of the night.

These controls work if the spirit of citizen journalism is understood and shared by the community at large, and is explained and taught by the "opinion leaders" within the community. With a site like CNN's iReport, the citizen journalist is given a structure to create and distribute content. When the citizen journalist "performs the norms" of the social network (Tilton 2012), he or she observes the stories that pique the interest of the community at large based on the views, comments, and shares of the story. Accordingly, he/she will try to shape his or her stories based on the aesthetics, language, and visuals of acceptable and shareable site content (Jenkins, Ford, and Green 2013). This informal training of the citizen journalist originates from a reasonable study of the user-generated content on the site. An analysis will lead the citizen journalist to understand the best practices for users of the system (Kaplan and Haenlein 2010). Johntw did not adopt these practices and the ethical standards of CNN and its sub-page called into question.

One of the questions that has been raised from this discussion of the protocol of iReport is the sense of collective responsibility present in iReport versus the communal bond of traditional social networks like Facebook or Twitter or even the content-focused networks like Digg or Reddit. Community building represents the foundation of all of the other systems mentioned. Profiles in those given systems represent a person better than the profiles created in iReport. The level of engagement on networks like Facebook and Reddit comes from a series of common interests communicated on the given networks (Tilton 2012). iReport is different than the other social networks, as the dominant forms of communication on iReport are the stories themselves instead of postings and group interactions. The stories themselves speak for the citizen journalists.

Citizen journalism as a social good

Central to the argument of the quality of citizen journalism online is the thesis that citizen journalism is a social good. Alan D. Mutter (2010), the former editor at the Chicago *Daily News* and the City Editor of the Chicago *Sun-Times*, defends the role of citizen journalism when he writes:

> Our democracy benefits from the scrutiny of a vigorous and unfettered press. That, in and of itself, is well worth championing. [In addition, the] decline in the protection of one class of journalists could lead to a decline to the protection of all journalists.

Citizen journalism supports a strong and unfettered press, in that the participation of citizens places the context of current events and stories in the voice of the local observer. Indeed, the product of the citizen journalist runs counter to that of the parachute journalist who covers events by "[stringing] together collection[s] of what seem like blogposts . . . with a few interviews to break up the predictability" (Malik 2014). A primary point in discussing the societal ideal of citizen journalism is that the stories break the prepackaged nature of modern journalism.

The raw nature of citizen journalism was made more refined during the London Bombings of July 7, 2005. The elements of the story that would be considered the beginning of citizen journalism were processed by the BBC. According to Torin Douglas (2006), a media correspondent for BBC News, "That day, the BBC received 22,000 e-mails and text messages about the London tube and bus bombings. There were 300 photos—50 within an hour of the first bomb going off—and several video sequences." Those texts, pictures, and videos allowed the BBC to construct a reasonably complete story about what was happening in the tunnels of London. These superior examples of citizen journalism came from the stories published by those who had firsthand experience of the attacks.

The ethical issues addressed by the media

The ethical issues related to the Jobs heart attack controversy of 2008 reveal a significant arena of discussion focusing on how the iReport represents the current state of citizen journalism. The questions raised by journalists reporting on the false story can serve as reference points for examining the moral integrity of professional news organizations when these entities use content from—and partner with—citizen journalists online. I conducted a study of the news articles posted about the iReport story[1] and discovered three common themes related to the ethical issues they reported: (a) The training of citizen journalists via the iReport site/becoming a member of the site, (b) iReport as audience and content creator, and (c) The credibility of the citizen journalist and the iReporter as journalist.

The training of citizen journalists

Commentators levied harsh criticism against CNN itself for neglecting to train citizen journalists on the ethical standards of reportage on the iReport site. These individuals also criticized CNN for not presenting sufficient barriers to entry for new journalists posting content on the site. In other words, CNN failed to teach citizen journalists about journalistic integrity, and the organization did not exercise adequate discretion when allowing users to join the community.

Becoming a citizen journalist on CNN is as simple as signing up for a new web app from an internet startup. The process involves nothing more than filling out a name, screen name, and e-mail address. Adding a phone number is optional and necessary only if a user wants the story to be considered by CNN. There's a CAPTCHA to prevent bots and an e-mail confirmation link; however, due to disposable e-mail addresses, such safeguards are rendered ineffective.

The fundamental ethical consideration when discussing this safeguard is the anonymity of the reporter. Journalism has a history of using anonymous sources to help journalists find the truth in a given story. "Deep Throat" from Bob Woodward and Carl Bernstein's "Watergate" in the Washington *Post* in 1972 is the most classic example of the practical use of anonymous sources (Zelizer 1993). The use of anonymous sources is accepted practice because of the vetting and the trust the writer and the editors have with the source. This relationship does not exist with a citizen journalist and the public if the citizen journalist is unknown. Sandoval (2008) discusses precisely the problem of anonymity and its potential for abuse with the following:

> Who is the reporter by the name of Johntw, anyway? As far as we could tell, the only way to get in touch with the reporter is through iReport's built-in messaging system. We sent him an e-mail asking him why he reported this story, but it remains unanswered. In our minds, we're already imagining an adolescent kid who's having a good laugh with their friends this morning over how they just "punked" CNN.

Sandoval's qualms are related to the idea that the ease of creating an account means that anybody can create havoc in the system if they wish. Given the possibility that users may willfully report misinformation and subvert the intended purpose of citizen journalism, an important ethical question must be engaged: Should online social media providers like CNN's iReport establish barriers to entry for citizen journalists? One such measure includes educating users about "best practices," a tactic that iReport employs. The organization provides the following tips on their website:

> Get the basics: First thing's first: Your story needs to include the basics. That's who, what, where, when, why, and how. It needs to be true, and it needs to be fair. Pinpoint the significance: Why should your audience care about your story? It's your job as a storyteller to explain why anyone should. Think about how you can connect your story with your audience. Talk like a human being: Your story should be told in words we all use and understand. If you were going to call your best friend and tell her the story, what would you start with? And how would you describe it? That's probably the best part, and the simplest way to get it across. Start there, and see where it takes you. (CNN iReport 2013)

The guidelines are a good start, but beg the question, should CNN have some responsibility to do more to ensure that iReport users publish their stories ethically? Similar websites, such as Current.tv, go to greater lengths in an attempt to promote user accountability. Current.tv uses user-generated content in the form of citizen journalism pieces and documentaries, implements an up-vote/down-vote system. Users and moderators vote what they consider to be the best, most level-headed content up—and polemics down—which tacitly educates the community about ethical standards. In other words, users learn by example and emulate preferred habits to garner up-votes. In addition, Current.tv embeds brief training exercises on their site and on their cable network to inculcate best practices and ethics (García-Avilés 2010). If an organization like CNN is serious about including citizen journalism as part of their coverage, there must be a clearly defined training process with some focus on ethically presenting stories. If the organization fails to do so, it risks becoming a form of entertainment rather than news source.

iReporters as audience and content creators

The dual role of iReport users as both audience members and content creators is a second source of contention in the case of the 2008 Jobs controversy. There are two major problems inherent within this duality. The first is that users may feel they should report on stories that interest them personally rather than write about the broader interests of the community. Writing about events and topics of personal interest can help citizen journalists demystify the production of news stories, but may also fail to convey information and viewpoints to larger audiences.

A second problem is that users may use reportage as a form of "ego boosting." This phenomenon is common in social media. The reporter is more concerned with likes, shares, and other artifacts signifying network success (i.e., popularity) and not with the underlying tenets of ethical journalism. While demand tends to increase the visibility of a given citizen journalist, this reputation can come at a cost.

Because iReport users are simultaneously audience and content creators, they must maintain a level of ethical credibility. There are no external checks and balances, so to speak, so they must work from within to ensure the integrity of the field. Despite this reality, the iReport community does not take this point seriously. For example, an iReport story appeared on May 26, 2014, with the headline "Giant Asteroid Possibly On A Collision Course With Earth" with the story reading as follows:

> If astronomers are right, all life on this planet could be extinguished in less than 30 years. Scientists at NASA's Jet Propulsion Laboratory have detected a large object the size of Manhattan possibly on a collision course with Earth. Using their Near-Earth Object Wide-field Infrared Survey Explorer (NEOWISE), the 10-mile wide object was found approximately 51 million miles from Earth. Scientists believe that during a close encounter with Mars, the asteroid was nudged slightly off its usual orbit and may currently be on a high speed collision course with our fragile planet. The asteroid is calculated to have a potentially lethal encounter with the Earth on March 35, 2041. (Lecher 2014)

The story was proven to be false. One of the key points proving this falsehood was the date of March 35, 2041. In addition, the tags for the story were "beiber, war, gaming, stocks, science, cyrus, space, obama, earth, states" [*sic*]. The story was up for more than thirty hours with over 250,000 views and more than 23,000 shares. If the community does not act quickly enough in the mind of the collective whole and report false stories, and CNN fails to remove them quickly once identified, iReport will continue to experience concerns about credibility and reputation.

The credibility of the citizen journalist and iReporters as journalists

Finally, the false Jobs story of 2008 impacted the credibility of citizen journalists and citizen journalism. The general response from the media was that CNN's credibility was negatively affected. Sarah Perez (2008) speaks to this point by stating, "The question was then raised: Do false reports like this damage CNN's credibility? The answer is yes, absolutely. This particular report may even lead to an SEC investigation where CNN will be asked to provide an IP address for the user who posted the story." The SEC was provided this information by CNN as they tracked the IP address back to an eighteen-year-old male. The investigation concluded that the teenager posted the story for fun (Benjamin 2012).

The problem amplified by the false Jobs story of 2008 is that its publication casts doubt on citizen journalism's relationship to modern journalism. Online citizen journalism especially is called into question by this case. Traditional journalism sources and networks will make mistakes occasionally without necessarily undermining journalism as a whole. The readership no longer believes those individual offenders when they break their social contract of ethical reporting. When individual citizen journalists commit the same unethical transgressions, however, there is generally a discussion about the quality and credibility of stories produced by citizen journalists. Services like Bellingcat are trying to deal with these issues of credibility via a crowd-sourced fact-checking system. For example, the service is checking to make sure that published images are purporting to depict the Syrian Civil War are, in fact, sourced from Syria (Higgins 2014). This Wikipedia-like method of fact-checking is one of the ways that citizen journalism can improve its standing in the overall world of journalism and enhance traditional journalism via more careful vetting.

Current state of iReport

One method to improve the credibility of citizen journalism would be to implement a general code of ethics that citizen journalists would agree to follow. There exists a nuanced interplay between the aggregation of news content and research, production, and distribution of stories. The latter element of the research, production, and distribution of stories was layered in "the public's trust of the news media in relation to social media, the relationship between local news organizations and social media, and how news is and will be covered using social media tools" (Harper 2010). Ultimately, is it possible for citizens to report important issues and events outside the journalistic system and still reach an audience while upholding a sense of credibility in the eyes of this audience? The ethical dilemma related to this is not centered on an internal code of ethics between the actors within a given system (e.g., the CNN newsroom). These rules allow the journalist to act as the "voice of the community" without needing the approval of the established journalistic networks. If the citizen journalist can do this, that person can then present news in front of a larger audience while maintaining their credibility.

Within this case study, the liability/breach of trust was not initially with the professional news organization but rather with the individual citizen journalist. Specifically, CNN's iReport represents the manual collection of citizen content. Their ethical guidelines are embedded within the "Terms of Use" within the site. These detailed rules of conduct could be a list of protective actions rather than a traditional code of ethics presented by a news organization. The primary standards of citizen journalism could be a much simpler set of bullet points given early in the account-creation process for the site. One of the reasons for the lack of a formalized code of ethics could be CNN's perception of the iReport site. If CNN is treating the site as a community of citizen journalists in which the network itself acts as a collection of the posting content where the community leaders act as the agents of aggregation, then CNN could make the argument that, since it wields no editorial authority over the site, the burden of the standards of content lies solely with citizen journalists themselves.

This type of relationship would limit the direct influence that CNN would have over the site. However, citizen journalism becomes an issue of free (or semi-free) labor if CNN uses one of the stories from this site. Labor issues beg several ethical questions:

- "What is the responsibility that CNN has to the iReport user if CNN uses content from that user?"
- "What agency does the iReport user have in this relationship?"
- "Will CNN offer the same level of legal protection to an iReport user if CNN uses their content for other CNN services (e.g., CNN.com, Headline News)?"
- "When CNN decides to pull content from iReport—or other social media services, like Twitter—to use for the traditional CNN networks, does CNN lose the 'ignorance of the source' argument that was used in this case?"

The second possibility regarding CNN's relationship with iReport is that CNN views iReport as a pool of pre-created stories and content. As described earlier in this article, many of the stories found on the iReport site have a similar aesthetic to those stories found on the primary site. There are several sections on the front page of iReport that are designed to focus user efforts on creating stories around a particular topic. For example, at the time of this writing, the primary assignments on the iReport's homepage were the 2014 summer supermoons, stories from the Middle East, and stories from the World Cup. Each of the assignment pages contains a photo gallery connected to the central theme of the story. An iReport user takes each photo and places that photo into the proper gallery. Additionally, there are serial stories and videos told from the viewpoint of the user and given the notice "Not Vetted by CNN."

Conclusion

Citizen journalism drives the feeds of information coming in from all corners of the Internet. Twitter, Facebook, YouTube, Instagram, and other social media services are providing multiple channels of distribution to citizen journalists and allowing them to have more direct communication with traditional journalist networks and figures within the networks. These relationships are not expected to diminish in the future. Many of the traditional leaders in the field have already "set up advisory boards, hired professional editors[,] and laid down editorial guidelines, ensuring greater accuracy and credibility" (Jurrat 2011). Those leaders (e.g., *The Washington Post, Huffington Post* and *The Guardian)* see the value in citizen journalism as long as it meets the quality standards established by those organizations.

The industry sees citizen journalism as a complement to the traditional material provided by the networks. As shown in the Steve Jobs' iReport example, much of the news covered by iReport has been focused on particular topics, or consist of stories and content focused on a specific global region to which traditional journalists would have little to no access. It is fair to make the argument that some of the most thoughtful, well-constructed stories coming from conflicts in the Middle East were produced by citizen journalists. Those stories created by people living in the area can provide a sense of context, showing how each story affects the local community. The future of citizen journalism depends partially on this type of writing, wherein the local reporter uses the means of distribution in order to present her or his story to an audience who cares about what is happening.

It is important to discuss how individual citizen journalists see themselves in the overall picture of writing in order to conclude this discussion and attempt to answer the question about the code of ethics for the citizen journalist. There could be a few variations on those codes. By conducting their reportage within these standards, they maintain their credibility within the industry. If citizen journalists perceive themselves as narrators of the events in their local community or "community of interest," they should be more likely to develop the ethos of those communities.

As technologies change, citizen journalism will continue to provide a necessary service to the larger journalistic community. These reporters can venture where traditional journalists are unable or unwilling to go and provide context to events as they develop. Those journalists producing this content must be ethical in their presentation. Otherwise, there will continue to be instances of false reportage similar to the false reporting that was at the heart of the Jobs controversy of October 2008.

Note

1   An article analysis of Google News search engine conducted on June 26, 2014, found the terms "Steve Jobs," "iReport," and "heart attack" used in approximately 249,000 postings from October 2008 to October 2009. By performing a content analysis of a randomly selected sample ($n = 300$) of the results from the search engine, we found that twenty-nine of the 300 articles were spam, fourteen of the articles were wiki or encyclopedia articles about the case, and thirty-seven were referring to other sources that would be considered less than "journalistic" (e.g., whitepapers, websites from an unknown source, and other problematic references).

Section Three

Professional Communication

10

Perfectly "Compliant": The Devaluation of Ethics in Corporate Communication Industry Discourse

Sam Ford[1]

In 2014, I was involved in a first-of-its-kind project in which several competing agencies came together to speak out on a pressing ethical issue facing the marketing, public relations, and advertising industries (referred to throughout this chapter as "corporate communications"): the strained relationship between corporate representatives and volunteer editors with the Wikipedia project.[2]

Corporate communicators have earned Wikipedia editors' skepticism—and, increasingly, cynicism—with a steady stream of missteps. Executives, employees, and agency representatives have flooded the site, pasting in marketing copy for every product their company offers, adding a bio for each senior executive, and including voluminous details of "corporate social responsibility" initiatives to the entry about their organization. To illustrate how overt and pervasive this practice has become, Shareen Pathak (2014), for a June 2014 *Digiday* article, conducted a "casual tour" through Wikipedia entries about several communication agencies. Pathak found that many featured a message at the top, "either warning that someone close to the business is involved in the editing of the page or that the article sounds like an advertisement."

Pathak provides various examples of agency representatives adding self-aggrandizing language to their own firms' entries. For instance, a March 2014 edit to agency JWT's page claimed that "a spirit of imagination and bravery is engrained in JWT's DNA." Meanwhile, Big Spaceship's page at one point "went into great detail about why the company wasn't credited on a Cannes Lion" award in 2008 and praised the "many accolades" the agency had received—language clearly inappropriate for an encyclopedia article.

Worse, some corporate representatives have been caught trying to remove unflattering information from their company's pages or adding unflattering information to competitors' pages. A 2011 UK examination by The Bureau of Investigative Journalism and the *Independent,* assisted by additional research from blogger Tim Ireland, brought mainstream attention to these issues (Pegg 2011). The project centered on the practices of large UK-based agency Bell Pottinger in intervening on Wikipedia entries for its clients. Bell Pottinger had, for instance, edited one client's entry to remove reference to his university drug conviction and made a range of additions and edits to the entry of another client being accused of commercial bribery. Because of the prominent coverage the investigation received, Bell Pottinger became the "agency poster child" for edits that extend beyond puffery and marketing-speak and into more potentially nefarious—and misleading—corporate manipulation of entries.

Especially troubling—and angering—for the volunteer Wikipedia editor community have been a few agencies and consultants that overtly sell their ability to "create and fix Wikipedia pages" in ways that violate the very spirit and purpose of the project. For instance, after an investigation by Wikipedia editors lasting more than a year, the Wikimedia Foundation issued a cease-and-desist letter to Texas-based firm Wiki-PR in 2013, banning the agency's employees and the various accounts they had created from making further edits to the site. The move came after the editors' investigation linked more than 300 "sockpuppet" accounts to the firm (Arthur 2013)—meaning that the accounts had been set up for the sole purpose of making controversial edits without disclosing the editor's ties to the company/person in question.

Some Wikipedia editors who have dealt with, or repeatedly heard about, this influx of conflict-of-interest edits have grown resistant to corporate edit queries. And that cynicism—combined with the fact that there aren't nearly enough volunteer editors to fully vet the information added to and edited on the site each day—has made it particularly difficult for transparent corporate representatives. Requests for simple and verifiable factual updates (replacing 2013's annual revenues with 2014's) or attempts to bring concerns or suggested changes to a more objective editor's attention can languish for months. And corporate representatives grow ever more frustrated at incomplete, incorrect, or outdated information indefinitely sitting on one of the most popular online destinations, while their requests go unanswered; they may even face pressure to find a quick way to "just fix it."

In response to this untenable situation, in January 2012, Edelman's Phil Gomes created a Facebook group called "Corporate Representatives for Ethical Wikipedia Engagement" (Gomes 2012). The group focuses on when, where, and how it would be ethical for corporate representatives to engage with the Wikipedia project. Some of those actively involved in the group planned a February 2014 day-long session in Washington, D.C., organized by William Beutler of Beutler Ink (Beutler 2014a). Representatives from several leading communication firms (I represented my employer, Peppercomm) were joined both by volunteer editors and academics who study Wikipedia to discuss these issues. We talked candidly about the strained relationship between professional communicators and volunteer Wikipedia editors.

A few months later, eleven agencies released a joint statement on Wikipedia that made public our commitment to take the goals of Wikipedia seriously ("Statement on Wikipedia from Participation Communications Firms" 2014). The statement was a small first step toward addressing unethical behavior from corporate representatives on Wikipedia. It also put our agencies directly on public record in affirming that each has internal policies in place to engage transparently and respect the Wikipedia editor community's principles, policies, and guidelines, as well as the Wikipedia reader's expectation to find information that is as objective and accurate as possible. At the time of this writing, a total of thirty-eight agencies, four professional organizations, and two academics were officially signed onto the statement.

The statement pledges that its signatories will continually promote greater understanding of Wikipedia's goals among their employees and clients. It also promises each agency will investigate and seek corrective action in any instance where a potential violation of Wikipedia's policies arises from someone within their organization. Our hope was that this statement would be a first step toward a productive conversation about how ethical corporate communicators can serve the Wikipedia editor community. We also wanted to make it clear that much of the corporate communication industry—and, at the very least, the organizations who signed—take the principles of the Wikipedia project (and other participatory spaces online) seriously and support ideals of a more participatory culture.

Of particular importance was the fact that each agency committed itself to push the corporate communication industry as a whole to have more deliberate conversations about a high standard of ethical engagement with the Wikipedia project, as well as better education in the corporate world about what the Wikipedia project strives to achieve. To that end, William Beutler partnered with the Council of Public Relations Firms and the Institute for Public Relations to publish a Wikipedia guide for corporate communication professionals (Beutler 2014b). Also, several involved with the statement have devoted significant time to writing about, and speaking on, ethical engagement with Wikipedia. We have sought opportunities wherever space for those discussions could be found—which can sometimes be a challenge (as this chapter will hopefully help illuminate).

The underlying issue: A lack of education on ethics

Most corporate edits of Wikipedia are not the acts of bad faith that the Bell Pottinger and Wiki-PR examples illustrate. Many of the more venial sins are the result of a widespread lack of understanding and education about Wikipedia's standards regarding conflicts of interest. For instance, Pennsylvania State University professor Marcia DiStaso's 2013 survey of PR professionals found that, although 40 percent of survey respondents had engaged in some way on Wikipedia, three-fourths were unaware of—or didn't fully understand—key norms within the Wikipedia community (DiStaso 2013).

For corporate communicators used to dealing with paid media professionals, a project like Wikipedia is particularly confusing. Corporate representatives often don't understand how one of the most popular online sites has no editorial hierarchy, which means that there is no one in particular to appeal to for retractions or to place requests with to amend incorrect information; how Wikipedia is a "publisher" that takes no legal responsibility for misinformation on its site (meaning the foundation itself has an active disinterest in updating an inaccuracy or mischaracterization); and that Wikipedia is managed by volunteer editors who increasingly struggle to vet the volume of daily edits made to entries. Most of all, though, I've found that, while corporate communication professionals understand Wikipedia is "the encyclopedia that anyone can edit," they don't understand the project's aims for accuracy and objectivity and its communally accepted conflict-of-interest policies. In other words, they think of Wikipedia as a repository of information anyone can add to, without realizing why having an employee add information to an entry on their company is a violation of the project's goals.

Some of us involved with the agency statement have a goal beyond the Wikipedia issue in particular. We hope to create a model for how corporate communicators can collaborate on ethics projects. To our knowledge, our statement was the first time so many prominent agencies had partnered directly—rather than via a trade organization—to commit to an ethical stance. The coverage and energy our work received in 2014 also demonstrated the promise for what might happen when corporate communicators concentrate moderate time and effort to a discussion of ethics.

Unfortunately, that concentration is often difficult to support institutionally. The Wikipedia statement is one of several ethics interventions in which I've been involved, primarily focused on education and advocacy for issues of disclosure and transparency. In the remainder of this chapter, I explore core flaws in how corporate communications operates as an industry—flaws which make a consistent dialogue about ethical issues difficult to achieve. In particular, I look at how certain pressures within corporate communications force conversations that do arise about ethics quickly into the space of legal compliance. In the process, I reflect directly on my own attempts in this space, as well as case studies that illustrate why these issues are a significant concern.

A dearth of "Big Picture Thinking"

Our industry's lack of commitment to discussing ethics has an even deeper root cause: a dearth of time and space dedicated to strategic thinking. "Thought leadership" (as "meta" discussions are called in corporate communications) spaces in which industry professionals can dedicate their focus to rethinking overarching approaches, strategies, and tactics, can be difficult to carve out, amid all the usual responsibilities and project deadlines. Those few moments for reading trade publications and couple of times a year for attending conferences may be a corporate communicators' only chance to sequester themselves from day-to-day tasks and projects and think more deeply about what they do.

However, even in these spaces, there's significant pressure to make every moment tie back to "actionable, measurable" immediate next steps. Thus, these rare opportunities for industry professionals to converse, away from (or between) their calendars and to-do lists, are primarily focused on efficacy and innovation: what new trend, or new platform, is coming down the pike that you need to learn about if you aren't going to become outmoded? Or what "best practice" or crisis case can you study to learn better what to do or what not to do in your own job?

Articles in industry publications and presentations at corporate communications industry events frequently have two tracks: strategies and tactics.

Tactical articles/sessions examine case studies and look at the "how-tos" of operating on various platforms and in various communities. Strategic articles/ sessions focus on how to adapt and shift logics—and related forms of measuring success—to new platforms and media environments.

Often, more than 75 percent of content in publications, and sessions at conferences, focus on tactics. For instance, in looking at a typical issue of prominent industry publication *Advertising Age* (April 2014), of the thirteen articles emphasized in the table of contents, only three are focused explicitly on broader-scale strategic questions. These were a report on the results of "The 2014 Agency Report" *Ad Age* conducted, an article about how the work of executive recruiters greatly shapes an organization's ability to do high-quality marketing work, and a piece about major shifts in how "social" and "digital" work is conducted between companies and their agencies.

Or consider the agenda for an event like the *Social Media 20/20 Summit* in San Francisco in August 2014, organized by industry trade publication *PR News*.[3] (This type of public one-day session is typical in the corporate communication space.) The agenda (*PR News* 2014) featured nine core presentations. Four of the sessions looked at particular types of corporate communication work (crisis communications, measurement, content creation, and community management). Three sessions looked at tactical recommendations for specific platforms (blogs, Facebook, and Twitter). That left only two sessions that were more "big picture" in their description: an opening keynote on the state of the corporate communication industry and a lunchtime keynote from a "digital futurist."

So, while there are occasionally specific magazine issues and corporate communications industry events focused entirely on larger questions and rethinking approaches, the examples above demonstrate the typical agenda or table of contents. Editors I've worked with cite reader feedback requesting "actionable insights" they can apply to their day-to-day jobs and enact "today." And corporate communication industry conference emcees often promise that attendees can justify the fees and travel expenses their employer paid with "concrete" insights and tips they can immediately put into action.

If 25 percent or less of thought leadership focuses on "big-picture questions," perhaps it is little surprise that it's especially rare for questions of ethics to be the focus. Scanning *Advertising Age*'s digital archive from October 2013 through September 2014, only three articles appear with "ethics" in the title (Full disclosure—one of them [Ford 2014a] was authored by me), and only fifteen articles include the word "ethics" somewhere in the piece (several of which are not even about ethics in corporate communications but rather about an ethics issue elsewhere in a company). Of course, ethical issues and considerations may be tackled without that word being used; but the statistics mentioned above does illustrate the larger trend aptly.

The ramifications of this lack of conversation on ethics pervade the corporate communication space. For instance, in fall 2014, the lack of clear disclosure and transparency surrounding many examples of "native advertising"—in which advertising space is dedicated to media texts meant to more closely adhere to the "editorial" material from the publisher—came under fire, particularly after comedian John Oliver aired a highly viewed segment on these practices on his HBO show, *Last Week Tonight with John Oliver* (Dumenco 2014). Oliver's routine critiqued the rhetoric of publishers about their increased investment in native ads. He also called out examples such as *The Atlantic* running a sponsored piece from the Church of Scientology and *The New York Times* running a sponsored article on the future of energy from Chevron, both of which generated significant concerns about the blurring of the editorial/advertising line. The concerns expressed in discussion surrounding Oliver's piece highlights the heightened reputational risk organizations may find themselves in if they don't think through the ethical ramifications of their campaigns.

Meanwhile, as I was working on this chapter in fall 2014, the FTC publicly scolded agency Deutsch LA for encouraging employees to tweet about the release of the PlayStation Vita from their personal Twitter accounts, which led to a range of posts about the game from agency employees who in no way disclosed that their agency was being paid to promote the gaming system (Tadena 2014). And, during the same time period, Mondelez, the parent company of Oreo, had a campaign banned by Britain's Advertising Standards Authority (ASA) after YouTube personalities were paid to create videos participating in an "Oreo Lick Race." While the personalities involved included messages such as "Thanks to Oreo for making this video possible," in some cases during the video and in others in the text comments below the video, the ASA ruled that these disclosures were not clear enough that the average viewer would realize they were watching marketing material (Sweney 2014).

When these organizations found themselves in the midst of government scrutiny, and/or significant reputational risk, such ethical issues became a primary concern. However, by that point, they were no longer issues of ethics at all but rather of "crisis communications." If professional communicators seek to provide the best strategic counsel to their organizations/clients, prioritizing these issues while they are "ethics" concerns rather than waiting until they become "crisis" situations or legal compliance questions seems like it should be a primary concern for them and, in general, the corporate communication industry.

Talking about ethics in "Industry Thought Leadership"

I entered the corporate communications space, first as a consultant in 2007 and as a full-time employee of a communication strategy firm in 2008. My background was not in corporate communications but rather in media studies. The company I have worked with since 2007—Peppercomm—actively sought someone from academia who didn't necessarily have any background in corporate communications. Their goal was to have a position "in-house" which could bring a different way of thinking and approaching the agency's work.

As I've detailed elsewhere (Ford 2011), my role (currently titled "Director of Audience Engagement") is divided into three equal pieces. My position is one part academic, allotted to teaching, researching, presenting at academic conferences, and writing for university press books and journals. I am one part consultant, working with our agency's clients and internal teams as they think through how they listen to, participate in dialogue with, and create texts for the audiences they seek to reach. And I am one part Peppercomm ambassador within the corporate communication space: speaking at industry conferences, writing for industry publications, and participating in industry groups or initiatives aimed at the sort of "big-picture thinking" on which this chapter is focused.

The ideal (and, usually, the reality) is that these three "parts" inform one another. I aim to bring what I've learned about the media industries through my work "from the inside" of corporate communications to bear on how I approach studying media texts and media audiences in my academic work. And Peppercomm sees value in my spending a significant portion of time not thinking about our industry or our clients so that I can introduce unexpected ways of thinking to the agency and our clients.

One of my primary motivations has been to bring the ethos and thinking I've encountered in my media studies work into direct conversation with those making decisions in the corporate communication world—at a macro-level, in "industry thought leadership," as well as at the micro-level, in my consulting work. As my coauthors and I write in *Spreadable Media* (Jenkins, Ford, and Green 2013), this approach "recognize[s] that the policies that most directly impact the public's capacity to deploy media power are largely shaped by corporate decision-makers—true in the U.S. in particularly and increasingly so in a global context" (xii). (For more reflections on the nature of this work between academia and the corporate communications world, see Ford 2014b.)

I first started explicitly writing about issues of ethics and empathy in corporate communications through my contributions at *Fast Company* (Ford 2010a, b, c). That writing brought me in touch with others actively advocating for issues of ethics to be included in the larger business strategy space. For instance, Carol Sanford—author of *The Responsible Business: Reimagining Sustainability and Success* (2011) and *The Responsible Entrepreneur: Four Game-Changing Archetypes for Founders, Leaders, and Impact Investors* (2014)—has argued that capitalist logic should have ethics at its core and that responsible behavior is closely connected to long-term business success. Sanford's writing—drawing from her own decades of consulting with companies, large and small—points toward the logical business flaws in an environment where "responsibility" is relegated to a department charged with "Corporate Social Responsibility." Such an approach seems akin to the ways organizations might think about "carbon offsetting"—a logic that the harm an organization causes in its core business practices can be rectified by the good the organization does through philanthropy.

Rather, Sanford convincingly argues that organizations must put responsibility to their key stakeholders at the center of their organization's *raison d'être*. Those stakeholders include their customers, their employees and business partners, the environment, their communities, and company shareholders—in that order. And she advocates that the responsibility for this approach must be "owned" by everyone in the organization, rather than by one division of the enterprise.

The Responsible Business articulates two concepts that have been key aspects of my own "boardroom advocacy" work, in trying to prioritize acting ethically within predominant neoliberal logic. First, Sanford argues that ethical behavior and a focus on the responsibility an organization owes to its customers and other stakeholders does not run counter to capitalism but rather should have a central place in business logic. And, second, she demonstrates how a central focus on responsible behavior strengthens long-term profitability and reputation for an organization.

My work with Peppercomm also gave me the opportunity to collaborate with Dr. Fred Kiel. Kiel's work has focused on the business need for a high level of ethical decision-making and strong character in corporate leaders at an individual level. His 2005 book, *Moral Intelligence: Enhancing Business*

Performance and Leadership Success, coauthored with Doug Lennick, argues that corporate leaders who have a strong moral compass also make better business decisions and that high ethical standards point to key business skills for leaders who want to be successful over the long term. Kiel's 2015 follow-up book, *Return on Character: The Real Reason Leaders and Their Companies Win*, builds on the work of Jim Collins (2001) to connect "strong character" with better business results. Kiel finds that leaders who are identified by their employees as having strong character are also found to achieve up to five times greater "return on assets" for their organizations than those identified as having weak character.

While these business consultants' work provided a larger framework and reference point for arguing how ethics should have a strong place in organizational and individual decision-making, the space for discussions of ethics in corporate communications in particular wasn't quite as clearly defined. (In fact, most of my writing about larger ethical issues has come through columns for broader business publications like *Harvard Business Review*, *Fast Company*, and *Inc.* For those publications, readers come from a wide range of business disciplines and not primarily corporate communication industries.)

Corporate communication trade organizations—such as the Arthur W. Page Society (for corporate communication leaders), the Public Relations Society of America, the Chartered Institute of Public Relations in the United Kingdom, the Word of Mouth Marketing Association (WOMMA), the Council of Public Relations Firms, and others—have a commitment to ethics in their organizational description.[4] They all also offer some degree of ethics resources to members, focused on ethical standards for the corporate communication profession and applying those standards to specific corporate communications functions or practices. (For a list of these—and other organizations'—ethics codes, see "Public Relations Society of America" in the references section.) But these high-level reference and philosophy statements often have difficulty filtering into prevailing industry thought leadership discussion. To borrow a phrase from my academic work, these projects have often had limited spreadability.

Conflating the ethical with the legal

WOMMA is arguably the organization that focuses most prominently on ethics. Among all the trade organizations previously mentioned, WOMMA is the only one that has "ethics" as a stand-alone category on its website.

And the organization's official "about" page states in the opening paragraph that WOMMA "is the leader in ethical word of mouth marketing practice" and that the organization is focused on "advocacy, education, and ethics."

For the past couple of years, I've helped lead WOMMA's Ethics Committee, and I currently sit on the organization's board of directors. As I have engaged in this work with WOMMA (and elsewhere), however, I've found that even the rare conference sessions and publications labeled "ethics" have often not really been focused on ethics. Rather, they are aimed at providing interpretations of how to comply with current governmental guidelines and regulations focused on addressing ethical issues.

For organizations like WOMMA that take membership education around issues related to disclosure and transparency seriously, it's perhaps not surprising that conversations about ethics quickly become focused on what the government has—or hasn't—yet set as guidelines. Regulatory bodies in the United States, from the FTC, The Federal Drug Administration, and the Financial Industry Regulatory Authority (FINRA) to the Securities and Exchange Commission and the National Labor Review Board, all have issued varying levels of guidance on how companies—and their employees and business partners—communicate in ways that respect proper transparency, disclosure, accuracy, reporting, privacy, and free speech. Professionals in corporate communications therefore struggle with how to make sense of these various federal guidelines and how to apply them to day-to-day industry practice.

In most cases, the regulators themselves remain unsure of how best to adapt "broadcast-era" policies for today's communication landscape. The result is that many rounds of regulatory guidelines have been purposefully broad or, if attempts are made to get specific, risk becoming quickly outdated when people can't figure out how they apply to particular communications practices online. These guidelines become especially tricky when applied to emerging industry or audience practices or new platforms that arise and confound existing regulation.

This happened, for instance, with the rise of character-restrained microblogging platforms like Twitter, which made the question of how to provide full and proper disclosure of paid relationships in social media activity difficult. The prevailing industry approach is to try to find plainspoken ways to disclose material relationships in tweets (such as, "My colleague XXXX" or "My client YYYY"). There has also been some industry practice of using hashtags to indicate material relationships in tweets—this received particular attention in 2013 when diet supplement brand Sensa terminated its relationship with actress

Octavia Spencer, in part due to its objection to her using the hashtag #spon to indicate her role as a paid endorser for the brand when she tweeted about them (Gardner 2013).

This question of proper disclosure is also challenging in the context of the rise of visual sharing platforms, as text-based approaches of transparency and disclosure are difficult to adapt to them. For instance, in 2014, the FTC issued a letter to fashion brand Cole Haan (Davis and Gilbert 2014).[5] The letter reacted to a Cole Haan Pinterest campaign that encouraged people to enter a contest by "re-pinning" images of its shoes onto their own Pinterest boards, including the hashtag "#WanderingSole." While the ability for disclosure in such a visual medium is limited, the FTC argued (compellingly) that the average viewer would not understand that #WanderingSole was a marketing campaign from the hashtag alone and that this method did not provide sufficient disclosure of the person's material incentive from Cole Haan to share pictures of the company's products.

This web of overlapping regulatory bodies can be especially confusing to agencies whose work spans multiple sectors; they find that the regulatory environment for their online communications work vary, depending on the field. Even companies operating in a single sector can find themselves facing confusing and competing regulations. For instance, take a company in the insurance or investment industry whose communications are regulated by FINRA.[6] FINRA has been traditionally concerned with ensuring that companies keep official records of all marketing and sales communications on behalf of the company. Meanwhile, the FTC has issued several guidelines over time that make clear that company employees or business partners talking online about industry issues, about the organization for which they work, and/or about their company's competitors are expected to disclose their "material connection" with the company. This FTC guidance is meant to ensure that audiences reading a statement from someone who has a tie to the organization involved have all the information they need to accurately assess the claims being made.

For insurance or investment companies regulated by FINRA, that disclosure immediately raises the question, then, of whether any communication from an employee about their professional lives or issues in the field, in which they acknowledge that they are a company employee, is considered official communication of the sort that the company would be expected to track, identify, collect, and archive for purposes of FINRA compliance.

In response, many organizations in this situation have, over the past several years, actively discouraged their employees from talking about their professional lives at all, for fear that they don't have the resources to actively monitor and collect all their employees' online communications in which business communications were present and/or that privacy issues present all sorts of challenges when attempting to comprehensively collect employee communications. In other words, the easiest way to avoid the expense, headaches, and privacy issues involved with collection is to take a prohibitionist stance on employee social media activity.

However, increasingly, decisions from the National Labor Review Board indicate that employees are seen as having a right to use social media platforms and other forms of online communication to talk about their work lives. This leaves companies in this space with difficulty in finding a way forward and feeling caught among various sets of regulations that, all adhered to closely, make it hard to imagine how to operate with comprehensive compliance.

Thorny questions of compliance like these pop up in every field. One of our clients in the accounting space spent significant time wrestling with the question of whether "independence" regulations which state that accounting firms cannot be in the practice of promoting the businesses of companies for whom they act as external auditor meant that employees of their firm could not share a news story on a social media platform from a publication whose parent company was audited by the firm. Would sharing a *Wall Street Journal* article on Twitter, for instance, equate to promoting a product of News Corp, which is against the law for its auditor?

In situations like these, then, it's perhaps no surprise that corporate communicators find themselves more focused on how not to inadvertently run afoul of regulators. What little time they do have to discuss ethical issues usually immediately turns to these questions of compliance, which seem more pressing and concrete than discussion of ethical obligations they have to the publics they seek to reach with their communications. Thus, again, we see organizations move quickly into "action" and practice rather than theory and rethinking approaches. This environment also explains why traditional corporate disclosures are particularly aimed at legal compliance, while little focus is given to whether it serves—or is legible to—the audience the company seeks to reach.

In part because of these reasons, an organization like WOMMA, which is publicly and prominently committed to education on ethical issues, has—for much of the organization's existence—had a significant portion of its time and bandwidth taken up in helping interpret regulatory guidance for member companies so that those companies can understand how guidelines filter down into daily corporate communications practice.

This has manifested itself in creating template social media policies, education sessions, white papers that explain federal guidelines on issues like proper disclosure and transparency in plain language, and other "translation" initiatives, reacting to federal policymakers more often than driving marketers to think about their own ethical obligations to audiences. (I, myself, have contributed to several of these initiatives aimed in large part at helping organizations think about how federal guidelines break down to day-to-day corporate communications activity; see WOMMA 2013, 2014a; Chernaik and Ford 2014.)

Such work has frequently brought WOMMA's Ethics Committee into direct conversation with the organization's Legal Affairs Committee, which—like the ethics group—is comprised of representatives from WOMMA partner organizations (in this case, all from member companies' legal teams or from law firms specializing in the corporate communication space). Collaboration between the Ethics (largely made of up marketers) and Legal Affairs committees have primarily focused on issuing this occasional WOMMA guidance for how to interpret and comply with existing federal regulation. These projects have been time-intensive and have had a fairly low level of output—in particular, because WOMMA wants to be careful and deliberate about any document that gives official guidance to its members on governmental regulations.

Of late, our two committees have begun to give much shorter compliance-focused guidance in order to free up more space for facilitating more frequent conversation—rather than official guidance—about emerging ethical questions for which there are not yet federal guidelines, and/or that goes beyond what WOMMA is willing to officially issue as guidance to examine core ethical questions. Frankly, this transition has been and remains a challenge. We have started focusing focusing on how WOMMA can help drive individual people whose companies are members to share opinions without necessarily making them official positions of the trade organization. Many of these ethical questions surrounding issues like native advertising (for instance) need to be vigorously discussed in ways that allow for divergent points of view, and none of us want to be given the responsibility for speaking on behalf of our whole industry on these issues.

Attempts to produce ethics-focused events—such as a November 2014 (WOMMA 2014b) stand-alone workshop I planned as I wrote this chapter—have been difficult to position and promote for attendees used to more tactical and clear-cut programming. Because of the time we wanted to dedicate to the workshop (a half-day) and these concerns about how it would be received, we ran the workshop as a stand-alone event. Despite significant promotional efforts, we had difficulty getting registered (paying) attendees and instead gave complementary invites to many of the people in the room. We ended up with a mix of corporate communication professionals, lawyers, academics, regulators, and publishers—and the workshop ended up being the highest-rated session among all of the events at the annual conference.

Despite our difficulties with making the workshop a reality, the reception the workshop received again indicated the great potential in investing in a greater concentration on ethics. WOMMA has demonstrated a long-term willingness to invest in trying to drive such conversations and a desire to recruit companies/individuals interested in making questions of what marketers owe the audiences they seek to reach, rather than (and beyond) what they must adhere to when it comes to pleasing regulators. I remain hopeful of what might be accomplished in carving out a higher percentage of space to focus on these larger questions of ethics.

Conclusion

My tri-part role as a media studies researcher, consultant, and ambassador within the unique position I hold at Peppercomm has given an explicit "advocacy" orientation to my work in the corporate communications world. Yet, even with an exceptional portion of my time dedicated to rethinking what our industry does and how we approach our audiences when compared to what's afforded to most other professionals in my space, I have often been dismayed at how rare it is to find space for discussing fundamental strategic issues as an industry—and equally dismayed at how rare it is, even within that small space for strategic discussion, to find ethics a prominent part of the conversation. As I wrote in *PRWeek* (Ford 2014d):

> Our industry conferences should have as many panels discussing how we are serving our audiences as they do talking about the ROI of campaigns. Our industry publications should have as many tips on how to act ethically as they do on how to best use the latest social platform. Our trade organizations must talk constantly about the nature of communities such as Wikipedia and what ethical engagement looks like.
>
> And our individual organizations have to reinforce to our employees the importance of ethics—and how we are serving our audiences—as often as we

talk about the efficacy of our client services. As an industry, we have failed ourselves on this front. And we have to work together to do better.

Nevertheless, I have found various others in the corporate communications space who are also passionate and dedicated to ethical issues, and have seen serious steps taken to bring those people into a common conversation—via WOMMA and other trade organizations and through initiatives like the Wikipedia statement I've been involved in over the past year. Consistently, when we are able to find space in event agendas and trade publications to raise ethical issues and get that conversation in front of an audience (often in front of those who didn't necessarily explicitly seek it out), there's been a great deal of engagement, support, participation, and even enthusiasm for tackling these more strategic ethical questions. The fact that publications like *PRWeek* have featured pieces like the one referenced above indicates a willingness within the corporate communications space to engage on ethical issues.

As I have suggested, the devaluation of discussing ethics in corporate communications is connected to much larger issues of lacking space to think through larger strategic questions as an industry and a symptom of broadcast-era logics of understanding audiences as target aggregate groups to be marketed to rather than complex networks of real human beings who should be listened to, empathized with, understood, and served by the organizations seeking to reach them. Those issues pose significant challenges to having more frank ethical discussion in this space. Yet, the potential benefits for pushing the corporate communications world to prioritize its "publics" is great—and the inroads made in this direction (I've been fortunate to be a small part of this) indicate that it's a cause that's worthy of receiving significantly more attention.

Notes

1   Sam Ford left Peppercomm in August 2015 to take a new position with the digital and television network Fusion. However, because this chapter was written while in his position with the agency, we have left the wording in the present tense.

2   This example is based largely on Ford (2014c).

3   In the spirit of full disclosure, I should note I have spoken at multiple *PR News* events, authored various pieces for the publication, and received awards from the organization in the past—in addition to conducting an internal workshop for their

parent company, AccessIntelligence. My Peppercomm colleague Ann Barlow was one of the opening "big picture" industry speakers at this event.

4 Peppercomm (and I) are active members of the Council of Public Relations Firms, and, I have spoken, without financial remuneration, at an event the Arthur W. Page Society conducted with the Council of Public Relations Firms and the Institute for Public Relations. Peppercomm's cofounder is a Page Society member. I have also spoken on a Public Relations Society of America webinar and written for its publication, *The Public Relations Strategist*, both without remuneration.

5 Davis & Gilbert represents many agencies in the corporate communication industry. It has also acted as Peppercomm's legal counsel.

6 I should note that FINRA is, itself, a client of Peppercomm.

11

The Emerging Ethics of Digital Political Strategists

Luis E. Hestres

Digital communication technologies have become key components of modern politics and issue advocacy. Most political campaigns and activist groups today rely heavily on websites, Facebook pages, YouTube videos, e-mail lists, and similar online tools to carry out their work. We now take for granted our ability to participate in politics with a mouse click or a tap on a glass screen. But few of us are aware of what it takes to run modern online political campaigns. Not only are the software and hardware that power these campaigns invisible to most of us; the people who run these campaigns are relatively unknown to us as well. Who decides what online tools a campaign should use to communicate with supporters, and how to use them most effectively? Who writes the e-mails we receive urging us to give money or sign petitions, the Facebook posts we like, or the tweets we share with our followers? Who writes and produces the YouTube videos we watch, or crunches the terabytes of data all these interactions generate?

The people who perform these duties go by many different job titles, such as online organizer, internet director, new media specialist, or e-advocacy coordinator, but in this chapter I will refer to them collectively as *digital strategists*. They are the professionals—or highly dedicated volunteers, in some cases—who are most responsible for the strategic use of digital tools, and they carry out the lion's share of online political work: blogging, mass e-mail copywriting and production, supporter data management, social media outreach, website design and management, online video production, fundraising, and other related tasks. These professionals are now key players in political associations and campaigns (Karpf 2012; Kreiss 2012).

As a profession, digital strategy is still taking shape. It draws heavily from preexisting political and communication professions, such as press relations, grassroots organizing, and web development, among others. Because of the emerging nature of their profession, digital strategists do not yet have a uniform code of ethics to follow. But this does not mean that digital strategists do not face ethical dilemmas that require careful consideration.

In this chapter, I discuss the state of digital strategy ethics today, focusing on the lack of ethical codes explicitly tailored to this profession. I then discuss several ethical theories that could underpin digital strategy ethical codes, and argue that theories that reflect the semipublic function of digital strategists—particularly Kantianism—are best suited to this task. Finally, I use three topics that are currently focal points of much discussion among political advocacy experts as examples of the ethical questions that digital strategists face:

Emotional manipulation: Digital strategists routinely manage large amounts of information connected to millions of citizens who support their campaigns and causes. But concerns about how corporations and other institutions track our online activities and use this data to influence our emotions and behavior have brought greater scrutiny to social media and related online tools that digital strategists rely upon. What ethical responsibilities do digital strategists have toward the people they engage and the organizations they serve in relation to data management?

Perceived vs. real political impact: There is an implicit contract between political organizations—and by extension, their digital strategists—and their supporters: participating through an organization or campaign will make an individual's efforts, combined with those of many others, more effective than they would be on their own. But online strategists sometimes present their supporters with actions that *appear* effective, but actually only lead to direct gains for the organization. What ethical responsibilities do digital strategists have toward their supporters regarding the impact of online campaigns?

Political polarization: Political scientists and other experts have voiced concerns about the growing divide in American politics, and the bitter rhetoric that usually goes with it (Nisbet and Scheufele 2013). This growing gap includes a tendency to demonize ideological opponents, and is associated with an alarming inability to tackle large-scale social problems. Yet digital tactics that contribute to political polarization can often help digital strategists achieve their goals. Do strategists have an ethical responsibility to take into account how they may worsen political polarization and lead to further erosion of our political climate?

Digital strategy ethics today

Because digital political strategists practice a still-emerging profession, they have not yet developed the types of professional associations that other communication professionals like journalists, marketers, and public relations specialists have had ample time to form. These organizations are important in the development of ethical codes because "as organized, self-governing social units authorized to represent the profession, these associations serve as the custodians of professional traditions and help to keep a profession's moral commitments relevant" (Frankel 1989, 114).

Instead of formal ethical codes—or those professional organizations upon which communications and political professionals rely to develop such codes— digital strategists turn to a loose network of conferences, trainings conducted by technology and strategy firms, and e-mail discussion lists. Professional "best practices" are discussed through these avenues, but typically they do not feature systematic examination of ethical concerns related to digital politics.

Some informal avenues through which ethical discussions occur include conferences like Netroots Nation, an annual gathering of progressive activists that regularly features panels focused on digital strategy.[1] Although the conference focuses on politics and grassroots activism, it features on its website a prominent statement of diversity and inclusion that lists several ways the conference strives for these ideals, such as "including topics on our agenda that push attendees to think beyond their own communities and experiences," "choosing panels that include a diverse group of speakers," and "elevating new, diverse voices on the big stage," among others. Given that Netroots Nation is an ideologically motivated conference, however, these concerns are probably based on an ideological commitment to diversity rather than a desire to put forward a cross-ideological digital strategy code of ethics.

Another possible avenue for discussion of digital strategy ethics is the annual Nonprofit Technology Conference, sponsored by the nonpartisan Nonprofit Technology Network. The 2014 Nonprofit Technology Conference, held in Washington, D.C., featured a panel titled "50 Shades of Social Media: Navigating Policies, Laws, and Ethics," that was described in the conference program:

> As the manager of your nonprofit's social media presence, knowing what you (and your colleagues) can say or how you should respond gets tricky. Establishing solid social media governance policies and understanding your

legal and compliance obligations are both important aspects of your overall social media strategy. But, where do you turn when you encounter a dilemma that isn't easily solved by turning to the law or an existing policy? In this highly interactive session, we'll discuss real-world situations, explore using ethical frameworks to resolve social media conundrums, and integrating [sic] ethical considerations into your social media policies, training, and practices.

Attendees will walk away with: 1) new ideas for how to set and manage the tone of your organization's social media community; 2) a better understanding of the legal implications of your social media policies and practices; and 3) ways to balance the ethics and opportunities of social media. ("2014 Nonprofit" 2014)

The New Organizing Institute (NOI) (2014), a progressive organization that trains digital strategists on the latest tactics and best practices for successful online organizing, is another potential avenue for discussions of digital strategy ethics. At first glance, NOI looks like a proto-professional organization for digital strategists. Its annual Rootscamp "unconference" serves as a clearinghouse for the latest in digital political strategy and as a valuable networking opportunity. Yet digital strategy ethics is not an issue featured in the NOI website, which addresses topics like online organizing, voter contact, data management, and "organizing your career," among others.

Progressive Exchange, an e-mail list for digital strategists and similar professionals committed to progressive American politics and advocacy, is yet another potential avenue for these discussions. Progressive Exchange was established in 2004 by the progressive political consulting firm M+R Strategic Services ("Progressive Exchange" 2004) "as a way to share information about online strategies, tactics and tools among people doing Internet organizing, advocacy, marketing and fundraising on behalf of the public interest." As of September 2014, the list had nearly 13,000 subscribers.[2] Discussions on Progressive Exchange tend to focus on the nuts and bolts of digital strategy: opinions on which tactics work best or how to modify online tools to meet certain goals, requests for contractors' referrals, circulation of job listings, and so on. Occasionally, however, participants do discuss ethical issues related to their work; in fact, some of the ethical questions I discuss below have also been discussed in Progressive Exchange.

In the absence of a formalized code of ethics, digital strategists do have some preexisting sources of guidance. Because digital strategy can be seen as a hybrid of different political and communication professions, digital strategists can turn to codes that most closely address various aspects of their work.

For example, digital strategists who engage heavily in blogging can turn to the Society of Professional Journalists Code of Ethics (2014), which stresses that "public enlightenment is the forerunner of justice and the foundation of democracy" and that it is the duty of journalists "to further those ends by seeking truth and providing a fair and comprehensive account of events and issues." A strategist working primarily on voting mobilization, meanwhile, could consult the American Association of Political Consultants Code of Ethics (2014), which asks its members to foreswear appeals to voters "based on racism, sexism, religious intolerance or any form of unlawful discrimination and will condemn those who use such practices" and commits them to "work for equal voting rights and privileges for all citizens." Strategists heavily involved in information management—for example, supporter or voter databases, social media user information, and similar data—could consult the Association of Information Technology Professionals' Code of Ethics & Standards of Conduct (2014), through which each member acknowledges that:

> I have an obligation to society and will participate to the best of my ability in the dissemination of knowledge pertaining to the general development and understanding of information processing. Further, I shall not use knowledge of a confidential nature to further my personal interest, nor shall I violate the privacy and confidentiality of information entrusted to me or to which I may gain access.

These ethical codes may be helpful to digital strategists in a piecemeal way, but ultimately do not provide a coherent ethical framework upon which they can rely. The ethical dilemmas that digital strategists face today—and given the rapid pace of technological development, are likely to face in the future—are unique enough to merit an ethical framework tailored to this emerging profession. Ideally, such a framework would reflect the profession's semipublic function of fostering greater political engagement.

From ethical egoism to Kantianism

The internet's history is closely tied to libertarian notions of radical freedom, perhaps best exemplified by John Perry Barlow's 1996 "Declaration of Independence in Cyberspace" (Barlow 1996; Castells 2001). These libertarian leanings are closely related to the philosophy of *ethical egoism*. Popularized by novelist Ayn Rand, author of *Atlas Shrugged* and *The Fountainhead*, this philosophy holds "man's life as the standard of value—and his own life as the ethical purpose of every individual man" (Rand and Branden 1964). In other words, an individual must measure the ethical value of all actions by how they affect or advance his or her own rational self-interest. This philosophy does not preclude one from helping others—so long as this act furthers one's self-interest. But ultimately, ethical egoism is inadequate as a basis for digital strategy ethics. Like relativism, it can blur the lines between doing what one believes to be ethical and what one simply wants to do. Second, it is too individualistic and inward looking to apply effectively to a profession like digital strategy that performs a semi-public function. This is probably why it is not broadly reflected in ethical codes from similar communication professions, like journalism (Roberts 2012). Ethical egoism's focus on the internet's potential to maximize liberty may be justified from an individual perspective, but institutions like governments, the press, advocacy organizations, and political parties, which act as custodians of liberal democracies, have responsibilities to their societies that go beyond narrow institutional interests—as do the digital strategists that conduct online campaigns on their behalf.

Kantianism offers a more promising approach. Kantianism originated with the writings of Immanuel Kant, who tried to arrive at universal moral norms through the use of reason (Kant [1781] 1998). Unlike divine command theory, which finds its universal moral norms from appeals to higher authorities, Kant discovered his universal norms through reason—a process in which we can all engage. Kant arrived at these norms through his Categorical Imperative, composed of three tests:

CI 1: "Act only on that maxim through which you can at the same time will that it should become a universal law" (Kant [1785]/1996). This maxim is designed to take cultural or personal biases out of moral decision-making and requires us "to view the issue from a multiplicity of perspectives" (Bowen 2013, 124).

CI 2: "Act in such a way that you always treat humanity, whether in your own person or in the person of any other, never simply as a means, but always at the same time as an end" (Kant [1785] 1996). This maxim aims to protect the dignity and equality of each individual, which makes it highly applicable to communication professions like digital strategy (Bowen 2013, 125).

CI 3: "If our conduct as free agents is to have moral goodness, it must proceed solely from a good will" (Kant [1775–80] 1963). This maxim aims to avoid self-serving motives behind ethical decisions.

Kantianism is a plausible basis for an ethics of digital strategy. It is based on reason, seeks to preserve the dignity of all (including would-be targets of political communication and mobilization efforts), and gives us a systematic way to arrive at moral judgments when confronted with ethically complex situations. Given that some communication scholars have found it useful in analyzing cases of social media, Kantianism also seems like a practical approach for digital strategy (Bowen 2013).

To show how such an approach would work in practice, below I present three examples of ethical questions digital strategists face daily, based on topics that are currently focal points of much discussion among political advocacy experts: emotional manipulation, the actual political impact of online campaigns, and political polarization.

Emotional manipulation

Ever since political campaigns and activists became serious about using the internet as a tool for political communication and outreach, experts have expressed concern about the ethical ramifications of such use. As far back as 2000, Gary Selnow was already expressing concern about cookies—that is, the ability of website operators to track their users' browsing habits without their knowledge by creating tiny text files called "cookies" in their computers—and their use in political websites.

Websites and related systems have come a long way since then. Thanks to the growing popularity of social media and increasingly sophisticated ways to collect, aggregate, and analyze data from our online interactions, campaigns and advocacy organizations now have a treasure trove of data about their supporters. Companies like Catalist and Aristotle can now cross-reference voter information with hundreds of additional consumer databases to build up demographic profiles of individuals, which they then provide to campaigns and advocacy groups (Delany 2013).

Combined with sophisticated content management and mass e-mail delivery systems, this bounty of user data allows digital strategists to fine-tune their online communication and mobilization strategies as never before. This includes the ability to run online experiments that let them know what content their supporters respond to most strongly—a practice known commonly as *A/B testing*.

In a typical A/B test, for example, a digital strategist working on health care reform would choose a random sample of her organization's supporter list (e.g., 1 percent of 500,000 supporters) and assign half of that sample one version of an e-mail message (version A), and the other half a different version (version B). Version A may emphasize the economic aspects of health care reform, while version B may instead emphasize a moral case in favor of reform. The strategist would then send whichever version performed best to the whole list.

The most controversial A/B online experiment to date was not performed by a political organization, but by Facebook. Without the knowledge or express consent of participants, Facebook partnered with academic researchers to test the idea of "emotional contagion" in social networks. The researchers divided a sample of more than 600,000 Facebook users into two groups. By manipulating Facebook's newsfeed algorithm, researchers exposed one group only to their friends' positive comments and postings, while the other half saw only their friends' negative comments and postings. The result: the group exposed to negative content tended to post negative content, while the group exposed to positive content tended to post positive content (Kramer, Guillory, and Hancock 2014).

Revelations about the experiment caused great controversy in summer 2014 (Booth 2014), sparking a conversation about the ethics of A/B testing. For example, TechCrunch's Josh Costine (2014) raised the issue of the impact that the emotional manipulation involved in experiments like this could have on users predisposed to mental illness. Although political organizations typically do not have the scale of Facebook's 1 billion-plus users, or the sheer number of data points to carry out something like the emotional contagion experiment, they routinely engage in various forms of A/B testing that involve emotions. Upworthy, a viral content curation and distribution site that works closely with progressive advocacy groups, has built a thriving online presence on this practice (Greenfield 2013).

Because emotion is an important part of successful political mobilization, digital strategists A/B test messages and related content loaded with different emotional contents to discover which messages lead to more engagement (Goodwin, Jasper, and Polletta 2009). A strategist, for example, might wonder whether a mass e-mail or Facebook post infused with a hopeful message will yield greater engagement than similar content infused with anger, run an A/B test to find out, and act on the results.

A Kantian analysis of this practice yields serious ethical questions for digital strategists to ponder. Applying Kant's CI 1 would yield the following universal law: "Digital strategists should be able to perform A/B tests of emotionally loaded content without obtaining users' informed consent." Such a universal law would ignore the potential risks that online emotional manipulation poses to users. It would also further restrict internet users' ability to control their online experience, and ignore the idea that they might have a right to such control. The less information users have about the content testing processes happening behind the scenes, the less they are able to control their online experiences and choose whether to expose themselves to emotional manipulation.

Kant's CI 2 also raises ethical issues for A/B testing of emotionally loaded content. A/B testing of emotionally loaded content tempts the digital strategist to treat supporters as means to strategic ends—getting out the vote during an election, raising money for a campaign or cause, directing e-mails or calls to a senator—while ignoring the potentially detrimental effects of such testing on the individual user.

Bowen (2013) argues that many public relations activities fail to meet Kant's third test of the categorical imperative because "they work in a mode of advocacy or self-interest, rather than serving truth" (125). Advocacy and political campaigns face a similar danger because of the deep conviction it often takes to work on them. Digital strategists are therefore vulnerable to rationalizing potentially unethical behavior because of the righteousness of the causes, candidates, or parties for which they work—especially when these are compared to what they may regard as unacceptable alternatives.

The preceding analysis shows that there are many unexamined ethical questions surrounding A/B testing that a digital strategy ethical code may help address. Given the rising popularity of A/B testing-driven online political engagement, strategists must put A/B testing under closer ethical examination so that it can be both a useful *and* ethical practice.

Political impact of online tactics

Digital strategists often deploy low-threshold online tactics to recruit supporters, donors, and volunteers to their causes and campaigns. Petitions are perhaps the most commonly deployed low-threshold online tactics. Not only can they be effective in their own right, but they are also considered effective tools to grow supporter lists (Packard 2013). But digital strategists often deploy online petitions whose potential for immediate political impact is questionable.

Here are two examples taken from the two major US political parties. In 2012, the Democratic Congressional Campaign Committee (DCCC), the Democratic Party's arm charged with electing Democrats to the House of Representatives, posted a petition aimed at Republicans, urging them to denounce conservative radio talk show host Rush Limbaugh:

> Sandra Fluke, the courageous Georgetown Law student who had the strength to stand up in Congress against Republican attacks on birth control coverage, is now under attack from the right wing.
>
> First, House Republicans refused to let Sandra testify. Now, they think they can shame us into silence. Standing up for women's health care does not make you a "slut" or a "prostitute."
>
> Sign our petition right now calling on Republican leaders to publicly denounce Rush Limbaugh's cruel tirade against women. (Petition 2012)

The second example comes from the Republican National Committee's (RNC) website (2014). In 2014, the RNC called for abolition of the Internal Revenue Service (IRS):

> The IRS abused its power, attempted to silence conservative groups and potentially spent years lying about it.
>
> As Congressman Paul Ryan said, the IRS can turn our lives "upside down." But Americans have almost no recourse when the IRS abuses its power.
>
> Tax collection should be simple, not scandalous.
>
> Sign the petition to abolish the IRS.

A politically dispassionate evaluation of these petitions would reveal that neither has had a real political impact. Rush Limbaugh's popularity with the political base of the Republican Party, the DCCC's mission to unseat Republican members of Congress, and the fact that the petition signatures must come overwhelmingly from partisan Democrats, make it highly unlikely that this petition had a direct political impact. Likewise, Democratic control of the White House and the US Senate at the time, along with the extremely complex ramifications of abolishing the federal government's tax-collecting arm, make this highly unlikely to happen anytime soon.

That neither petition guarantees its signatures will be delivered to anyone— and in the Republican Party's case, is not even addressed to a decision maker— suggests that neither of them were intended to accomplish their stated goals.

Instead, they were most likely conceived as vehicles to collect e-mail addresses from new supporters who might later be converted to donors and activists, or as ways to sustain engagement with existing supporters. But we must assume that at least *some* petition signers expected their signatures to have a direct impact on these issues. Most internet users are not privy to the behind-the-scenes tactical calculations of online political campaigns. We must therefore assume that most users who sign a petition do so in the hopes of achieving what the petition says it wants to achieve—for example, a denunciation of Rush Limbaugh, or abolition of the IRS.

This gap between user and strategist intent raises ethical questions for digital strategists. Kant's CI 1 would yield a universal law stating that all digital strategists can deploy online petitions to recruit new supporters and re-engage existing ones, regardless of the petition's potential for impact. Such a law would leave us with millions of politically engaged individuals signing thousands of petitions every year that will not have obvious political impacts. With enough time and enough ineffectual petitions, cynicism about online political participation could rise, to the detriment of the broader body politic. Continuous deployment of petitions-as-recruitment-devices may also run afoul of Kant's CI 2, which enjoins us to avoid treating individuals as means to an end—in this case, as means to raise money and sustain campaigns. As with the A/B testing case, digital strategists may also be at risk of rationalizing the use of online petitions by upholding the worthiness of their causes and campaigns. None of this makes deployment of online petitions for recruitment purposes patently unethical, but the practice does raise ethical questions worthy of discussion among digital strategists.

Political polarization

Political polarization—the hardening of political attitudes and intransigence associated with it—is one of the most hotly debated topics in political science today (Nisbet and Scheufele 2013; Fisher, Waggle, and Leifeld 2013; Stroud 2010). This is closely related to growing concerns over incivility in online political discourse and its interaction with polarization (Anderson et al. 2014). Virtually no major social problem can be tackled without some measure of compromise and dialogue between political opponents. Political polarization makes dialogue and compromise less likely, which makes solving large-scale social problems increasingly difficult. But digital strategists often rely on inflammatory language that can perpetuate polarization, or even worsen it. Language that demonizes opponents while reinforcing the recipient's worldview can stir emotions that motivate participation and strengthen bonds with causes or candidates, but it can also raise the bar for compromise and dialogue down the road.

Here are two examples of this type of language from opposite ends of the American political spectrum: The first comes from an e-mail by Democracy for America, a progressive advocacy group; DFA founder and former presidential candidate Howard Dean (2014) signs the message:

> When Tea Party extremists won gubernatorial races across the country that year, Republicans found a new and powerful way to undermine President Obama— and pushed a radical agenda that takes our country in the wrong direction. Governors like Scott Walker and Rick Snyder have attacked women's rights, made it harder to vote, smashed labor unions, and gutted funding for public schools and health care.
>
> The battle for America's future is often won in the states. As a former governor myself, I know that they have a lot of power to decide what that future looks like. We can't afford to see four more years of radical extremism in our states.

The second example comes from an e-mail by Heritage Action for America, a conservative advocacy organization, and is signed by executive director Michael Needham (2014):

> Liberals like George Soros and labor bosses are pouring huge sums of money and resources into campaigns and grassroots activism right now.
>
> They're coordinating their spending through the so-called Democracy Alliance, a secret partnership of rich bigwig liberals, who are arguably more powerful than the Democratic Party itself.
>
> Their plan is to use huge influxes of cash—up to $39 million this year alone— to influence elections and policy and force through a radical liberal agenda.
>
> The Democracy Alliance is in *direct opposition* to the conservative ideas you stand for and which Heritage Action promotes.

Setting aside the objective merits of the accusations bandied about in these e-mails, the polarizing quality of their language is strikingly similar. Opponents are "radicals" and "extremists." Their "radical agenda" is in "direct opposition" to the recipient's values. They are taking the country "in the wrong direction." Through "secret partnerships," these "powerful" opponents "smash" and "gut" all the recipient cares about—a situation that all but requires the reader to join a "battle for America's future." This rhetoric paints those who disagree with the recipient's political ideology as dangerous enemies, instead of mere political opponents.

As with the first two scenarios, the use of polarizing rhetoric in online appeals raises ethical issues worth considering. A Kantian universal law based on this rhetorical practice would allow all digital strategists across the ideological divide to use highly polarizing language in online appeals. A likely consequence of this law is an increasingly polarized political environment that makes dialogue and compromise across the ideological divide less likely. As with the cases raised above, this practice may run afoul of Kant's CI 2 by treating supporters as means to an end. In this case, supporters' natural inclination toward polarization is stoked for political gain without regard to the long-term effects of polarization on society. Finally, digital strategists may be tempted to rationalize polarizing messaging by upholding the worthiness of their causes and campaigns. Use of polarizing messaging may not be clearly unethical, but it raises ethical questions for digital strategists worth discussing.

Conclusion

Digital political strategy shows signs of increasing and inexorable profes-sionalization. Conferences like Netroots Nation, organizations like NOI, and online communities like Progressive Exchange provide spaces where those who practice digital politics for a living can slowly but surely lay the foundations for this emerging profession. Ethics will need to become part of this process.

The examples I have provided in this chapter show that digital strategists face unique ethical dilemmas that require guidelines specific to this emerging profession because they are not fully addressed by other codes. As our digital media environment becomes more complex, we can expect these dilemmas to proliferate, making the need for a digital strategy code of ethics more obvious. The examples raised in this chapter show that a Kantian approach to these dilemmas could be useful in developing such a code. By emphasizing the semi-public function that digital strategists fulfill in political systems, reasserting the dignity of all individuals, and forcing rigorous examination of the motives behind digital strategies, Kant's work provides a practical framework for discovering and dealing with the ethical dilemmas digital strategists encounter every day. It is important that digital strategists, regardless of their ideological leanings, embrace common ethical guidelines to govern their profession. Otherwise, the emerging ethics of digital political strategists, like so much else in public life, could fall victim to political polarization and petty partisanship.

The framework I have discussed could also apply to other semipublic professions and institutions wrestling with ethical dilemmas arising from a constantly shifting digital media landscape. For example, journalists and editors who work primarily online may wonder about the ethics of optimizing their copy for search engine optimization (SEO), or writing headlines that draw a high number of clicks but do not accurately reflect the content of an article (these are sometimes derisively referred to as "click-bait"). By allowing news consumers to find news online quickly and drawing more traffic, these practices may shore up a news organization's bottom line, but do they compromise the public functions we have come to expect from these organizations? A Kantian ethical framework may help clarify this and similar questions, and help semipublic professions and institutions navigate the new media landscape without compromising their missions.

Notes

1 While it is possible that similar discussions are happening on the conservative side of American activism, evidence is not easily available. A search of the 2014 schedule of the Conservative Political Action Conference (CPAC), sponsored by the American Conservative Union, yielded just two digital strategy panels and no panels on ethics.

2 As a Progressive Exchange subscriber, my comments are based on non-systematic observations of traffic and discussions happening through the list.

12

Cash Out: Philanthropy, Sustainability, and Ethics in Nonprofit News

Joe Cutbirth

The only way to save journalism is to develop a new model that finds profit in truth, vigilance and social responsibility.
—Philip Meyer, *The Vanishing Newspaper*, 2004

As the economic system that's traditionally sustained American journalism falters, many in the news industry are looking to nonprofit organizations as both a source of funding and as a potential model for restructuring legacy media. The relatively new, increasingly digital enterprises that have embraced this trend have gained widespread recognition in recent years as internet technology continues to reshape the public sphere. Yet, questions remain about whether the grants and gifts nonprofit organizations use to launch their operations are viable sources of long-term revenue—and whether news operations that rely on them can keep their journalistic integrity as people and foundations with social and political agendas fund their work.

Issues of transparency and conflict of interest are not new to the news industry nor to its revenue model. Nor, given the long-standing history of the Associated Press and public broadcasting, is much new about the general idea of nonprofit news. The *Chicago Reporter* and (New York) *City Limits Magazine*, established in 1974 and 1976 respectively, set a modern standard for nonprofit coverage of urban policy matters. More recently, *Voice of San Diego*, *MinnPost*, *ProPublica*, and the *Texas Tribune* have caught the eye of both investors and industry leaders by producing the type of professional work community leaders and active citizens traditionally seek. They also have begun experimenting with long-standing editorial rules and pushing against traditional ethical practices.

As media ethicist Stephen Ward (2009) notes, nonprofit news organizations tend to be smaller in size and scope; they offer some content with more narrow or single sourcing; and many of them collaborate through content sharing with organizations that also may be competitors. Almost all of them rely on a handful of major funders (sometimes one major foundation). Finally, and a chief source of concern, is that in many cases the professional distance between journalists and their funders in a typical nonprofit newsroom is greatly reduced.

This chapter explores the rise of nonprofit digital journalism and the ethical questions that come with it. It uses *ProPublica* and the *Texas Tribune*—two nonprofits that are widely seen as successful models—to show how ethics come into play in both organizational structure and high-level reporting. It places them in a social and historic context that includes ethics codes that traditionally have shaped editorial and business practices for legacy media. Finally, it lays out criticism of both publications as well as some concerns that are starting to emerge from media ethicists and concludes with answers to some key questions: (1) What are acceptable sources of revenue for nonprofit journalism? (2) How transparent should nonprofit news organizations be with the identity of its funders? and (3) What steps should nonprofit news take to protect its editorial independence?

It's against that backdrop of changing social values, new technology, and economic restructuring that *ProPublica*, the *Texas Tribune*, and other digital nonprofit news organizations have begun to emerge and must be examined.

Nonprofit news: Two models

When Ira Glass opened a 2013 edition of *This American Life* with a report that alleged the active ingredient in Tylenol (acetaminophen) kills people, he was offering listeners a story built on an investigation by *ProPublica*, the Pulitzer Prize–winning nonprofit news organization whose reporters spent two years and $750,000 on that story alone (Osnos 2013, ¶6). "During the last decade more than 1,500 Americans died after taking too much of a drug renowned for its safety," the report claimed, referring to Tylenol's familiar advertisements that it's the pain reliever "hospitals use most" (Gerth and Miller 2013, ¶1). The story, titled "Use Only as Directed," also showed the Food and Drug Administration had long been aware of the situation and failed to respond adequately to it or to implement a full series of recommendations to address it (Glass and Cole 2013, act 2).

More than 500 stations and about 2.1 million listeners tune in weekly to the public radio show created by Glass, produced by Chicago Public Media and distributed by The Public Radio Exchange (PRX) (*This American Life* 2014). Collaboration with *This American Life* and other well-established outlets is part of the market strategy for *ProPublica,* one of the new nonprofit digital news organizations to come on the scene in recent years. *ProPublica* doesn't have a traditional distribution system for the investigations its founding editor in chief Paul Steiger calls "deep dive" content. Instead, its editors give their projects as short-term exclusives to news organizations they believe will provide the greatest audience or where they think the reports will have the most impact.

Since it began operation in 2007, *ProPublica* has developed a network of more than one hundred publishing partners, and twenty-six of them carried *ProPublica* content of some sort in 2013 (Pilkington 2014, ¶8). The partners include familiar and highly respected names in the news business: *ABC News,* the *Atlantic, CNN, Frontline, Los Angeles Times, 60 Minutes,* and *The New Yorker.* The exclusive investigations help *ProPublica's* partners broaden their audiences and finance their operations, since partners are free to place content they get from *ProPublica* on pages with advertising. That works fine for *ProPublica* because its 501(c)(3) status means it can't profit from its stories (Hirschman 2008, ¶3). Eventually, *ProPublica* posts the work on its own website and shares it more broadly under the Creative Commons no-derivative, noncommercial license. In 2013–14, the New York-based organization had a staff of about forty working journalists and an annual budget of roughly $12 million, most of which came from contributions by board members and major grants and gifts of more than $50,000 (ProPublica Inc 2013, 13–14).

The *Texas Tribune,* a digital nonprofit news group that covers Texas politics and state government, began operations in 2009. It also shares content with other news organizations, though its partners often are print and broadcast outlets in Texas that cannot afford full-time reporters and bureaus at the state capital. Like *ProPublica, Tribune* editors hope their partner-sharing arrangements will give their work broader exposure and more impact. Unlike, *ProPublica,* the *Tribune* offers a broad range of journalistic work that includes news interviews, polling, and more traditional and frequent news reports, all of which are published primarily on its website. It competes with traditional news organizations, often scoops them, and regularly shapes the agenda for public interest reporting in Texas. In 2013–14, the Austin-based company had a staff of eighteen reporters and a budget of roughly $4.5 million ("Texas Tribune" 2014c).

When state senator Wendy Davis, from Fort Worth, donned pink tennis shoes and launched a filibuster in the waning hours of the 2013 legislative session to kill a bill that would restrict abortion services in Texas, a deal the *Tribune* struck months earlier with state leaders finally paid off. The *Tribune* had secured exclusive rights to live stream legislative proceedings, but for most of the session, the viewership barely averaged in the hundreds (Lapin 2014, ¶3). That changed virtually overnight. Suspense mounted as Davis' opponents tried a series of parliamentary moves to scuttle her effort. Word of the clash spread across Austin on social media, and thousands of supporters made their way to the capital, filled the senate gallery and rotunda. President Barack Obama's Twitter feed helped steer hundreds of thousands of viewers to the *Tribune's* site, which hit its peak viewership of roughly 183,000 just after midnight (Lapin 2014, ¶6).

The *Tribune* raised more than $23,000 in donations, mostly from first-time contributors in more than thirty states, during the eleven-hour marathon (Lapin 2014, ¶8). More importantly, its editors saw a demand they could fill by using live stream technology in their coverage of the upcoming 2014 statewide elections, which would include Davis as the Democratic Party's candidate for governor. They launched a fundraising drive with a Kickstarter campaign and asked people to contribute $60,000 for portable transmitters, switchers, and encoders. In less than a month, 1,269 backers pledged $65,310 for the project (Kickstarter 2014). The equipment has allowed *Tribune* staff to report political events in real time from remote locations across the state with digital technology.

The *Texas Tribune* has received two Online Journalism Awards for general excellence, four Edward R. Murrow national awards, and national recognition by the Society of Professional Journalists and Gannett Foundation for investigative and watchdog journalism. *ProPublica* content published in conjunction with its partners has twice won the Pulitzer Prize (for national reporting and for investigative reporting) and been a finalist two other times. It also has received the Peabody Award and the George Polk Award for radio reporting. The awards show that the journalism these organizations are doing can have the same impact as the best work done by legacy media. What they don't show is whether these organizations are playing by the same rules.

Advertising and objectivity

Experts agree there is no way to restore American journalism to what it was during most of the twentieth century (Anderson, Bell, and Shirky 2012, 7). The advertising model used to underwrite production costs since the 1880s is collapsing, thanks to the direct outreach ability of social media and free digital options such as Craigslist. The idea of drawing on venture capital, foundation grants, and corporate funding to support a new business model is alluring, but it also is full of ethical pitfalls. Examining the ethical framework among journalists at nonprofit organizations, the sources of journalists, and those who fund the activities of journalists at a time when so much in the industry is changing gives insight into whether these new nonprofit news groups can contribute to participatory democracy with the quality of journalism many in the industry want to preserve and whether they can do so with their integrity intact.

Publishers such as Benjamin Day, James Gordon Bennett, William Randolph Hearst, and Joseph Pulitzer have used new technologies and found innovative revenue streams to fund operations since the nineteenth century, when the Penny Press experimented with options other than the subscriptions and political patronage that supported the partisan and commercial papers of the Revolutionary and Early American Eras (Schudson 1978, 12–60). The circulation-funded model penny publishers adopted was designed to take advantage of mass production technology and egalitarian ideals that marked the final stages of the industrial revolution and the onset of Jacksonian democracy. It took another fifty years and the growth of department stores, trademarks, and brand names to convince publishers to abandon their long-held resistance to commercial advertising and to accept significant revenue available from selling ad space to businesses that wanted to showcase their products (Schudson 1978, 93). Meanwhile, the roots of nonprofit American journalism took hold with the creation of the Associated Press. Formed in 1846, it initially was an arrangement between five New York newspapers that wanted to share stories about the Mexican-American War. A century and a half later, the AP staffs about 280 offices in more than 100 countries and remains a nonprofit cooperative owned by 1,500 American newspapers, which are both its customers and members (Associated Press 2014, ¶4). Despite the AP's early success and relative longevity, advertising eventually became the chief revenue source for corporate newspapers and for network broadcasting as America moved into the twentieth century.

As the modern business model for American newspapers developed, so did expectations of what a newspaper should be. Industry leaders who saw advantages to professionalization moved away from the sensational headlines and dubious sources that marked the newspaper wars of the 1890s between William Randolph Hearst and Joseph Pulitzer. Adolph Ochs, who bought the fledgling *New York Times* in 1896, favored a newer concept of "objectivity," which in its early incarnation simply meant less dependence on official sources, particularly government and public relations practitioners, and a shift away from the sensationalism Hearst and Pulitzer used so effectively. In the decades that followed, news organizations separated the responsibilities of editorial employees from the business operation. Simply put, reporters didn't sell ads and advertisers didn't attend news meetings. Many organizations took it a step further and literally segregated the advertising and editorial departments into different areas of their buildings.

The purpose of the divide was to demonstrate to readers, viewers, and the public (and perhaps the occasional advertiser and employee) that news coverage couldn't be bought—this demonstration was expected to enhance its credibility and thus its value. As professional organizations and individual companies developed ethics codes, the idea of separating the two functions became routine practice. The voluntary standards set by the Society of Professional Journalists note that journalists should "deny favored treatment to advertisers and special interests and resist their pressure to influence news coverage" (Society of Professional Journalists 2014). The *New York Times* ethics code states:

> The relationship between the *Times* and advertisers rests on the understanding, long observed in all departments that news and advertising are strictly separate— that those who deal with either one have distinct obligations and interests and neither group will try to influence the other. (*New York Times Co.* 2004, 23)

Locking the idea of "objectivity" into ethics codes was another matter. The Society of Professional Journalists ethics code doesn't mention objectivity *per se*, though it does call on journalists to be independent, accurate, and fair. The sole mention of objectivity in the *New York Times* ethics code comes in an admonition to members of the news department to "maintain disinterest and objectivity by avoiding discussion of advertising needs, goals and problems" except when they are related directly to the business of the news department (*New York Times Co.* 2004, 23).

The idea that objectivity somehow equates to presenting opposing viewpoints in a neutral voice has been one of the constant debates in the news industry for the last fifty years. Many journalists and some media critics hold onto that idea as the foundation for the work American journalists do. Increasingly, however, media scholars and a rising chorus inside the industry disagree.

Historian Michael Schudson (1978) argues that the neutral-voice paradigm for objectivity began to unravel during the Vietnam War as government management of news collided with a growing adversary culture on college campuses, inside the news industry, and among readers and viewers. He notes that social and political events of the 1960s led to "a radical questioning of objectivity" and a resurgence of reporting practices that the objective style had long overshadowed. Writes Schudson (1978), "The idea of objectivity has by no means been displaced, but more than ever, it holds its authority on sufferance" (10). More recently, Bill Kovach and Tom Rosenstiel (2007) have claimed that the original intent of objectivity has been corrupted to the point that twenty-first-century journalism should move away from the term as its ideal and instead should emphasize professional fairness and factual verification (84–86). Geneva Overholser (2004), a former ombudsman for the *Washington Post*, sees the allegiance to objectivity as a touchstone that has "has grown worse than useless" and says that allowing voice and reasoned perspective into journalism will result in "clarity, strength and purposefulness from the democratization and the questioning and the critiques that accompany the transition" (¶5).

As the challenges to objectivity that Schudson noted a half-century ago have intensified, the economic base that had sustained American journalism began to unravel in the 1990s with the launch of the commercial web (Anderson, Bell, and Shirky 2012, 2). A report by the Tow Center at Columbia University notes that American media weren't really selling content as a product during the twentieth century; they were in the service business with vertical integration of content reproduction and delivery. They essentially were using a tightly wrapped hierarchical model to deliver eyeballs to advertisers.

> The Internet wrecks vertical integration, because everyone pays for the infrastructure then everyone gets to use it. The audience remains more than willing to pay for reproduction and distribution, but now we pay Dell for computers, Canon for printers and Verizon for delivery, rather than paying Conde Nast, Hearst or Tribune Co. for all those services in a bundle. (Anderson, Bell, and Shirky 2012, 8)

So, in the end, contrary to popular belief, American news media have long been veiled advertising companies. Readers and viewers widely assumed news organizations were selling them news. In fact, news organizations were using news to capture readers and viewers, then shrewdly selling that audience's attention to businesses who wanted exposure to their products.

Digital nonprofit news

Nonprofit status is basically a legal designation and business model. Under the Internal Revenue Service Code section 501(c)(3) nonprofit organizations, also known as "charitable organizations," are exempt from federal income taxes as long as their activities involve a specific focus, such as education, charity, religion, and amateur sports. They must be careful not to: (1) operate for the benefit of private interests or for the benefit of individual owners or shareholders; (2) attempt to influence legislation as a substantial part of their activities; or (3) participate in any campaign activity for or against political candidates (Internal Revenue Service 2014).

American journalists like to claim that their ethics are grounded in independence—particularly from government and institutions it is supposed to cover—but there is a long history of government involvement with and on behalf of American media, beginning with the Postal Clause in the US Constitution, which was intended specifically to aid interstate communication. By the 1930s, highly profitable commercial broadcasting licenses allowed government-selected individuals and corporations exclusive rights to public airwaves. And during the 1960s, states and universities subsidized public radio stations with help from national foundations. The Carnegie Corp. helped create the Carnegie Commission on Education Television, which in 1967 issued a national plan for public television that eventually became the nonprofit Corporation for Public Broadcasting (Charles Lewis 2007, ¶15). The Corporation for Public Broadcasting receives virtually all of its funding from Congress and provides key support for the Public Broadcast Service and National Public Radio. Ethics for the Corporation for Public Broadcasting are written into federal law. The Public Broadcasting Act (1967) mandates that the organization follow a "strict adherence to objectivity and balance in all programs or series of programs of a controversial nature" and that it review national programming for objectivity and balance and report on "its efforts to address concerns about objectivity and balance" (Corporation for Public Broadcasting 2014, Sec. 396g). The act also sets guidelines for advertising. Public Broadcast Stations may offer services, facilities, or products in exchange for remuneration, but they aren't allowed to accept typical commercial advertising (Corporation for Public Broadcasting 2014, Sec. 396g). In contrast, the BBC, which is funded by a license fee set by the British government, operates under a well-established public remit reaffirmed in a widely publicized 2013 study. The organization noted: "The BBC's mission is to inform, educate and entertain audiences with programmes and services of high quality, originality and value" (Reynolds 2013, 2).

A 2013 study by Pew Foundation found that 172 active nonprofit news sites were launched in the United States from 1987 to 2012 (Mitchell et al. 2013a, 3). They joined a group that already included: *The Chicago Reporter* (est. 1974), *City Limits Magazine* (est. 1976), and the Center for Investigative Reporting (est. 1977). Most nonprofits either follow practices set in the Society of Professional Journalists ethics code or have their own ethics codes posted on their websites. The Center for Investigative Reporting, for example, has an extensive ethics code posted on its site that addresses: anonymous sourcing, aggregation of information, conflicts of interest, crediting other media, gifts, plagiarism, political activity, and undercover work. It also addresses the notion of a professional separation between editorial employees and donors.

> We have no sacred cows. We will not shy away from stories that we deem newsworthy. In the name of transparency, when we produce stories that involve donors to CIR or board members, we will always disclose the relationship. When these situations arise, please notify your editor. To keep a firewall between development and editorial staff, our newsroom personnel should use common sense when engaging in a dialogue with our funders, foundations and major donors. If there is any confusion about this, please consult with the editorial director or executive director. (Center for Investigative Reporting 2014, ¶15)

So, there were plenty of models and precedents by 2007 and 2009, when *ProPublica* and the *Texas Tribune* were launched with high expectations and great fanfare. Yet, despite the praise and recognition both have received, both have been questioned and criticized for ethical issues beginning with their funders.

ProPublica received most of its early funding from the Sandler Foundation, whose principals Herbert and Marion Sandler earned roughly $2.4 billion in 2006 from the sale of Golden West Financial Corp (Perez-Pena 2007, ¶7). The Sandlers pledged $10 million annually to help get *ProPublica* started, and other foundations provided smaller amounts (Perez-Pena 2007, ¶6). (Herbert Sandler also served as founding chairman of *ProPublica's* governing board.) An article in the *New York Times* about *ProPublica* two months before it began operation described the Sandlers as "major Democratic political donors and critics of President Bush." *Slate* media critic Jack Shafer published an article around the same time titled "What Do Herbert and Marion Sandler Want?" It drew on information from the Federal Election Commission database and Center for Responsive Politics, and the research showed that the Sandlers gave hundreds of thousands of dollars to Democratic Party campaigns (Shafer 2007, ¶6). The list included: Moveon.org voter fund ($2.5 million) and Citizens for a Strong Senate ($8.5 million), a group with close ties to former North Carolina senator John Edwards. Shafer wrote, "If I were a newspaper editor considering *ProPublica* copy for a future issue, the first thing I'd want is proof of a firewall preventing the Sandlers and other funders from picking—or nixing—the targets of its probes." In the case of *ProPublica*, however, the ethical firewall seems to be working.

The organization has been aggressive about answering criticisms of its work. When a columnist for the *Rocky Mountain News* challenged its reporting on hydraulic fracking, *ProPublica* offered a digital update with links to pdf versions of studies and reports by the EPA and state environmental commissions and agencies (Lustgarten 2009, 8–14). It also has not shied away from reports that shed unfavorable light on the Democratic Party, and people associated with it, with reports such as "How Democrats Fooled California's Redistricting Commission" (Pierce and Larson 2011) and "The New Democrats: The Coalition Pharma and Wall Street Love" (Jones and Stern 2010).

ProPublica also posts financial statements, such as its annual report to stakeholders and IRS 990 forms, on its website. In a section titled "supporters," it provides links to websites for several dozen high-profile foundations, trusts, and other organizations who provide financial assistance. A "media kit" details opportunities and policies for advisers and the *ProPublica* code of ethics, which focuses more directly on issues that might constitute conflicts of interest by individual employees.

In comparison, BuzzFeed, which some argue deliberately attempts to blur advertising and journalism, uses social media such as Facebook and Twitter to distribute a product that Bloomberg News describes as "everything from weighty political journalism and long-form stories that rival traditional publications to auto correct mishaps and quirky photo lists, such as '10 Pieces of Proof that Shar-Peis Are Actually Fuzzy Land Manatees'" (Bloomberg 2014, ¶12). In 2014, it received a single $50 million fund infusion from the venture capital firm Andreessen Horowitz. It was BuzzFeed's fifth round of venture funding, and it easily eclipsed the $46.3 million raised during the four other rounds combined (Stelter 2014, ¶1). BuzzFeed has been criticized for shoddy editorial practices—these have been outlined in articles such as

Gawker's "Remix Everything: Buzzfeed and the Plagiarism Problem" (Chen 2012a) and the *Atlantic Wire's* "Buzzfeed's 'Happiest Facts of All Time Were Mostly Plagiarized from Reddit'" (Bump 2013). Yet, Chris Dixon, a partner in Andreessen Horowitz, said he was very keen on the product:

> We're presently in the midst of a major technological shift in which, increasingly, news and entertainment are being distributed on social networks and consumed on mobile devices. We believe BuzzFeed will emerge from this period as a preeminet media company. (Stelter 2014, ¶2)

The *Texas Tribune* also received a significant amount of its initial funding from a single source. Venture capitalist and cofounder John Thornton and his wife directly contributed $1 million of about $3.5 million raised for the site, which had a first-year budget of $1.6 million (Tenore 2011, ¶7). Another $1 million came from three foundations: the Houston Endowment ($500,000), the Klein Foundation ($250,000), and the Knight Foundation ($250,000) (*Texas Tribune* 2014b). Thornton also pledged to continue to support the operation for several years out of his pocket (James Moore 2014, ¶46). The *Tribune* also had contributions from dozens of corporate sponsors, government entities, and other non-profit groups as well as hundreds of donors and members who gave $100 or less. A significant part of its financial strategy has depended on increasing that base which includes a wide range of businesses, public institutions, and political interests as well as lobbyists and lawmakers affiliated with both political parties.

In the case of the *Texas Tribune*, it's the smaller-and medium-sized regular contributors—not the large individual founders and charitable foundations—that have drawn public criticism. Jim Moore, best-selling author and frequent MSNBC political analyst, claims the *Tribune's* large member and donor base has so many members who are public officials and lobbyists, or are otherwise tied to institutions with business at the state capitol, that reporting offered by the *Tribune* cannot be independent in the journalistic tradition. In a lengthy report published by the *Huffington Post*, Moore pointed to the Texas Tribune Festival, an annual weekend with hundreds of speakers and panelists who discuss pressing policy issues. The event is a mixture of networking and social events, all designed to raise money and visibility for the *Tribune*. Moore notes that the festival is underwritten by "policy junkies and sponsors with vital interests in the topics of the program, which, bluntly, means corporations and lobbyists." He concludes:

> In less than five years, the *Texas Tribune* has gone from being an exciting start up to a hypocritical money-grubbing promotional operation wearing a coat

of many colors that it wants to convince everyone is actual journalism. But it is not. There is no reason to any longer take the *Tribune* seriously as a news organization. They simply cannot be trusted. (James Moore 2014, ¶109)

Tribune editors acknowledge that they are trying new financial models, but they insist they are not sacrificing ethical integrity, and they point to extensive transparency as evidence of that claim. The *Texas Tribune* website publishes extensive financial information, including financial reports, audits, and the annual IRS form 990, which details income and expenses for nonprofit organizations. A section of the site titled "Who Funds Us" lists every individual contribution and amount by every corporate sponsor, donor, or member by year since 2009. In 2014, the *Tribune* announced that stories that referred to or quoted a corporate sponsor who has given $1,000 or more would include a note to that effect. The *Tribune* also publishes its own ethics code, which attempts to construct the traditional wall between employees who raise revenue and those who write stories. It states among other things that editorial decisions are made by journalists alone and that all corporate support will be solicited by the business staff and no sponsored content will be produced by *Tribune* employees (Texas Tribune 2014a, ¶19).

Criticisms of the *Texas Tribune* are less about partisan slant than about its grand relationship with lobbyists and political insiders. Indeed, its funders include six-figure contributions from high-profile Republicans and Democrats and foundations associated with their families. The *Tribune's* lengthy list of contributors, who also are registered lobbyists with political business at the capital, has drawn considerable attention. R. G. Ratcliffe, a former *Houston Chronicle* reporter who has covered money and influence in Texas politics for three decades, sums up the criticism others have offered: "When the *Texas Tribune* people first told me in 2009 that their financing plan would include corporate sponsors, I envisioned the kind of sponsorship you see for the cancer race or the music festival or public broadcasting. Instead, what we've gotten is a fundraising scheme that is more like that of a political action committee" (James Moore, 2014 ¶69).

For his part, *Tribune* publisher Evan Smith is unapologetic. He sees the trend away from printed products and toward digital production—and an ethics code based on disclosure and transparency—essentially a *fait accompli*. "The hand-wringing about native advertising will give way to hand clapping at the prospect of someone paying for serious journalism" (Smith 2013).

Conclusion

The transition to digital production and distribution of news has so fundamentally changed the relationship between owners, advertisers, and their audiences that virtually everyone who understands the news industry believes that the news organizations of the twenty-first century will have to adopt a different economic model than their twentieth-century ancestors. America has moved into an era where what doesn't work is more evident than what does, and long-held beliefs about how to manage news organizations are giving way to a more variable set of practices than those accepted as routine in the twentieth century (Anderson, Bell, and Shirky 2012, 16). Given that dynamic, deep discussions about sustainability—the current buzzword for long-term financial viability—have emerged as a key ethical challenge for nonprofit digital news.

Leaders in the growing field of nonprofit journalism are optimistic about the future, though most of them face serious challenges on the road to sustainability, according to a recent study by the Pew Research Center (Mitchell et al. 2013a, ¶1). Bill Kovach, founder of the Committee of Concerned Journalists, believes the industry needs to count on philanthropic organizations for support, at least in an interim period while the destabilization continues. "Most news organizations are so scared and so unsure of themselves, they are not protecting their franchise," says Kovach. "And somehow a philanthropy that believes in democracy has to help stabilize it" (Charles Lewis 2007, ¶27). Yet, those who want foundations and philanthropies to step in and sustain nonprofit journalism on a long-term basis may fail to account for the way most of those organizations operate.

The large seed grants that help many nonprofits get started work well for their intended purpose, but the Pew study found that digital nonprofit news operations often lack the professional talent to build innovative financial models and to broaden the revenue base in ways that meet their long-term financial needs (Mitchell et al. 2013b). More than half of the nonprofit organizations that took the Pew survey (54 percent) identified business, marketing, and fundraising as the areas where they need to bolster staff, while a little more than a third (39 percent) said their top need was more editorial employees. When asked about major challenges, nearly two-thirds of them (62 percent) cited "finding the time to focus on the business side of the operation," while only about half (53 percent) cited increased competition for grant money.

Indeed, some nonprofits told Pew they operate in an economic catch-22: They don't have sufficient business side resources to develop the revenue streams that would help them hire the business employees they need to become financially sustainable; yet, they feel pressured not to devote resources to raising revenue because the nonprofit culture emphasizes spending on services (editorial content) over business development (Mitchell et al. 2013b, ¶3). Ruth McCambridge, editor in chief of *Nonprofit Quarterly*, believes that "anybody who is not playing around with emerging sources of revenue at this point is being pretty silly," because philanthropy is often "fad driven and impatient" (Mitchell et al. 2013c, ¶10).

Clearly, foundation grants are not a panacea for sustainability. In fact, no one knows how the economic model for American journalism will evolve during the next decade. That means it is especially important to consider the fundamentals of journalism ethics as the news industry and the American public examines alternatives to legacy media.

Separating advertising from reporting seemed to be the best course for everyone—newspaper owners, reporters, advertisers and consumers—as long as objectivity was the goal. However, as noted earlier, that ideal fell into question by the 1970s. As James Carey (1997) wrote a decade or so later, but still before the internet and digital journalism had turned objectivity and the ethics and economics of legacy media on its head:

> Modern journalism and modern democracy invented around the 1890s have had a pretty long run. But there was democracy before modern journalism; there will be democracy after it, though there are difficult and dangerous transitions to be negotiated. (234)

Indeed, a central question in the twenty-first century is whether Americans and the journalists who serve them want to hold onto that utilitarian tradition and if so how will the industry move from ethics codes written to reflect twentieth-century economics and values to codes written for a twenty-first-century digital culture.

Media ethicist Stephen Ward (2009) notes that ethics are not static. They are principles that constantly change to reflect our primary values.

> They define who we are and give us an ethical identity. Ethics are the process of inventing new and better ethical responses to problems and conflicts. This process is driven not only by social change but also by our ethical imagination, which continually pushes on existing boundaries. (¶5)

Given the social history of nonprofit news and information from the Pew survey, how does the news industry make these changes and hold onto the core values that define it and the expectations of its American audience?

First, news organizations must accept the fact that change has happened and that more change is on the way. Virtual integration and objectivity may be part of American journalism, but they are no longer the industry standard. Technology has radically changed the way news is reported and delivered as well as how those activities are funded. So, it's more important than ever to remember that journalism is more than using technology to create content. Ethics in the new digital age need to recognize this duality.

Second, news organizations must search broadly for revenue sources. Seed money and foundation grants are not long-term funding. There is a temptation to hope a foundation may continue to support an enterprise beyond an initial gift, but that is a dicey strategy. They may also want to charge for some premium content. Individuals may have political ties and agendas, too, and there may be times when a nonprofit news organization, like anyone in the public realm, should look at its contributor list and, in some cases, possibly return contributions that raise questions about its operation or agenda.

Third, transparency is important, but it's not a cure-all. Digital publication makes it so easy to show documents and basic information that not making that information public can raise questions about what may be hidden. Contributor lists and income tax records let people check funding sources and expenses that may include salaries of key personnel. Enterprising readers can cross-reference news stories and sources in them to contributors and draw their own conclusions about fairness and truth. Putting that information in public view also places it more directly in the minds of reporters, who may choose to change their reporting habits—for better or worse—to avoid those individuals and corporations. Generally, however, when it comes to transparency, the ethical choice should be to reveal as much information about the operation of the business as possible.

Finally, remodel the wall. Ethical codes that required an absolute professional wall between editorial and advertising departments were crafted for an industry supported by commercial advertising. It may not be that simple in the future. That doesn't mean it's time to abandon the idea altogether and have reporters selling advertising. In fact reporters shouldn't sell ads or otherwise raise money for operating expenses. News must never appear to be for sale. The professional wall rarely focused on subscribers, and it may be time to reexamine that relationship. As revenue sources shift toward foundations, large donors, and sustaining members, the professional separation between reporting on those people and institutions and raising money from them should be a prime ethical concern.

13

When Privates are Public: Ethical Issues in News Media Coverage of Transgender People

Susan Wildermuth

On February 4, 2013, the *Los Angeles Times* covered a story about a transgender prostitute who was robbed and then shot to death on Santa Monica Boulevard (Quinones 2013). The paper was later forced to issue an apology for referring to the victim, Cassidy Vickers, as "heshe." This story highlights both the high rate of violence against transgender people in the United States, and the need for journalists who cover news stories related to transgender issues to be more sensitive in their reporting. According to the 2011 National Transgender Discrimination Survey, conducted by the National Center for Transgender Equality, transgender people in the United States face heightened levels of harassment, physical assault, and sexual violence at school, at the workplace, in politics, within religious institutions, within the family, within the social justice system, and within the health care setting (Grant et al. 2011). These heightened rates of discrimination are pervasive, in part, because news media coverage like the above story contributes to a culture of misunderstanding and marginalization of transgender people. Through a detailed analysis of two prominent news stories involving coverage of transgender people (*Grantland* magazine's story of "Dr. V's Magical Putter" and Katie Couric's interview with Carmen Carrera and Laverne Cox), I will argue that journalists need to recognize their larger social role in teaching the general public about how to understand and talk about transgender issues. At the conclusion, I also recommend specific changes in journalistic practices to help journalists cover transgender issues ethically and reduce the current climate of discrimination and violence toward transgender people.

Having an understanding of the progression of news media coverage of transgender issues and people over time helps us to understand these specific cases. As early as 2001, organizations and commentators that monitor media coverage were noticing a drastic increase in the presence and representation of transgender people in the media (Leo 2001). The increase in coverage gave rise to claims that a media boom was underway on behalf of transgender men and women in the United States (Leo 2001). According to the American Psychological Association (2011), transgender is an umbrella term for persons whose gender identity or gender expression does not conform to that typically associated with the sex to which they were assigned at birth. Gender identity refers to a person's internal sense of being male, female, or something else; gender expression refers to the way a person communicates gender identity to others through behavior, clothing, hairstyles, use of voice, and body characteristics (Butler 1993). Transitioning from one gender to another is complex and may involve a move to a gender that is neither traditionally male nor female. While there is no "right" way to transition, there are some common social changes transgender people experience that may involve one or more of the following: adopting the appearance of the desired sex through changes in clothing and grooming, adopting a new name, changing sex designation on identity documents, using hormone therapy treatment, and/or undergoing medical procedures that modify their physical body to conform with their gender identity. An estimated 0.3 percent of adults, or about 925,000 people, identify as transgender in the United States (Gates 2011).

While the increased representations of transgender people in the media during the early 2000s was welcomed by those in the transgender community, there was concern that the coverage was primarily limited to fictional characters in film and television, and that it was often stereotypical and limiting. In a 2012 report, the Gay and Lesbian Alliance Against Defamation (GLAAD) stated that in ten years of media coverage from 2002 to 2012, transgender characters were cast as victims 40 percent of the time and as villains 21 percent of the time. Additionally, the most common profession for transgender characters was that of a sex worker (20 percent of the time). Finally, anti-transgender slurs, language, and dialogue were present in 61 percent of the storylines and episodes reviewed in the study. During that same time period, news coverage of transgender individuals slowly began to increase such that today, media coverage of transgender people includes factual news stories as well as fictional media characters. As society has become more accepting of transgender people, there has been a rise in transgender public figures, and associated news coverage of transgender people. Examples of transgender people recently in the news include Chelsea Manning, Chaz Bono, Laverne Cox, Janet Mock, and Carmen Carrera.

Many view this increase in visibility and news coverage as a positive step. For example, Zack Ford (2014) argues that *TIME* magazine's recent cover story on Laverne Cox was a huge step forward for transgender equality. He describes the cover story and its other components as perhaps the most positive and in-depth representation of transgender life experiences ever presented in mainstream print media. The *TIME* magazine article argued that society has reached a transgender tipping point and that the increased media visibility and public acceptance of transgender people indicates a shift in deeply held cultural beliefs about gender (Steinmetz 2014). That this increased media presence has a positive impact on the transgender community is reflected in the multiple social policy changes that have been made recently to address transgender rights. From reviewing the ban on transgender individuals openly serving in the military, to updating policies on gender designation on birth certificates, to decreasing red tape for legal name changes, to Medicare coverage of gender reassignment surgery, and to a president that publicly expressed support for transgender rights, multiple national policy changes have reflected a more inclusive and accepting attitude toward transgender persons (Anderson-Minshall 2014). By getting the stories out, traditional and social news media coverage of transgender individuals has been integral to lesbian, gay, bisexual, transgender, queer (LGBTQ) political organizing and to achieving policy changes for transgender people (Petrow and Milan 2014).

However, some pundits argue that the increase in news coverage could be potentially harmful to the transgender community because the coverage is primarily negative and presents inaccurate and/or disrespectful viewpoints of transgender people (Jones 2014). Only eight percent of people in the United States know a transgender person, so for 92 percent of the population, everything they know about transgender people comes from the media (Jones 2014). This makes misinformation and misrepresentation of transgender people in news coverage especially problematic (Petrow and Milan 2014). Problems with news coverage about the transgender community include misuse of pronouns and other signifiers, a focus on news stories where transgender people are victims, and a focus on topics related to the use of the presence or absence of certain genitalia to determine policy (bathroom usage, military service, sports participation, etc.) (Callahan 2014). Some argue that these negative and misleading news portrayals can result in increased violence against members of the transgender community (Truitt 2014). The 2013 National Coalition of Anti-Violence Programs (NCAVP) study of hate violence against the LGBTQ community found that while rates of violence against the LGBTQ community as a whole remained stable from 2012, there was a substantial increase in the severity of the violence reported against transgender people (National Coalition 2013). Additionally, the study found that transgender women face the highest risks of homicide and that people who identify as transgender are almost 30 percent more likely to experience physical violence than those who are gender normative. Thus, there is a fear that the increase in inaccurate or negative news coverage could be problematic as it could serve to accelerate hate crimes and violence against transgender people.

Covering news is more than just reporting the facts. News coverage can have a significant impact on how a group of individuals is viewed and treated by the broader society. Thus, the increased visibility and coverage of transgender people in the news is an opportunity for journalists, editors, reporters, and others involved in the news media to reflect on how transgender topics can be treated ethically in news coverage. Some issues are relatively simple to address such as should news coverage use the "he" or "she" or "ze" (gender neutral) pronoun when referring to transgender people who are transitioning or who identify as queer (DiBlasio 2013)? Or, should news organizations use a transgender person's legal name (which may reflect one gender) or their "preferred" name (which may reflect a different gender) in news coverage? While news organizations vary in how they handle names and pronouns, there are clear AP standards in place to help guide journalists on issues like this (DiBlasio 2013). In other areas, there are no clearly developed guidelines and that is where media ethics gets more challenging. Two ethical questions that emerge in this discussion are: 1. the public/private controversy and 2. the politics of outing. The chapter will use the case study of Katie Couric's interview with Carmen Carrera and Laverne Cox and the case study of Dr. Vanderbilt and the Magical Putter to frame these questions, providing historical context to help develop each issue and exploring perspectives on what various parties involved believe is the "ethical" way to approach each question.

The public/private conundrum: The case of Katie Couric, Carmen Carrera, and Laverne Cox

The first case study covered in this chapter explores the public and private conundrum in relation to coverage of transgender persons. On January 6, 2014, Katie Couric interviewed two transwomen, Carmen Carrera and Laverne Cox, on her talk show. During the interview, Katie Couric asked the two women about their surgeries and their associated genitalia; questions which many people in the transgender community considered inappropriate. Her question was, "Your private parts are different now, aren't they?" A similar incident happened with Piers Morgan when Janet Mock appeared on his show. While Piers did not ask direct questions about "private parts" like Katie Couric did, Morgan's entire interview seemed to focus on Mock's genitalia. He repeatedly referred back to her given name, suggesting time after time that she "used to be a man" and was "formerly a man" (Ford 2014). In both cases, the transgender women were asked questions about their transitions by journalists who seemed more interested in talking about the particulars of transgender bodies than about transgender lives (Truitt 2014). This outraged many in the transgender community who argued that the newsworthiness of transgender persons does not come from their physical body, but from their struggles, accomplishments, and goals, and thus, that questions about their physical bodies which dehumanize them, reducing them to nothing more than breasts and penises and distracting from the real reasons they are newsworthy, are inappropriate.

In contrast, the other side of the argument is that famous people's private lives, and in some cases "private parts," do become journalistic fare. When individuals gain attention, even if only partially because of who they are, then, all aspects of who they are are fair game for media coverage. People in the public eye often depend for their success on the image they project, and many deliberately blur the distinction between their private and public personalities to maintain public interest. For journalists, the issue centers on whether or not public figures use media to promote a particular image of themselves to the public. In the case of transgender celebrities, if such persons are open about their transgender status, and use that status, even in a small way, to gain interest from the public, then some journalists would argue that questions about all aspects of their transgender lives are potentially relevant. For example, Amy Holmes, an anchor at *TheBlaze. com*, argues that the reason that Janet Mock was asked about her genitals on the Piers Morgan show, and was getting national attention, was because she was born with male genitalia, went through surgery, and is now female (Ford 2014). The transformative aspect of her gender identity is central to her public persona, and is therefore, newsworthy. This perspective argues that transgender people have to balance the right to privacy with the desire to have a voice in the public debate through access to media attention. If transgender advocates want access to national media in order to advance conversations about discrimination, violence, and other issues facing the transgender community, then they must accept that in their role as public figures, they give up some of their right to privacy (Vivienne and Burgess 2012). Legally, persons who are "public figures," and who have placed themselves in the public light, through politics or voluntary participation in the public arena, have a significantly diminished privacy interest than others (Reporters Committee for Freedom of the Press 2014).

Additionally, some journalists and some members of the transgender community argue that the job of the news media is to meet the public where they are. The increased visibility of transgender people has increased the natural curiosity of the public about what it means to be transgender, therefore making questions about the physical and emotional aspects of transitioning more likely (Ghazali and Nor 2012). This perspective argues that if the public is open to learning about transgender people, but is currently interested in the physical side of being transgender, then that is the place where journalists need to start the conversation. Hedegaard (2012) states that the transitioning process is an undeniable audience-drawing curiosity factor for the general viewer. Thus, a journalist is not behaving in an unethical or insensitive manner when asking questions about the physical process of transitioning, but rather is doing his or her job by attempting to provide information that addresses the general public's central questions. These critics go on to argue that when transgender people respond to the public's interest by stating, "I don't want to answer questions about my body," they are effectively shutting down a potential avenue for dialogue. While answering questions about genitalia and surgery may be awkward, it is a starting place for opening up broader public dialogue about many more complex and important issues (Vivenne and Burgess 2012). Shutting down the conversation eliminates the opportunity for both educating and learning (James 2007). From this perspective, for advocates that are trying to reach out to unknown, imagined, and potentially antipathic audiences, refusing to discuss certain topics might allow those audiences to create misinformed, inaccurate, and biased understandings from other potentially non-reliable sources (Vivenne and Burgess 2012).

Chaz Bono is an example of a transman who supports the media's role in meeting the audience where they are. Chaz shares his story, hoping that talking about the physical aspects of the transgender experience (that aspects that currently capture the general public's imagination) will spark a deeper dialogue about other issues. Chaz explains that his goal is to educate: "I was put on Earth in this incredibly famous family, and then I'm transgender, and because of that life experience, hopefully, I can educate people" (Hedegaard 2012, 42–45). When interacting with the news media, Chaz is open to questions about his hormonal treatment, his top surgery, and his contemplation of bottom surgery. For example, in a piece for *Rolling Stone* magazine, Chaz discussed the differences between phalloplasty and metoidioplasty, both forms of penile construction surgery (Mocarski et al. 2013). He discussed his top surgery and how his male nipples were constructed and he explained the effects of taking testosterone. Experts argue that by doing so, Chaz has helped to reduce fear and misinformation and to promote normalization of the transitioning process (Mocarski et al. 2013).

Another example that illustrates the reality of great public interest in the physical side of the transgender experience is Thomas Beatie. Thomas Beatie is a transman whose pregnancy got him book deals and interviews with Oprah and numerous magazine spreads (Halberstam 2010). The public consumed news about the "pregnant man." For some, the whole story was sensationalized fluff that catered to public voyeurism and detracted from the real news facing the transgender community—violence and discrimination. For others, the news coverage of Beatie's pregnancy enabled the public to ask direct questions about penis implants, transgender genitals, and other previously off limit topics and thus, helped the public begin to contend with shifts in their understanding of family, belonging, normativity, and gender stability (Halberstam 2010).

A final argument that is raised when it comes to this question of what is private and what is public stems from some transgender advocates' concerns about the transgender community's obsession with extreme gender stereotypes. This perspective argues that the transgender community has adopted as the ideal the hyper-feminine, hypersexualized Barbie aesthetic for transwomen and the hyper-masculine, hypersexualized, macho-man aesthetic for transmen (Ghazali, Suriati, and Nor 2012).[58] The acceptance of these aesthetics as the ideal leads to transgender people feeling like they have to be hyper-feminine or hyper-masculine to pass as "true" males or females (Siebler 2012). Currently, the only way to obtain such a "hyper" masculine or feminine appearance is through surgery. For example, for both non-transgender women and transwomen, it is impossible to get the large breasts, full cheekbones, and tiny chin necessary to meet the hyper-feminized Barbie ideal without surgery. This perspective argues that in order to meet this idealized standard of "man" and "woman," the transgender community has become obsessed with surgery and hormone treatments. To support this claim these critics argue that there are few representations in popular mainstream media of a transgender fictional character or a real-life public figure who defies the pre-op, post-op categories (Siebler 2012). Additionally, locating a transgender identity online that is not transitioning with hormones and/or surgery to a specific gender identity is also extremely rare (Siebler 2012).

Thus, while the "freakshow" storyline (that transgender advocates such as Janet Mock and Laverne Cox are fighting to overcome by arguing that certain types of questions are unethical) is a highly problematic storyline, so too, is the tragic, "I was trapped in the wrong body but now I am a normal man or woman, just like you, let's move on" storyline. Both of these storylines are too one-dimensional (McBee 2012). Media portrayals that are either soft-focused empathy or tawdry headlines are both inaccurate (McBee 2012). Many transgender people don't feel there is anything "wrong" with the body they have, and they don't want to be anything different from what they are. With the focus of media attention on figures that have chosen their gender expressions with the goal to pass fully as the gender they identify with, there is less space in the conversation for transgender people who don't choose surgery, or whose goal is to express as genderqueer rather than to pass as one gender or the other.

Thus, the question of what is considered public or private when dealing with transgender public figures in the news is complex and one that journalists and editors will need to explore in news coverage moving forward. Perhaps the most ethical solution to this question is to write and produce news stories that articulate a more complex view of transgender identities. The more comprehensive story of what it means to be transgender may be the one about the process of transitioning to a fully male, female, or queer identity—including reflections about decisions for or against surgery. These stories may include a discussion of surgery, hormones, and genitalia, as they explore what it means to decide for or against physical changes as a transgender person, but they should also focus on the lived experience of being transgender—the discrimination, the fear of violence, and the acceptance or rejection by family and friends. The real ethical need is for journalists who present complex story lines, who include potential physical changes as an important part of understanding a transgender person's journey, but not as the whole of their identity (McBee 2012). In this way, the conversation can be broadened to include transgender people who choose a queer identity as well as to address issues of violence and discrimination felt by transgender people (Truitt 2014).

The politics of outing: The case of Dr. Vanderbilt and the Magical Putter

The second case study discussed in this chapter moves the conversation from the question of how someone's transgender body is covered by the news media, to the question of how (or if) someone's transgender status is covered by the news media. In January 2014, the online magazine *Grantland* published a story entitled, "Dr. V's Magical Putter" (Hannan 2014). The piece documented the reporter's eight-month investigation to unravel the truth about the Essay Anne Vanderbilt, the inventor of a new piece of golf equipment. In the investigative piece, the reporter revealed that the inventor was a con artist. Dr. Vanderbilt lied about getting her education at MIT and lied about working in the defense industry. Using those lies, she convinced an investor to give her $60,000; money the investor never recouped. Hannan also discovered, and chose to report, that Dr. Vanderbilt was a transwoman, born Stephen Krol. Prior to the publication of the piece, when she learned that Hannan was going to reveal her as a transgender woman as well as reveal her misrepresentation of her educational and professional history, Ms. Vanderbilt committed suicide. Other journalistic outlets, bloggers, transpeople, and social media sites were outraged by the piece, and some blamed Hannan for Dr. Vanderbilt's death. The story provides a powerful case study for exploring media ethics and the practice of outing transgender people through news coverage.

While outing someone as transgender is relatively rare, exploring how the news media have historically approached revealing someone's sexual orientation can help us understand journalistic perspectives on the practice of outing in general. Sexual orientation was once considered similar to other forms of illegal or "immoral" behavior, and thus, was viewed as appropriate news coverage about public figures. If there was evidence to support a claim that a public figure was engaging in homosexual behaviors, then that information was reported in the news coverage surrounding that person. Starting in the 1980s, the mainstream media became reticent to report on someone's sexual orientation. Because being a gay/lesbian/bisexual was still considered a shameful condition, to allege inaccurately (or without sufficient evidence) that someone was gay/lesbian/ bisexual could constitute slander or libel and result in a lawsuit (Newmann 2006). As litigation increased and costs escalated, including sexual orientation as part of the news coverage about a public figure decreased. Instead, during this time, outings in the news were conducted almost exclusively by LGBTQ journalists who chose to out public figures whom they believed were hiding an LGBTQ identity while being publicly anti- LGBTQ (Signorile 2009). Recently though, the practice of including sexual orientation among the descriptive variables provided about subjects of news stories has reemerged. Those in support of this journalistic practice argue that the LGBTQ community has fought long and hard to affirm that gay/lesbian/bisexual orientations are nothing to be ashamed of, and thus, to reveal someone's sexual orientation is simply to indicate a benign aspect of their life. Further, by leaving it out, one perpetuates the idea that it is shameful (Newmann 2006). This perspective is supported by Morris (2004) who argues that resistance to outing famous historical figures perpetuates the idea that there is something negative about being gay. In his essay on Abraham Lincoln's sexual orientation, for instance, Morris argues that historians and journalists should present evidence regarding the sexual orientation of famous figures because it is relevant to understanding that person's lived experiences, and because it reinforces the idea that there is nothing "wrong or bad" about being homosexual. Additionally, Morris argues that by denying the evidence that famous and well-respected historical figures might have been homosexual, society is denying a legacy of role models for LGBT people.

Many journalists currently make the same arguments used in support of revealing one's sexual orientation in the press as arguments in support of revealing that someone is transgender. They argue that being transgender is simply a part of someone's description, like age, political affiliation, or name, and to hide it implies it is something shameful. This perspective argues that society's impressions and stereotypes about transgender can be eliminated if the press more fully informs viewers and readers about the key facts in a newsworthy transgender case, including the transgender status of the key persons involved. Additionally, in cases like the Dr. Vanderbilt case, the fact that Dr. Vanderbilt once lived under a different name is not irrelevant to the story (Levin 2014). When the goal of the piece is in-depth investigation, finding that the subject of an investigation changed their name and created a new persona is important to cover, and likewise, finding that someone changed their name and gender expression and created a new persona might be relevant. A change in gender identity could help explain to the reader why a reporter might have had difficulty researching a subject's background, for example (Levin 2014).

Other journalists, however, condemn the practice of outing someone in the news as an invasion of privacy that makes a decision for someone else that should properly be his or her decision alone. Additionally, while one might claim that being transgender is "nothing to be ashamed of," the reality is that hate crimes against people who are transgender exist. The Transgender Murder Monitoring Project estimates that once every three days a transgender person is murdered (Walkley 2014). Additionally, over 41 percent of those who identify as transgender have made a suicide attempt (Walkley 2014). With such high rates of violence and depression, transgender people may be more uniquely vulnerable to the negative effects of public "outings." Many transgender people make great efforts to align their gender identity (the gender they feel they are) with their gender expression (the gender they present to others). Getting "read" (identified as transgender) can be a demoralizing blow to the individual's self-confidence, and it can negatively impact their safety. Passing is about survival (James 2007). Because transgender people are often targets for violence, being able to walk down a street or enter a club or restaurant without having people recognize you as transgender keeps you safe from potential attacks. For these reasons, fear that newspapers will reveal their transgender status might reduce the likelihood that transgender people report crimes against them (Denno 1993).

In addition to concerns about violence, individuals in the transgender community also need to be concerned with discrimination as a result of outing. Not all transphobia results in violence (Cram 2012). Transphobia can also be expressed in employment, education, housing, health care, the military, and legal discrimination. Once someone is outed as transgender in the news, the original news outlet has no control over where that information goes. The individual may lose his or her job, military benefits, and access to affordable health care, safe educational environments, and housing.

A final argument that is raised in the discussion of whether or not it is ethical to out someone in print is the argument that in the case of transgender people, revealing their transgender status is equivalent to revealing private, medical information. Steps that a transgender individual may make to transition are recognized by the American Medical Association and the United States Tax Court as medical treatments for the misalignment of their physical sex and gender identity (American Trans Man 2014). Some journalist therefore, argue that information about a trans person's status and/or transition should be held in confidence just like any other person's private medical issues and treatments and should not be disclosed in print.

Legally, the Supreme Court has addressed the issue of privacy and ruled on the side of publication of names in crime-related news. The court ruled that information relative to the commission, investigation, and persecution of crimes is public interest (Johnson 1999). Once a news organization learns information about a public matter, its publication of that information cannot be restricted (Johnson 1999). The Supreme Court has given the press near immunity for publishing accurate information that is obtained from public documents and governmental proceedings, and information obtained legally from other sources is also protected. Judges argue that courts cannot logically rule that a basic fact, such as a name, is private in one situation and not in others. Additionally, they argue that a press that systematically omits information (in this case names related to crime and punishment) cannot be a reliable monitor of the criminal justice system (Johnson 1999). The legal justice system has left the door open by stating that speech can be restricted if it poses a clear and present danger of causing substantive harm. However, "clear and present danger" and "substantive harm" are terms that are difficult to define, and courts have consistently ruled that news organizations cannot be prohibited from or punished for, publishing truthful information even if it has some potential to harm victims (Johnson 1999).

Thus, the question of whether or not to out someone as transgender in a news story is an ethical one that has no easy answers. Is someone's transgender identity newsworthy? Is it relevant to the story at hand? Is it unethical not to report it, as deliberately leaving out information such as names or gender identity decreases credibility and is unethical reporting? These are questions that those involved in presenting the news to the general public must address more fully as news coverage of transgender people increases. Perhaps the best guidance on this issue comes from newsman Josh Levin who stated in regard to Hannan's piece on Dr. Vanderbilt that the issue was not that Hannan revealed Dr. Vanderbilt's identity as a transwoman; rather the issue was *how* he revealed it (Levin 2014). His choice of words such as "remarkable," "strange," "odd," and "deceitful," "liar," and "a chill ran up my spine" in reference to finding out Dr. Vanderbilt's birth name, were all choices that made the piece feel cold-hearted and unsympathetic to the reality of life as a transgender person (Levin 2014). Hannan could have avoided much of the negative reaction he received simply by using more neutral and objective language in his writing of the piece.

Additionally, editors and reporters do not have the luxury of being uneducated about issues that are foreign to them. When they are uneducated, they may inadvertently contribute to a tragic confluence of events by simply not understanding the real level of risk of tragedy (Tracy Moore 2014b). Dr. Vanderbilt's story should have been handled with care and concern, with the understanding that the very hardship of being transgender could impact an individual's way of managing her life and her own past and the extent to which she'd be comfortable disclosing it (Tracy Moore 2014b). Thus, it is imperative that journalists educate themselves about the facts and the implications of revealing those facts to others.

Conclusion

While the answers about how best to address the various ethical questions that arise when covering transgender issues will likely evolve along with the coverage of such issues, there are choices and approaches that journalists and editors can make in order to ensure that media coverage of transgender issues meets high standards of professionalism. Included here are some key suggestions about how to approach covering transgender issues in the news media:

1. Use the gender pronoun and name preferred by subject of the news item whenever possible. If you are not sure and cannot ask, use the name and pronoun that match the way in which the person is living their life and presenting themselves to the world. If the individual presents as gender neutral, be sure to inquire as to what pronoun they prefer you use.
2. Do not ask a transgender person unexpected questions relative to surgery, intercourse with partners, or genitalia while "live on the air." Ask permission in advance to address those kinds of questions and only ask the questions of this nature that you have prior permission for. Additionally, remember that the presence or absence of surgery/hormone therapy is often irrelevant to many news stories, and thus, should not be addressed at all.
3. If your media outlet supports a decision to "out" someone for a transgender identity, do not "out" them without notice. Inform the individual that the piece will be running and when it will be released. Remember that publicity and outing may destroy a life or career, so be certain that your news organization fully understands the potential impact of public outing.
4. A lot of how you present an issue is in the language and word choice you use. In the Dr. Vanderbilt article, author Caleb Hannan describes the moment he realized that the subject of his story was a transwoman by writing, "a chill ran down my spine." As this phrase in popular use is typically in reference to something scary, haunted, or horrifying, using it

in this context was a poor choice. Be careful of word choice and terms you use to discuss transgender issues. Stating, "Bonnie Cullen, a transgender woman, was killed last night," versus, "A man who lived life as a woman was murdered last night" changes the tone of a piece. Be very reflective about the language you use when writing about people who are transgender. GLAAD (2014) has a good reference guide that helps identify terms to avoid when writing about transgender issues.

5. Be certain to create ways that you can be open and responsive to comments and feedback on your news piece. For example, news media now are online and the social media element allows the people who are subjects of news to respond to the news coverage about themselves. Be certain the opportunity for the transgender community to help set the news agenda and tell a story from their perspective is in place.

6. When covering news about transgender people, be certain to provide definitions and background for the reader to ensure clarity. What is gender, biological sex, sexual orientation, gender expression, and so on? Being careful about the terminology that you use and define those terms for others to ensure clarity and understanding and give the public a language they can use to discuss transgender issues (GLADD 2014).

7. If your news organization questions whether or not to run a piece, or has concerns about the reception of a piece, it might be a good idea to have someone from the transgender community read through the piece prior to publication. This can be helpful to ensure that the language use is objective and appropriate and that there is no negative bias. However, this is only appropriate when there is no possibility that the news would be significantly altered or denied publication as a result of the feedback, as it could be taken as news being suppressed due to outside influence.

14

The Harm of Video Games: The Ethics Behind Regulating Minors' Access to Violent Video Games in Light of the Supreme Court Ruling

Ryan Rogers

Violent tragedies, such as the Columbine massacre, the 2011 mass murder in Norway, and the Sandy Hook shootings are often linked to violent video games (Rotunda 2004), with some politicians and video game regulation advocates claiming violent video game content might cause children to act violently (Gaskill 2010). For years, these same advocates have attempted to regulate children's access to video game content. Regulation of harmful content in video games has been attempted many times before in the United States; in 2005 there were more than sixty bills designed to limit access to violent and sexual content in video games (Sweeting 2005), but the *Entertainment Merchants Association* case marks the first Supreme Court evaluation of the issue. To date, considerable attention has focused on both the legal ground and the attitudinal/behavioral aspects of this topic, but a thorough examination of the ethical underpinnings is lacking. Thus, now is a critical time to examine how ethics fit into the issue of violent video game regulation.

One of the most important developments in this debate was the recent Supreme Court of the United States decision in *Brown v. Entertainment Merchants Association* (formerly known as *Schwarzenegger v. Entertainment Merchants Association*).[1] In this case, the Supreme Court decided to strike down a statute banning the sale of violent video games to minors. In light of this landmark case, it is as important as ever to understand the role of ethics in the Court's decision. This study will examine previous arguments and literature regarding the regulation/effects of violent video games with special attention to ethical considerations. In particular, this case raises an ethical debate: Is it better to protect minors from potential harm and empower parents or allow individual freedom to produce and consume video game content? Specifically, this study will discuss this case within the context of harm, paternalism, and responsibility as well as detail the author's conclusions on the issues.

In the United States, many cases concerning regulation of minors' access to video game content exist. *Video Software Dealers Association v. Maleng* (2008), *American Amusement Machine Association v. Kendrick* (2001), *Entertainment Software Association v. Blagojevich* (2005), *Interactive Digital Software Association v. St. Louis* (2003), and *Entertainment Software Association v. Granholm* (2005) are just some of the cases from various states that have addressed statutes similar to the statute challenged in the *Entertainment Merchants* case.[2] Despite the desire to protect children from harm, the outcome has been universal in all of these cases. None of the courts have upheld these laws as they were found to be in violation of the First Amendment. While this chapter focuses on United States law and policy, the regulation of violent video games is a global issue with different countries reaching different conclusions on regulating video games. For example, a German ban on violent video games was abandoned in favor of better consumer education (Purchese 2010). In the Netherlands it is illegal to sell violent video games to minors based on the premise that violent content is harmful (Wetboek van Strafrecht 2004) and Switzerland opted to completely ban violent video games (Parfitt 2010). Meanwhile, specific video games have been banned all over the world for a variety of reasons: China banned *Command and Conquer Generals* for its portrayal of China, Australia banned *Getting Up: Contents Under Pressure* because it featured graffiti which is illegal in Australia, and United States military bases banned *Medal of Honor* because an early version of the game allowed players to assume the role of a Taliban member (GlobalPost 2010). The global scope and diverse conclusions surrounding this issue highlight the importance of using ethical concepts to interpret the Supreme Court of the United States decision. For the purposes of this chapter, and for the sake of feasibility, I will focus on the United States policy. Specifically, this chapter will tease apart how ethical concepts like harm, paternalism, and responsibility factor in to this debate.

Background of the Case and the Ethics in Play

In 2005, California passed a statute banning the sale of violent video games to anyone under the age of eighteen, requiring labeling beyond the existing

Entertainment Software Ratings Board (ESRB) rating system, and imposing a fine for any infraction. The law was set to go into effect in 2006. In anticipation of the harmful effects of this legislation on the video game industry, the Video Software Dealers Association filed suit against the state of California in the United States District Court for the Northern District of California. The Video Software Dealers Association, a trade organization in the video game industry, obtained a preliminary injunction in December of 2005 to block enforcement of the statute (note: the Video Software Dealers party is replaced by the Entertainment Merchants Association in the Supreme Court ruling).

Essentially, California argued that the regulation protects children from harmful video game content. Conversely, the video game industry argued that regulating this content is a violation of the First Amendment and is thus harmful. Based on the state's argument that violent video games are harmful to minors, it is worthwhile to examine ethical conceptualizations of harm. John Stuart Mill's (1863) harm principle states "the only purpose for which power can be rightfully exercised over any member of a civilized community, against his will, is to prevent harm to others." In other words, individual rights should only be limited when exercising them is harmful to someone else. Mill's harm principle allows for a large amount of individual liberty while highlighting the importance of protecting the freedoms and rights of others. While the principle is straightforward, application may be more complicated. One important question that comes to mind is: what constitutes harm?

Joel Feinberg (1984, 1985) has further examined harm. Feinberg's definition of harm is often understood as a wrongful setback to another's interests. The operative word in this case is wrongful, which Feinberg describes as an unjustified faulty act. In other words, the setback must be unfair. This means that an act could not be considered wrongful if the victim consented to the harm or possibility of harm, like partaking in a competition where risks are assumed. Also, a setback is an obstruction to progress.

Feinberg (1984) states that liberty might be limited in light of the harm principle or the offense principle. This harm principle is a refined version of Mill's harm principle that reflects Feinberg's definition of harm as a wrongful setback to interests. The offense principle indicates that acts that are seriously offensive to others should be prohibited by law. Feinberg (1984) suggests that when these principles are fulfilled individual rights might be limited and a regulation such as the video game ban would be ethical. That is, something that is upsetting to another might be regulated ethically.

Feinberg (1984) also describes aggregative harm and accumulative harm. Aggregative harm describes acts that as a whole are harmful, but may actually be positive on an individual level. Feinberg uses the example of drinking alcohol by proposing that, generally, alcohol consumption causes harm and banning it would have positive effects. However, a ban would also restrict many people from casual, harmless, enjoyable drinking. Accumulative harm refers to acts that on a small scale are harmless but on a large scale are harmful. Feinberg uses the example of pollution; one person polluting by driving a car is not nearly as harmful as large-scale industrial pollution. Stewart (2001), however, points out that these harms, as defined by Feinberg, do not address acts that are inherently harmful, but rather acts that are harmful in particular contexts.

Accordingly, Deni Elliot (2007), in a more recent work, suggests that Mill has been misunderstood such that aggregate good is confused with arithmetic good. Arithmetic good refers to the idea that an action is just because it is good for the majority but may harm the minority. Elliot argues that this is different from Mill's central argument which, according to Elliot, can more accurately be described as aggregate good or the importance of considering the well-being of *all* people impacted by the action. As a result Elliot offers a decision tree to determine if an action is just that will be implemented later:

Utilitarian Decision Tree

1. What is the intended action?
2. Will it cause harm? If not, no analysis needed. If yes, review principles of justice.
3. Is someone being denied legal rights? If so, action is unjust.
4. Is someone being denied moral rights? If so, action is unjust.
5. Is the person being harmed getting what he/she deserves? Or, is the person being helped getting what he/she deserves? If so, action is just.
6. Has the person being harmed had a promise broken to him/her? If so, action is unjust.
7. Has everyone in the situation been treated impartially? If so, the action is just. In the rare occasions that exceptions to following these rules are justified, it is essential to show how the exception will lead to the aggregate good and how following the rule will not lead to the greatest good for the whole group. Only if the action has been determined to be just, advance to the utilitarian calculus:

8. How will harming this individual promote the overall good of the community? Consider whether the community will be better or worse if everyone knows that individuals can be harmed in this way for this reason.
9. How will the community be harmed if the proposed action is not taken? Consider whether the community will be better or worse if everyone knows that individuals will NOT be harmed in this way for this reason.

The state also contended that, under the First Amendment, sexual content can be regulated for minors, while violent content is protected. This means it is illegal to sell depictions of nudity to children but legal to sell children depictions of violence. Ultimately, the Supreme Court came down on the side of the First Amendment. First, violent video game content does not meet the standard for either obscenity or variable obscenity. Obscenity refers to content that appeals to prurient interests, lacks political or social value, and violates reasonable community standards.[3] Obscene material is not protected by the First Amendment and can thus be regulated by the government. California argued that violent video game content should be considered under the *variable* obscenity standard found in 1968's *Ginsberg v. New York*.[4] The variable obscenity standard suggests content not considered obscene for adults might qualify as obscene for minors, such as certain sexual content. The implementation of the variable obscenity standard is meant to address how some content may be particularly harmful to minors but not to adults. Thus, California claimed that the variable obscenity standard was appropriate because regulating access to violent video games protects minors from harmful content but allows adults unrestricted access to violent video games. The Supreme Court did not agree. The ethical issue at play here is empowering adults to control the content their children consume. This highlights the ethical concept of paternalism.

Paternalism prohibits actions in order to prevent harm to the one performing the act (Feinberg 1971). Legal paternalism refers to the justification of the state in preventing harm to the self or guiding individuals to their own good (Dworkin 2010). Dworkin (2010) offers the following procedure for classifying a policy as paternalistic: X is paternalistic of Y by doing Z. Doing Z must interfere with the freedom of Y. X does Z without Y's consent. X does Z in order to promote the welfare of Y. For example, the state might prohibit the consumption of alcohol by making it illegal. Making this illegal interferes with the people's freedom to drink. The state has done so without the approval of the people. The state has made consuming alcohol illegal to reduce crime and death of the people.

According to Feinberg (1971), there are two types of paternalism, strong and weak. Strong paternalism suggests that a government can prohibit someone's self-inflicted harm against his or her will. Weak paternalism allows the government to protect an individual from harm to the self when the act in nonvoluntary. Feinberg notes that in order for the government to interfere with an individual's actions, the action must create a high level of risk and be unreasonable. High level of risk is fairly self-explanatory especially in light of the preceding harm discussion, but Feinberg admits that "unreasonable" can change depending on the context. The example Feinberg uses suggests that it is unreasonable to drive at sixty miles per hour in a twenty-mile-per-hour zone, but it might be reasonable to speed in order to get a pregnant woman to the hospital. This means that speeding is, in large part, risky and unreasonable, but in certain cases there might be a justified reason for doing so.

Lastly, the Supreme Court ruled that without applying the variable obscenity standard, the regulation of violent video game content is considered a content-based regulation and content-based regulations must survive strict scrutiny. Strict scrutiny refers to a judicial test that a statute must pass in order to justify a restriction of citizen's rights, in this case, free speech. Strict scrutiny requires the statute to serve a compelling government interest, meaning that the regulation is necessary and undoubtedly serves the public good and the government's interest. Strict scrutiny also requires that the regulation be narrowly tailored such that it is not overbroad and directly addresses the government interest. The act failed the test of strict scrutiny and is unconstitutional. The Supreme Court's opinion—written by Justice Scalia—noted that the Court is not responsible for deciding if violent video games are harmful toward children but only if a regulation can be legally justified. In other words, even if the government wants to protect children it must work within the Constitution. Thus, the Court's decision seems to hinge on legal precedent as opposed to the ethics involved in protecting children from possibly harmful content; the Court does not suggest that regulation of video game content is unethical but rather that the *type* of regulation is paramount. Indeed, the Court raised such issues. For example, Justice Alito argued that while the California statute is unconstitutional, there are certain depictions of violence that are inappropriate for minors so there may be justification for regulation of violent video game content. Similarly, Alito expressed concern over the unknown effects of video game technology, saying that the Court should make a better effort to understand the technology before making a ruling. This clearly positions the Court as an organization that does not necessarily adjudicate on ethics but instead focuses on legality.

The passages from the Court's judgment referred to here raise the following questions: Who is responsible for protecting children from this content? Is it the responsibility of the government to protect children from violent video game content or does the responsibility belong elsewhere? If the government is not responsible for regulation, then responsibility belongs to one or a combination of the following: game developers/studios, video game retailers, parents, and video game players. Where, ethically, does responsibility lie?

Dworkin (1999) suggests that citizens should be afforded moral freedom to be responsible for their own decisions. Likewise, video game players are not responsible for avoiding violent content if it appeals to them (McCormick 2001). However, corporations should bear some social responsibility for what they produce (Robin and Reidenbach 1987). In fact, Peter Molyneux, former CEO of video game company Lionhead Studios, has stated that the video game industry has a moral responsibility to the lessons they teach (Takahashi 2005). This suggests that the responsibility may be divided among multiple parties, primarily, the individual, and the content producers.

Currently, the ESRB is a self-policing organization that can punish publishers for not fully disclosing controversial content like harsh language and violence (ESRB.org 2014a). But some may question the effectiveness of the ESRB as a self-policing organization because there exists a conflict of interest between maximizing profit and protecting audience members. In other words, why would the industry deliberately try to limit their sales and thereby damage their profits?

The ESRB has also been criticized for not playing through an entire game before deciding on a rating, so some argue the ratings are uninformed and sometimes inaccurate (Grabianowksi 2014). Indeed, content producers are asked to provide the most controversial aspects of the game to the ratings board and a decision on the rating is made based on that. As a result, it would be easy for content producers to obscure some of the game's content or for some content to be overlooked. One famous example of this is the "Hot Coffee" incident in *Grand Theft Auto San Andreas* (Feldman 2005). In this sequence the player has sex with an in-game girlfriend. This scene was not reported to the ESRB but many players found the sequence when using a mod (a shift in the game's code to provide a different experience than what the content producers provided).

The ESRB is open to further criticism because of their lack of authority over retailers. All of the ratings from the ESRB can be rendered worthless if retailers do not adhere to them. Currently, retailers do not face any penalty, besides possibly bad public relations, if they sell mature video game content to minors. Retailers could be an effective instrument to practice regulation of video game content because they can actually control the product without compromising creative license. But again, this creates a conflict of interest because retailers do not want to limit who can purchase games for reasons of profitability.

The ESRB tries to increase media literacy, such that consumers are informed about video games and video game content (ESRB.org 2014b). Media literacy refers to the ability of someone to evaluate and produce media in a variety of formats (Kubey 1997). The idea is that someone who is media literate can understand media without being too influenced by it. This is a worthwhile goal and is critical to protecting minors from potentially harmful content. The efficacy of the ESRB on this goal is up for debate.

The last group that may be responsible for regulating violent video game content is parents. Parents should be afforded some authority to determine what media their children consume. Arguably, parents can control what content their children are exposed to. However, obvious concerns arise here as well. Some parents may not be available to watch over their children or some parents may lack the media literacy to effectively regulate content. Similarly, some children may be able to access content when their parents are not around. Also, there is no uniformity as far as what different parents may deem appropriate or inappropriate. Furthermore, this is already practiced in some capacity. Parents already have the option to oversee their children's video game play, determine which games they buy, etc. In short, parents cannot control everything their children have access to.

Analysis of Supreme Court decision through ethical lenses

The Supreme Court held, citing *Erznoznik v. Jacksonville* (1975), that minors can only have their First Amendment rights limited in very narrow circumstances.[5] *Erznoznik* states clearly that a state cannot restrict the rights of minors to access nonobscene material simply because the state thinks it is unsuitable. Despite this, Justice Thomas disagrees claiming that even if minors have First Amendment protection to express themselves, this does not allow for any message, such as violent video games, to reach minors without parental consent.

From here, it is important to understand whether or not the California statute qualifies as paternalism. The statute could be considered paternalistic because it restricts minors' access to video game content for their own good (Feinberg 1971). According to Dworkin (2010), X (the state) is paternalistic of Y (minors) by doing Z (restricting access to violent video games). Doing Z must interfere with the freedom of Y—it does because the free speech rights of children are impeded. However, Justice Thomas argues in his judgment that this is *not* a violation of children's rights. X does Z without Y's consent—this is fulfilled as well. Children, or even parents, did not consent to this regulation. X does Z in order to promote the welfare of Y—the statute is meant to prevent harm to children. Each of these items is satisfied so the statute does indeed qualify as paternalism. Also, the statute would qualify as strong paternalism according to Feinberg (1971) because the harmful act of playing violent video games is voluntary. It is difficult to imagine a situation in which an individual would play a violent video game involuntarily. In order for the government to uphold such a statute, the act of playing violent video games must be considered a high level of risk and unreasonable (Feinberg 1971). The Supreme Court asserted that the act of playing violent video games is not adequately risky. Determining whether or not it is "unreasonable" is a bit more difficult. In the case of video games, it may be reasonable to play violent games once in a while and in a private setting but it may be unreasonable to play them constantly or publicly. Barring extreme cases, like prolonged play, it is difficult to qualify violent video game play as unreasonable. Of course, these arguments rely on providing minors with the rights of an adult. If the rights of minors are classified differently, then we should expect paternalistic regulation to be applied and the Court may have been wrong in this instance.

The Court claims that the state, by asking for application of the *Ginsberg* standard of variable obscenity, is asking them to substantially reconsider the definition of obscenity as it relates to the First Amendment. The Court ruled that the variable obscenity standard is only relevant as applied to sexual content, not violent content which is presumed protected. If the Court allowed the use of variable obscenity, it would create a whole new category of restricted speech. In other words, regulating violence as obscenity would redefine obscenity. While *Ginsberg* does cite the rights of parents and the protection of children from harmful content as interests of applying the standard, it currently can only be applied to sexual content.

The Supreme Court has been clear in limiting obscenity to sexual content. *Memoirs v. Massachusetts* (1966) does not address violent content in its definition of obscenity.[6] In *Memoirs*, the Supreme Court ruled that a work with any social or literary value should not be considered obscene. An argument could be made that most violent video games have some social or literary value, as violence is often just a piece of a larger narrative. While violence is a major component of *Grand Theft Auto 4*, the violence is just a portion of a larger story about an illegal immigrant surviving in the United States (Calvert 2008). *Call of Duty: Modern Warfare 2* features a lot of violence and gunplay, but takes place in the context of Russian politics and global security (Thorsen 2009). It would be unfair to classify video games as a medium lacking meaningful characters, stories, and themes when other media are defended based on this premise. Justice Breyer is careful to point out the anomaly that, based on the majority opinion's logic, a video game can only be regulated for minors when it features sexual content regardless of how violent the game may be or how valuable it might be artistically or educationally. This anomaly is distressing and highlights the difference between what is legal and what is ethical.

Legally, the Court has created a paradox where children are protected from sexual content but not violent content. The Court does not offer a convincing reason for this distinction outside of the established legal definition of obscenity and Justice Breyer points this out. Thus the Court's argument against the application of the variable obscenity standard is not necessarily getting at the ethics of the issue—potential harm to children. The Court acknowledges the importance of the ethical concern in protecting children but based on legal precedent, arguments, and definitions regarding obscenity, violent video games cannot be regulated in this way. According to Mill's "harm principle" access to violent video games can be regulated if they cause players to act violently against others. The Supreme Court ruled that there is no proof of harm in this context and thus the statute does not qualify as a justified restriction under the harm principle.

If video games were proven harmful more thoroughly, the regulation would qualify under Mill's harm principle, but it still would not qualify as a "wrongful set-back" according to Feinberg. For a setback to be wrongful the victim must not consent to the act. Again, it is difficult to imagine a situation where someone would be forced to play a video game against his or her will. Video games are rarely thrust upon individuals and thus the act of play could be considered implicit consent. Further, Mill argues that, as long as others are not hurt, one has the right to harm him or herself.

Feinberg actually discusses legislation similar to the California statute in detail. When discussing the assertion that violent pornography promotes rape and violence toward women, Feinberg (1984) states that the regulation of pornography should only be allowed if strong, causal evidence was presented. In fact, the evidence would have to be so strong that the connection between rape and pornography could qualify as incitement. Legally, incitement refers to words or communication that will incite violence or an immediate breach of the peace.[7] The regulation of video games is not much different from this example; in order to regulate violent video games, there must be strong evidence that games incite violent behavior. At this point, this degree of evidence does not exist. To date, social science researchers have not reached a consensus on the issue of violent video games and harmful effects on children; researchers are careful when they interpret their data and often suggest that a deeper understanding of video game effects is necessary. A small cross-section of studies indicate that violent video games may not produce higher arousal nor do they induce more aggressive thoughts than nonviolent games (Ivory and Kalyanaraman 2007), games might be a unique tool to aid education (Gee 2007) and video games might actually be used to promote prosocial behaviors (Gentile et al. 2009). Meanwhile, a meta-analysis on the effects of violent video games indicates that playing violent video games increases aggressive thoughts and behaviors (Anderson 2003) but another meta-analysis indicates that playing violent games does not increase violent behavior (Ferguson 2007). While video games can have an influence on people exposed to them, the exact effects have not been clearly defined. As such, the Court appropriately points out that there is not substantial evidence to indicate this regulation would help to serve the interest of protecting children. While violent video games *may* cause violent behavior, the evidence thus far is not definitive so it should not be treated as such. Consequently, video game play does not result in an immediate breach of the peace even if games do raise arousal, heart rate, etc.

In *Brown v. Entertainment Merchants Association*, the government's interest was in protecting children from harmful content. But the Court rejected the state's argument that the government can regulate content if it merely anticipates harm.[8] The Court stated that a more appropriate standard can be found in the 2000 *United States v. Playboy Entertainment Group* case.[9] Accordingly, the Supreme Court ruled that the evidence presented by the state was insubstantial as the evidence relied on correlations to harm and did not test causality. Furthermore, the Court asserted that other media, like cartoons, can have the same so-called negative effects as video games, though there were concerns about the unique effects of video games. There may be effects unique to video games but the effects are still being researched and some of the effects might actually be positive. For example, video games can be effective educational tools (Gee 2007).

For aggregative harm, one might concede that video game play can cause violent behavior in *some* minors but in many cases it would not. For accumulative harm, violent media might contribute overall to violent perceptions and attitudes but playing violent video games on an individual level is not necessarily harmful (Gerbner and Gross 1976). Even so, Feinberg would reject these arguments by arguing this expression should not be restricted even if harmful outcomes are more than chance occurrences (Stewart 2001). Lastly, Feinberg's "offense principle" can be applied to violent content in video games. Some people may be offended by violent video game content, thus it could potentially be regulated under the offense principle. However, this restriction does not seem necessary for one to avoid offensive game content. If one believes that a game is offensive, he or she does not have to be exposed to it. As such, the statute would not qualify under the offense principle either.

In order to more fully explore this decision, I will now run the Court's ruling through Elliot's (2007) decision tree. First, we ask what the intended action is. In this case, the intended action is protecting children from harm. Then, will it cause harm? This legislation may limit the First Amendment rights of children as well as those in the video game industry. Is someone being denied legal rights? Yes. First Amendment rights are infringed. As a result, the action is unjust. However, for an intellectual exercise, I will examine the rest of the decision tree. Is someone being denied moral rights? When Elliot talks about moral rights, she is referencing civil rights that may not necessarily be recognized as legal rights. As such, we might say that the paternalism inherent in the law denies children their moral right of self-determination. Thus, the legislation is unjust. Is the person harmed receiving a just punishment? No, as those harmed are being done so a priori. But is the person being helped getting what they are entitled to? Perhaps. One could argue that children are getting help that they deserve as they are being protected. Has a promise broken to someone? Given that the First Amendment is a right, this could be conceived as a broken promise. Has everyone in the situation been treated impartially? No. Children are being treated as a special population, which may be acceptable, but more importantly the video game industry is treated differently than other media industries that produce violent content.

Based on this analysis, the legislation is not just. However, Elliot (2007) indicates that sometimes exceptions are made if they serve the aggregate good. Thus, there are two more questions to answer. How will this action promote the overall good of the community? And how will a lack of the action harm the community? Infringing on the rights of the video game industry and the rights of children could, at the very least, protect children from experiencing distressing content. At most, it could reduce the number of violent acts committed by those who play violent video games. Conversely, the video game industry will be hurt financially and many people would not be able to play video games that give them enjoyment.

Lastly, the Court also states that a regulation must be narrowly tailored and be executed in the least restrictive means possible. If the government interest can be served by a less restrictive means, then the less restrictive means must be sought. The Court suggests the statute is not narrowly tailored because it unjustly singles out the video game industry. Likewise, the Court suggests the statute is not the least restrictive means because the current self-policing rating system (ESRB) is sufficient (ESRB.org 2014a). Justice Breyer, however, asserts that this system is flawed, while Justice Alito worries the self-policing system will deteriorate if the video game industry does not have the perpetual threat of government regulation.

There is no obvious answer to the question of how to regulate violent video games. According to Dworkin (2010), moral sovereignty should be given to individuals and thus individuals are responsible for their own decisions. While this is certainly true for adults, it may not always be the best approach for children. But limiting children's access to video games is limiting access to modern culture and informative aspects of the world (Calvert 2009). Also, video games might offer a litany of positive effects that would be stagnated through video game regulation. Currently, there is no perfect answer. Perhaps the ideal regulation would be video game developers and publishers regulating themselves. Corporations have a responsibility to society (Robin and Reidenbach 1987). The government has denied responsibility for regulating this issue and parents may not be capable. For now, rating systems like the ESRB are likely the best solution. The ESRB is not flawless, its authority is limited, and it does create a conflict of interest, but improving the functionality of the ESRB is a reasonable way to protect children from harmful content. Rather than spend time and money pursuing government regulations that fail, advocates of video game regulation should spend time and money trying to improve unsatisfactory aspects of the ESRB.

Conclusion

When looking at the ethical issues of this case holistically, interesting findings emerge. First, in virtually every instance the harm of video games is questionable. Similarly, the statute qualifies as strong paternalism. However, considering that the statute is aimed at children, a paternalistic statute might be appropriate. Indeed, sometimes it may be effective to limit children's autonomy in order to educate or protect them. Without paternalistic rules, children can harm or upset themselves. A child may not know how a certain action will impact him or her. Based on this premise, the statute might be justified under paternalism. This is a particularly valid point considering the variable obscenity standard. Again, this standard indicates that some content may be considered obscene for children but not for adults. In this instance the Court is willing to uphold paternal laws when related to sexual content but not violent content. From a legal perspective, this decision follows precedent. From an ethical perspective, this is confounding. The Court required clear causal evidence that games harm children to justify the statute. That degree of evidence does not exist; neither does such a degree of evidence exist for sexual content. The question remains: Why was the Court willing to be paternalistic in relation to sexual content but not violent content? Ethically, a justification for this statute exists under paternalism.

However, this legislation does not only impact children. Issues arise when the law starts to impact others, that is adults who may be limited by this law. In this case, the legislation restricts the rights of content producers. The law did two things. One—it banned the sale of violent video games to those under the age of eighteen. While this does impact vendors and the video game industry, this portion can likely be justified as paternalism. Two—the law required the video game producer to adopt a state-run labeling system. This was considered compelled speech and thus violated the rights of the video games industry. This dimension of the law is difficult to justify especially given the current ESRB labeling system. The ESRB provides thorough information on game content. There is no evidence to suggest that these labeling measures are ineffective. Further, the ESRB already prohibits the sale of violent video games to minors. Essentially, the ESRB already voluntarily practices the things the law aims to enforce. As a result, the law is redundant. It seems the law would be more effective, and ethical, if it focused on enhancing the ESRB rather than replacing it.

Based on the foregoing analysis, the Supreme Court was legally correct in affirming the Ninth Circuit's opinion to enjoin the statute in *Brown v.*

Entertainment Merchants Association. The statute should not be considered under the variable obscenity standard because variable obscenity does not include violence. Likewise, the statute should not survive because multiple courts have found no substantial evidence that the statute serves the compelling governmental interest and, furthermore, the statute has not been considered the least restrictive means to serve the governmental interest. The statute also does not adequately address harm to minors, according to Mill and Feinberg but the law might be considered paternalistic. Minors' rights in this country are loosely defined and that makes ethical considerations difficult but worthwhile.

Notes

1 Brown v. Entertainment Merchants Association, 564 U. S. (2011); Brief of Respondents, Schwarzenegger v. Entertainment Merchants Association, 130 S. Ct. 2398 (2010) (No. 08–1448).

2 Video Software Dealers Association v. Maleng, 325 F. Supp. 2d 1180 (2008); American Amusement Machine Association v. Kendrick, 244 F.3d 572 (7th Cir. 2001); Entertainment Software Association v. Blagojevich, 404 F. Supp. 2d 1051 (N.D. Ill. 2005); Interactive Digital Software Association *v. St. Louis*, 329 F.3d 954 (8th Cir. 2003); Entertainment Software Association v. Granholm, 404 F. Supp. 2d 978 (E.D. Mich. 2005).

3 Miller v. California, 413 U.S. 15 (1973).

4 Ginsberg v. New York, 390 U.S. 629 (1968).

5 Erznoznik v. City of Jacksonville, 422 U.S. 205 (1975).

6 Memoirs v. Massachusetts, 383 U.S. 413 (1966).

7 Chaplinsky v. New Hampshire, 315 U.S. 568 (1942).

8 Turner Broadcasting System, Inc. v. FCC, 512 U.S. 622, 664 (1994).

9 United States v. Playboy Entertainment Group, 529 U.S. 803 (2000).

Section Four

Identity in a Digital World

15

Paradigm Shift: Media Ethics in the Age of Intelligent Machines

David J. Gunkel

During the first conference on cyberspace convened at the University of Texas in 1990 (ancient times as far as the internet is concerned), Sandy Stone provided articulation of what can now, in retrospect, be identified as one of the guiding principles of new media ethics: "No matter how virtual the subject becomes, there is always a body attached" (Stone 1991, 111). What Stone sought to point out with this brief but insightful comment is the fact that despite what appears online, behind the scenes of the screen there is always another user—another person who is essentially like us. This other may appear in the guise of different virtual characters, screen names, profiles, or avatars, but there is always some*body* behind it all.

This insight has served us well. It has helped users navigate the increasingly complicated interpersonal relationships made possible by network-connected computers. It has assisted researchers in examining the social aspects and effects of new media technology. And, perhaps most importantly, it has helped all of us sort out difficult questions concerning individual responsibility and the rights of others in the era of virtual interaction and computer-mediated communication. But all of that is over. And it is over precisely because we can no longer be entirely certain that "there is always a body attached." In fact, the majority of online activity is no longer (and perhaps never really was) communication with other human beings, but interactions with machines. Current statistics concerning web traffic already give the machines a slight edge, with 51 percent of all activity being generated by something other than a human user (Foremski 2012), and this statistic is expected to increase at an accelerated rate (Cisco Systems 2012) as algorithms take over not just search operations but also content recommendation and generation. Even if one doubts the possibility of ever achieving what has traditionally been called "strong AI," the fact is our world is already populated by semi-intelligent artifacts, social robots, learning algorithms, and autonomous decision-making systems that increasingly occupy the place of the other in social relationships and communicative interaction.

The following chapter investigates the opportunities and challenges made available by these increasingly social and communicative machines. The examination of this subject matter will proceed in three steps or movements: The first will assess the way we typically deal with the computer. It will, therefore, target and reconsider the instrumental theory of technology, which defines the machine as nothing more than a tool or contrivance serving human interests. The second will consider the opportunities and challenges that socially aware and autonomous technologies pose to this standard default understanding. Recent developments in autonomous technology, learning algorithms, and social robotics exceed the conceptual boundaries of the instrumental theory and ask us to reassess who or what is (or can be) a legitimate social actor. Finally, and by way of conclusion, the third part will draw out the consequences of this material, explicating what this machine incursion means for us, the other entities who communicate and interact with us, and the social situation of the twenty-first century.

Default setting

When employed for the purposes of communication, the computer has customarily been assigned one of two possible functions. It has either been situated as a medium through which human beings exchange information, or it has occupied, with varying degrees of success, the position of the other in communicative exchange, becoming a participant with which (or with whom) human users interact. These two alternatives were initially introduced and distinguished in Robert Cathcart and Gary Gumpert's "The Person-Computer Interaction" (1985). In this relatively early essay, the authors differentiate communicating *through* a computer from communicating *with* a computer. The former, they argue, names all those "computer facilitated functions" where "the computer is interposed between sender and receiver." The latter designates "person-computer interpersonal functions" where "one party activates a computer which in turn responds appropriately in graphic, alphanumeric, or vocal modes establishing an ongoing sender/receiver relationship" (Cathcart and Gumpert 1985, 114). Despite early identification of these two alternatives, the field of communication in general and media studies in particular has (for better or worse) emphasized one alternative over and against the other. With few notable exceptions, communication scholars have predominantly considered the computer and computer networks, like the internet, as a medium *through* which human users interact, exchange ideas, and communicate with one another. This approach is immediately evident in and has been institutionalized by the relatively new field of computer-mediated communication (CMC), which is routinely defined as "communication that takes place between human beings via the instrumentality of computers" (Herring 1996, 1).

Situating the computer in this fashion is completely reasonable and has distinct theoretical and practical advantages. First, it locates the machine at an identifiable position within the process model of communication, which was initially formalized by Claude Shannon and Warren Weaver (1963) in *The Mathematical Theory of Communication*. According to Shannon and Weaver, communication is a dyadic process bounded, on the one side, by an information source or sender and, on the other side, by a receiver. These two participants are connected by a communication channel or medium through which messages selected by the sender are conveyed to the receiver (Shannon and Weaver 1963, 7–8). This rudimentary model is not only "accepted as one of the main seeds out of which Communication Studies has grown" (Fiske 1994, 6) but also establishes the basic components and parameters for future elaborations and developments. In accordance with this model, CMC locates the computer and related technology in the intermediate position of channel or medium. As such, it occupies the position granted to other forms of communication technology (print, telegraph, telephone, radio, television, etc.) and is comprehended as something *through* which human messages pass.

Second, this intermediate position is substantiated and justified by the usual understanding and definition of technology. According to Martin Heidegger's (1977) influential analysis in the essay "The Question Concerning Technology," the presumed role and function of any kind of technological apparatus is that it is an instrument or mere means employed by human users for specific ends. Heidegger terms this particular characterization of technology "the instrumental definition" and indicates that it forms what is considered to be the "correct" understanding of any kind of technological contrivance. And because a tool "is deemed 'neutral,' without valuative content of its own" (Feenberg 1991, 5) a technological artifact is evaluated not in and of itself, but on the basis of the particular employments that have been decided by its human designer, manufacturer, or user. This is what is typically called "instrumental neutrality."

Third, characterized as a tool, instrument, or medium of human endeavor, technical devices are not considered the responsible agent of actions that are performed with or through them. "Morality," as AI scientist J. Storrs Hall (2001) points out, "rests on human shoulders, and if machines changed the ease with which things were done, they did not change responsibility for doing them. People have always been the only 'moral agents'" (2). This decision not only sounds level-headed and reasonable, it is one of the standard assumptions of computer ethics. According to Deborah Johnson (1985), who is credited with writing the field's agenda-setting textbook, "computer ethics turns out to be the study of human beings and society—our goals and values, our norms of behavior, the way we organize ourselves and assign rights and responsibilities, and so on" (6). Computers, she recognizes, often "instrumentalize" these human values and behaviors in innovative and challenging ways, but the bottom line is and remains the way human agents design and use (or misuse) such technology. Understood in this way, computer systems, no matter how automatic, independent, or seemingly intelligent they may become, "are not and can never be (autonomous, independent) moral agents" (Johnson 2006, 203). They will, like all other technological artifacts, always be instruments of human value, decision-making, and action.

Finally, all of this has been and remains largely unquestioned, because it constitutes what is routinely called "normal science," which not only codifies accepted methods of research but can also have the unintended effect of restricting alternative possibilities and innovation. The term "normal science" was introduced by the philosopher Thomas Kuhn in *The Structure of Scientific Revolutions* to describe those undertakings that are guided by an established and accepted *paradigm*. Paradigms, according to Kuhn (1996), are "universally recognized scientific achievements that, for a time, provide model problems and solutions to a community of practitioners" (x). Normal sciences, as Kuhn demonstrates, have distinct theoretical and practical advantages. Operating within the framework of an established paradigm provides students, scholars, and educators with a common foundation and accepted set of basic assumptions. This effectively puts an end to debates about fundamentals and allows researchers to concentrate their attention on problems defined by the discipline, instead of quibbling about competing methodological procedures or basic substructures. For this reason, a paradigm provides coherent structure to a particular area of research. It defines what constitutes a problem for the area of study, delimits the kind of questions that are considered to be appropriate and significant, and describes what research procedures and resulting evidence will qualify as acceptable. When computer technology is understood and examined as an instrument or medium facilitating human communication, research typically focuses on the quantity and quality of the messages that can be distributed by the system or the kinds of relationships established between the human senders and receivers through its particular form of mediation. Evidence of this can be found, as Kuhn (1996) argues, in the contents of standard textbooks, which "address themselves to an already articulated body of problems, data and theory, most often to the particular set of paradigms to which the scientific community is committed at the time they are written" (136). Without little or no exception, standard textbooks in the disciplines of communication studies, media studies, and media ethics, whether introductory or advanced, address the computer and computer networks as an *instrument* of human communication and seek to investigate the effect this new technology has on the quantity and quality of human interactions and relationships (Barnes 2002; Consalvo and Ess 2013; Dutton 2013; Herring 1996; Jones 1998; Ess 2013).

The new normal

The instrumental theory of technology not only sounds reasonable, but also is obviously useful. It is, one might say, instrumental for figuring out questions of moral conduct and social responsibility in the age of increasingly complex technological systems. And it has a distinct advantage in that it locates accountability in a widely accepted and seemingly intuitive subject position: in human decision-making and action. At the same time, however, this particular formulation also has significant theoretical and practical limitations, especially as it applies (or not) to recent technological innovations.

Theoretically the instrumental viewpoint reduces all technology, irrespective of design, construction, or operation, to a tool, an instrument, or medium of human activity. "Tool," however, does not necessarily encompass everything technological and does not exhaust all possibilities. There are also *machines*. Although "experts in mechanics," as Karl Marx (1977, 493) pointed out, often confuse these two concepts calling "tools simple machines and machines complex tools," there is an important and crucial difference between the two, and that difference ultimately has to do with the location and assignment of *agency*. For Marx, the machine is not a kind of complex tool, but occupies the position of the user of the tool. "The machine," Marx (1977) explains, "is a mechanism that, after being set in motion, performs with its tools the same operations as the worker formerly did with similar tools" (495). This alternative viewpoint is taken up and further developed by Langdon Winner in his book *Autonomous Technology*. "To be autonomous," Winner (1977) argues, "is to be self-governing, independent, not ruled by an external law of force" (16). The phrase "autonomous technology," therefore, refers to technical devices that directly contravene the instrumental theory by deliberately contesting and relocating the assignment of agency. Such mechanisms are not mere tools to be directed and used by human users according to their will but occupy, in one way or another, the place of an independent and self-governing agent. Understood in this way, the machine occupies not the place of the hand tool of the worker but the worker himself or herself, the active and self-directed entity who had wielded the tool.

Autonomous machines are not only a perennial favorite of science fiction (from the monster of Mary Shelley's *Frankenstein* to the HAL 9000 computer of *2001: A Space Odyssey* and more recently the AI "Samantha" from the film *Her*) but are rapidly becoming science fact, if not already part of social reality. According to Ray Kurzweil's estimations, the tipping point, what he calls the "singularity," is near: "Within several decades information-based technologies will encompass all human knowledge and proficiency, ultimately including the pattern recognition powers, problem solving skills, and emotional and moral intelligence of the human brain itself" (Kurzweil 2005, 8). Similar forecasts have been offered by Hans Moravec (1988) and Rodney Brooks (2002), both of whom predict the achievement of human-level capabilities in a relatively short period of time. "Our fantasy machines," Brooks (2002) writes referencing the popular robots of science fiction (i.e., HAL, C-3PO, Lt. Commander Data, etc.), "have syntax and technology. They also have emotions, desires, fears, loves, and pride. Our real machines do not. Or so it seems at the dawn of the third millennium. But how will it look a hundred years from now? My thesis is that in just twenty years the boundary between fantasy and reality will be rent asunder" (5).

Predictions of human-level (or better) machine intelligence, although fueling imaginative and entertaining forms of fiction, are, for the most part, still hypothetical. That is, they address possible achievements in the fields of AI and robotics that might occur with technologies or techniques that have yet to be fully developed, prototyped, or empirically demonstrated. Consequently strict instrumentalists are often able to dismiss these predictions as nothing more than wishful thinking or speculation insofar as actual achievement in AI research and development has been much more mundane and limited. In fact, if the history of AI is any indication, there is every reason to be skeptical. We have, in fact, heard these kinds of fantastic hypotheses before, only to be disappointed time and again. As Terry Winograd (1990) wrote in an honest assessment of progress (or lack thereof) in the discipline, "artificial intelligence has not achieved creativity, insight, and judgment. But its shortcomings are far more mundane: we have not yet been able to construct a machine with even a modicum of common sense or one that can converse on everyday topics in ordinary language" (167). Despite these shortcomings, there are current implementations and working prototypes that appear either to possess or to be assigned some significant degree of autonomy, and they complicate the standard instrumental understanding of things.

There are, for instance, learning systems: mechanisms designed not only to make decisions and take real-world actions with little or no human direction or oversight but also programmed to be able to modify their own rules of behavior based on results from such operations. These machines, which are now rather common in commodities trading, transportation, health care, manufacturing, and even culture appear to be more than mere tools. Consider, for example, what has happened in the financial and commodities exchange markets in the last fifteen years. At one time, trades on the New York Stock Exchange or the Chicago Board Options Exchange were initiated and controlled by human traders in "the pit." Beginning in the late 1990s, financial services organizations began developing algorithms to take over much of this effort (Steiner 2012). These computer programs effectively analyzed the market, executed trades faster than human comprehension, and were designed with learning subroutines that could alter their initial programming in order to respond to new and unanticipated opportunities. And these things worked. They generated incredible revenues for the financial services industry. As a result, over 70 percent of all trades are now machine generated and controlled (Patterson 2012, 8). This means that our financial situation—not only our mortgages and retirement savings but also a significant part of the national and global economy—is now directed and managed by machines that are designed to operate with a considerable degree of autonomy.

The unanticipated social consequences of this can be seen in a remarkable event called the Flash Crash. At about 2:45 p.m. on May 6, 2010, the Dow Jones Industrial Average lost over 1,000 points in a matter of seconds and then rebounded almost as quickly. The drop, which amounted to about 9 percent of the market's total value or $ 1 trillion, was caused by a couple of trading algorithms interacting with and responding to each other. In other words, no human being initiated the action, was in control of the transaction, or could be considered responsible for its outcome. It was something undertaken and overseen by the algorithms, and the human brokers could only passively watch things unfold on their monitor screens not knowing what had happened, who had instituted it, or why. To this day, no one is quite sure what actually occurred (Slavin 2011). No one, in other words, knows exactly who or even what was responsible for this brief financial crisis.

A less nefarious illustration of machine autonomy can be found in situations involving the consumption and production of culture. Currently recommendation algorithms at Netflix, Amazon, and elsewhere increasingly decide what cultural objects we access and experience. It is estimated that 75 percent of all content obtained through Netflix is the result of a machine-generated recommendation (Amatriain and Basilico 2012). Consequently, these algorithms are, in effect, taking over the work of film, book, and music critics and influencing—to a significant degree—what films are seen, what books are read, and what music is heard. But machines are not just involved in distribution and exhibition; they are also actively engaged on the creative side of the culture industry. In the field of journalism, for example, computer applications now write original content. Beyond the simple news aggregators that currently populate the Web, these programs, like Northwestern University's Stats Monkey, automatically compose publishable stories from machine-readable statistical data. And organizations like the Big Ten Network currently use these systems to develop content for web distribution (Slavin 2011, 218). These applications, although clearly in the early stages of development, led Kurt Cagle, managing editor of XMLToday.org, to provocatively ask whether an AI might compete for and win a Pulitzer Prize by 2030 (Kirwan 2009, 1).

Similar transformations are occurring in music, where algorithms and robots actively participate in the creative process. In classical music, for instance, there is David Cope's Experiments in Musical Intelligence or EMI (pronounced "Emmy"), an algorithmic composer capable of analyzing existing compositions and creating new, original scores that are virtually indistinguishable from the canonical works of Bach, Chopin, and Beethoven (Cope 2005). And then there is Shimon, a marimba playing jazz-bot from Georgia Tech that not only improvises with human musicians in real time but "is designed to create meaningful and inspiring musical interactions with humans, leading to novel musical experiences and outcomes" (Georgia Tech 2013; Hoffman and Weinberg 2011).

Although the extent to which one might assign "creativity," "originality," or "inventiveness" to these mechanisms remains a contested issue, what is not debated is the fact that the rules of the game seem to have changed significantly. As Andreas Matthias points out, summarizing his survey of learning automata:

> Presently there are machines in development or already in use which are able to decide on a course of action and to act without human intervention. The rules by which they act are not fixed during the production process, but can be changed during the operation of the machine, *by the machine itself*. This is what we call machine learning. Traditionally we hold either the operator/manufacture of the machine responsible for the consequences of its operation or "nobody" (in cases, where no personal fault can be identified). Now it can be shown that there is an increasing class of machine actions, where the traditional ways of responsibility ascription are not compatible with our sense of justice and the moral framework of society because nobody has enough *control* over the machine's actions to be able to assume responsibility for them. (Matthias 2004, 177)

In other words, the instrumental theory of technology, which had effectively tethered machine action to human agency, no longer adequately applies to mechanisms that have been deliberately designed to operate and exhibit some form, no matter how rudimentary, of independent action or autonomous decision-making. This does not mean, it is important to emphasize, that the instrumental definition is on this account simply refuted. There are, and will continue to be, mechanisms understood and utilized as tools to be manipulated by human users (e.g. lawn mowers, cork screws, telephones, digital cameras, etc.). The point is that the instrumental theory, no matter how useful and seemingly correct in some circumstances for explaining some technological devices, does not exhaust all possibilities for all kinds of devices.

Finally machine intelligence—however it is characterized and defined—is not necessarily the deciding factor. Even if our smartphones and computers remain essentially "mindless" instruments, it is what we do with and in response to them that makes the difference. This is the unique insight obtained from what Clifford Nass, Jonathan Steuer, and Ellen Tauber (1994) have called the Computer as Social Actor (CSA):

> Computers, in the way that they communicate, instruct, and take turns interacting, are *close enough* to human that they encourage *social* responses.

The encouragement necessary for such a reaction need not be much. As long as there are some behaviors that suggest a social presence, people will respond accordingly. When it comes to being social, people are built to make the conservative error: When in doubt, treat it as human. Consequently, any medium that is close enough will get human treatment, even though people know it's foolish and even though they likely will deny it afterwards. (see also Reeves and Nass 1996, 22)

The CSA model, which was developed in response to numerous experiments with human subjects, describes how users of computers, irrespective of the actual intelligence possessed (or not) by the machine, tend to respond to technology as another socially aware and interactive subject. In other words, even when experienced users know quite well that they are engaged with a machine, they make the "conservative error" and tend to respond to it in ways that afford this other thing social standing. Consequently, in order for something to be recognized and treated as a social actor, "it is not necessary," as Reeves and Nass (1996) conclude, "to have artificial intelligence" (28).

This outcome is evident not only in the tightly constrained experimental studies conducted by Nass and his associates but also in the mundane interactions with "mindless" (Nass and Moon 2000) objects like online chatter bots and non-player characters, which are encountered in online communities and massively multiplayer online role playing games (MMORPGs).

> The rise of online communities has led to a phenomenon of real-time, multi-person interaction via online personas. Some online community technologies allow the creation of bots (personas that act according to a software programme rather than being directly controlled by a human user) in such a way that it is not always easy to tell a bot from a human within an online social space. It is also possible for a persona to be partly controlled by a software programme and partly directly by a human. . . . This leads to theoretical and practical problems for ethical arguments (not to mention policing) in these spaces, since the usual one-to-one correspondence between actors and moral agents can be lost. (Mowbray 2002, 2)

Software bots complicate the one-to-one correspondence between actor and agent and make it increasingly difficult to decide who or what is responsible for actions in the virtual space of an online community. Although these bots, like Rob Dubbin's "Olivia Taters" (Madrigal 2014), which emulates the behavior of a teenage Twitter user, are by no means close to achieving anything that looks remotely like intelligence or even basic machine learning, they can still be mistaken for and pass as other human users. They are, in the words of Nass and Reeves, "*close enough to human to encourage social responses.*" And this approximation, Miranda Mowbray (2002) points out, is not necessarily "a feature of the sophistication of bot design, but of the low bandwidth communication of the online social space" where it is "much easier to convincingly simulate a human agent" (2).

Despite this knowledge, these software implementations cannot be written off as mere instruments or tools. "The examples in this paper," Mowbray (2002) concludes, "show that a bot may cause harm to other users or to the community as a whole by the will of its programmers or other users, but that it also may cause harm through nobody's fault because of the combination of circumstances involving some combination of its programming, the actions and mental or emotional states of human users who interact with it, behavior of other bots and of the environment, and the social economy of the community" (4). Unlike artificial general intelligence (AGI), which would occupy a position that would, at least, be reasonably close to that of a human user and therefore not be able to be dismissed as a mere tool, bots simply muddy the water (which is probably worse) by leaving undecided the question of whether they are or are not tools. And in the process, they leave the question of social responsibility and subjectivity both unsettled and unsettling.

Apocalypse now

In November of 2012, General Electric launched a television advertisement called "Robots on the Move." The sixty-second spot, created by Jonathan Dayton and Valerie Faris (the husband/wife team behind the 2006 feature film *Little Miss Sunshine*), depicts many of the iconic robots of science fiction traveling across great distances to assemble before a brightly lit aircraft hanger for what we are told is the unveiling of some new kind of machines—"brilliant machines," as GE's tagline describes it. And as we observe Robby the Robot from *Forbidden Planet*, KITT the robotic automobile from *Knight Rider*, and Lt. Commander Data of *Star Trek: The Next Generation* making their way to this meeting of artificial minds, we are told, by an ominous voice-over, that "the machines are on the move." Although this might not look like the typical robot apocalypse (vividly illustrated in countless science fiction films and television programs like *Terminator*, *The Matrix Trilogy*, and *Battlestar Galactica*), we are in the midst of an invasion. The machines are on the move. They are everywhere and doing everything. They may have begun by displacing workers on the factory floor, but they now actively participate in many aspects of our intellectual, social, and cultural life. This invasion is not some future possibility coming from a distant alien world. It is here. It is now. And resistance is futile.

So what does this mean for us? What are the ethical consequences and significance of this machine invasion? Let me respond to these questions with three statements that inevitably have, at this particular juncture, something of an apocalyptic tone. First, life as we have known it is over. Communication studies as we have understood and practiced it is at an end. We need, however, to be cautious with how we characterize and employ the word "end" in this particular context. In the field of communication studies (and the related disciplines or subdisciplines of media studies and media ethics), the operative paradigm—the framework that has defined what is considered normal science—situates the computer as a tool or instrument of message exchange between human users. This is clearly evident within the last three decades of the twentieth century with the phenomenal growth of CMC as a recognized field of investigation and its institutionalization within professional organizations, university curricula, and standard textbooks and scholarly journals.

At the same time, however, it is increasingly clear that recent technological innovations do not necessarily fit into this paradigmatic structure and effectively challenge long-standing assumptions about the role and function of technology in human society. These occurrences constitute what Kuhn (1996) calls an "anomaly" (52). In one way or another, they exceed the conceptual grasp of the dominant paradigm and call into question many of its basic principles, presumptions, and procedures. For this reason, mechanisms like learning algorithms, autonomous decision-making systems, and even "mindless" chatterbots are not necessarily new technologies to be accommodated to the theories and practices of communication studies as it is currently defined but introduce significant challenges to the standard operating presumptions of communication research, initiating what Kuhn calls a "paradigm shift." What is at an "end," therefore, is not communication studies per se but the dominant paradigm that has, until now, structured and guided both the theories and practices of the discipline. Like the highly publicized "end" predicted by the Mayan calendar to occur in late 2012, this is not "the end of the world" but of a certain conceptualization and ordering of it.

Second, a new paradigm, especially during the time of its initial appearance and formulation, does not simply replace, reject, or invalidate the preceding one.

For this reason, the previous *modus operandi*, although clearly in something of a state of crisis, or at least bumping up against phenomena that it is no longer able to contain fully, can still be useful, albeit in a restricted capacity and circumscribed situation. Within Newtonian physics, for example, what is true and what is false is determined by the entities, rules, and conditions that come to be exhibited within the Newtonian system. As long as one operates within the framework or paradigm established by this system, it is possible to define what is and what is not valid for the Newtonian characterization of physical reality. All this changes, of course, when the normal functioning of Newtonian physics is confronted with an alternative, like that formulated by Albert Einstein. Einstein's innovations, however, do not simply invalidate or foreclose the Newtonian project. They merely reinscribe Newton's laws within a different context that reveals other entities, rules, and conditions that could not be conceptualized as such within the horizon of Newtonian thought. In an analogous way, the change in paradigm that is currently being experienced in communication studies does not disprove or simply put an end to CMC research in general and media ethics in particular. Instead it redefines CMC as a highly specific and restricted case of what needs to be a much more comprehensive understanding of the social role and function of computer technology within the field of communication. In other words, CMC has clearly provided researchers and scholars with a useful instrument for explaining various forms of human-computer involvement. We should not, however, conclude from this particular success that it is the only or even the best possible theoretical model.

Finally, although recent innovations challenge the current paradigm, placing its normal functioning in question, what comes next is only now beginning to make an appearance. And if the history of science is any indication, it may be quite some time before these innovations come to be formulated and codified into the next iteration of what will be recognized as "normal science." At this preliminary stage, however, we can begin to identify some aspects of what the next generation of communication research might look like in the wake of this paradigmatic alteration. For now, the shape of the new paradigm is, for better or worse, influenced (or clouded) by the current one, which provides the only conceptual apparatus and vocabulary we have at our disposal. We are, therefore, in the somewhat cumbersome situation of trying to articulate what will exceed the current situation by employing the words and concepts that it already defines and regulates. This will, of course, affect what can be said about the new possibilities, but we have no other way by which to proceed.

From what we already know, it is clear that it is no longer accurate to define the computer exclusively as an instrument that is to be animated and used, more or less effectively, by human beings. Computers and related information systems are beginning to be understood as another kind of subject—another kind of communicative other, who confronts human users, calls to them, and requires an appropriate response. This other aspect of the computer, as we have seen, was predicted by Cathcart and Gumpert back in 1985 and further developed by Nass et al. in the CSA model. Communication studies, however, had (for reasons that are both understandable and justifiable) largely ignored it, mainly because this alternative did not fit the established instrumentalist paradigm. In reframing the machine according to the stipulations of this other and marginal possibility (or "repressed content," to use psychoanalytical terminology), all kinds of things change, not the least of which is our understanding of who, or what, qualifies as a legitimate social actor. For Norbert Wiener, the progenitor of the science of cybernetics, these developments fundamentally alter the social landscape. "It is the thesis of this book," Wiener (1988) writes at the beginning of *The Human Use of Human Beings*, "that society can only be understood through a study of the messages and the communication facilities which belong to it; and that in the future development of these messages and communication facilities, messages between man and machines, between machines and man, and between machine and machine, are destined to play an ever-increasing part" (16). In the social relationships of the not-too-distant future (we need to recall that Wiener wrote these words in 1950), the machine will no longer comprise merely an instrument or medium through which human users communicate and socialize with each other. Instead it will occupy the position of another social actor with whom one communicates and interacts.

In coming to occupy this other position, one inevitably runs up against and encounters fundamental questions of social standing and responsibility—questions that not only could *not* be articulated within the context of the previous paradigm, but if they had been articulated, would have been, from that perspective, considered inappropriate and even nonsense. What, for example, is our responsibility in the face of this other—an other who is otherwise than another human entity? How do or should we respond to this other form of otherness, and how will or should this machinic other respond to us? Although these questions appear to open onto what many would consider to be the realm of science fiction, they are already part of our social reality. And how we decide to respond to the opportunities and challenges of this machine question will have a profound effect on the way we conceptualize our place in the world, who we decide to include in the community of socially significant subjects, and what we exclude from such consideration and why. But no matter how it is decided, it is a decision—quite literally a cut that institutes difference and makes a difference. We are, therefore, situated at a crucial juncture or shift in the operative paradigm. And what we decide to do in the face of these increasingly social interactive machines will have consequences that affect not just us but others.

16

Race, Gender, and Digital Media:
The Mis-Adventures of Awkward Black Girl and Representations of Black Female Identity

Erin Watley

Right now, pitching your idea to a network exec or an industry liaison just isn't working because they have this limited perception of black women and what they think black women want to see on screen. I think the Web is the best way to go right now, and I've seen a lot of great shows come off the Internet.—Issa Rae (creator and star of "The Mis-Adventures of Awkward Black Girl")[1]

I remember the very first time I saw ABG ["Awkward Black Girl"], and it felt right at home. Everything was (and still is) just right. I'm so glad Issa gave voices to people just like me! Part of the reason I even make YouTube videos are so that people like me can relate to what I say and are interested in. Issa gave me a voice and I want to be just like her—successful, intelligent and hilarious! LOVE YOU ISSA!—CourtneyRevolution (ABG YouTube commenter)

Digital media spaces are not usually considered ideal venues for initiating change regarding issues of cultural diversity and communication. Popular memes, hashtags, and website comment sections can become riddled with disparaging remarks and representations about race and gender, but some online trends and movements have also vividly displayed how digital media distribute varying narratives and facilitate diverse interactions about culture that might not otherwise take place. The use of #blacklivesmatter on Twitter to center discussions about police violence against Black Americans and the success of a viral video of a woman getting repeated catcalls from passers by to spur more awareness about the street harassment that many women experience on a regular basis are just two examples of digital media's useful contributions in connection to cultural matters. Digital media are similar to more traditional mass media outlets, like television and film, in that the ability to present content to large groups of culturally diverse people does not automatically equate to the representations of those different groups and ideas being evenly featured. However, there are ways that digital media outlets are uniquely equipped to promote more dynamic representations, especially for groups that have been marginalized, that are not available in other mass media spaces. From a media ethics perspective, it is important to recognize the pitfalls and the potential in digital media that come with increasing representations of different cultural groups.

One particular group that has consistently been misrepresented throughout mass media is Black women. Historically, mass media depictions of Black women have frequently relied on stereotypes and narrow narrative frames to portray their lives and experiences. This chapter identifies the problematic portrayals of Black American women as an ethical issue that continues to be perpetuated throughout popular television and film but does not reflect the range of actual everyday experiences for Black women and discusses the societal impact of these representations. Then, the essay looks to the web series *Mis-Adventures of Awkward Black Girl* (ABG) as an example of how the internet, as a form of digital media, is a space that is uniquely equipped for social intervention by countering hegemonic representations, creating discourse about diverse identity intersections, and connecting cultural content to broader societal concerns. These characteristics collectively contribute to the promotion of more balanced media representations of Black women.[2]

It is particularly important to evaluate these media representations from an ethics perspective because of the impact that misconstrued portrayals can have. "Mass media's tendency to blur the lines between fact and fiction has important consequences for perceptions of Black culture and Black people" (Collins 2005). Cultural stereotypes in television and film are not only representatives of entertainment; they are also reflective of "what is widely agreed upon and believed to be right" (275) within the society in which the media is produced (Dyer 2012). When individuals have limited exposure to a group they learn about them through media texts (Moon 2008).The gravity of media misrepresentations can be observed in the ways Black people are viewed by others and in how members of the group perceive themselves in media. Media have been shown to influence the perception that Black people are inherently "cool" (Brown 2008) and also fuel the notion that Black people are more likely to be criminals (Dixon and Linz 2000). In her discussion of oppositional gaze and Black women viewing representations of themselves in television and film, bell hooks (1999) notes that the women "never went to the movies expecting to see compelling representations of Black femaleness . . . they were all acutely aware of cinematic racism—its violent erasure of Black womanhood" (119). A lack of diverse portrayals also helps to impose limits on how Black women should perceive themselves, and Melissa Harris-Perry (2011) states that the overrepresentation of the stereotypical strong and self-reliant Black woman in media can diminish the emotional well-being of Black women in real life (199). If stereotypical media portrayals are any influence on real-life perceptions and experiences then the topic is also an issue of ethics and along with critiquing problematic representations we should also advocate those sources that provide agency and intervention for historically misrepresented groups.

ABG is an award-winning web series and a poignant case study that demonstrates how digital media can be used to resist and counter narrow and stereotypical media portrayals of Black American women. The first episode of ABG was posted to YouTube in February 2011. The web series has since completed its second, and final, season in April 2013. The series is a scripted comedy that follows the work, home, love life, and related antics of the main character J, a Black woman in her mid-twenties (played by the show's creator Issa Rae), alongside her friends and coworkers. The series—as well as J herself—challenge prominent hegemonic depictions of Black women frequently encountered in mass media spaces by presenting a narrative about a Black woman who is not cool, does not look like most Black actresses with leading roles, and is in a romantic, interracial relationship.

Along with the content of the series itself, ABG's exclusive distribution through a digital media venue plays a role in the presentation of representations that confirm elements of Black women's identities that are typically constrained in popular television and film. A Multimodal Critical Discourse Analysis (MCDA) allows for evaluation to take place through multiple levels of discourse because ideologies are present not just in the spoken content, but also in the physical appearance and actions of the actors, and interactions through the YouTube comments. I viewed the first season of the series along with 100 of the top comments in the comments section for each of the twelve first-season episodes. Looking at the top comments allowed me to see the ones that got the highest rankings, meaning that they had the most likes, shares, and replies, and brings me to the comments that people have been engaging with the most. Pulling the top comments also allowed me to easily include comments that have posted recently along with ones that are from 2011 when the episodes were first posted. The results of the study show that ABG exemplifies how digital media can be used to act ethically as another "powerful site for critical intervention" (Hooks 1999) by providing unique access for the production and consumption of more diverse representations of Black women. The technical format allows for a direct connection between the ABG series and viewers, and the series' content and viewer comments illuminate critiques of the way Black women are frequently portrayed, the need for more nuanced characters, and a connection between the fictional characters and the lived experiences of Black women not usually seen on screen. Evaluation of ABG within this digital media space, and in direct connection to popular stereotypical representations of Black American women, complements prior research that emphasizes digital media as a tool for positive exchanges about racial identity that create connections that are resistant to prominent hegemonic depictions (Cunningham 2013). The ABG series does not eliminate the presence of stereotypical portrayals or prove on its own that the internet is equitable and diverse, but it can demonstrate that a need has been created by the lack of diverse representations of Black women on television and film, and an alternative and resistant product that is "produced outside of market forces and the state" (3) as one way to address the issues of problematic cultural representations in media spaces (Atton 2004).

The need for more diverse imagery: A brief history of Black female stereotypes in television and film

Jezebel, Mammy and Sapphire are the angles in the crooked room where [B]lackwomen live. They do not reflect [B]lack women's lived experience; instead, they limit African American women to prescribed roles that serve the interests of others.—Harris-Perry (2011)

The portrayal of Black women on television and film is tied to a prevalent history of invisibility and caricature. In the years prior to the American Civil Rights movement, Black women were rarely on the big and small screens, and even when they were offered roles, they were often models of subservience or a warning about how not to behave (Mastro and Greenberg 2000). Media stereotypes are generally present in three ways: limited exposure, lack of range in type of characters that are portrayed, and relegation to simple characters (Holtzman and Sharpe 2014). Presently, there are many more Black women playing a variety of roles on television and in film. Characters like Olivia Pope (Kerry Washington) on *Scandal* and Annalise Keating (Viola Davis) on *How to Get Away With Murder* portray Black women with multiple dimensions. However, just because Black women are more likely to be present, and some more dynamic characters have emerged, does not mean that the representations of Black women in mass media contexts are no longer problematic (Stephens and Phillips 2003). From an ethical perspective, it is troubling that the character templates for Black women on television and in film still contain many older stereotypical characteristics. The Jezebel, Mammy, and Sapphire archetypes are historically grounded but continue to frame the experiences of Black women in a stereotypical fashion. The continuing presence of these caricatures can have an impact on how Black women are perceived by others, as well as the way that they conceptualize themselves.

These caricatures are relevant because they have been a part of the mass media landscape for decades. While the names of these portrayals might sound foreign or dated, the corresponding characteristics still ring true. The Jezebel character is a seductress who fulfills male sexual fantasies. She is good looking and sexually aggressive, and usually has physical features that adhere closely to white standards of beauty (Jewell 1993). Coffy, played by Pam Grier, in the 1973 Blaxsploitation film *Coffy*; Halle Berry, as Leticia Musgrove, in *Monster's Ball*; and video vixens often featured in music videos are all Black women who fit the Jezebel media portrayal because they are seductive, have sex as a key element of their personas, and also have physical features that are closer to hegemonic beauty norms. The Jezebel's portrayal has its origins in nineteenth-century slavery when Black women's sexuality was juxtaposed against the gentility and chastity of white womanhood to justify the sexual relationships that male masters had with female slaves and to use the perceived insatiable sexual appetite to deny Black women true femininity (Morton 1991; West 1995).These depictions are ethically problematic because of the dual hegemonic norms that are enforced through the Jezebel media caricature. First, Black women deviate from "normal" femininity and are sexually promiscuous in comparison to sexual depictions of white women (Cox 2013). Second, that Jezebel aligns more closely with white standards of feminine beauty (long hair, slight nose, thin lips, fair skin, and a relatively slender body) sends the message that Eurocentric features make a

Black woman more attractive. Current iterations of the Jezebel can be found featured as nameless models in music videos or in the mold of pop stars like Nikki Minaj or Rihanna, whose physical assets are often played up for sex appeal while other personality traits or talents become less significant.

There is a striking contrast in media depictions of Black women's sexuality, because while the Jezebel trope is hypersexualized and valued for her body the Mammy character, typically an older Black woman, is valued for her virtue. Mammy is wise, strong-willed but jovial, a good caretaker, overweight with dark skin, and traditionally asexual (e.g., not depicted in sexual situations, or given romantic interests).The origins for Mammy are also rooted in the nineteenth-century American South when Black female maids and cooks worked and cared for white families (Bogle 1997). The hegemonic messages embedded in this portrayal are that Black women should be subservient and nurturing, and happy about it. These Black women with darker skin and fewer Eurocentric facial features are considered less attractive and better suited for service work (Jewell 1993).The advertising icon Aunt Jemima, the maids in *The Help*, or Ella Payne from the Tyler Perry sitcom *House of Payne*, are all remaining links to the Mammy portrayal of Black women in current popular television and film. The replication of this portrayal perpetuates a notion that a darker complexion is not attractive or that a valuable Black woman is one involved in service work.

The Sapphire media trope falls in between characterizations of the Jezebel and the Mammy, taking on some similar traits from the others and unique because she is usually a younger woman who is quick-witted, verbally aggressive, and often emasculating during her interactions with Black men. Sapphire was originally a character on *The Amos'n'Andy Show*, which began as a radio program and then moved to television in the 1950s. On the series, Sapphire was brash, sassy, and often talked down to the Black male characters; the success of her portrayal has carried over prominently into television sitcoms and reality shows (Yarbrough and Bennett 1999). Common modern imagery that meets the Sapphire criteria would be Black women who are bitchy, wise-cracking, "ghetto," and/or domineering: "Of the most frequent stereotypes of African-American women to appear in today's sitcoms, the [S]apphire is the most consistent" (Cox 2013, 275).The characters Donna Meagal (Rhetta) on *Parks and Recreation* or Angela Williams (Tasha Smith) on *For Better or Worse*, and the majority of the women on *Love & Hip-Hop* and *The Real Housewives of Atlanta* would fit in closest to this Sapphire depiction of Black femininity. Sapphire tinged media characters reinforce hegemonic ideas that Black women do not appropriately display anger or know how to maintain relationships (Jewell 1993). Overrepresentation of this type of character causes an ethical complication because it easily lends itself to the limiting assumption that Black women must be loud, aggressive, and angry.

Most of the representations of Black women on television and in film are not purely one of these three tropes; rather, different traits might be combined within one character to create varying depictions of Black femininity. However, ethically the concern is that when those media depictions still revolve around stereotypes, the impact goes past the screens where the portrayals are viewed. Entertainment media can be a major source of information about society's dominant ideologies, how we understand others, and the world around us (Holtzman and Sharpe 2014). When portrayals of one group are consistently skewed then viewers are likely to apply biased ideas toward that group in real life (Dixon and Linz 2000; Wood 2003). For example, people who have been exposed to lots of television news where Black people were mostly shown as suspects are more likely to think that Black people are violent and criminals (Dixon and Linz 2000). Media stereotypes are not neutral; we use them to make ethical choices about our interactions with others and to interpret the ethical choices of others. They ultimately work to maintain a status quo that is only to the benefit of dominant groups (Lind 2013). Gerbner and Gross (1976) emphasize that mass media function as a tool for "the socialization of most people into standardized roles and behaviors" (175). In a more recent evaluation, Gabbadon (2006) notes that the images specifically found on television are important to consider because "they form a mirror (albeit a distorted one) of society" (4). What we consume about other cultures through mass media can impact our view of those cultures. However, "mass media's tendency to blur the lines between fact and fiction has important consequences for perceptions of Black culture and Black people" (Collins 2008, 151). The consequence for Black women is a limitation to what is generally regarded as acceptable or authentic behavior. We have become very familiar with the portrayal of the "sexy Black woman," the "independent Black woman," or the "independent and funny Black female sidekick," but those depictions continue to reinforce those hegemonic cultural lines of what is and is not Black femininity because they are only partial accounts of a broad set of characteristics and experiences.

What we see most frequently on film and television are snippets of Black femininity that do "not describe the actuality of being Black but rather references a particular way of thinking: it is not about *being* Black but being *thought* of as Black" (Ross 1996, 5). As a result, when limited representation is combined with economy, politics, and ideology, it falls right into a hegemonic system that keeps conceptions of Black women in assigned places and spaces (Collins 2008; Morton 1991). The Black woman who has "non-Black" interests, is outwardly vulnerable, is socially awkward, or is not a depiction of white beauty norms, is rarely seen in our mass-marketed entertainment media. These are some of the gaps that digital media can be observed as working to fill through the ABG Web series.

Digital media space

The digital media space does not have to be as concerned with the concentration of media ownership as do television and film environments. McQuail (2010) explains how consumers of media assume that media present a diversity of information, opinions, and types of content; the reality is that media do not serve the interests of all sectors of society, and yet they are the shapers of how we see the world and interpret meaning (Hall 1980). Mass media outlets are owned by a group of just seven corporations, and they are run by people with a high degree of shared values (Holtzman and Sharpe 2014, 41). The combination of business and cultural interests at the top of these media corporations means that there is an overrepresentation of majority groups and constricted or nonexistent portrayals of minorities (Haridakis and Hanson 2009). The ownership of media is concentrated in the hands of a few companies, and most of those making the decisions about what images of Black women make it to production and stay on the air are white, upper-class males (Heider 2000). How can this controlling and diversity-deficient group be expected to produce, or even advocate for, more dynamic voices and representations? It is not necessarily the ethical concern of those companies to make sure that alternative voices are present and that the characterizations of marginalized groups are balanced and well developed (Holtzman and Sharpe 2014). Because the driving force of most mass media companies is not geared toward the production of balanced cultural representations, challenging stereotyped portrayals of Black women is not easily accomplished through traditional mass media sites. A less constrictive medium for the distribution of mass media, like YouTube, could offer more diverse ownership and production of content that is a more culturally effective intermediary for institutions within civil society (McQuail 2010).

Digital media have more space for the wide distribution of user-generated content that can be representative of a greater range of voices than those represented on television and film because ties to market and ownership forces are weaker (Nerone 1995). While digital media are not completely free—they still have connections to markets and ownership and limits to use according to access and knowledge of technology that create a variety of ethical problems— they do have the potential to circumvent some of the ethical issues that befall other mass media outlets. When posting a video to YouTube, one individual has an immediate platform with the potential to reach an audience of millions of people without being filtered through an approval process, market testing, or checks for sponsorship compatibility. A series like ABG can bypass the middlemen in the production process and take its story directly to the potential consumers. By examining digital media content, we can see what can be created and distributed on a mass media scale without conforming to market and ownership restraints. Digital media give us a tool that can be resistant because of their broad potential for diversifying cultural representations of others and providing space for greater agency resistance to hegemonic portrayals by those groups that have historically been the subject of stereotypical portrayals (Jansen 2007; Dahlgren 2005).

Audience participation is another facet of digital media that distinguishes its liberating nature. When Jansen (2007) and Dahlgren (2005) characterize the internet as a tool of resistance, they do so because of the accessibility that it creates and its user-friendly ability to create content (Atton 2004). Traditional one-way interaction with mass media involves limited direct interactions that the audience can have upon the text (Downey and Fenton 2003). With interactive digital media, there is a greater sense of immediacy of interaction and the discourses here could be significant because it is communication that has the potential to impact individuals and radiate outward to provoke systemic changes (Ruesch and Bateson 1987). In these digital media spaces, an individual has the access to give immediate commentary and engage other viewers in the same space where the content is being produced and share it with other digital locations.

If the ethical framework we use when encountering others is built in part from the media we encounter, then digital media technology has the potential to play a role in connecting users and fostering community where alternative representations of Black femininity are promoted. Starting in 2013, YouTube, which is owned by Google, has been encouraging its users to link their YouTube account to their Google identities (Gmail, Google+, Google Search) in order to engage other people through YouTube. As a result of this merger, many of the comments that appear under a video are the feeds from Google+ users sharing a video with their circle and people from the circle posting replies and reactions. For example, YouTube commenter SLAP J shared an ABG episode with friends, and that correspondence shows on the ABG YouTube page:

> Yo, what up my G's? You gotta check out this show that some of my business associates are a part of. If you like to laugh, or if ur black, or a guy or a girl, you should watch this. Guarantee you'll watch up to episode 8. Feel free to Reshare& +1 it![3]

Because of this formatting, viewers are not limited to correspondence in this space just with strangers who are viewing the video at the same time—there is the option to bring in your own community and engage with them through this platform. Sharing content, emotion, and information are all elements of engaging a community environment, and these examples of discourse have demonstrated how they present uniquely in this ABG-themed space and can be harnessed as a tool that contributes to an ethical response to media stereotypes of Black women.

Creating discourse through content and conversation

Along with a digital media platform that makes it easier for alternative voices to produce programming and get access to viewers, ABG contributes directly to discourses about more diverse character portrayals of Black women through the series' content and the viewers who leave comments on YouTube. The original content and responses all demonstrate awareness about common media portrayals of Black women and a desire to advocate for representations that are less stereotypical. Within the web series, J's physical appearance and behavior contrasts with many aspects of the Jezebel, Mammy, and Sapphire stereotypes. In the first episode, for example, J introduces herself by declaring that she is in fact both awkward and Black: "the two worst things that anyone could be." J is not "cool." She mishandles or avoids social situations and does not look or act the part of most leading Black actresses seen on television and film. "Black cool" is an attitude, a social skill, and an entertainment ability that most portrayals of Black women on television and film possess. Black women are typically shown as quick-witted, fashionable, self-assured, dominant, and entertaining, while an underrepresented characteristic is the expression of awkwardness and uncertainty. The lack of portrayed awkwardness or general uncertainty tells Black women that they have an unattainable standard to live up to and leaves little room for a multifaceted being equipped to experience a range of emotions and capabilities.

By declaring the intersection of her awkwardness and Blackness as the worst combination ever, J acknowledges a cultural dilemma from the very start. This conflict is caused by not fitting into this Black "cool" notion. J is what people do not think she should be, stigmatized across multiple identities for her race, gender, and awkwardness. For example, in the second episode J has an interaction at work with her boss, who is making inappropriate comments to J about her private life. J comments in her voice-over, "Situations like this make me angry and uncomfortable. I would love to express that." But J does not speak out, instead playing out more aggressive reactions to her boss in a daydream. Usually, Black women are shown on television and film as women who speak their minds regardless of the situation and refuse to be disrespected—characteristics that align with the traditional Sapphire character. J is not quick-witted and outwardly aggressive. Her passive aggressive nature negates that assumption and familiar persona. Yes, "awkward" is in the title of the show and is J's defining characteristic, but it is most significant in the discussion of mass-mediated portrayals, where Black women have an impenetrable presence and cannot be clumsy, insecure, or socially unaware. This is not to say that Black women on screen never show flaws; however, traditionally when they do, the flaws are seen as character breaks or as present only in extreme emotional moments. The consistent portrayal of Black women as strong and without awkwardness is an ethical threat because the imagery is contributing to problematic notions by outsiders that Black women "have it together." Contrary to the characteristics of Mammy, Jezebel, or Sapphire who are knowledgeable and assertive in their own ways, awkward is a prominent part of who J is. In the series her awkwardness is not a lapse, and the intentionality of these characteristics makes for a broader depiction of the Black female experience.

Issa Rae's portrayal of J on ABG recalls long-standing beauty codes and challenges them with her presence and role. Stuart Hall (1980) reminds us that codes embedded in media become significant because of their connection to the signification of power and identity in society, and that those encoded or decoded meanings cannot be impactful unless they connect to a salient ideology. J's skin color and hair are two physical examples that are reflective of, and a challenge to, encoded and decoded beauty standards often applied to Black women. The history for preference of lighter-skinned Black women dates back to the days of slavery when Blacks with fairer skin were often given more privileges and less manual labor to do (Kerr 2005). Lighter skin and adherence to white standards of beauty have been equated with attractiveness and a friendlier disposition. While there are many more prominent Black female entertainers now in 2013 than in the past, remnants of colorism remain. Audiences are still more likely to see lighter-skinned Black women in mass media contexts than darker skinned ones, especially in the spotlight of leading roles. Issa Rae has a darker complexion and her presence alone as the show's leading character, and without an outwardly aggressive attitude, recasts the typical media portrayal of dark skinned Black women.

Hair is also an aesthetic for defining the beauty of Black females. Long straight hair is still the preferred look for prominent Black female figures. Despite the fact that women who are of African descent usually do not have hair that grows straight, it is extremely rare to see a Black woman on television or in film who wears her hair "natural" (e.g., does not have her hair chemically treated to be straight or wear wigs or extensions that present the illusion that hair is long and straight). Some scholars regard the display of straight hair as a reflection of attempts to match white beauty standards and an enforcement of that hegemonic structure (Byrd and Tharps 2001; Patton 2006), while others argue that straight hair is more of a style preference that is another part of Black beauty norms. J impulsively cuts all of her hair off in the first episode of ABG and wears a short, natural afro for the duration of the series. J embraces the look, despite receiving comments about looking like a man and inquiries about her sexuality because of the short hair. But J makes no other statement about her hair after cutting it. Her hair is not a statement piece; it is another reinterpretation of what a Black leading lady can be and look like. This hair choice is also reflective of the strong natural hair community that has grown through online connections over the last ten years, where emphasis is on embracing and taking care of natural hair, not necessarily making a statement.

J might not be an overtly sexual, Jezebel type character, but her love life is a prominent part of the show's storyline and the dominant story arc in the first season is the love triangle that J gets caught in. She has to decide between her Black coworker Fred and his best friend White Jay First, considering that the complexion of J's skin is darker than other Black women playing lead roles, it is unique that she is an object of romantic affection at all. Second, the final partner choice that J makes is also resistant to the usual narrative because J chooses to date White Jay exclusively. Black woman/white male romantic pairings are rarely depicted in media, and when they are present they are treated as novelty.

By choosing White Jay over Fred, J challenges the notion that the Black woman should automatically be coupled with the Black man and presents a positive image of a Black woman in a romantic relationship with a white man. The popular culture narratives tends to say that Black women are unable to find romantic partners, or that they are less attractive in the eyes of white men, or that they are reluctant to date white men (MN Editor 2012). This narrative persists even when the actual experiences of Black women in interracial relationships differ (Childs 2005). The presence of this romantic pairing adds dimension to the media depictions of Black women's sexuality. J's desirability is presented in a more ethical fashion because she is in direct opposition to Jezebel characters who are hypersexualized and the Mammy who is not considered at all for romantic appeal. J reinforces that Black women with darker complexions are desirable partners for more than just Black men. Despite more prevalent conceptions, J chooses the white male as her partner, and plays a part in reframing media depictions of Black womanhood in the process.

Each of these deviations from a more stereotypical norm highlights a piece of what has been missing in media portrayals of Black femininity. This is reflected in how the viewers respond to and create their own discourse in response to the show. Fans often explain real-life identification with the fictional character J, as, for instance, seen in this comment from DeeDee Stanley—"I think i can kinda relate to this show . . . i'm am kinda awkward . . ."[4]—and from this one from cocopuff79—"I'm watching #awkwardblkgrl series aka the story of my life again for the second time in two months. @issarae is awesome."[5] These are viewers of the show who see the awkward portrayal of J as a reflection of themselves, and the connection to this conception of awkward is not a source of shame. Viewers are excited to assert that this character is relatable to their sense of selves: for example, greendo2456 writes, "Oh my gosh, my life. I'm an awkward black girl too everyone!!"[6] and "Yay, I'm not alone" gets expressed by Kyra Brown.[7] It is not just the traits of the main character that ring true for the commenters, as eibbit12 shares an identical hair experience to the one that J has to deal with at work: "OMG when her boss says her hair reminds her of pubic hair . . . a guy said that to me once he was like its so curly like pubic hair is that a common thing that people say to Black people or what?"[8] Similarly, J's interracial relationship strikes a personal chord with Nkenge Ragan.

> I want to see couples like the one I'm in portrayed as normal and natural, not as a "special episode about race" or as being made up of a stripper and her deadbeat boyfriend (saw that on an MTV True Life: I'm in an interracial relationship)

or some other such mess to show that interracial relationships are somehow inherently deviant.[9]

These examples show that the viewers of the show are able to utilize the space to engage in interactions that highlight both their experiences and what is missing from the stereotypical portrayals of Black women in media. This type of interaction infuses an ethical element by facilitating space for critique from multiple voices.

Connections to broader societal issues

Critiques about media representations of Black women are not only for cultural critics. Viewers feel the lack of balance when it comes to the portrayals of Black women in more traditional media platforms: "So so funny! I hope you get to replace *In Living Color*. We need some fresh female comedy on tv," says Hairbiz74.[10] Shattisbaddis also makes a judgment about what traits in Black women are marketable and commoditized when replying to a comment that questioned why the ABG videos do not have even more views and popularity, arguing it's "because they don't [portray] the ratchet behavior and they are natural looking Black women playing the roles . . . natural Black women in a positive light are not hot commodity . . . hair hatted hooligans are!"[11] These respondents know that something is missing in mainstream representations of Black women and within this interactive digital media space of YouTube, viewers are able to see portrayals that are relatable and resonate with their own lived experiences. They can also use the space to turn around and critique media trends that they consider to be doing a disservice to the realities of Black femininity. One step toward increasing media ethics is in moving past the mere presence of diverse faces and toward the elimination of stereotypical representations and maintaining critical evaluations of the media being consumed (Dixon 2013). With ABG the digital space allows for the simultaneous presentation of a narrative that injects more diversity into the media representations of Black women while allowing viewers to engage in critique of the broader hegemonic system.

Looking toward the future, researchers should continue to monitor the resistant discourses taking place through interactive digital media. Van Dijk (1987) has stated that much of what we know about "others" who are from different perceived cultural backgrounds is learned from the mass media.

That interaction between the viewer and the mass-mediated texts is a form of intercultural communication (Moon 2008). As audiences of mass media, we construct and deconstruct cultural notions about others and ourselves. If these tenets apply to digital media as well, and the use of digital media is rapidly increasing, then the scholar of ethics should look closely at the interactive aspects of digital media that might have just as much potential to resist hegemony as it does to replicate it. Can we promote and advocate for those resistant elements in digital space? That engagement might be key to chipping away at the constraints of hegemony.

Notes

1 Interview with Black Girl With Long Hair (2011), http://blackgirllonghair. com/2011/06/interview-with-issa-rae-writer-star-producer-of-misadventures-of-awkward-black-girl/.

2 Black American is used consistently throughout this chapter as an all encompassing cultural description of people of the African diasporas. It is used instead of the often more popular "African American" to also include those who are part of the diasporas but cannot identify an ethnic connection to any African country. "Black" is written purposefully with an uppercase 'B' when referencing people of the African diaspora because the term is a proper noun that represents people of a specific racial and ethnic category (not unlike Korean, Native American, American, or Kenyan) and is not merely a descriptive color.

3 SLAP J, Comment on "The Stop Sign"—Awkward Black Girl (2011), https://www. youtube.com/watch?v=nIVa9lxkbus.

4 Dee Dee Stanley, Comment on "The Job"—Awkward Black Girl (2011), https:// www.youtube.com/watch?v=xv0ahGRkaKE.

5 Cocopuff79, Comment on "The Stop Sign"—Awkward Black Girl (2011), https:// www.youtube.com/watch?v=nIVa9lxkbus.

6 greendog2456, Comment on "The Stop Sign"—Awkward Black Girl (2011), https://www.youtube.com/watch?v=nIVa9lxkbus.

7 Kyra Brown, Comment on "The Stop Sign"—Awkward Black Girl (2011), https:// www.youtube.com/watch?v=nIVa9lxkbus.

8 Eibbit12, Comment on "The Stop Sign"—Awkward Black Girl (2011), https:// www.youtube.com/watch?v=nIVa9lxkbus.

9 Nkenge Ragan, Comment on Awkward Black Girl "The Check," https://www. youtube.com/watch?v=iiNpSVXbWU&index=9&list=PL854514FC0EBDCD8.

10 Hairbiz74, Comment on "The Hallway" Awkward Black Girl (2011), https://www.youtube.com/watch?v=GzGHeZSwgCA&list=PL854514FC0EBDCD8E&index=3.

11 Shattisbaddis, Comment on "The Job"—Awkward Black Girl (2011), https://www.youtube.com/watch?v=xv0ahGRkaKE.

17

"Be a Bully to Beat a Bully": Twitter Ethics, Online Identity, and the Culture of Quick Revenge

Scott R. Stroud

More high-profile cases are coming to light involving mobs of people on Twitter shaming people who supposedly deserve to be shamed. Whether it's getting alleged racists fired, punishing those who post their distasteful Halloween costumes, or battling sexist tweets by revealing them to the public, users are increasingly using Twitter as a prime way of generating the desire for revenge against those who have done or said something wrong. For a communicative technology seemingly so minor in range (tweets are limited to 140 characters), the ethical implications run deep. Online identity is inherently malleable, obscured, and separable from one's offline identities (Baym 2010). On Twitter, one can pick a name, an avatar picture, and define who he or she is and what you know about him or her via his or her tweets. While previous work has looked at the benefits and drawbacks of pseudo-anonymity for web forums and blogs (Donath 1999; Stroud and Pye 2013), few have looked at the ethics of Twitter, especially in the interactions it fosters among those anonymously tweeting, "listening in," and acting on appeals made by popular voices on this platform.

The combination of magnifying communicative action, coordinating disparate others, and enhancing anonymity are all reasons that Twitter has now become a vital implement for the online activist collective known as Anonymous to execute its operations (or "ops") (Coleman 2014). This inquiry into the ethical problems raised by Twitter will focus on two operations pursued on Twitter: (1) "OpAntiBully," a concerted effort to harass and shame alleged online bullies and (2) "OpPedoFear," an operation to identify (through civilian online sting operations) and publicly shame putative pedophiles. These two cases are interesting for those studying communication ethics because they take advantage of Twitter's incredibly responsive and interconnected forms of communication. Furthermore, both cases employ "doxing" (d0xing), the revealing of private identifying information of online selves that are accused of nefarious online and offline conduct, as a basis for pursuing offline revenge. Is seeking justice online against those that deserve it this clear and ethically simple? This chapter explicates the empirical aspects to online revenge-seeking. Beyond this descriptive function, this chapter hopes to show that in the case of both anti-bullying operations and operations exposing supposed pedophiles is a deep ethical conflict in how we are to use our potential power for action to affect others and the common good.

One side says we have the power and ability to speak and criticize, so why not use this communicative ability to maximize public good and minimize obvious harms? Some false accusations of being a pedophile, some overreactions to what exactly it means if one's employee is listed on a website as a "cyberbully" are allowable *if* we can strike a blow at the larger phenomena of cyberbullying and online exploitation of children. Call this the *utilitarian* intuition: the right thing to do is that action which tends to produce the greatest good for the greatest number (e.g., Bentham (1781) 2007). Some harm is allowable, as long as the good outweighs this small drawback to a path of action. The police fail to see *this* person as the threat that *we* see him as; am I to let him go without doing something about this situation? Twitter gives me the insulation and power to do something very loud and effective about it. It also lets me marshal others in this endeavor, increasing feelings of justification and multiplying my ability to do something to this person who so deserved it. On the other side is what can be called the *Kantian* intuition: one should not treat humans—individually or as a mass—in certain ways (e.g., Kant (1785) 1996). This applies even if disrespectful treatment is still legally allowed. They should always be granted respect, regardless if this treatment postpones consequences we may desire, and they should never be used as a mere means to some end that you happen to value highly. This person reacts with skepticism to the bullying of bullies and the extra-judicial setting up of online strangers as threats to children; they worry about the issues of accountability, proportionally, and reversibility of punishments meted out. They do not demur to the pursuit of justice; instead, they would be motivated to seek it in a way that *respects* the humanity of all individuals, victims and those who might be accused of harming victims. The point of this chapter is to muddy the waters here, and to argue against reading these practices of pursuing online revenge as simply just and wholly ethical.

OpAntiBully and Twitter

Bullying is a new form of harassment that is receiving more attention from scholars. One central feature of bullying is that it usually involves communicative means that hurt the emotional or physical well-being of its target. As danah boyd (2014) points out, bullying is often defined by repetitive aggressions in contexts involving a power differential. Online, however, the traditional elements of bullying get muddied—online relationships are not as saturated with power structures as they may be in school settings, for instance. Additionally, many cases of online bullying involve a collection of non-repeated utterances from a mob of individuals. What makes the analysis of online bullying even trickier is that there is a blurry line between harsh but legitimate criticism of some person and their actions and illegitimate, harmful bullying. Bullying seems to take hurtful speech to unnecessary extremes, but when it comes to matters of law, the precision needed to coercively legislate such matters is often hard to achieve. Add to this the "cyber" element of cyberbullying, and one has a tough ethical issue. Instead of verbally pushing someone around on the playground in a face-to-face interaction, one can fire off mean tweets or Facebook posts at them and their friends, using hard to trace online identities. Legislating all of these grades of behavior *and* upholding First Amendment rights is difficult (Hudson 2014). One cannot outlaw all speech that hurts feelings, since there are more rights involved than those implicated by a vague appeal to a right to live a life free from fear or worry caused by others (e.g., Bazelon 2014b). While "true threats" can be legally proscribed, there is an expanse of criticism and public statement that does cause anxiety that seems difficult to identify, legislate, and justifiably crush.

One of the more well-known cases of online bullying was that of Amanda Todd, a Canadian teenager who committed suicide in October 2012. While any suicide is awful news, this one was deemed particularly newsworthy because it was one of the growing number that were seemingly caused by online and real-life bullying. Todd was a user of "BlogTV," a website that allowed users to chat with other online users. She was twelve years old when she made a fateful decision to flash her breasts on camera to strangers with whom she was chatting. One observer had taken a "screen grab" of that image, thus immortalizing her nudity in digital form. The stranger then contacted her on Facebook and demanded more sexual images and videos. If she didn't comply, he would release the captured images of her topless (Morris 2012). Eventually, the photos were posted to Facebook and other online sites, enabling the original harasser and others to bully Todd. She changed schools repeatedly, but the photos and harassment would inevitably follow her. Some have pointed out how this is a complex case of online stalking that begat real-life bullying by male and female classmates (Bazelon 2012). Its tragic conclusion only further emphasized the harmful potential of online forms of abusive communication.

While the legal authorities floundered when addressing this tragedy and those who enabled it, the online activist group Anonymous opened a "white knight" operation to do something about it. This operation was titled "OpRIP," and focused on "dismantling the collection of child porn that proliferated after the 15-year-old's [Todd's] death" (Murphy 2013). Beyond reporting Twitter accounts that forwarded and linked to her nude images, the anonymous hackers running this operation began to focus on revealing who originally stalked and harassed Todd. Acting on their own leads, Anonymous activists eventually identified the man they said was responsible for Todd's death: "They released a roundup of personal information—that is, they 'doxed'—a Vancouver-area man, claiming he was the one behind Todd's suicide. They released a cache of identifying information including his Facebook, Twitter, and Google+ accounts, links to his accounts at perv sites like Jailbait, photos, chat transcripts, and home address. And, as is traditional, a bombastic 'Expect Us' video" (Murphy 2012b). This information was publicly (and anonymously) shared on internet sites such as Pastebin. Yet all was not perfect. It turns out that the address that had been listed was not the correct one for that man, thus inconveniencing and endangering those who lived in that house. Furthermore, the age was incorrectly listed among his information, making one wonder what other inaccuracies made it into this "proof." Eventually, Canadian authorities announced that this individual wasn't the culprit (Murphy 2012a), and an arrest was made of a Dutch citizen in Amsterdam ("Who Is the" 2014). Accuracy and good intentions did not necessarily correlate in such operations.

Many of the online activists (or "hacktivists") involved in this operation became associated with an ongoing operation named "OpAntiBully" (Murphy 2013). Hacktivists had honed their revenge-seeking procedure: identify which online persona was doing the harassing or original distribution of harmful content, and then connect that persona with a real-life identity that could be shared (via a "dox") with the online community, news outlets, and governmental authorities. Most of the information in the dox is publicly available. Yet when it is connected to an online persona who is accused of questionable actions, it becomes worrisome because of the harms it could hold to the offline identities of those accused. In one op, the wrong boy was doxed as a harasser of a girl who had committed suicide. This error was later noticed by the online avengers, the damage was done—the accused boy stated, "My life right now is falling apart because of this. . . . I always have to look out, behind my back" (Bazelon 2014a).

Through "tagging" and "retweeting," Twitter enhanced OpAntiBully's ability to identify bullies and the exact words or threats that they were uttering. Twitter's ability to quickly convey links with sparse descriptive text allowed OpAntiBully members to publicize anonymously posted content on Pastebin and other sites. This linking activity gave anonymous Twitter accounts a sheen of protection should this information be harmful or incorrect, since in some cases it is not clear who posted the original dox. This publicity is said—by members of OpAntiBully—to have led to police action in some cases. Emily Bazelon (2014a) describes the psychology and the tensions behind Anonymous operations such as OpAntiBully:

> Anons tend to see the cases in which they intervene in polarized terms, parables with an innocent victim, evil perpetrators and ineffectual (or corrupt) law enforcement. There have been notable instances in which the pressure they created from a distance brought needed scrutiny to a case that had otherwise been ignored or buried. But because these activists have no local roots, they can also be blind to important subtleties and wind up falsely accusing or demonizing innocent people. Whether an op does good or ill depends entirely on the care of the people who sign on, because there are no built-in checks, no authority figure who can call off Anonymous.

The choice of targets, the means of retaliation, and the sort of evidence that allows for a positive identification are all subject to the diffuse organizational structure of Anonymous. Anonymous operations often contain minor or major errors about who (in real life) did what online. Sometimes, they are accurate. They are always trumpeted, however, as being driven purely by the cause of social justice and the common good.

One very public figure who joined the anonymous legions of Anonymous in its anti-bullying operations was James McGibney, the man associated with the BullyVille and CheaterVille websites. McGibney would use his Twitter account, @BullyVille, to identify and attack alleged bullies. McGibney's aggressive style embodies his motto, "Sometimes you have to be a bully to beat a bully" (Kushner 2014). His forceful online publicity campaign was effective in shutting down a variety of revenge pornography sites; as part of his leverage on Hunter Moore, one of the webmasters he targeted, he was aided by Anonymous hackers obtaining

Moore's address as well as stolen photos of Moore doing drugs. McGibney's website, BullyVille, is also a way that he and others fight against alleged bullies. This website allows for the posting of "evidence" (largely narrative) of others' bullying behaviors. The victims detailed on this site are normal denizens of the Web as well as some celebrities. The most notable of the latter group was Kate Gosselin, a reality television star who polarized segments of the online world. McGibney identified a blog where many of the anti-Kate posters posted mean comments and alleged death threats (such as a photoshopped picture of Gosselin impaled on a stick), and eventually convinced its owner to sell the domain to him. He then quietly used IP addresses and embedded information in posted pictures to "identify" the posters' real identities and locations. He posted their mean comments on BullyVille next to their real names for internet searches to find (Kushner 2014), and contacted their employers with their tweets as "proof" of the claim that they are bullies (Carpenter 2013). As McGibney tweeted, "Revenge is never pretty but when done meticulously, intelligently, and psychotically, it sure is a thing of beauty" (Kushner 2014). His controversial tactics of naming and shaming people he dubs as "bullies" has earned him the ire of many online, and has cost him most of his advertising revenues. Celebrity sponsors such as actress Becca Tobin pulled away from BullyVille, claiming "I believe in providing strength to those who have been bullied . . . but not in bullying a bully" (Kushner 2014). In all of these cases, we see the means of Twitter being used extensively to get word out about certain individuals and to help craft (or hide) the identities of those acting in extra-legal manners to pursue justice. While McGibney used identifiable Twitter aliases, most others do not. This allows them to "reincarnate" as a slightly different Twitter persona if they are reported or suspended for violating Twitter's terms of service (which vaguely prohibit harassment and the disclosure of private information). In the cat-and-mouse game of pursuing and shaming bullies, Twitter only multiplies the rapidity of moves toward perceived justice.

OpPedoFear and Twitter

In some cases, cyberbullying is worrisome because it correlates with real-world, physical harm. In other cases, hacktivists worry about it because it *could* lead to offline harms. Both of these are part of the utilitarian impetus to shame and hurt alleged online bullies. One online activity that does seem to correlate with real-life harm is child predation. Connected with this is child pornography, an activity that has direct or indirect links to the exploitation of children. The ease and anonymity of Twitter communication has made it a hub for those expressing interest in children and in some cases, sharing nude images of children. In common usage, such predators who sexually abuse children are called "pedophiles." Online, this term is molded by Anonymous to fit those who might potentially abuse children by "grooming" (preparing) children for abusive relationships. The subgroups of Anonymous who fight online pedophiles mounted an operation in 2012 called "OpPedoChat." This operation targeted a range of websites that putatively facilitated discussion among those who identify as "minor attracted"; Anonymous announced its intentions in a Youtube video:

> Anonymous aim to diminish if not eradicate this plague from the internet. For the good of our followers, for the good of mankind, and for our own enjoyment we shall expel from the internet and systematically destroy any such boards that continue to operate. Anonymous recognises this as a serious undertaking and do not expect it to be completed in a short period of time. Factions of Anonymous from all over the globe are participating in sub-operations. Information on paedophiles is being gathered and released. (Steadman 2012)

Such operations go beyond simply reporting the tweeting of child pornography to Twitter. They involve civilian members of Anonymous destroying such online communities by publicly naming and shaming their members. These operations involved Anonymous members going to websites and forums where minor-attracted individuals gather and eventually get enough information to "out" such alleged pedophiles. Anonymous's Pastebin entry for #OpPedoChat even provided a list of websites that were "targets" and implored "Those that can attack are asked to fire their lazors [sic]; those that cannot are encouraged to learn."

Much can be learned from Anonymous's tactics in such operations by watching their publicly accessible Twitter feeds. Twitter is both how they ascertain targets and how they hurt such targets. I will discuss some findings from observations taken from publicly accessible Twitter feeds in 2012–13 connected to "OpPedoFear." A few notes about the following description. First, all of these pedohunter Twitter feeds were unlocked and publicly available for anyone (including those without a Twitter account) to see. Part of the power of these Anonymous operations comes from their publicity, so a secured Twitter account would work against the operation's aims. Second, none of these feeds from OpPedoFear contained illicit material such as child pornography.

Indeed, this lack points to major ethical quandaries raised by this operation—OpPedoFear's pedohunters locate and target people who could *potentially* do something illegal (viz., child predation), but not those actually or observably doing that act *now*. Third, all or almost all of the Twitter pedohunter accounts observed are now suspended or defunct. I will change the names of the accounts and leave out identifying tags.

The method of the OpPedoFear operators seemed to be pretty standard. First, the Anonymous member would post a Craigslist personal advertisement for a person seeking a "platonic" friendship, or initiate contact through the sorts of forum websites noted in OpPedoChat pastebins (Steadman 2012). Second, the pedohunter would chat with a target online. During this chat, the pedohunter (using a fake alias, typically female) will reveal that they are underage (often claiming an age of 14 or 15). All this takes place in text-based chat—no pictures are being supplied by the pedohunter of any child (other than a clothed headshot avatar); they simply assume the online persona of a minor through their words. The pedohunter attempts to get the target to reveal his (in all the cases reported on Twitter, it was a male target) identity. This could be inferentially gained through IP addresses associated with the target's online identity (or e-mail correspondence); some targets seem to give away names and/or phone numbers quite freely to the disguised pedohunter. Third, and essential to the rhetoric of evidence prevalent in Anonymous operations, the pedohunter must screen-capture the chat activities with the target to document the problematic act. Pastebin entries of the chat log often show a few lines of text, usually involving the target talking with the pedohunter, the pedohunter dropping in their (young) age, and sometimes (although not always) the target asking for the pedohunter to send them some erotic pictures. Of course, the pedohunter does not send such pictures. This is simply a ruse to establish that the target *wanted* something illegal (pictures, or even a physical meeting).

Fourth, the pedohunter ends the interaction abruptly (without sharing any promised content). They then set out to compile a full "dox" of the target, now labeled by the pedohunter as a "pedophile." Such doxes, posted on anonymous online sites as Pastebin, attribute no authorship beyond the operation hashtag (i.e., #OpPedoFear), and in some cases the Twitter handle of the doxer (e.g., "DrX,"). Like the doxes of bullies in OpAntiBully, these typically contain the target's full name, e-mail address, real-life address, social media links, occupation title and business name, phone numbers, and similar demographic and contact information for bosses, family members, and friends. One thing that must be noted—as was the case with the anti-bullying doxes, none of this information gathered is strictly illegal. What is worrisome is the potential for harm through the *use* it is put to, and the inferential connections explicitly or implicitly made about this person's *character*, *actions*, and *potential actions*. In some cases, chat logs of the offending interaction are screen captured and linked in this Pastebin dox. Fifth, the pedohunter turns to Twitter in order to distribute this dox to other anonymous members.

This linking or redistributing information about a "pedophile" via Twitter allows some distance between those who merely announce a pedophile and those who punish such actions. For instance, DrX, a pedohunter, announced a target as follows: "Pedophile [real name] at [town, state]. Feel free to destroy. #NASTY! #OpPedoFEAR d0x--> pastebin.com/XXXXXX <--d0x." The pedohunter simply announced this, or so it can be said. Plausible deniability is established, since this is just a link being redistributed. The "destroying" is done by others receiving this tweet. The same DrX announces in another tweet (to two other tagged friendly accounts): "I'm a purveyor of information. The Hive, however . . . #AllBetsAreOff." It is at this point that the "Hive" or the collective of Anonymous members takes over. Sixth, anonymous members respond to the information-passing tweet in an attempt to publicly shame the target. The anonymous members often tweet about what they will do or have already done to the target. As with many things online, one needs pictures or screen captures to prove something actually happened. Some say they've added another address to the target's dox, and provide the link again. Others share another Pastebin link to a letter they claim they've sent to the target's family and local police department, or a screen capture of a link to the dox that they supposedly posted on a family member's Facebook page. Others tag the target's family members in retweeting the link to the dox (and the claim that this person is a pedophile). In the case of the formal letters (via e-mails), the anonymous member invokes the name of Anonymous to air the link to the original Pastebin dox and to claim that this demonstrates "grooming" and "solicitation of child pornography" on behalf of the chatting target. They then ask the family to ostracize "this dangerous predator" or police to arrest him as soon as possible. Judging from the reaction of some targeted individuals on the various pedohunter's Twitter feeds, consequences from this Twitter-enabled campaign include separation from their spouse and children, along with losing significant work positions. In the case of corporate-or military-affiliated target individuals, the pedohunters announce (on Twitter) their accusations that "*x* is a pedophile" (along with link to their dox) and "tag" related corporate or military Twitter accounts to further shame the accused individual. Such negative publicity, regardless of whether it is true or false, clearly motivates many businesses and entities to distance themselves from the accused individual for their own sake.

There has been some pushback to pedohunting tactics on Twitter from other anonymous individuals. Some of them decry the light that these operations cast on Anonymous. The supporters of doxing and shaming putative pedophiles see this as the best way to proceed in the face of a legal system that does too little to address these predators. For instance, one supporter replied in a tweet to DrX: "You do more to protect children than any law enforcement I know. Public exposure beats long expensive trials." Yet others fail to see this as the perfect solution in an imperfect world. Their concerns, judging from their Twitter interactions with the pedohunters, fall into a few categories. First, the critics of the pedohunters worry about false positives being created through these internet setups. One even tweeted that this is "destroying the real meaning of what a pedophile is because of these fake 'pedo hunters.'" The critics seem to view this as entrapping lonely men online to eventually talk about incriminating topics; the idea is that they would not have asked these questions or broached these topics without the pedohunter's intense prodding in the course of private chats. Second, critics worry about the deceptive aspect to these setups. A pedohunter quickly replied "better THAT then a real child." Here the conflict seems to be between notions of deception that see it as bad only when it is harmful to the greater number of people and the idea that it is bad because it implicates a failure to treat another human with the appropriate level of respect due. Third, some critics worried about the avatar picture used by the pedohunters in their chats. Some claimed that they identified the real-life (and unaffiliated) teenage girl that unknowingly supplied one main pedohunter's fake avatar picture through Google reverse image searches and other means. This is worrisome, some argued, because that identifiable picture placed that unaffiliated, real child at risk during the course of the pedohunter's operations. Fourth, some critics worried that the pedohunters weren't going after the *real* pedophiles—actual individuals who were accosting and sexually assaulting real children. Some critics suggested stings, but of individuals who were "demonstrably" predisposed, meaning those previously convicted of sexual assault on a child or on sex offender registries. This standard of "demonstrably" predisposed, of course, comes into play in legitimate police sting operations because it mitigates concerns of police entrapment. Anonymous, however, doesn't have to worry about such matters in pursuing justice in the court of public opinion. Spread the dox and screen caps of what the target has said, and the truth will win out, or so it is believed.

Fifth, some criticized the pedohunters for faking screen-captured evidence or chat logs through photoshop or similar programs. This is worrisome, as some pedohunters fought off accusations that a member of their op was himself a child-predator by dismissing evidence against him for the very same reason. When their evidence is questioned, another Twitter account with a pseudonym chimes in and says that "I can VERIFY that those Facebook messages posted by DrX are in fact LEGIT and very real." Of course, no one knows how such verification happened, nor can they replicate or check it themselves. A technique that the pedohunters created was to confront their targets, before going public with a dox, with their "real identity" (viz., as the Twitter account associated with the pedohunter) and give them a chance to avoid public shaming. The pedohunter gave them a few minutes to get a marker, write "PWNED [pawned/owned] by DrX" or "I love DrX" on their forehead, and take a picture of their face in the mirror. This was then passed on to the pedohunter, who then reneged on the agreement, and posted this picture as indisputable "proof" that this individual agreed and admitted to doing what he was accused of doing. As one publicly accessibly pedohunter Pastebin explained: "The reason for this is because often times the child-predator will deny that the person on the other end of those calls, texts, e-mails, etc was them. This puts HUGE holes in their story because why would an INNOCENT person humiliate themselves like this. Plus . . . I mean . . . it's funny."

Ethical challenges to the pursuit of online revenge

What both of these cases show is the potential for using the malleable means of Twitter—and the public sharing of information it enables—to identify and shame those that have supposedly committed some egregious offense ranging from offensive joking to racist utterances to trolling forums looking for children to "groom" for illegal activities. Perhaps the means that Anonymous must engage in are justified only by the end—in the two cases noted here, that of protecting children. But must one "be a bully to beat a bully," as McGibney so often puts it (Kushner 2014)? Why would one *not* want to err on the side of the good and the right, especially in terms of protecting the children? What these cases of using Twitter illustrate is the ease at which online actors can identify what they judge to be injustice and then seek to right these wrongs on their own terms, even if it means harming or using another person as a mere means to do so. In other words, these are cases of using Twitter to pursue revenge on those supposedly deserving it. Sir Francis Bacon said, "Revenge is a kind of wild justice" (French 2001, 3). It is "wild," of course, because of the unpredictability and bias introduced by the one pursuing justice being conflated with other important roles in the pursuit of the justice, namely judge and punisher. Revenge is often pursued because of a moral wrong to one's own interests (Nozick 1981). The internet adds a new dimension to revenge-seeking—pursuing revenge for unknown others. When the "Hive" of anonymous Twitter users publicizes, harasses, and harms people labeled as "pedophiles" or "bullies," the common feature is not personal knowledge or relational connection; it is a real-life individual's conviction that this (largely unrelated) person is worthy of punishment.

With this online culture of quick revenge (Stroud 2014), we no longer ask, "Am I the right one to pursue this retribution?" or "Why should I become involved in this matter?" Instead, Anonymous members ask, "Is this a chance to swiftly and harshly punish some evil in the world?" If there is such an opportunity, then they must. That seems to be the superhero mind-set behind pursuing revenge against bullies or alleged pedophiles that one has no real connection to. The internet can make us seem all powerful, and all connected—at least in terms of affecting consequences on others. These targets usually cannot affect us, of course, since our real-life identity is not fixed to the avenging Twitter persona (if we are careful). This is the power of being anonymous online, and the secret to Anonymous as a group. If you can remain anonymous, you can remain Anonymous. Segregating your online persona from your real-life identity gives you the power and the safety to decide to "be a bully to beat a bully."

Why resist the simple idea that this legal use of counterspeech is ethical solely because of its Potential to prevent significant evils? There are three ethical challenges posed by these two operations that should give one pause. First, one must worry about the lack of *accountability of those involved in a pursuit to avenge an injustice.* Courts and law enforcement agencies have known actors and procedures precisely for this reason—it gives them (and the system) a measure of accountability. If the system goes tragically wrong (say, with a wrongful conviction), we can at least see who was involved, what their interests or blindspots may have been, and publicly create binding solutions to prevent future instances of such a lapse. If a judge was swayed by inappropriate or biased concerns—and one can convincingly prove that to other known, accountable officials—that judge could be removed or replaced. The real-life person is affected by bad decisions, creating a deterrent for them *and* for similarly placed others in future instances comparable to that bad decision. But in the case of the pursuit of revenge via Twitter, all similar bets are off. One labels person X as a cyberbully, and unknown others pile on. Who knows who originally made this claim and what their evidence was? The important factor is the accusation that now resides next to person X's name in Google searches and a growing amount of public discourse. In the case of the pedohunters, this concern is magnified. From their public Twitter feeds, it is clear that their pursuit of revenge against putative pedophiles destroyed marriages and careers. What if these accusations were wrong? Even more prescient, what if these accusations are taken in the most damaging light possible (e.g., instead of as a certain kind of online discussion playing out, they are taken as clear evidence of criminal intent to sexually assault a child)? Law enforcement worries about entrapment and the rights of the accused because the situation is so serious, and because they are accountable. The best that Anonymous can hope for is that its distributed membership uses the best judgment available; as it puts it in one of its Pastebin entries listing "pedophile" websites to hack or attack, some of these sites "have not been screened at all yet and are 'innocent until proven guilty by a court of Anonymous.'" What this court is, who is involved, and how accountable they are, are all issues shrouded in the mist of online identity, exemplified by (but not unique to) Twitter's quick and malleable format. Online revenge is emphasized in these ops, not accountability or respect for the value of all people that transcends any specific operation or pursuit of justice.

Second, there are worries about *the proportionality of punishment for the alleged infraction*. Some of these instances of bullying could be chalked up to very bad taste, and seen as utterances that needed to be stopped without seriously harming the utterer. Yet many of the anti-bullying and pedohunter operations, especially those involving the public naming and shaming of identifiable persons, get very damaging quickly. They loudly and publicly label a real-life person something that society despises—a "bully," or worse, a "pedophile." Twitter's ability to be accessed by search engines *and* to quickly respond to information sharing needs is a deadly combination. Twitter users can quickly disseminate the "fact" that person X is a cyberbully or pedophile, but this quickly gets distanced from the context and any change that may have occurred in that person. Doxes and accusations are as permanent as the web archives that continue to chronicle them, and their harm does not change if the circumstances alter or the facts turn out differently. Some of those pursuing their own brand of justice against pedophiles or bullies might also be accused of not matching their passion and ire to the infraction. For instance, some of the alleged pedophiles are accused of soliciting meet-ups in real life; others are only accused of soliciting nude pictures. Still others, not doing either of these other two actions, are accused of vaguely "grooming" or preparing the child for these acts later. Yet all of these online, text-based acts are connected to the damning label of "pedophile," wielded by individuals who feel glee in sharing this judgment with families, churches, employers, and others. One could worry about the proportionality of the harms of public shaming in relation to the range of actions involved in the ambiguous worlds of online bullying and harassment. This concern is evoked in an observed instance where the public worlds of OpAntiBully and OpPedoFear overlapped—in defending one pedohunter from a critic on Twitter, a self-identified leader of OpAntiBully tweeted to the critic: "You have 10mins to shut up before your friends, family, work, previous work and local community get a nice little dossier." This was followed by the same anti-bullying individual exclaiming: "Goodluck. I'm going to ruin your life." Regardless of whether the anti-bullying advocate had the fixed, real-life identity of the critic to create these consequences, one can still notice the ethical concern here. Should one suffer a "ruined life" and public shame (probably as a "pedophile supporter") in all realms of their life because they worried about accountability and evidentiary issues implicated in pedohunting practices? This seems like a characteristic *overreaction*, but it is precipitated by the same conditions as the actions comprising the pursuit of justice—giving an insulated, online identity the simultaneous opportunity to (1) judge wrongs, (2) decide punishments, and (3) enact these punishments in a public fashion. What guarantee do we have that any given action of a pedohunter or anti-bully isn't a similar overreaction? An important way of operationalizing respect to persons is proportionality between offense and punishment—each ought to get their *just* desserts.

Lastly, there is the concern about *the corrigibility of punishments*. If a mistake is made and punishment applied, are there ways to correct it? If one suffers ruined relationships and loses their business because of anonymous public pressure being exerted that indicated they are a "cyberbully" or a "pedophile," and these claims turn out to be false or not exactly true, how can one proceed? No court can give them back their reputation, or all the thoughts and judgments that these claims cast upon them in the eyes of family, friends, and business associates. Even the normal method of redress through civil action is not available. If one knows who accused them of being a pedophile, then one could pursue civil legal action on the grounds of defamation, invasion of privacy, false light, and so forth. But if one maintains their anonymity on Twitter (meaning, uses a non-identifiable Twitter handle, a proxy to log in, and so forth), one is hard pressed to identify the revenge-seeker who wrongly harmed them. Even a subpoena for IP addresses only works if the offender failed to cover their tracks with means such as Tor or a proxy. And civil corrections would only include monetary damages, hardly a replacement for the relational and reputational harm wrought by this anonymous pursuit of revenge through Twitter publicity. There seems little that one can do to put the genie back into the online bottle from which well-intentioned avengers let it out.

Conclusion

But what if the law does not eradicate—quickly and completely—some evil we see in the world? Should we not use our legally allowed freedom of speech to punish, silence, or respond to this evil? Or are we to remain silent and abused by this evil in the world? Ethics, of course, deals with how we are to justifiably act in situations free from legal constraint or force. Even if an action is legal, the question of ethics still stands: *should* we do this action? This chapter's overriding point is that there are deeply conflicting intuitions at stake in the pursuit of online revenge—some of which are oppositional to revenge-seeking and important enough (e.g., the idea of respecting persons regardless of the good or bad consequences) that we should be very hesitant at marshaling online mobs to seek justice. Clearly, if one is bullied or harassed, one should respond. But this chapter has shown us that magnifying this response via online services such as Twitter will be ethically problematic primarily because it simplifies a complex moral situation solely out of concern for one way of thinking (that of maximizing what one agent thinks of as the good). Concerns with proportionality, reversibility, and accountability should not be forgotten as these principles are key ways we protect the respect due even to people we don't care for. In some cases, this conflict of deeply held values may even force us to see the reason behind tempering a quest for justice we could initiate with others and at the expense of a disagreeable target, all because we cannot guarantee that we are doing justice to the Kantian intuition at play in how we treat targeted others (and in how we expect them to treat us). Yes, we can swiftly and safely point our virtual finger at others, and bring down the wrath of wide swaths of society if we tie into the right issues and narratives. How can we do this, and achieve a great good, while protecting and respecting all of the parties involved?

18

Branding Feminism: Corporate Blogging and the Shaky Relationship between Ideology and Profitability

Molly Bandonis with Paul Booth

In today's neoliberal online environment, "[the women's blogosphere] feels like a much more insular, protective, brittle environment than it did before" (Goldberg 2014, quoting *Jezebel* founder Anna Holmes). Further, author Carrie Hamilton (2009) shows that, despite some solid community-building and consciousness-raising work that has been accomplished, the feminist blogosphere continues to adhere to old-media patterns of "exclusion and division" within feminism through practices of privileging certain voices and oversimplification of various contexts (86). The historical splintering of feminism and the hostile environment of online discussion forums are, in many ways, a perfect match. In this article, we hope to elucidate the ways that corporate blogging practices facilitate a neoliberal and patriarchal style of discourse in purported feminist spaces online.

Examining the ethics of the feminist web presents an opportunity for studying some of the most self-professed "feminist" sites online. One such site is *Jezebel*, a site billing itself as "general interest women's website" that is "more critical" than other women's websites (Jezebel Staff 2011). According to internet traffic tracking website Alexa.com,[1] *Jezebel* is one of the highest-trafficked websites in the United States (ranked 271), especially when compared with other popular feminism-oriented sites such as *The Mary Sue* (2,393), xojane.com (ranked 2612), and *Feministing* (11,193). *Jezebel* contributor Tracie Egan Morrissey (2014) offers her own perspective on the feminist blogosphere:

> Jezebel is *not* a place of unconditional support of women just because they're feminists. Feminism itself isn't even like that. The movement has been rife with infighting and debate about its direction since its inception. Dissent is important because it's what helps keep a movement from becoming static. (¶6)

By examining fourteen to fifteen daily posts on *Jezebel* for fourteen consecutive days, and conducting textual analyses on the two of the most popular (viewed) articles from a given day (July 23, 2014), we will explore patterns in terms of language and structure, and discuss the pageview goal of the site. This 24-hour period was chosen to reflect the "everyday pattern" of publishing (and the pattern that an everyday reader might follow) that *Jezebel* follows. No single event dominated *Jezebel*'s coverage.

A key question this chapter aims to address is: What does a feminist ideology look like when it hinges on a pageview-generating model? In a reflection about the early days of cyberfeminist discourse, Faith Wilding (1998) argues that cyberfeminists have "the chance to . . . address the complex new social, cultural, and economic conditions created by global technologies" and that a successful feminist environment online will "challenge . . . [traditional] gender, race, age, and class structures" (12). We argue in this chapter that such challenges are combated by the formalization of structures of online discourse— structures that are created by corporate interests and guided by an inherently patriarchal understanding of web discussion. In other words, the pageview model reinforces typical power structures, as opposed to the internet creating spaces for new models of discourse. Using a framework based on Richard Holt's (2004) analysis of Robert A. Dahl's tenets of civic discourse, we argue that the language and perspectives of *Jezebel* inhibit opportunities to engage in dialogue with others. Given *Jezebel*'s responsibility to parent company Gawker Media and its various revenue strategies (specifically, the monetization of user discussion via aggregator Kinja), we argue that the site contradicts its aspirational view of feminism by maintaining the status quo in terms of gender norms, dogmatic language, and the "memeification" of larger social issues specific to women. The "dissent" *Jezebel* editor Morrissey aspires to runs counter to cyberfeminist goals and creates further splintering in the interest of fostering online conflict. *Jezebel* is creating its own brand of feminism that illustrates a muddled relationship between commerce and identity politics/online forums.

Cyberfeminism and the ethics of corporate blogging

Ultimately, we argue that *Jezebel*'s brand of feminism targets different goals than those of cyberfeminism, and we locate our discussion within a framework that analyzes interdependence (Ess 2013), coalition (Keating 2005), and activism

(Desai 2009). In *Digital Media Ethics*, Charles Ess (2013) discusses a variety of ethical frameworks and their applicability to the digital media environment. In his application of feminist ethics to digital media situations, Ess characterizes the framework as emphasizing the importance of "interdependent relationships," and "our emotional bonds with one another" (235). A feminist ethical framework privileges collective experiences over individual gain—Ess connects this to "sharing" media online, and, broadly, "caring for others beyond our immediate circles" (235). As a distinct variant of this ethical framework, cyberfeminism explores the feminist possibilities and limitations within a digital technological sphere from a perspective of activism, solidarity, and cultivating spaces and dialogues of cultural/social/political change. Cricket Keating (2005) argues that dialogue with oppositional perspectives can help dismantle systems of oppression. Rather than using a universal perspective to effect change, Keating argues that identifying and investigating oppositional perspectives is integral to the "work of building coalitions" (94). Finally, Manisha Desai (2009) defines cyberfeminism in the context of globalization—cyberfeminism takes the shape of "collective connections . . . between virtual and place-based power and feminism" which create opportunities across borders for far-reaching political and social engagement (91). According to Desai, cyberfeminism exists at an intersection of previously existing activists' practices, and the development of the internet as a digital space within which physical borders or boundaries are less tangible.

The internet is a cultural construct, a space which can afford both resistance and complacency at the same time. Internet spaces are always-already gendered, part of larger gendered constructs, with a technological discourse. As offline assumptions about characteristics of gender migrate online, it becomes impossible to separate gender issues from technological issues. Nancy Baym (2009) states that "cyberfeminist practices are important because they do not stay online" (130). They are always factored in and a factor of offline-gendered discourse as well (see Nakamura 1995; Sundén 2003). One such example is the interaction between deliberately gendered spaces like *Jezebel* and the economic forces shaping online content. Although some sites can work as spaces of rebellion (see Pierce 2010), many others become subsumed under larger corporate, patriarchal forces. For instance, in a neoliberal economic climate, market forces establish a particular focus for online discourse. Is a true, or productive, feminist discourse possible in a climate where "a relative handful of private interests are permitted to control as much as possible of social life in order to maximize their personal profit" (McChesney 1999, 7)? Where "the last vestiges of private, intimate life, relationships and emotions are, often unwittingly and gradually, sacrificed to work" (Harvie 2013, 53)?

Today, as corporate blogging practices take center stage in contemporary social media cyberfeminism, and as civic discourse becomes muddled by corporate interests, a diffused sense of feminist discourse manifests online. Keating (2005) and Desai's (2009) iterations of cyberfeminism denote an active engagement with oppositional voices in order to create collective understanding. Corporate blogs diffuse these ideals, necessarily, in the interest of profitability and adherence to a pageview-generating model. Democratic potential within online content is at risk, given the amount of power wielded by corporate interests and their control of both author and commenter content.

Professional feminist bloggers are faced with two often-conflicting interests when publishing online: their own individual sense of ethics and the larger media conglomerates and/or corporate bodies for whom they work. The lines between these interests become blurry as popular models for blog spaces are built by online media companies like BuzzFeed and Gawker, companies owned and operated in largely male-dominated businesses and housed within a patriarchal economic structure. These companies represent a kind of melding of two previously distinctive blogging agendas: that of the individual/independent blog and that of the "blogolas" or flogs—blog-for-hire writer who would promote products and/or services for money. Bart Cammaerts (2008) notes that "even though the Internet was initially based on a nonprofit philosophy," examples and overall trends illustrate "that market forces have established themselves as the hegemonic paradigm of the medium" (363). He describes this as the exploitation of an individual blogger by large media companies. In terms of what Cammaerts calls the internet's "nonprofit philosophy," Richard Holt's (2004) *Dialogue on the Internet* discusses the ideals of an expansive democratic forum. Holt proposes four tenets to "bring the Internet into civic discourse," modeled on Robert A. Dahl's qualities of "ideal democracy." The tenets are: (1) effective participation, (2) voting equality, (3) enlightened understanding, and (4) control of the agenda. While utopian in its reach, these characteristics call attention to inconsistencies within the realm of online discussion. Holt (2004) describes effective democratic participation online as needing a space where these core tenets of civic discourse can be expressed: "If enough alternative representations are generated, there is a better chance of choosing among them to fashion more effective and appropriate thoughts and utterances" (216) Such a utopian digital "virtual sphere" is the hope of many cyberfeminists working on feminist discourse, but as Papacharissi (2002) warned over a decade ago, internet-based technologies seem to adapt to the political climate rather than creating a new one.

Directly engaging with and "choosing" content is a model which many websites privilege in their layout. Reddit, for example, allows users to "upvote" content and only the most popular content is listed on the front page. BuzzFeed engages users via social media, listing Facebook comments underneath articles, and allowing users to vote on whether the article itself represents a "fail," a "win," or a number of other internet language–specific codes. Because social media voting represents the harnessing of individual readers' affect and labor for a particular article (Terranova 2000), and because such voting can be controlled by a corporation working with goals incompatible with an egalitarian discourse, in practice such sites become shaped by neoliberal impulses of hierarchy and, in doing so, have become more hostile to feminism and feminist discussions. As Jen Harvie (2013) notes, audience labor

> offers the pleasures of action, self-determination and discovery; it appears quite straightforwardly to empower its audiences as co-makers. But *its benefits are much more compromised than they at first appear.* The engagements it offers are actually very limited, even illusionary. *Its equalitarianism is compromised by its tendency to retain authorial status for the producing company* or "real" artist. (50, emphasis ours)

Holt's (2004) third tenet might represent the greatest threat to successful corporate blogging: the user's "enlightened understanding" of content. Education in internet political discourse has to do both with knowledge about how internet messages are fashioned and conceived and with the ways in which the idiosyncratic qualities of the medium work in aiding or hindering these processes (219). This kind of understanding is also referred to as media literacy—a critical thinking skill set applied to various forms of media messaging. For cyberfeminists and cyberfeminism, media literacy helps reveal the underlying political and economic forces shaping online discourse, and thus offers a way to revisit so-called open forums as feminist spaces.

The fourth and final tenet of democratic online discussion, Holt (2004) argues, lies in the ability of the user to "control the agenda" (214). Such equal participation lies at the heart of what Henry Jenkins, Sam Ford, and Joshua Green (2013) refer to as "spreadable media," or content that can be controlled and distributed by anyone. However, just as Jenkins, Ford, and Green note that control over content shapes online discourse, Holt's own suggestions focus on a broader definition of the internet as a whole, addressing only the more theoretical shape online communication may one day take. With this conceptualization of democratic online discussion in mind, we now turn to how corporate blogging strategies can conflict or agree with Holt's tenets—illustrated by Gawker Media (*Jezebel*'s parent company), and their discussion platform, Kinja.

Gawker Media and Kinja

Commenting platform Kinja illustrates the contentious negotiations around cyberfeminist goals, creating dialogue and drawing consistent pageviews while ultimately creating a regulated meritocracy. The meritocracy of Kinja emerges through what Nick Denton, owner/founder of the Gawker Media online media company, describes as "the big board"—past strategy for creating competition among writers by displaying top-performing posts, those which drew the most new readers (McGrath 2010). Both this profile and an *Ad Age* article published two years later point to 2010 as a turning point for Gawker employees, a transformation from flat $12-per-post salary to near six-figure incomes and 401k's (Bercovici 2012).

In May 2012, Denton noted the inevitable demise of the era of revenue from banner ads, and predicted that Gawker's "primary offering to marketers will be our discussion platform" (Morrissey 2012, ¶3). Enter Kinja, Gawker's commenting platform. Interestingly, the language Kinja uses is somewhat reminiscent of Holt's (2004) descriptions of a democratic forum. The following description is taken directly from the Kinja (2014) site:

> With Kinja, you can now create your own discussions on your blog and control who gets to be a part of those discussions. You have the power to curate the conversation using the same tools of engagement as our editors, such as reply, dismiss, follow, like, and share.

Columbia Journalism Review writer Felix Salmon (2012) interpreted Denton's memo and the dawn of Kinja as a new monetization of user comments, and advertiser's control thereof: "If an advertiser buys a sponsored post . . . the advertiser will have a reasonably large degree of control of the conversation that most people see in that post" (¶11). Salmon observes that Gawker's emerging model aims to capitalize on the fact that "commenters are faster and funnier and more knowledgeable than the staff of any website." On the one hand, this newer, more democratic approach to commenting privileges discussion. On the other hand, this discussion is used for profit and embedded advertiser-consumer conversation runs counter to Kinja's claim to being a meritocracy, in which comments and discussions are voted into visibility. *Jezebel*'s commenting structure, as we will demonstrate, relies on profits more than on opening up spaces for feminist discourse.

The mechanics of commenting on *Jezebel*

This section will address how users engage with *Jezebel*, and how different kinds of engagement are encouraged or penalized and shape the kinds of discourse the site ultimately fosters. We demonstrate the responsibility that forum moderators and site admin wield in enforcing parameters of discussion and the ways in which feminism is allowed to be interpreted.

Anna Holmes founded *Jezebel* in 2007 with ambitions of creating a self-aware and more intelligent approach to everyday, women's magazine-style content: celebrities, fashion, and pop culture (Mulkerrins 2013). Currently, *Jezebel* is one of the 1,000 most visited websites in the United States, and has about 10 million unique page views each month (Alexa.com; Quantcast.com). Threaded comments were introduced to *Jezebel* and all of Gawker Media's sites in September 2008. Former editor Holmes (2008) originally introduced the changes to commenting via a September 22 post "The Girl's Guide To Commenting On *Jezebel*: Version 1.2," which said that comments would be "newly organized by conversations, ordered by popularity." In August 2010, new editor Jessica Coen posted a set of commenting guidelines reiterating some of this information and introducing more specifically interpreted rules of comment content. At this point, the site and its moderators were handing out "stars" on a case-by-case basis, a responsibility which would be handed over to commenters themselves two years later. Coen's (2012) advice for earning stars included suggestions such as "we love your funny, so bring it," and "back yourself up" when it comes to post criticism (¶3, ¶10). On the topic of problematic or overly critical commenting, Coen describes the threat of punitive measures, including removing posts or stars, or banning a user. In terms of "bullying" or "sass," Coen argues, "A commenter's tone is everything" (¶14). She also warns, "Arguing with editors regarding 'censorship' or the violation of 'free speech' is just silly, and it will almost certainly have some kind of consequence" (¶9). Ironically, the discussion space at the end of the post is empty, as small gray font informs the reader "this discussion is closed." Ultimately, the stars-based system ended up creating a hierarchical system rather than the open discourse purportedly desired by Holmes (and Coen), thus maintaining the old system rather than developing a new one.

In 2012, Gawker introduced a new system for comments and for the monetization of those comments—Kinja. Kinja's meritocratic structure rewards humor over ideology-based discussions that might threaten the *Jezebel* brand. On June 27, 2012, Cohen (2012) posted an announcement and a how-to guide for Kinja, which first addressed the issues with *Jezebel's* previous system of moderating discussions:

> The system *was* broken. We created it, and we got it wrong. Stars inevitably created a hierarchy; suspending/banning/moving threads just created drama. And most frustrating of all, the best conversations got lost in the fray. (¶3)

Coen then emphasized how Kinja is a "meritocracy" where the "best" (most popular) discussions rise to the top, and users moderate their own discussion threads (i.e., have the power to "dismiss" unwanted replies). Other changes include mandatory verification of *Jezebel* accounts through third-party accounts (e.g., Facebook, Twitter, or other social media outlets), and the ability to create "burner *Jezebel* accounts" for more sensitive information or one-time posting purposes. In Coen's words: "It makes it very easy to tell us your secrets—we're always looking for good scoops or stories." Additionally, the editor in chief frequently uses aggressive user-specific antagonism in order to keep discussions on-topic and questions about *Jezebel's* ideology to a minimum. All of these changes point to Denton's memo about the future source of Gawker Media's revenue: the discussion boards.

Yet, practical considerations contradict the utopian goals of Kinja. On *Jezebel's* (2014) "About" page, commenters are urged to find external spaces to discuss *Jezebel* content: "Commenters can make their own spaces outside of moderated posts for discussions, investigations, live-blogs, and spirited debate. This is where you can stray off-topic and hold court with friends and foes." Anna Holmes recalls "growing pressure from Gawker to make it less incendiary in order to increase its appeal to advertisers." According to Holmes: "I didn't want to get fired, and I didn't want to fight with them, but I didn't want to turn the site into something I didn't want it to be" (Mulkerrins 2013). Coen's more commercial brand of management mirrored Holmes', and the pressure from

Gawker in terms of *Jezebel* content did not exist as a one-sided power play: *Jezebel* published a blog post openly demanding Gawker take action against a repeated pattern of "trolling" (deliberately antagonizing others online), which involved unlabeled links to violent pornography images/gifs. *Feministing* blog contributor Maya Dusenbery (2014) commended *Jezebel*'s "leadership" in identifying Gawker's ill-advised silence. However, the type of trolling that was going on seemed to be a direct result of the structure of Kinja and the nature of certain economic spaces online: ultimately, pageviews are pageviews, and when merit is denied, negative behaviors can return. Moments like this illustrate a push-and-pull between the tiers of a corporate blogging hierarchy—and such dynamism pervades *Jezebel* content as well. A blog ran a piece on the corporate forces behind Vice Media in May 2014, and one commenter sarcastically posted: "What? The subculture, underground media machine turns out to be super capitalist and not underground at all? I'm *shocked*" (montycarlo 2014). Despite framing itself as a site of feminist dialogue, *Jezebel*'s economic model and textual discourse reveal the fragility of this space.

What are *Jezebel* readers reading?

Each of our analyses of *Jezebel* posts reveal patterns of rhetoric that can easily be traced to a model of website profitability. The effect of these patterns in readers' comments is a destabilization of feminist practices within this online space through the imposition of dominant discourses. We believe that to truly represent a feminist ethic, *Jezebel* (and, following it, Gawker) should encourage *and create* content that directly articulates an intervention into the status quo; a break with the standard, dominant discourses. What we found in our survey was not just that this intervention did not happen, but that the most popular content from *Jezebel* actually courted dominant discourses.

The following is an excerpt from a log of *Jezebel* post titles on July 23, 2014 (Table 18.1). We chose this day at random, although we did not want to choose a day where "big news" stories occurred and would skew our interpretation of the quotidian on *Jezebel*. Using this list as a representative microcosm of *Jezebel* content, several patterns become apparent. First, a great deal of the content here is reposting and/or commenting on trending items from elsewhere online—for example, the sex spreadsheet post, a movie trailer, a Chris Pratt interview.

Table 18.1 *Jezebel* July 23, 2014

Time	Article title	User responses
5:00 p.m.	Beach Body Horror Story: Life's a Beach and Then You Die	(26,125 views, 78 commenters, 10 recs)
5:15 p.m.	Adorable Chris Pratt Expertly Braids Intern's Hair During Interview	(22,735 views, 86 replies, 17 recs)
5:30 p.m.	Man Needs Your Money to Create World's Largest Dong Drawing	(6,969 views, 51 replies, 1 rec)
5:45 p.m.	Dude Vows Abstinence for a Year, Finds Out It's Not That Difficult	(22,594 views, 198 replies, 19 recs)
6:00 p.m.	Let's Settle This Once and For All: Is Sex Sexy or Not?	(34,760 views, 362 replies, 10 recs)
6:15 p.m.	Pennsylvania Woman Demands Truckers Stop Exposing Themselves To Kids	(19,931 views, 153 replies, 6 recs)
6:30 p.m.	Here's The Website You Will Never Ever Leave	(16,762 views, 43 replies, 4 recs)
6:45 p.m.	Sex Spreadsheet Details Wife's Frustration With Husband	(112,435 views, 624 replies, 13 recs)
7:00 p.m.	Woman Recites Beyoncé's Single Ladies as a Monologue and It's Genius	(151,869 views, 25 replies, 13 recs)
7:15 p.m.	Musical Based on Woody Allen Movie Flops on Broadway	(5,570 views, 92 replies, 1 rec)
7:30 p.m.	The Struggle Is Real for Rumer Willis	(29,602 views, 64 replies, 1 rec)
7:45 p.m.	Teen Girl Raped on Field Trip, Treated Horribly by Seattle High School	(132,910 views, 786 replies, 87 recs)
8:00 p.m.	Lauryn Hill Is Late to Her Own Concert, Yells at Fan About "Respect"	(45,224 views, 345 replies, 6 recs)
8:30 p.m.	Bartender Sets Customer On Fire	(21,716 views, 132 replies, 3 recs)
9:00 p.m.	The income threshold where money stops making you happier	(35,646 views, 268 replies, 18 recs)
9:30 p.m.	*Sex and the City* Really, Really Loved Name Dropping Brands	(46,774 views, 245 replies, 12 recs)
9:59 p.m.	Stop asking me "Why are you single?"	(28,706 views, 467 replies, 75 recs) (Shared from Groupthink)
10:30 p.m.	This Movie Trailer Will Break Your Mind With Nostalgia	(17,781 views, 139 replies, 5 recs)
11:00 p.m.	This Picture Perfectly Captures All My Emotions About the Royal Baby	(16,645 views, 48 replies, 1 rec)
11:30 p.m.	Man Says Southwest Airlines Kicked Him Off Plane Over Tweet Complaint	(47, 013 views, 458 replies, 3 recs)

Second, celebrity names, sex, and sexual violence are present in nearly every title. To a certain extent, many of these headlines reveal important stories, but like many "clickbait" headlines (titles that attempt to garner click-throughs by hinting at stimulating or salacious content), these titles seem more like the hallmarks of yellow journalism and invoke a type of sensationalism more familiar to viewers of gossip sites like *TMZ* or *PerezHilton.com*. While some headlines reflect undoubtedly important news, the contrast between serious headlines such as "Teen Girl Raped on Field Trip, Treated Horribly by Seattle High School" and facile headlines like "Man Needs Your Money to Create World's Largest Dong Drawing" (posted just two and a quarter hours apart) make *Jezebel* seem more glib than serious, exploitative rather than empowering.

Third, the titles often directly address the reader ("Here's the Website You Will Never Ever Leave"), reminiscent of pop-up ads ("You Won't Believe This Weight Loss Trick!"). Directly addressing the reader positions the titles as personal and focused, revealing a desire to generate more pageviews.

In what follows, we analyze two articles to detail further content-specific descriptions of the discourse on *Jezebel*. Specifically, these two pieces are: "Teen Girl Raped on Field Trip, Treated Horribly by Seattle High School," and "Sex Spreadsheet Details Wife's Frustration With Husband."

1. Teen Girl Raped on Field Trip, Treated Horribly by Seattle High School

Tags: Rape-Rape, Campus Rape, High School, Garfield High School, Rape Reporting, Title IX

Contributor Lindy West (2014) uses dogmatic language to address the issue of campus rape. While successful in drawing attention to an important social issue, both the framework West uses and the site's commenting system leave little room for dissent or dialogue. West draws the majority of the case information from a single *Al Jazeera America* report, and supplements the larger issues at play with statistics from RAINN and older *Jezebel* posts. An introductory paragraph uses twenty-nine of the thirty-three characters in the sentence as individual hyperlinks to other "campus rape" posts. This is used to illustrate how pervasive an issue is sexual violence on American college campuses, which segues into how this issue is handled in secondary school systems. West outlines the case where a fifteen-year-old girl was anally raped by a classmate on a field trip, and Garfield High School/Seattle Public Schools mismanaged the case, violating Title IX of the Education Amendments of 1972 which prohibits sex discrimination, under which sexual violence is categorized. The victim was unable to return to school, as the alleged rapist "retained full control of the story," and support from the high school. Much of West's editorializing is kept at a minimum and is limited to adding her own adjectives such as "horrifying" when describing the school's treatment of the rape victim. West's concluding paragraphs posit that this model of mismanagement represent why few victims report rape (here she includes a hyperlink to the Rape, Abuse and Incest National Network's page on "Reporting Rapes," where low stats on reporting are graphed and interpreted). West (2014) also offers several oppositional platitudes ("Oh, everyone knows rape is bad." "Last time I checked, rape was illegal." "We put rapists in jail") that, she argues, these statistics disprove. Her final argument is that "being raped and then being punished for it is currently built into our education system, much as it's built into the culture at large. It is inescapable. It follows our kids like a pestilence" (¶15–17).

The use of we/our/our kids is the rhetorical shadow of community building around a single issue. West uses this us/them construction to drum up further support for her or the victim's case, but, arguably, in a closed-circuit fashion. The pathos, the moving words and warnings of the "pestilence" of "rape culture" lead to the final paragraph in which West (2014) writes, "Based on past experience, it's easy to be skeptical that this investigation will enact lasting, visible change on such a historical, entrenched problem. But it's something. It's a start" (¶18). This post has a built-in audience ("when WE talk about rape culture"—the reader is implicated as part of the *Jezebel* community, assigned a viewpoint regarding the concept of rape culture), opposition (the all-purpose "people" who are paraphrased in discounting rape culture), and a foregone conclusion regarding the future of the investigation—that the systematic mistreatment of rape victims will continue unchecked. So, unlike consciousness-raising, this article does not do the work of finding new readers or activists. Despite a seemingly-empowering message, this article instead represents a marriage of clickbait and a serious "women's issue": dogmatic "us/them" rallying, and the exploitation of "rape" as a buzzword.

The us/them language is mirrored in the comments. Several survivors of sexual violence express their horror at the situation described, and share details of their own struggles. In this instance, a safe online discussion space is created. Users express their frustration and pain, adopting several of West's rhetorical choices. "We really are just 'things' to them, aren't we?" one commenter posts. Another notes that he or she read the post and had to then "get my rage under control." Another demands that the alleged rapist's name be given out, while yet another claims that he or she is offering money for the rapist's name to be revealed. The language used in the comments is reminiscent of a culture of fear and alarmism, a sort of "derivative fear" that Zygunt Bauman (2006) defines as "a steady frame of mind . . . the sentiment of being *susceptible* to danger; a feeling of insecurity . . . and vulnerability" (3). For Bauman modern life is a cacophony of fears that shape and mold us into hyper-aware citizens: importantly, these fears also turn us into complacent followers, uncritical thinkers who consume more than we think. It's not that this isn't a serious issue, and it isn't that *Jezebel* doesn't take it seriously. Rather, the corporate mechanics behind the promotion of this post (make it dogmatic, make it communal, make it memeified) shape the online discourse.

2. Sex Spreadsheet Details Wife's Frustration With Husband

Tags: Sex, Sex Spreadsheets, Relationships

Contributor Tracy Moore (2014a) reposts content found on another site in order to generate pageviews, and punctuates her evaluation of the content with a broader gender/sexuality-oriented message. This repost-post lures readers with a sexy title, utilizes in-text advertising, and the static commenting system negates reader contradiction. Moore begins by describing a *Reddit* user's original content from July 18 in which a husband's unsuccessful attempts at initiating sex had been logged and dated in a Microsoft Excel spreadsheet. Moore quotes a BuzzFeed article that points to another site, Guyism, and a second spreadsheet of this variety, this time from a wife's perspective. The Guyism article cites that this spreadsheet came from the author's personal e-mail correspondence with the unhappy wife in question. Moore addresses the potential falsehood of the second spreadsheet with an introductory disclaimer: "In this case (if it is even real because who knows about anything ever)."

Following the description of the second spreadsheet, Moore (2014a) writes seven "rules" ("things we can learn from spreadsheets") regarding the future of sex spreadsheets, written in a part-humor, part-socially conscious and/or reflective BuzzFeed-esque list (¶10–16). The first rule asks for more spreadsheets, as Moore argues that "over time they will probably show predictable patterns of rejection and rejoicing, the two R's of a sex life." Moore notes in the second rule the both "funny and sad" aspects of chronicling sexual behaviors on a spreadsheet: "first spreadsheet is all lolololol," while the "second one is all *disintegrating marriage.*" The third and fourth rules address whether or not husbands or wives owe their partner sex. Moore cites a related *Salon* article on the circulating (first) spreadsheet, who "declared correctly that wives don't owe their husbands sex," though, according to Moore, it's a "reasonable expectation." In terms of what husbands do or don't owe their partners, Moore writes that sex not happening "can be for all sorts of reasons," including partners feeling "tired and vommy or sweaty and gross." Fifth on the list, Moore observes that "if you are documenting your sex life, something is probably wrong." The sixth rule states "not having sex is a symptom." Moore inserts a hyperlink to another article, written by herself (2014c) and posted to *Jezebel* in February, titled "The Truth About How Much a Happy Couple Should Have Sex." This post includes an interview Moore conducted with a urologist, several citations from posts or articles and books—including an illustrated link to a Lifehacker (also owned by Gawker Media) post—and an illustrated in-text ad for the book *Where's My Sanity?: Stories that Help* by Dr. Claudia Luiz which included a link to Amazon, a yellow "Buy this" button, and text that reads "6 readers bought this." Moore's seventh and final rule suggests that if "talking is no longer an option" one should "have at" said spreadsheet-creating. This final rule is a self-aware jab at the inherent meanness of publishing/exploiting individuals' sexual failures for pageviews. "Two spreadsheets came from hate, but how many do you think we can generate FROM LOVE, PEOPLE? No? Better from hate? Yeah. Prolly right." Arguably, this afterthought reads as a lukewarm admonishment tacked onto the end of a featured post. The site has successfully plumbed the content in order to generate pageviews of its own, as well as link back to earlier pages, related Gawker Media blogs, and merchandise.

Both selections of curated comments and discussions ("Popular Discussion" and "All replies") involve a blend of puns, photo gags (i.e., "here's my sex spreadsheet" above an image of a blank spreadsheet), and personal anecdotes about sex habits within the commenter's relationship. Buried are several critical comments about the article, including a reaction to the "men vs. women" method of analyzing the two spreadsheets, an observation that "too many people are trying to put this in a black-and-white situation. It goes far deeper than that. Every person is different, and every couple is different," and another comment containing just ellipses followed by "never mind."

The posts expressing frustration are recommended in the single digits, while the comments or discussion threads that express agreement with Moore's points can reach triple digits. Although it is possible for dissenting comments to rank as highly or higher than those in agreement, users must manually sort comments by "all replies." The default thread which appears is "popular discussion," comments which have been selected by *Jezebel* editors/moderators. "Popular discussion" criteria appear to dismiss critical comments, and privilege those which align with the author's perspective. Rather than being used as a space for dissent, the site appears to focus on assent as the most common—and therefore, more acceptable—reaction.

Conclusion

Corporate blog *Jezebel* occupies an online space in two, conflicting ideological spheres: cyberfeminist activism, and corporate interests. *Jezebel's* version of feminism is, we argue, shaped by the economic forces which govern the site's layout and content. We are not arguing that this site is not representing feminism, but that it is representing a feminism beholden to Gawker Media, a feminism without the sort of critical role that, for instance, Wilding (1998) argues is central to the digital age. The maintenance of an online space devoted to feminist discussion is a tall order, and the new forms in which these issues can be made more visible is, in itself, exciting.

The content however, when aligned with feminism, is unsettling. By making feminist/women's issues palatable to a wide audience *Jezebel* sacrifices a space for radical and counter-hegemonic feminist discourse. Cyberfeminism, as defined by Stephanie Schulte's (2011), works to re-create the internet and manifest offline change. *Jezebel's* brand of feminism maintains the status quo through not only the patterns of its content, but the moderating tools used to tailor user discussion. Infighting and perpetual dissent, as Tracie Egan Morrissey (2014) categorized it in her response to *Girls*, may be or may not be pillars of an ever-evolving ideology, but it is *definitely* a lucrative model for a daily blog.

One shortcoming of the textual analysis is the emphasis on the numbers of pageviews as the determinants of representative content. A future analysis might examine less-read content to investigate whether more serious political news, or social issue items are being comprehensively discussed but not viewed as much as, say, posts with the word "Beyoncé" in them. This also runs the risk of negating the reader's responsibility, as it could be argued that *Jezebel* content is shaped as much by reader demand as by Gawker Media's profit margins. Ultimately, any sort of feminist discourse that appears on *Jezebel* must be guided by the underlying economic forces that shape Gawker's commercial interest—and as such, always reflect a negotiated view of hegemonic feminism.

Note

1   © 2014, Alexa Internet (www.alexa.com).

19

Not Your Mother's Video Game: The Role of Motherhood in Video Game Advertising

Shira Chess

The video game industry has long been dominated by masculinity. Researchers and industry figures have noted that, for many years, video games were primarily made by men for male audiences (Fron et al. 2007; Fullerton et al. 2008; Cassell and Jenkins 1998a). In the last ten years, this paradigm has rapidly begun to shift, opening spaces for new kinds of gamers through casual gaming, mobile gaming, and social gaming. In turn, a broader and more diverse audience has begun to play video games (Chess 2014). In fact, in 2014 the number of adult women gamers exceeded the number of teenage boy gamers in industry reports ("Women Significantly Outnumber Teenage Boys in Gamer Demographics | The Rundown" 2014). Given this shift, it would seem logical that roles and appearances of women in the gaming industry would be rapidly expanding; instead these shifts have often caused major rifts between players and industry professionals (Salter and Blodgett 2012; Chess and Shaw 2015).

While the identity of what a "gamer" consists of continues to shift, one demographic remains consistently at odds with traditional gamer culture—the mother. The mother sits in a complicated place with respect to gaming culture. An increasing number of women (not necessarily mothers) are becoming players, facilitating new kinds of growth across the industry. This information, unsurprisingly, does not come with easy statistics. The number of mothers playing video games is primarily speculative, but (after all) if more women are playing, many of those women are surely mothers. Despite this, reputations of video games as being violent, addictive, or generally unhealthy for children create a perceived tension between mothers and gaming. Furthermore, the cultural constructions of motherhood often do not include the notion of play. Given these factors, motherhood and gaming rarely align. This conflict has been occasionally reconciled when popular games have used mother characters (such as the *Cooking Mama* game series), or when video games and systems are deliberately marketed to women (as done with the Nintendo Wii). Yet, a kind of tension remains—in order for a game to be considered cool, gamers wouldn't want to think of that game as being one played by a mother in general, or their mother in particular.

Advertising functions as an ideal focal point to understand how the industry positions video games within a dominant ideology with respect to marginalized gamers—mother gamers in particular. The reason for this is twofold. First, advertising is a way to gage existing attitudes toward our already existing consumption practices. Second, as a persuasive medium, advertising is able to influence people with already dominant ideologies. According to Judith Williamson (2005):

> Advertisements are one of the most important cultural factors molding and reflecting our life today. They are ubiquitous, an inevitable part of everyone's lives: even if you do not read a newspaper or watch television, the images posted over our urban surroundings are inescapable. Pervading all the media, but limited to none, advertising forms a vast superstructure with an apparently autonomous existence and an immense influence. (11)

Studying video game advertising becomes a convenient means of illustrating the ways in which video games are understood, interpreted, and used in American culture.

The following essay explores the tension between motherhood and video games, specifically by considering video game advertising. When we study ethics in media, it is important to consider how groups are left out or marginalized from specific media and technologies. The relationship between motherhood and video games offers one such case. In this way, advertising serves to illustrate a larger theme in video game culture—a perception that motherhood has a limited, if not nonexistent, role in video game play. In short, advertisements tell us how things "should" be done through the mass-mediated images they provide. Advertisements of video games suggest that good mothers may not play games for their own pleasure, but continue to purchase games for others or play to make others happy. By studying specific examples of how mothers are portrayed in video game commercials, it becomes obvious that the mother player is excluded and becomes a kind of taboo. In this way, the role of the mother is necessarily "Othered" by the gaming industry. She is necessary to the process of purchasing video games, yet always must be represented as a non-player. Yet, while the mother is the ultimate Other in a video game world constructed from the perspective of the young male (perceived) primary demographic, as that demographic ceases to be dominant this role will necessarily need to change.

Gender and gaming

The subfield examining gender and gaming has shifted considerably in the past two decades. In the 1990s, there were relatively few video games specifically aimed for a female audience and early research focused more on the question, "How do we get girls to play more video games?" (Cassell and Jenkins 1998b; Kafai et al. 2008). This question made sense at the time—research showed that an interest in gaming resulted in more interest in STEM careers (Cassell and Jenkins 1998b). This focus, however, resulted in an increased number of "pink games"—games that played off of traditional stereotypes of femininity. Often this resulted in research that conflated women and girls and ignored shifts in taste, and interests in play, that might occur over the course of a person's life cycle (Taylor 2006).

The emergence of new gaming systems in the mid-2000s, though, helped to shift expectations of who might be considered a gamer. In particular, gaming consoles such as the Nintendo Wii and Nintendo DS increasingly attempted to get at a range of audiences, which included both women and families. Magazine advertisements for the Nintendo Wii often highlighted how mothers can use gaming systems to suggest that gaming can help create better bonding time with one's family (Chess 2011). While this kind of advertising campaign, on the one hand, does not create a chasm between motherhood and gaming, on the other hand, it does suggest that gaming would only be of interest to mothers as a means of spending time with their children. These advertisements leave out the possibility that mothers would want to play for the sake of play. Similarly, Nintendo DS advertisements in women's magazines often highlighted feminine stereotypes such as beauty and time management. As I (2011) have previously written, these advertisements are selling more than just play: "By collapsing play with productivity, there is something larger being sold about how women are expected to play. In turn, video games are able to maintain status as masculine play spaces, reinforcing subtext that women should only play in specific circumstances" (236). Play shouldn't be just *fun* for women, it must necessarily be for a purpose.

As the market for console gaming began to open up to a larger audience, computer games saw an emergence of what are often referred to as "casual games." Casual games are games that are cheap or free, easy to learn, are highly replayable, and can be stopped and started without significantly impacting gameplay (Casual Games Association 2007; Juul 2010). Given the ability to fit casual gaming into busy schedules, they often were designed specifically for women audiences who had not previously been involved in gaming (Chess 2014). Frequently, the content of popular casual games builds on stereotypes and expectations of women's styles of play. For example, the computer game series *Diner Dash*, which had its first release in 2005, has the player playing as Flo—a waitress and restaurateur—whose primary game tasks involve emotional labor and keeping customers satisfied. I (2012) have previously noted of the *Diner Dash* series:

> Emotional management is the common denominator of all of the Dash game narratives, and many of the mechanics and designs. The themes that are being negotiated throughout the play of the games—those of work/play, empowerment, and "going with the flow"—they all contribute to this game space where emotional play becomes . . . a kind of emotional labor. And just as emotional labor takes a toll on many women, so might emotional play. (287)

Essentially, many casual games, such as mobile games, hidden object games, and puzzle games use narratives, themes, and tropes that evoke anxieties specific to femininity, turning these games into a form of labor which reinforces standards and expectations of motherhood.

Casual gaming sits in contrast to what is often referred to as "hardcore" gaming—games that are expensive (usually meant for console systems such as the PlayStation or Xbox), difficult to learn and master, and penalize players for not being able to dedicate larger periods of time to play (Juul 2010; Chess 2014). Hardcore gaming is most commonly associated with masculinity—at the same time it is often perceived as the primary monetary and cultural force in the gaming industry (Chess 2014). This supposition makes sense since it is more socially acceptable for men to have leisure time at home, whereas women do not necessarily have that same surplus of time to devote to play. So while casual gaming might be designed for or advertised to women gamers, hardcore gaming is rarely purposefully advertised to women.

The problem, in part, rests on the video game industry, which, even with shifting audiences, is still made up of only an 11 percent female workforce (Consalvo 2008). Because the majority of games are still primarily marketed at men and boys—with occasional exceptions such as the Nintendo Wii and DS (as described above)—fewer women enter the video game industry as designers, producers, and programmers. Additionally, women who do enter the video game industry often find that the working conditions are not amenable to women with families, due to heavy crunch periods in the game development cycle (Consalvo 2008). This suggests some larger ethical issues in the industry that go beyond simply game design and advertising, supporting what has been described as a kind of "hegemony of play" (Fron et al. 2007) where the majority of higher-profile and hardcore video games are still designed for and marketed to male audiences, by a primarily male workforce. While new audiences continue to embrace gaming, the video game industry mostly remains stalwart in its dedication to masculinity.

Industry response about emerging styles of gaming, and the new influx of women players, has been somewhat mixed. On the one hand, new video game companies, such as Big Fish Games and Zynga, have emerged as industry leaders that in large part try to open games up to broader audience bases—including women. At the same time, the video game industry itself has had an underlying push-and-pull with women audiences—both inviting in new audiences while simultaneously snubbing female players (and casual game play) as being inferior. Often, this tension comes into play in social media spaces where bloggers, microbloggers, and video bloggers have argued fiercely over whether or not more women should be welcomed into the video game industry, and whether or not women players and new styles of play are jeopardizing the existing industry (Salter and Blodgett 2012; Blodgett and Salter 2013). Thus, women are both sought out as a new revenue source in the video game industry and accused of being central to the downfall of that very industry—this accusation has been increasingly made since the August of 2014 when an all-out war broke out between independent game developers and hardcore gamers under the Twitter hashtag "GamerGate." During this series of events, several women involved in the gaming culture have received both rape and death threats (Chess and Shaw 2015).

The problems with motherhood

Motherhood sits in a precarious position in our culture. Motherhood—both the act of birthing as well as the involved and lengthy commitment to raising a child—is a necessary component to humanity. We honor and fetishize the role of motherhood as a kind of feminine ideal. As a result, we also tend to both fetishize and marginalize maternalism and its subjects. According to Shari L. Thurer (2004) in *The Myths of Motherhood: How Culture Reinvents the Good Mother*:

> For thousands of years, because of her awesome ability to spew forth a child, mother has been feared and revered. She has been the subject of taboos and witch hunts, mandatory pregnancy and confinement in a separate sphere. She has endured appalling insults and perpetual marginalization. She has also been the subject of glorious painting, chivalry, and idealization. Through it all, she has rarely been consulted. She is an object, not a subject. (229)

In this way, there is a culturally constructed desire to idealize the mother, but at the same time marginalize her. Motherhood is both necessary to the continuation of the human race, yet often a source of insult. The realities of motherhood seem to sit somewhere between Mother's Day cards and "Yo Mama" jokes.

Motherhood is not only related to the act of giving birth; it is a set of culturally learned and performed practices. According to Nancy Chodorow (1978), the practices of motherhood have become internalized, produced, and reproduced. She explains, "Women's capacities for mothering and abilities to get gratification from it are strongly internalized and psychologically enforced, and are built developmentally into the feminine psychic structure" (39). This internalization results in a form of mimetic performance—while the realities of mothering practices may vary, dominant ideologies dictate what "good" motherhood looks like.

Regardless of who is the primary consumer of a product in the household, the "mother" figure is likely the purchaser. This has been long culturally established, beginning in the period of the postindustrial revolution when "shopping emerged as a new recreation for women" (Satterthwaite 2001, 131). This practice has remained—women do most of the primary shopping in a household. According to a 2013 *Wall Street Journal* report, women are responsible for 80 percent of household spending. This means that part of the role and performance of motherhood is making purchases.

In the context of video games, this understanding of women as the primary contributors to household spending creates an uncomfortable yet contradictory position. On the one hand, as the primary household shoppers, women are often a likely target market for advertising video game purchases. But at the same time, stereotypes of motherhood and femininity do not suggest that women will be playing the games they are purchasing. In other words, television commercials for video games are likely advertising to women to purchase for other members of their households.

Mothers and games

While women are certainly a growing audience as consumers of video games— regardless of whether or not the video game industry feels that this transition is a good one—*motherhood* appears to be a special case. Of course, not all women are mothers. Yet, women are still treated like mothers. As I elaborate, below, the expectation of women-as-mothers in video game spaces is often assigned to and inferred upon adult women, irrespective of whether they occupy this identity in the real world.

The clearest place that one can see the dichotomy between motherhood and gaming is in television commercials. As already noted, commercials can function as a barometer to better understand popular perceptions, stereotypes, and assumptions. The role of mothers and motherhood in television commercials reflects how motherhood sits in a space of perceived resistance in gaming culture. Yet, at the same time, commercials need to be written in such a way that video games might have enough appeal that mothers—the primary purchasers of a household—will still buy the games.

While I have noted that the number of female gamers has changed drastically in recent years, little has changed about the way women are advertised to. This essay compares two advertisements from the past ten years to an advertisement from the 1980s. The comparison demonstrates the gaming and advertising industry's lack of willingness to respond to changes in demographics. Also, looking at advertisements created almost thirty years apart, we can see that attitudes toward motherhood have evolved little in the tech industry. The lack of evolution establishes that while the mother might be a primary purchaser of hardcore games, she rarely is induced to be the player. While it might be acceptable for a mother character to be a player of casual games, this kind of gaming is rarely seen in television commercials.

The advertisements discussed below often speak to two audiences distinctly and simultaneously. On the one hand, they attempt to make the primary target audience—young males—interested in purchasing a game that is decidedly different from the kinds of casual games their mothers are likely to be playing. On the other hand, they attempt to make an appeal to women—the primary purchasers in a household—to buy the games for their families. In short, while the video game industry may have changed in some ways since the 1980s, its commercials retain ambivalent attitudes toward the involvement of mothers in gaming.

Motherhood 30 years ago: Atari Anonymous

As one of the first home video game systems, the Atari 2600 became a highly popular consumer product starting from the 1970s and through the very early 1980s (Montfort and Bogost 2009). As early gaming (in the 1970s and 1980s) was often not as gendered as gaming was by the 1990s (Ray 2004), it would have been expected that advertising for the Atari would have been more inclusive and open, with the mother seen as a potential player. However, this did not prove true.

One of the first television commercials for home video game systems was for the Atari 2600. The commercial, airing in 1981, featured the voice-over of the matriarch of a family, reading aloud a letter she had composed to "Atari Anonymous." The mother character is never seen in this commercial, she is only heard; we see each of the other family members while she reads her letter of concern to the audience, expressing concern that her family has become addicted to the Atari system. Between each description of "addiction" in her letter, we see a family member playing an Atari game and either making some weird remarks or behaving weirdly.

Mother:	Atari Anonymous . . . My son Boris has a *Missile Command* problem.
Boris:	My mission in life is to save all of mankind.
Mother:	Lately my daughter has developed a similar problem with *Atari Warlord*.
Daughter:	[screams in anguish]
Mother:	Now, with *Video Pinball* my husband is acting funny.
Husband:	[laughs maniacally]
Mother:	With Atari games so ingenious, so involving, so intense, I ask you, Atari Anonymous, is this problem contagious?

After this final question, the commercial ends with a shot of the family dog playing the Atari system (*1981 Atari 2600 Commercial* 2010). The commercial places the mother character in an unusual position, with respect to gaming: everyone else in the house is permitted to play, to enjoy themselves—even the family dog is included in the pleasures of play. Yet, the mother, herself, not only is not permitted to play but also is completely excluded from the actual commercial, beyond a disembodied voice of concern. Her physical absence makes her a moral authority, situated figuratively above her embodied family of game players. Her voiced non-presence makes her appear as the voice of God.

That voice of concern articulates the beginnings of the complicated place that the mother is put in, with respect to players. The mother cannot possibly be a game player; she must necessarily be apart from the games in order for them to appear "fun." The mother character gets to articulate concerns that (potentially) other mothers might have had at that time regarding gaming and addiction. Yet, as the primary purchaser of the household, it is also the mother who is being marketed to—the advertisement features a happy family involved in something "ingenious," "involving," and "intense"—descriptions that sit as foil to the potentially "addictive" aspects of the game. The mother is necessary for the commercial, as the reserved character who does not desire fun for herself but instead seeks fun experiences for the rest of the family.

To reiterate the point made earlier, this commercial reflects the fact that even early in gaming—before the gendered nature of the gaming industry and gaming culture was fully developed—the mother was situated as necessarily distinct from other gamers.

Motherhood today: "Your Mom Hates Dead Space 2" and "Don't Tell Mom . . ."

The Atari 2600 advertisement seemed to assume that moms still wanted to be cool—the mother in the advertisement was depicted as attempting to comprehend video game spaces, even if she was overwhelmingly concerned about their addictive qualities. In recent years, the mother in commercials has become more of a villain. While mothers were (are) seen both then and now as being necessarily antigaming, the difference is that now mothers are actually seen as the villains of gaming, even as being potentially capable of destroying the video game industry. So the response to the demographic shift has not been to reconceptualize motherhood in relationship to gaming; it has been to place mothers even more in the role of villains who are trying to destroy gaming.

Dead Space 2, a follow up to the Electronic Arts console science fiction/ horror game *Dead Space*, was released in 2011. The game, which involves a character attempting to escape a space station inhabited by monsters, was critically acclaimed for its storytelling and gameplay (Miller 2011). Additionally, the game became well known for its advertising campaign that used the slogan,

"Your Mom Hates *Dead Space 2*." As part of this campaign 200 women were interviewed—they were selected because they were not previously gamers and because they reported more conservative values. Clips from the interviews were featured on the game web site, and select interviews were aired as television spots ("Your Mama Plays '*Dead Space 2*'" 2014).

The interviews seen in the longer promotional clips for the "Your Mom Hates Dead Space 2" campaign each took place in an experimental room. In each of these interviews, an older woman, who is alone, is asked to respond to video footage from the game. In some ways, this recalls the 1980s Atari advertisement, where the mother character talked about video games, but did not play them. The final cuts of the promotional clips featured footage from the game interspersed with both closeup shots of the women articulating their unsurprising disdain and visceral sound effects from the game. Each of the longer interviews (featured on the website) ends with the slogan, "Your Mom Hates *Dead Space 2*."

The official advertisement intended for television put together several of the interviews and showed mothers gasping, hiding their faces, and looking overwhelmingly repulsed by the game. Sound bites were abstracted from the longer videos with participants saying things like: "I think it could make a person become insane," "This game is an atrocity," and "Why would they even make something like this?" (*Your Mom Hates Dead Space 2* 2011). The commercial spot ends with a male voice-over explaining the context of what the women have just said: "It's revolting. It's violent. It's everything you love in a game. And your mom's gonna hate it" (*Your Mom Hates Dead Space 2* 2011).

The campaign received much criticism at the time, and many felt that the campaign was sexist and agist. Critics remarked that it was unclear who the advertisement was intended for. In an article for the game web site *Kotaku*, Winda Benedetti analyzes the perceived ironies of the campaign: "EA is making moms everywhere the fall gals so that they can sell their game to … who exactly? Rebellious teenagers? Don't make me go all mom on you, but I'm pretty sure that the vast majority of teenagers aren't old enough to play this M-Rated game. You're supposed to be at least 17 years old to buy Dead Space 2" ("Your Mama Plays '*Dead Space 2*'" 2014). While the 1980s Atari advertisement had the mother watching over the family of game players with a God-like presence, the *Dead Space* advertisements place the mother character deeply removed from any notion of play. The concern expressed in the older advertisements has given way to outright repulsion.

The implication of the point made by Benedetti and others was that *Dead Space 2* was being surreptitiously marketed to younger audiences than the ones the game was meant to be for. But considered another way, the *Dead Space 2* advertising campaign was not necessarily about the player's mom—after all, we don't even know for certain that these women were, indeed, mothers. The advertising campaign focuses on constructing motherhood as an "other" to the game's players. While the games themselves feature monstrous antagonists, the real monster is the mother figure, a killjoy whose revulsion makes players like the game more—in other words, the game is attractive because mothers, in general, find it horrific. The campaign, thus, suggests that regardless of the number of games being aimed at women audiences, hardcore gaming will always be situated apart from this constructed version of the mother character.

The *Dead Space* commercial may just be one example of the role played by mothers in current commercials on video games, but other commercials advertising new gaming systems continue to have the problematic depictions of mothers seen in the *Dead Space* commerical. The year 2013 saw the release of three new console systems: The Wii U, the Xbox One, and the PlayStation 4. Even with changing audiences, the mother character is still often othered, particularly in hardcore gaming. While the mother might not be portrayed as neurotic and overconcerned, as in the Atari commercial or as monstrous as in the *Dead Space* commercial, mothers are still shown as neither approving nor partaking in hardcore video game culture.

A Wal-Mart commercial for the new Xbox One system, advertising an upcoming system release, helps to establish that mothers, still, are not really gamers. The commercial begins with a father and son sitting in the son's bedroom playing a newly opened Xbox One—the opened box is still visible. The commercial continues:

Father:	So, what do you think?
Son:	Dad, best Christmas gift ever.
Father:	And it's for the whole family. But remember, mom can't know that we opened it early.
Mother (off screen):	Guys . . . dinner . . .

As this happens, the father and son scramble around the room, hiding packaging and evidence. The mother's feet slowly approach the bedroom, and threatening non-diegetic music begins to play. The music is not dissimilar to the Jaws theme or audio themes that are played to announce the presence of a villain. But the father and son are safe: by the end of the commercial the father and son are "studying"—the father is heard saying, "And that's when Ben Franklin discovered fire . . . with his kite" (*Don't Tell Mom We Opened the Xbox One—Walmart TV Commercial* 2014).

The commercial continues a division between gaming and motherhood. While the Xbox One might be "for the whole family," we quickly learn that at least one family member—the mother—is less likely to indulge in playing it than the male members of her household. The mother, of course, is established as the villain of play—the suspenseful music tells us as much. While she may have been the person who initially purchased the gaming system, she is an enemy of play. The mother's role functions as a foil to the father who is willing to play at any time, in any situation—without that play being authorized. The mother, on the other hand, is positioned as a disciplinarian. Much as with the Atari commercial, the whole family can enjoy the game, except for mom.

As we can see, there looms an ethical issue in how women are depicted in the two time periods under discussion. While there might be an increasing diversity of women players—and even mother players—getting involved with video games, the gaming industry, advertising, and gaming culture all situate the mother as the villain of the gamer. In the 1980s advertisements, the mother was simply the voice of concern; now, she directly opposes gameplay. As wars continue across gaming culture, on social media, and elsewhere (whether under the label of GamerGate or other related movements), it is important to consider the ways in which certain audiences are completely disassociated from digital play. Audiences may be growing, but perceptions have remained stagnant and stalwart.

Conclusion

There is no question that there exists an inherent tension between motherhood and gaming. Perhaps this tension is most cleverly articulated in one parody Twitter account: @momsagainstgam. The Twitter account allegedly speaks for a fictional organization, "Mothers Against Videogame Addiction and Violence." The account tweets fictionalized outrage over gaming using the voice of "mothers" who supposedly have had enough of gaming culture and its alleged detriment to society. For example, on August 4, 2014 the account tweeted: "America spends more on violent video games than it does on medical research and feeding hungry children. We demand change #BANViolentVideoGames." When the account was first created, many thought that it was legitimate ("'Moms

Against Gaming' Is My New Favorite Twitter Account," 2014). Even after being debunked, many on Twitter still respond angrily to tweets from the account. The @momsagainstgam account illustrates how easily audiences expect a resistance between motherhood and gaming. Similarly, the commercials analyzed above help to illustrate that while audiences may have changed in thirty years, perception has not.

When considering media ethics, it is important not only to look at legal and corporate matters, but also to consider the complicated issues behind media representation. What is represented in advertising, television, film, music, and other popular forms of mass media helps to define the status quo. In the case of video games, representational issues help to maintain a video game industry that primarily gears itself toward masculine audiences (although this may be slowly changing). Women are slowly being permitted into this space, but motherhood still functions as a gaming monster—the mother is the person who allows or denies gaming to their families. In the advertisements discussed, the mother character functioned as a gatekeeper, allowing or disallowing play to members of her family.

Yet, we need to be conscious of *who* we are advertising to, and why. There seems to be a kind of perversity to advertising play to an audience who we do not want nor expect to play. Motherhood, being culturally performed, is learned through a variety of spaces. It is apparent through the performance of motherhood in these commercials that mothers might be expected to purchase games, but never to actually interact with them. This places the mother forever in the role of an onlooker—she is never seen as someone who interacts directly with the games. The complicated role of motherhood in these commercials is not something that can be blamed on one systemic force. While it would be easy to apply blanket blame to the video game industry, the advertising industry, or gamer culture in general, the representations of motherhood have deeper roots in American culture. By comparing video game commercials from thirty years ago with recent commercials, we can see that these representations of motherhood have only strengthened, showing no connection to the actual composition of gaming audiences.

Afterword: Ethics—and Emancipation—for the Rest of Us?

Charles M. Ess

Controversies in Digital Ethics represents a significant step forward in the expanding literatures of what can be called digital media ethics, a name I enjoin because of its explicit conjunction in my own writing with what I have termed an ethics for "the rest of us" (Ess 2013, 198). With this phrase, I seek to capture a key thematic that defines this volume here. Manifestly, digital media technologies are increasingly being diffused throughout developed countries and therefore shape and define the lives of the vast majority of those living in such countries: consequently, the ethical issues and concerns that were once the provenance of specialists in information and computing ethics (ICE) are increasingly confronted and resolved by the rest of us, that is, by folk who are specialists neither in applied ethics nor in digital technologies. Despite our lack of (formal) expertise, we are forced, whether we like it or not, to recognize and come to grips with the ethical dimensions and challenges evoked by these new technologies. In my terms, we must all become ethicists—and I will argue, ultimately, philosophers.

Along these lines, both the editors, Amber Davison and Paul Booth, and the multiple contributions gathered here extend these literatures in the best possible ways. To begin with, the collection sharpens the focus within digital media ethics, as the editors narrow in on defining shifts in media production and consumption, indexed by the now well-traveled notion of the "prosumer" (Bruns 2008). Even more helpfully, in my view, the work here locates itself within the domains of participatory culture(s) and (digital) media literacies—where the latter is especially critical as it foregrounds the active roles and agencies of people who, when otherwise examined through the analytical concept of "consumer," are often denied this critical agency. As I hope to make clear here, one of the most important contributions to emerge here is precisely the heightened focus on individual and collective agency. I will argue that both the volume's guiding foci, and the contributors' particular insights and reflections, promise to foster such agency in what I think of as the most significant and important ways— most especially through the shared attention to matters of identity and human nature, gender, virtue ethics, deontological ethics, and the promise often made regarding digital media, which is that they will enhance and expand democratic processes and norms.

Metaethical beginnings

The volume does so first of all by beginning at the beginning—namely, by setting the stage for where we (a term I will return to shortly) are in terms of our engagements and confrontations with digital media. As the editors point out in their introduction, the focus on participatory culture(s) as facilitated by new media technologies immediately raises a central metaethical question: Do such new technologies require new ethical frameworks, norms, and processes of decision-making, and/or will extant norms, processes, and frameworks prove to be adequate in confronting the new behavioral and thus ethical possibilities evoked by these technologies? In ICE, this is taken up under the rubric of the uniqueness debate (Bynum 2010, 32). While there are good reasons and occasional cases that argue for radical novelty in these ways (consider in this volume Scott Stroud's discussion of anonymity and vigilante "justice")— both the editors and contributors mostly find themselves in agreement with prevailing views within contemporary ICE: as the editors put it here, the focus of the volume is "not whether or not we need a new system for evaluating the way we use media" (Davisson and Booth, this volume). Rather, the case studies and reflections gathered here, as I would paraphrase their point, help us focus on specific and fine-grained ethical challenges arising within the lives of "the rest of us." They do so, moreover, by taking up extant ethical frameworks in analyses and insights that help resolve at least many of these conundrums in ethically sound and legitimate fashion. At the same time, as Ryan Gillespie makes explicit, a good portion of the work here is to uncover and clarify the ethical principles in play in our analyses and debates—in part just so as to make these principles explicit, thereby foregrounding them for critical evaluation and debate. Such articulation and "unpacking" of ethical principles and norms that otherwise can remain tacit and unspoken are especially central to our critical debates on politics, policies, and law in the public sphere (Gillespie, this volume).

Identity, gender, sexuality, and human nature

Of course, the phrase "the rest of us" evokes a foundational question: who is the "we" referred to here? The question manifestly defines Section 4 ("Identity in a Digital World") and is further addressed from several of the standpoints represented in this volume, beginning precisely with identity politics and feminism (Molly Bandonis and Paul Booth). At the same time, from the standpoint of philosophical ethics, the questions of identity and selfhood are foundational first of all as we attempt to think through matters of agency and responsibility. Specifically, in what we can call high modernity, ethical agency and responsibility have been conceived almost entirely in terms of the *individual*—whether a more atomistic Cartesian rational self or Locke's "punctuated self" (Taylor 1989, 159ff.). By contrast, as I have argued elsewhere, the rise of "electric media" as McLuhan and Ong have analyzed it, and, more specifically, the emergence of networked communications as facilitated via the internet and instantiated in social networking technologies, correlate with the (re)turn to more *relational* emphases in our conceptions of selfhood and identity (Ess 2010, 2014). Such shifts in our foundational understandings of who we are as human beings and moral agents hold immediate and far-reaching ethical implications, first of all, for our notions of agency and responsibility. Such shifts are at least implicit in many of the chapters collected here, beginning precisely with the defining observation that participatory cultures entail the blurring of earlier lines between producer and consumer, and specifically in the focus on digital or citizen journalism. As multiple actors—whether more professional or more nonprofessional—engage in the construction of such journalism, the result is not only a blurring of earlier lines of demarcation between producer and consumer, but also, more fundamentally, a blurring and distribution of the ethical *agencies* and *responsibilities* affiliated with this construction. In this light, the several chapters devoted to digital journalism are thus instructive, not only for what each brings to the foreground in terms of specific case studies and reflections, but also for what they may suggest for these larger questions of what happens to our sense of selfhood and thus responsibility in a digital era. As we will further see below, these chapters are equally vital for concerns with the democratic impulses and potential of digital media.

To my eye, such shifts toward more relational senses of selfhood are in the background of several additional chapters and themes here, beginning with Amber Davisson's "Passing Around Women's Bodies Online: Sex, Power, and

Privacy on Reddit." Without question, the violation of women's privacy as documented by Davisson is a foundational problem for the women involved. At the same time, as the editors note from the outset, this is but one of innumerable examples of how *individual* privacy is rendered so profoundly problematic in online spaces (Davisson and Booth, this volume). Still more fundamentally: our received notions of privacy as a positive good in high modernity rest precisely on the emergence of *individual* notions of selfhood, identity, and agency. By contrast, in both the premodern West, and in those countries and cultures where more relational conceptions of selfhood and identity still prevail, "privacy" is consistently understood in strongly *negative* terms. This makes perfect sense for relational identities. Why would those whose identities entirely depend upon active and engaged relationships with others to define their significance and place in the community ever want to be "alone," that is, cut off from those relationships? The uniform answer across multiple societies is: only in order to hide something negative or shameful (cf. Lü 2005).

Such sensibilities, in fact, are at work in many contemporary responses to and justifications of the manifold losses of privacy online. To paraphrase the mantras of both Google and the National Security Agency, if you have nothing to hide, you have nothing to fear (Streitfeld 2013). Chairman Mao would be pleased. This sense of constant surveillance and sousveillance as justified by the public good thus clashes with not only our received notions of individual privacy but, more fundamentally, our received notions of individual selfhood. As the editors have commented with regard to Davisson's chapter, "Constant digital surveillance by average netizens leads to the belief that individuals need to censor themselves continually or face potential public humiliation" (Davisson and Booth, this volume). Similarly, such self-monitoring and self-censoring in the face of ubiquitous surveillance has been recently documented to contribute to the "spiral of silence" on social networking sites: that is, *contra* our best hopes that networked communication technologies will foster more democratic forms of discourse and deliberation, we are increasingly frightened of posting items or views that we know will disagree with those of our online (and, sometimes, thereby offline) friends and acquaintances (Hampton et al. 2014). The implications for greater democratic discourse and deliberation via online venues are dire—as are the implications for democracy more broadly of these shifts from more individual toward more relational selves. That is, historically such relational selves are affiliated with hierarchical and nondemocratic regimes (Ess and Fossheim 2013). In my view, how far we can conjoin relational selves with democratic norms and processes is one of the most compelling questions of digital media ethics, and thereby media literacies (Ess 2015a).

These foundational conceptions of selfhood and identity are further entangled with basic assumptions regarding human nature, gender, and sexuality. Several chapters cut into these primary notions, such as Susan Wildermuth's attention to the ethical issues surrounding reporting on transgender persons (more on this below), along with Erin Watley's examination of Black female identity. Questions about human nature and sexuality are further occasioned by Ryan Rogers' observation that the US Supreme Court seems very concerned to "protect" children from "pornography"—but not against violent content. In my view, such concerns index a characteristically US set of assumptions regarding human nature and sexuality—ones that are not only challenged in important ways by Wildermuth and Watley, but are further called into question by contrasting views in Europe and Scandinavia. Indeed, Scandinavian assumptions about sexuality, including the sexuality of children, along with approaches to violence and violent content, are more or less the inverse of those at work in the US Supreme Court ruling and, by implication, among at least many individuals and communities across the United States.

To begin with, sexuality, including the sexuality of children, is taken to be basically natural and thereby good—interests and curiosities to be carefully nurtured and educated, to be sure, but not moralistically condemned, much less regarded as something children require "protection" from (Ess 2013, 160–62). In these directions, the massive EU Kids Online studies couched its work not on "pornography" (a notion that is wildly variable across cultures: *ibid*) but on encountering unwanted "Sexually Explicit Materials" (SEM) online. Perhaps surprising to some in the United States, these studies have consistently found that young people are far more upset and concerned about online bullying than encountering SEMs (Livingstone et al. 2011, 25). From these perspectives, prevailing American attitudes toward sexuality, most especially the sexuality of children, appear to be unreasonably prudish, if not simply silly (e.g., Facebook's practice of removing photos of women nursing their babies because this exposure of women's breasts is taken as unacceptable nudity).

Similar comments hold concerning violence and how it is best to be responded to. On the one hand, Hobbesian assumptions regarding violence and competition, coupled with "natural" hierarchies—assumptions made explicit in both neolibertarian views and social Darwinian versions of *laissez-faire* capitalism—may be in play in the peculiar US view (again, Rogers) that children need protection from sexuality but not violent content. *Par contra*, the social-democratic societies of Scandinavia aim toward income and gender equality—accompanied by vanishingly low murder rates and relatively low incarceration rates: here, violence is not seen as somehow acceptable, much less admirable—but in significant measure the outcome of specific, and avoidable, social conditions. Violence, including violent content, *is* seen as a threat to children: it is illegal to hit a child, and, *contra* comparative US *laissez-faire* regarding violent content as defended under First Amendment rights, there are strict content regulations that seek to minimize exposure to violent content among the young.

The point here is not to make comparative judgments, nor to defend one view as the right one. It is rather to make more articulate these divergences concerning foundational assumptions regarding human nature, and thus to highlight the fact that they are (culturally variable) assumptions. Along with the other assumptions regarding identity and selfhood, these must hence be critically evaluated and justified, ultimately on philosophical grounds—rather than, say, specifically religious ones (most especially in the highly secular-rational cultures of Scandinavia and northern Europe).

Relational selves and virtue ethics

More positively (somewhat), the shift toward more relational selfhood also characteristically brings in its train an increasing emphasis on *virtue ethics*. We see such a turn here in Matthew Pittman and Tom Bivins's analysis of the game *Defense of the Ancients* (*DotA*), as they explicitly take up MacIntyre's virtue ethics as a framework for analyzing how this game issues in "an environment of democratized accountability," one marked by "greater civility, selflessness, and teamwork" (Pittman and Bivens, this volume). As they go on to point out, such an environment is sharply distinct from those in which "hate language, cyber-bullying, or trolling regularly occur" (ibid.). At the risk of painting with overly broad strokes, the latter can be seen to emerge from explicitly "neo-libertarian values" Davisson identifies as oft-cited justifications for the exploitation of women and the co-optation of women's bodies. To be sure, I at least would welcome virtue ethics insofar as it might thereby help counter such values, whether expressed in the exploitation of women or hate language and cyberbullying.

Along these lines, Sam Ford's "Perfectly 'Compliant': The Devaluation of Ethics in Corporate Communication Industry Discourse" is striking first of all for its finding that much corporate discussion on possible improvements in business practices focuses on efficiency and innovation rather than on ethics. And when the latter arise, as he documents, the emphasis is less on ethics per se and more on compliance with the many regulatory bodies that literally govern business practices. His antidote includes a call for the development of greater empathy within marketing and communications spaces, where such empathy would arguably enhance corporate senses of responsibilities toward its customers (and perhaps even their own employees?). From my perspective, this call is both important in its own right as well as deeply interesting insofar as *empathy* is precisely a *virtue* that is often argued to be foundational for such communicative virtues as patience and perseverance, and thereby for long-term friendships and intimacy, and so for good lives marked by deep contentment and flourishing (e.g., Vallor 2011).

Democracy?

At the same time, however, as interwoven with the shifts toward more relational selves, virtue ethics correlates with a turn from more individual conceptions of selfhood, agency and privacy: but this also implies, as we have begun to see here as well, possible shifts away from correlative (high modern) notions of democratic norms and polity, including equality and most precisely gender equality (Ess and Fossheim 2013; Ess 2015a). Additional threats to democratic processes and norms are helpfully brought forward in this volume. That is, beyond the threats of self-surveillance and self-censorship (Davisson), we can add here Luis Hestres' analysis of how strategies aimed at enhancing political organizations and campaigns through their manifold online manifestations and engagements may contribute to the polarization of American political discourse. As they do so, such strategies are accompanied "by high levels of incivility in political discourse and demonization of ideological opponents"—in other words, the language of hate and bullying that we have seen elsewhere described in this volume as marking several forms of online engagement (so Davisson, Pittman and Bivens, Wildermuth, and Stroud). In this instance, however, the threat is to the core of (American) democracy. As Hestres continues, these communicative strategies are thereby "associated with near-paralysis of the public policy process and a growing inability to tackle large-scale problems" (this volume). Hestres thus foregrounds a core ethical question: "Do strategists have an ethical responsibility to take into account how their strategies and tactics may exacerbate polarization and lead to further deterioration of the public sphere?" (this volume). In light of the above, we can now see that our response to this question will turn in part on our assumptions about the nature of selfhood and identity. Crudely, those advocating strongly atomistic conceptions of the individual—including those underlying neo-libertarian views—might well argue that one is only responsible for the immediate consequences of one's acts, and the longer-term well-being of the larger community is not one's concern or responsibility. More relational senses of selfhood, by contrast, as accompanied by distributed senses of agency and responsibility, would ground strongly communitarian responses to this question—namely, in the direction of "yes, strategists are responsible" for the polarizing outcomes of such tactics.

Regrettably, democratic discourse and norms are threatened in still other ways. As we have seen, the emergence of citizen or digital journalism is a primary instantiation of the blurring between producer and consumer in participatory culture(s)—one that entails precisely an increasing sense of shared agency and responsibility in the construction of journalism. This blurring is not entirely a happy one, at least in view of well-established journalistic criteria and aims, beginning with some sort of objectivity or disinterestedness, accuracy and truthfulness, and respect for at least some boundaries of privacy. So Joe Cutbirth is concerned with the emergence of nonprofit journalism and the specific ethical questions it raises, including how such journalism is to sustain editorial independence. Similarly, Shane Tilton investigates what emerged to be a false report of Steve Jobs' death on CNN as an important entrée into emerging ethics of digital journalism. Still more fundamentally, as Cutbirth and Antony and Ryan highlight, both traditional and contemporary journalism derive much of their prominence and *raison d'être* from their putative service to democratic goals and aims—for example, fostering democratic discourse through forwarding diverse points of view, fostering corporate and political accountability through a critical eye on how far these institutions indeed serve public interests, and so on. Here, these critical connections are perhaps most fully explored in Ryan Gillespie's analysis of Julian Assange and Wikileaks—more precisely, just what is meant by "freedom" and "democracy" when used to defend the exposure of state secrets online. As a last example, Susan Wildermuth makes clear in her exploration of the (somewhat) new challenges to media and journalism with regard to reporting on transgender persons of how old journalistic dilemmas regarding what information serves the public interest and what information should be kept private in order to avoid harms to particular persons are taken up with new force in online environments, especially as such online environments make it easier for the persons under discussion to offer information on their own that others might regard as private and thus off-limits instead.

In addition to the insights offered and arguments made by these contributors, I would further suggest that looking more closely at a virtue ethics approach vis-à-vis digital journalism, both for its own sake and, most especially, with a view to advancing its service of democratic norms and principles, would be salutary. This is, in fact, the approach taken up by Nick Couldry (2013), who, like Pittman and Bivens, builds on MacIntyre's virtue ethics to develop and justify a journalistic ethics that he sees as being required for digital and citizen journalism to retain at least some of journalism's traditional virtues and thereby legitimate themselves as institutions critical to democracy. Specifically, Couldry (2013) argues for the cultivation of three key virtues: accuracy, sincerity, and care (25f.). Couldry's arguments are especially pertinent here, as they add a virtue ethics approach to shared problems and concerns in digital journalism; at the same time, Couldry reinforces the overarching thread defining this volume as a contribution to digital media ethics. That is, Couldry observes that "media ethics in the digital age involves all of us, not just media professionals" (25). This is to say, he reiterates the defining understanding that digital media entail the blurring of the distinction between professional and citizen journalists, and between producers and consumers more broadly. This means that his media ethics—including his arguments for the three virtues of accuracy, sincerity, and care—are thereby not solely arguments for virtues within digital journalism; they are, in my terms, ethics for the rest of us. Indeed, for Couldry, the justification for such virtues is not restricted to concerns with journalistic integrity and legitimacy within democratic polities: most broadly, these are ethics for the rest of us because they derive from the classic virtue ethics focus on the *flourishing* of both individuals and communities at large. As he puts it, these three virtues are his answer to the larger question,

> What are the virtues or stable dispositions likely to contribute to us conducting the practice of [journalistic] media well—"well," that is, by reference both to the specific aims of media as a human practice and to the wider aim of contributing to a flourishing human life together. (25)

Nor is Couldry alone: rather, virtue ethics plays increasingly central roles in media and communication studies more broadly (Ess 2015b).

A new enlightenment?

It is further salutary that Kant is also represented in this volume—in Scott Stroud's analysis of how anonymous "mobs" on Twitter seek some form of justice by bullying the bullies. As these mobs point out, such efforts might be justified from some sort of utilitarian effort to establish the greatest good of the greatest number—but at the cost of individual rights to due process, legal representation, and so on. In this way, such vigilante justice—even when aimed at the "right" targets (and not, as Anonymous has done on more than one occasion, by outing the wrong person)—are profoundly problematic for deontological reasons, specifically for those reasons flowing from "Kantian views of the respect afforded to individuals" (Stroud, this volume).

Kant, in fact, is in play here in two ways. To begin with, Kantian deontologies, for all their faults and limitations, have grounded high modern notions of autonomy that thereby ethically fund basic notions of respect, equality, and gender equality, as well as high modern conceptions of democratic polity. If we are concerned, for example, that women be treated as persons, not as "just meat" (see for example, Davisson) or as subordinates to men (see for example, Shira Chess), we can (perhaps most) strongly justify these concerns on such Kantian grounds. The same holds true for the widely shared interests in sustaining and expanding participatory democracy manifest here. Moreover, in addition to virtue ethics as a useful ethical framework (most explicitly, in Pittman and Bivens—and, by extension at least, via Couldry), Kant is also close by. That is, Kant takes up virtue ethics approaches in central ways, especially in his later, more practical ethics (Myskja 2011).

Indeed, Kantian interest in virtue ethics resonates in a last but most critical way with the editors' response to J. J. Sylvia's analysis of how far prevailing practices of notice and consent in fact fail to protect user privacy. They note that "the essay raises serious questions about the ethical obligations of consumers to protect their data" (Davisson and Booth, this volume). To put this slightly differently: it seems to me that a direct consequence of the stress in participatory culture on the agency and engagement of what used to be categorized as "the consumer" is to foreground not only how far they may be able, for example, to contribute content to various forms of social media—but thereby how far these new capacities for engagement at the same time all but require that individuals and communities likewise elevate their attention to and care for new capacities and possibilities to act as ethical agents and citizens. This is to say, as several of the contributors highlight and seek to endorse, participatory culture and digital media promise new ways of realizing and expanding our engagements in participatory democracy and its practices (here, perhaps most notably, journalism). Negatively, as many of these chapters also highlight, digital media offer equal if not greater threat to core notions of democratic processes and norms, whether in the forms of government and corporate surveillance and (self-) censorship, or the forms of vigilante "justice" and ongoing exploitation of women and consumers. Especially in light of the latter, it seems to me that the rise of digital media and participatory culture *heightens* both the possibilities and necessity of individuals and communities engaging as fully as possible as moral agents and citizens.

Such an increase in individual and collective responsibility is already explicit in the notions elucidated here of "ethics for the rest of us." Again, digital media ethics is centrally defined by the recognition that as computational devices and networks increasingly infuse and define our lives, what were once ethical matters of concern for a relatively few professionals perforce become ethical issues that more or less each of us confront on a regular, if not daily basis.

By the same token, the rise of digital media heightens the necessity of our further taking primary responsibility for our social and political lives. For some, if not many, it is profoundly daunting and discomforting to encounter such news. In particular, such demands run directly contrary to the thematic work of technology—to (ostensibly) make our lives easier by selling us convenience, coupled with the correlative message that to consume thus entails less responsibility and so agency. Kant argues against these pitfalls to emancipation in his famous 1784 essay, "What is Enlightenment" (1991). To paraphrase: Kant announces here the motto of the Enlightenment as *sapere aude*—have the courage to think (and act) for yourself. Such critical independence is the necessary condition for Enlightenment as the movement from a "self-imposed tutelage," the inability to direct our own reason and affairs: it is self-imposed because we are, bluntly put, lazy and afraid to take up the responsibilities of thinking and acting freely. It is easier, in Kant's examples, to pay others to make decisions of conscience, to tell us what is best for our health, and so on. As long as I can pay others to do the tiresome work of thinking for me, I need not think for myself.

By contrast, if both individuals and societies are to move from servitude to emancipation and autonomy, the clear implication is that we must take on the irksome work of determining for ourselves what we think and believe. In our terms, emancipation thus requires taking responsibility for our ethical and social views, especially as these intersect with our political roles and responsibilities in a democratic polity. Moreover, Enlightenment dismisses irrational dogmatism as a convenient authority that saves us the trouble of thinking for ourselves. But this means, most broadly, that we all must become philosophers—that is, we all must think through for ourselves our views on such basic philosophical issues as human nature, gender, sexuality, and identity, along with ethics, politics, and so on. Especially for Kant and his successors in both Europe and the United States, becoming a citizen in these ways thereby required a virtue ethics—that is, cultivating the capacities and abilities required for responsible freedom and constructive engagement as a citizen of a democracy (cf. Ess 2014, 630f.) (In this light, Norbert Wiener's uptake of virtue ethics in his cybernetics—most especially his affirmation of the Enlightenment focus on liberty as the full development of our best capacities—thus constitutes a direct connection with these Enlightenment arguments and impulses toward emancipation.)

Certainly, I am not the first to take Kant as an inspiration for a new Enlightenment in a digital era: this is precisely the work, for example, of the Digital Enlightenment Forum, including in its yearly *Handbooks* that gather the sorts of insights and reflection needed to foster greater citizen engagement and democratic flourishing in the contemporary world (see http://www. digitalenlightenment.org/). By the same token, the insights and findings gathered here may contribute not only to a digital media ethics as an "ethics for the rest of us": at the risk of sounding extravagant or utopian, they likewise have every potential to thereby contribute to further emancipation and Enlightenment. Given the stakes involved, and given the manifold threats to both individual autonomy and democratic norms and processes, nothing less will do.

References

"13 Events Bidding Adieu to 2013." 2013. *Ad Gully,* December 27. Retrieved from Lexis-Nexis.

"2014 Nonprofit Technology Conference." 2014. Accessed August 17, 2014. http://14ntc. sched.org/list/descriptions.

"2014 Sales, Demographic, and Usage Data: Essential Facts About the Computer and Video Game Industry." 2014. *Entertainment Software Association.* http://www.theesa. com/facts/pdfs/esa_ef_2014.pdf.

"American Association of Political Consultants Code of Ethics." 2014. Accessed August 19, 2014. http://www.theaapc.org/default.asp?contentID=701.

"Association of Information Technology Professionals' Code of Ethics & Standards of Conduct." 2014. Accessed August 19, 2014. http://www.aitp. org/?page=EthicsConduct.

"Bush Administration's Warrantless Wiretapping Program." 2008. *Washington Post.* http://www.washingtonpost.com/wpdyn/content/article/2007/05/15/ AR2007051500999.html.

"Galt's Gulch Chile." 2014. http://galtsgulchchile.com.

"Global Video Games Revenue from 2012 to 2015 (in Billion U.S. Dollars)." 2014. *Statista: The Statistics Portal.* http://www.statista.com/statistics/237187/global-video- games-revenue/.

"Government Secrecy Continued to Rise in 2004." 2005. *Newsletter on Intellectual Freedom* 54 (3): 100–01.

"Kinja Support Center." 2014. Accessed August 08. http://help.gawker.com/customer/ portal/articles/1099535-what-is-kinja-.

"'Moms Against Gaming' Is My New Favorite Twitter Account." 2014. *Kotaku.* Accessed August 26, 2014. http://kotaku.com/moms-against-gaming-is-my-new-favorite- twitter-account-1597931312.

"Obama to Iran: 'The Whole World is Watching.'" 2009. *CNN.com.* http://www.cnn. com/2009/POLITICS/06/20/iran.obama/.

"PETITION: Tell Republican Leaders to Denounce Rush Limbaugh's Anti-Women Tirade." 2012. Accessed September 2, 2014. http://archive.dccc.org/pages/denounce-rush.

"Principles and Practices for Advertising Ethics." 2011. *Institute for Advertising Ethics.* Accessed December 05, 2014. http://www.rjionline.org/institute-for-advertising- ethics.

"Progressive Exchange." 2004. Accessed August 17, 2014. http://www.progressive exchange.org/welcome.htm.

"Role." 2014. *Dota2 Wiki.* http://dota2.gamepedia.com/Role.

"Scam Ads: Here's Why Ford, JWT India Are in a Mess." 2013, March 28. *CNBC TV-18 MoneyControl.*

"Standards of Practice." 2011. *American Association of Advertising Agencies,* June 7. http://www.aaaa.org/about/association/Pages/standardsofpractice.aspx.

"Statement on Wikipedia from Participating Communications Firms." 2014. *Wikipedia.* https://en.wikipedia.org/wiki/Wikipedia:Statement_on_Wikipedia_from_participating_communications_firms.

"Studio Smackdown. 2013: Warner Bros. Rules World With $5.04 Billion, Disney Close Behind." 2013. *The Hollywood Reporter.* http://www.hollywoodreporter.com/news/studio-smackdown-2013-warner-bros-668302.

"The Chip Shop Awards." 2014. http://www.chipshopawards.com/pages/about#name.

"Universal Declaration on Human Rights." 2014. *United Nations.* http://www.un.org/en/documents/udhr/.

"Who Is the Dutch Man Arrested in Connection with the Death of Amanda Todd?" 2014. *CTV News,* April 18. http://www.ctvnews.ca/canada/who-is-the-dutch-man-arrested-in-connection-with-the-death-of-amanda-todd-1.1781755.

"Women Significantly Outnumber Teenage Boys in Gamer Demographics | The Rundown." 2014. *PBS NewsHour.* Accessed August 26, 2014. http://www.pbs.org/newshour/rundown/female-adults-oust-teenage-boys-largest-gaming-demographic.

"World Report 2013." *Human Rights Watch.* http://www.hrw.org/worldreport/2013/country-chapters/ecuador.

"Your Mama Plays 'Dead Space 2'." 2014. *Kotaku.* Accessed August 26, 2014. http://kotaku.com/5739837/your-mama-plays-dead-space-2.

1981 Atari 2600 Commercial. 2010. http://www.youtube.com/watch?v=YZD-siXEQ9wandfeature=youtube_gdata_player.

Advertising Age. April 2014. http://adage.coverleaf.com/advertisingage/20140428.

Alfonso, Fernando. 2011. "Reddit Wrestles with Violence and Misogyny." *The Daily Dot,* January 15. http://www.dailydot.com/society/reddit-beatingwomen-misogyny-images.

Alfonso, Fernando. 2012. "Reddit's Most Notorious Troll Loses Job after Gawker Profile." The Daily Dot, August 15. Accessed August 22, 2015. http://www.dailydot.com/news/violentacrez-reddit-troll-fired-gawker-profile/.

Alfonso, Fernando. 2014a. "Creepshots Never Went Away—We Just Stopped Talking about Them." *The Daily Dot,* January 15. http://www.dailydot.com/lifestyle/reddit-creepshots-candidfashionpolice-photos/.

Alfonso, Fernando. 2014b. "Reddit Is Creeping on Your Facebook Photos." *The Daily Dot,* January 15. http://www.dailydot.com/lifestyle/reddit-creeping-your-facebook-photos.

Alighieri, Dante. 2003. *The Divine Comedy,* Translated by John Ciardi. New York: New American Library.

Aljalian, Natasha N. 1999. "Fourteenth Amendment Personhood: Fact or Fiction?" *St. John's Law Review* 73 (2): 495–540.

Allan, Stuart, and Einar Thorsen. 2009. *Citizen Journalism: Global Perspectives.* New York: Peter Lang.

Allen, David S., and Elizabeth Blanks Hindman. 2014. "The Media and Democracy: Using Democratic Theory in Journalism Ethics." In *The Ethics of Journalism: Individual, Institutional, and Cultural Influences*, edited by Wendy N. Wyatt, 185–203. New York, NY: I. B. Tauris & Co.

Amatriain, Xavier and Justin Basilico. 2012. "Netflix Recommendations: Beyond the 5 Stars." *The Netflix Tech Blog.* http://techblog.netflix.com/2012/04/netflix-recommendations-beyond-5-stars.html.

Amazeen, Michelle A. 2013. "Making a Difference: A Critical Assessment of Fact-Checking in 2012." *New America Foundation Media Policy Initiative Research Paper.* http://mediapolicy.newamerica.net/publications/policy/making_a_difference_a_critical_assessment_of_fact_checking_in_2012.

Amazeen, Michelle A., and Susan A. O'Sullivan-Gavin. 2014. "Unrestrained Creativity or Industry Irresponsibility? Testing Attitudinal Effects and Corrections of 'Rogue' Advertising." Paper presented at the Walter Cronkite Conference on Media Ethics and Integrity, November 2014. St. Joseph, Missouri.

American Psychological Association. 2011. *The Guidelines for Psychological Practice with Lesbian, Gay, and Bisexual Clients.* February 18–20. http://www.apa.org/pi/lgbt/resources/guidelines.aspx.

American Trans Man. 2012. *14 Reasons Why It Is Not Okay to Out Someone as Trans: A Public Service Announcement From Your Friendly Neighborhood Trans Person.* April 18. http://americantransman.com/2012/04/18/14-reasons-why-its-not-okay-to-out-someone-as-trans-a-public-service-announcement-from-your-friendly-neighborhood-trans-person/.

Anderson, Ashley A, Dominique Brossard, Dietram A Scheufele, Michael A Xenos, and Peter Ladwig. 2014. "The 'Nasty Effect': Online Incivility and Risk Perceptions of Emerging Technologies." *Journal of Computer-Mediated Communication* 19 (3): 373–87.

Anderson, C. W., Emily Bell, and Clay Shirky. 2012. *Post-Industrial Journalism: Adapting to the Present.* New York: Tow Center For Digital Journalism.

Anderson, Craig A. 2003. "An Update on the Effects of Playing Violent Video Games." *Journal of Adolescence* 27 (1): 113–22.

Anderson-Minshall, Diane. 2014. "Is Obama the Most Trans-Friendly President Ever?" *The Advocate,* June 21. http://www.advocate.com/politics/transgender/2014/06/21/obama-most-trans-friendly-president-ever.

Andrejevic, Mark. 2002. "The Kinder, Gentler Gaze Of Big Brother: Reality TV In The Era Of Digital Capitalism." *New Media and Society* 4 (2): 251–70.

Andrejevic, Mark. 2004. *Reality TV: The Work of Being Watched.* Lanham, MD: Rowman & Littlefield Publishers.

Andrejevic, Mark. 2006. "The Discipline of Watching: Detection, Risk, and Lateral Surveillance." *Critical Studies in Media Communication* 23 (5): 391–407.

Andrejevic, Mark. 2008. "Watching Television Without Pity: The Productivity of Online Fans." *Television and New Media* 9 (1): 24–46.

Andrejevic, Mark. 2009. "The Twenty-First Century TeleScreen." In *Television Studies After TV: Understanding Television in the Post-broadcast Era*, edited by Graeme Turner and J. Tay, 31–40. London: Routledge.

Andrejevic, Mark. 2013. *Infoglut: How the Digital Era Is Changing the Way We Think About Information.* New York and London: Routledge.

Angwin, Julia. 2014. "You Know Who Else Collected Metadata? The Stasi." *ProPublica.* http://www.propublica.org/article/how-the-stasi-spied-on-social-networks.

Antony, Mary Grace, and Ryan J. Thomas. 2010. "'This Is Citizen Journalism at Its Finest': YouTube and the Public Sphere in the Oscar Grant Shooting Incident." *New Media and Society* 12 (8): 1280–96.

Aristotle. 1984. *The Complete Works of Aristotle, Vol. 2.* Edited by Jonathan Barnes. Princeton: Princeton University Press.

Arthur, Charles. 2013. "Wikipedia Sends Cease-and-Desist Letter to PR Firm Offering Paid Edits to Site." *The Guardian*, November 21. http://www.theguardian.com/technology/2013/nov/21/wikipedia-cease-and-desist-pr-firm-offering-paid-edits.

Associated Press. 2014. *AP's History.* Accessed August 10. http://ap.org/company/history/ap-history.

Atton, Chris. 2004. *An Alternative Internet.* Edinburgh, UK: Edinburgh University Press.

Aufderheide, Patricia, Erik Barnouw, Richard M. Cohen, Thomas Frank, Todd Gitlin, David Lieberman, Mark Crispin Miller, Gene Roberts, and Thomas Schatz, eds. 1997. *Conglomerates and the Media.* New York: New Press.

Bagri, Neha Thirani. 2013a. "India's Ad Industry Shaken after Ford Figo Controversy." *The New York Times,* April 1. http://india.blogs.nytimes.com/2013/04/01/indias-ad-industry-shaken-after-ford-figo-controversy/?_r=1.

Bagri, Neha Thirani. 2013b. "India Winces at Ad Reactions." *The International Herald Tribune,* April 2: Finance 19.

Bahadur, Nina. 2014. "'Facebook Cleavage' Subreddit Reminds Us Just How Incredibly Creepy the Internet Can Be." *Huffington Post*, January 15. http://www.huffingtonpost.com/2014/03/14/facebook-cleavage-reddit-forum_n_4963780.html.

Baker, C. Edwin. 2002. *Media, Markets, and Democracy.* Cambridge, UK: Cambridge University Press.

Baker, Katie J. M. 2012. "How to Shut Down Reddit's CreepShots Once and for All: Name Names." *Jezebel*, January 15. http://jezebel.com/5949379/naming-names-is-this-the-solution-to-combat-reddits-creepshots.

Balkin, Jack M. 2014. "Old-School/New-School Speech Regulation." *Harvard Law Review* 127: 2296–342.

Barlow, John Perry. 1996. "A Declaration of the Independence of Cyberspace." Accessed August 17, 2014. https://projects.eff.org/~barlow/Declaration-Final.html.

Barnes, Susan B. 2002. *Computer-Mediated Communication: Human-to-Human Communication Across the Internet*. Boston: Allyn and Bacon.

Barnlund, Dean C., and Franklyn Saul Haiman. 1960. *The Dynamics of Discussion*. Boston: Houghton Mifflin.

Barocas, Solon, and Helen Nissenbaum. 2009. "On Notice: The Trouble with Notice and Consent." Proceedings of the Engaging Data Forum: The First International Forum on the Application and Management of Personal Electronic Information.

Bauman, Zygmunt. 2006. *Liquid Fear*. Cambridge, UK: Polity Press.

Baym, Nancy. 2009. "Response: Toward Understanding the Liberatory Potential of Elective Affinities Online." In *Webbing Cyberfeminist Practice Communities, Pedagogies, and Social Action*, edited by Kristine Blair, Radhika Gajjala, and Christine Tulley, 127–34. New York, NY: Hampton Press.

Baym, Nancy. 2010. *Personal Connections in the Digital Age*. Malden: Polity.

Bazelon, Emily. 2012. "Amanda Todd Was Stalked Before She Was Bullied." *Slate*, October 18. http://www.slate.com/blogs/xx_factor/2012/10/18/suicide_victim_amanda_todd_stalked_before_she_was_bullied.html.

Bazelon, Emily. 2014a. "The Online Avengers: Are Antibullying Activists the Saviors of the Internet—or Just a Different Kind of Curse?" *New York Times*, January 15. http://www.nytimes.com/2014/01/19/magazine/the-online-avengers.html.

Bazelon, Emily. 2014b. "Do Online Death Threats Count as Free Speech? *New York Times*, November 25. http://www.nytimes.com/2014/11/30/magazine/do-online-death-threats-count-as-free-speech.html.

Beckford, Martin. 2010. "Sarah Palin: Hunt WikiLeaks Founder Like Al-Qaeda and Taliban Leaders." *The Telegraph*. http://www.telegraph.co.uk/news/worldnews/wikileaks/8171269/Sarah-Palin-hunt-WikiLeaks-founder-like-al-Qaeda-and-Taliban-leaders.html.

Benjamin, James. 2012. "Tweets, Blogs, Facebook and the Ethics of 21st-Century Communication Technology." In *Social Media: Usage and Impact*, edited by Hana S. Noor Al-Deen and John Allen Hendricks, 271–87. New York, NY: Lexington Books.

Benkler, Yochai. 2006. *The Wealth of Networks*. New Haven: Yale University Press.

Benkler, Yochai. 2011a. "A Free Irresponsible Press: WikiLeaks and the Battle Over the Soul of the Networked Fourth Estate." *Harvard Civil Rights-Civil Liberties Law Review* 46: 311–97.

Benkler, Yochai. 2011b. "The Real Significance of WikiLeaks." *American Prospect* 22 (5): 31–33.

Benkler, Yochai, and Helen Nissenbaum. 2006. "Commons-based Peer Production and Virtue." *Journal of Political Philosophy* 14 (4): 394–419.

Bennett, Lucy. 2011. "Delegitimising Strategic Power: Normative Identity and Governance in Online R.E.M. Fandom." *Transformative Works and Cultures* 7. http://journal.transformativeworks.org/index.php/twc/article/view/281/226.

Bennett, Lucy. Forthcoming. "Singer-Songwriters in the Digital Age: New Trajectories in Connectivity and Participation between Musicians and Fans." In *Cambridge Companion to the Singer-Songwriter,* edited by Katherine Williams and Justin Williams. Cambridge: Cambridge University Press.

Bennett, Lucy, and Bertha Chin. 2014. "Exploring Fandom, Social Media and Producer/Fan Interactions: An Interview with *Sleepy Hollow*'s Orlando Jones." *Transformative Works and Cultures* 17. http://dx.doi.org/10.3983/twc.2014.0601.

Bentham, Jeremy. (1781) 2007. *Introduction to the Principles of Morals and Legislation.* New York: Dover Publications.

Bentham, Jeremy. 1823. *A Fragment on Government; Or a Comment on the Commentaries: Being an Examination of What Is Delivered on the Subject of Government in General, in the Introduction to Sir William Blackstone's Commentaries: With a Preface, in Which Is Given a Critique on the Work at Large.* 2nd ed. London: E. Wilson and W. Pickering.

Bercovici, Jeff. 2012. "From Digital Sweatshop to Perk Palace: Why Gawker's Nick Denton Started Spoiling His Staff." *Forbes,* October 11. Accessed August 8, 2014, http://www.forbes.com/sites/jeffbercovici/2012/10/11/from-digital-sweatshop-to-perk-palace-why-gawkers-nick-denton-started-spoiling-his-staff.

Beutler, William. 2014a. "Can Wikipedia and PR Just Get Along? Here's a Possible New Way Forward." *The Wikipedian,* June 10. http://thewikipedian.net/2014/06/10/can-wikipedia-and-pr-just-get-along-heres-a-possible-new-way-forward.

Beutler, William. 2014b. "Wikipedia and the Communications Professional: A Manual." Council of Public Relations Firms and Institute for Public Relations. http://www.instituteforpr.org/wp-content/uploads/Wikipedia_Manual_Beutler_91614.pdf.

Black, Jay. 2010. "Who Is a Journalist?" In *Journalism Ethics: A Philosophical Approach,* edited by Christopher Meyers, 103–16. Oxford, UK: Oxford University Press.

Blasi, Vincent. 1977. "The Checking Value in First Amendment Theory." *American Bar Foundation Research Journal* 2 (3): 521–649.

Blodgett, Bridget Marie, and Anastasia Salter. 2013. "Hearing 'Lady Game Creators' Tweet: #1ReasonWhy, Women and Online Discourse in the Game Development Community." *Selected Papers of Internet Research* 3 (0). http://spir.aoir.org/index.php/spir/article/view/694.

Blood, Rebecca. 2002. *The Weblog Handbook: Practical Advice on Creating and Maintaining Your Blog.* Cambridge, MA: Perseus Publishing.

Bloomberg. 2014. "BuzzFeed's Valuation Tops Tribune's, 'Validates' New-Media Approach." *NEWSMAXFINANCE,* August 12. Accessed December 2, 2014. http://www.newsmax.com/Finance/BuzzFeed-Valuation-New-Media-Approach/2014/08/12/id/588370/.

BlueKai. 2013. "A Top Wireless Telco Creates 6x Lift in Facebook Ad Performance & Reduces 3rd Party Data Costs 50%." *Bluekai,* December 1. Accessed April 14, 2014. http://ci33.actonsoftware.com/acton/attachment/4189/f-005b/0/-/-/-/file.pdf.

BlueKai. 2014. "BlueKai: Little Blue Book." *Bluekai,* March 1. Accessed April 27, 2014. http://www.bluekai.com/bluebook.

Bodó, Balázs. 2014. "Hacktivism 1–2–3: How Privacy Enhancing Technologies Change the Face of Anonymous Hacktivism." *Internet Policy Review* 3 (4): 1–12.

Bogle, Donald. 1997. "Black Beginnings: From *Uncle Tom's Cabin* to *The Birth of a Nation.*" In *Representing Blackness: Issues in Film and Video,* edited by Valerie Smith, 13–24. New Brunswick, NJ: Rutgers University Press.

Bogle, Donald. 2001. *Toms, Coons, Mulattoes, Mammies, and Bucks: An Interpretive History of Blacks in American Films.* New York, NY: Bloomsbury.

Bohman, James. 2004. "Expanding Dialogue: The Internet, Public Sphere and Prospects for Transnational Democracy." *The Sociological Review* 52 (1): 131–55.

Booth, Robert. 2014. "Facebook Reveals News Feed Experiment to Control Emotions." Accessed August 20, 2014. http://www.theguardian.com/technology/2014/jun/29/facebook-users-emotions-news-feeds.

Bowen, Shannon A. 2013. "Using Classic Social Media Cases to Distill Ethical Guidelines for Digital Engagement." *Journal of Mass Media Ethics* 28 (2): 119–33.

Bowman, Shayne, and Chris Willis. 2003. *We Media: How Audiences Are Shaping the Future of News and Information.* Reston, VA: The Media Center at the American Press Institute.

boyd, danah. 2014. *It's Complicated: The Social Lives of Networked Teens.* New Haven: Yale University Press.

Boyle, Kris, and Carol Zuenger. 2012. "News Staffs Use Twitter to Interact with Readers." *Newspaper Research Journal* 33 (4): H4, S6–19.

Brooker, Will. 2002. *Using the Force: Creativity, Community and Star Wars Fans.* New York: Continuum.

Brooks, Rodney A. 2002. *Flesh and Machines: How Robots Will Change Us.* New York: Pantheon Books.

Brown, Laurel. 2013. "Benedict Cumberbatch, Martin Freeman Forced to Read 'Sherlock' Fan-fic." *Zap2It.* http://www.zap2it.com/blogs/benedict_cumberbatch_martin_freeman_forced_to_read_sherlock_fan-fic-2013-12.

Brown, Timothy J. 2008. "'I Am Who I Am': Black Masculinity and the Interpretation of Individualism in the Film *Barbershop.*" *Qualitative Research Reports in Communication* 9 (1): 46–61.

Bruns, Axel. 2008. *Blogs, Wikipedia, Second Life, and Beyond: From Production to Produsage.* New York: Peter Lang.

Buber, Martin. 1958. *I and Thou.* Translated by Ronald Gregor Smith. 2nd ed. New York: Scribner.

Bugeja, Michael. 2007. "Making Whole: The Ethics of Correction." *Journal of Mass Media Ethics* 22 (1): 49–65.

Bump, Philip. 2013. "BuzzFeed's 'Happiest Facts of All Time Were Mostly Plagiarized from Reddit.'" *The Atlantic Wire,* March 8. Accessed December 2, 2014. http://www.theatlanticwire.com/business/2013/03/buzzfeeds-happiest-facts-all-time-were-mostly-plagiarized-reddit/62918/.

Burleigh, Nina. 2013. "Sexting, Shame and Suicide." *Rolling Stone,* January 15. http://www.rollingstone.com/culture/news/sexting-shame-and-suicide-20130917.

Burton, Lee. 2012. "Underage & Overexpossed." *Screen Education* 65 (1): 58–70.

Busse, Kristina. 2009. "Attention Economy, Layered Publics, and Research Ethics." *FlowTV.* Accessed July 16, 2014. http://flowtv.org/2009/05/attention-economy-layered-publics-and-research-ethics-kristina-busse-university-of-south-alabama.

Busse, Kristina, and Karen Hellekson. 2009. "Fan Privacy and TWC's Editorial Philosophy." *Organization for Transformative Works.* Accessed August 15, 2014. http://transformativeworks.org/projects/twc-citation.

Busse, Kristina, and Karen Hellekson. 2012. "Identity, Ethics and Fan Privacy." In *Fan Culture: Theory/Practice,* edited by Katherine Larsen and Lynn Zubernis, 38–56. Newcastle upon Tyne, UK: Cambridge Scholars Publishing.

Butler, Judith. 1993. *Bodies that Matter.* New York: Routledge.

Butterly, Amelia. 2014. "The Fappening Creator Does AMA on Reddit's Shutdown." *BBC Newsbeat,* January 15. http://www.bbc.co.uk/newsbeat/29105802.

Bynum, Terrell Ward. 2010. "The Historical Roots of Information and Computer Ethics." In *The Cambridge Handbook of Information and Computer Ethics,* edited by L. Floridi, 20–38, Cambridge, UK: Cambridge University Press.

Byrd, Ayana, and Lori Tharps. 2001. *Hair Story: Untangling the Roots of Black Hair in America.* New York, NY: St. Martin's Press.

Callahan, Kat. 2014. "Reporting around R. Kelly's Child Shows Depth of Trans Ignorance." *Jezebel,* June 8. http://roygbiv.jezebel.com/reporting-around-r-kellys-child-shows-depth-of-trans-i-1587876454.

Calvert, Clay. 2009. "Sex, Cell Phones, Privacy, and the First Amendment: When Children Become Child Pornographers and the Lolita Effect Undermines the Law." *Journal of Communications Law and Policy* 18 (1): 1–66.

Calvert, Clay, and J. Brown. 2000. "Video Voyeurism, Privacy, and the Internet: Exposing Peeping Toms in Cyberspace." *Cardozo Arts & Entertainment Law Journal* 18 (3): 469–568.

Calvert, Justin. 2008. "Grand Theft Auto IV Review." *Gamespot.com,* December 8. http://www.gamespot.com/ps3/action/grandtheftauto4/review.html.

Cammaerts, Bart. 2008. "Critiques on the Participatory Potentials of Web 2.0." *Communication, Culture and Critique* 1: 358–77.

Campus Reform. 2014. "Mission." *Campus Reform.* Accessed February 20, 2014. http://www.campusreform.org/about.

Canter, Lily. 2013. "The Misconception of Online Comment Threads: Content and Control on Local Newspaper Websites." *Journalism Practice* 7 (5): 604–19. doi:10.108 0/17512786.2012.740172.

Carey, James. 1997. "The Press, Public Opinion and Public Discourse." In *The James Carey Reader*, edited by Eve Stryker Munson and Catherine A. Warren, 228–60. Minneapolis: University of Minnesota Press.

Carpenter, Cassie. 2013. "Anti-Bullying Group Rushes to Kate Gosselin's Aide by Outing Reality Star's Twitter Haters to their Employers." *Daily Mail*, April 1. http://www.dailymail.co.uk/tvshowbiz/article-2302557/Anti-bullying-group-rushes-Kate-Gosselins-aide-outing-reality-stars-Twitter-haters-employers.html.

Carpenter, Serena. 2008. "How Online Citizen Journalism Publications and Online Newspapers Utilize the Objectivity Standard and Rely on External Sources." *Journalism and Mass Communication Quarterly* 85 (3): 531–48.

Carpenter, Serena. 2010. "A Study of Content Diversity in Online Citizen Journalism and Online Newspaper Articles." *New Media and Society* 12 (7): 1064–84.

Cassell, Justine, and Henry Jenkins, eds. 1998a. *From Barbie to Mortal Kombat: Gender and Computer Games*. Cambridge, MA: MIT Press.

Cassell, Justine, and Henry Jenkins. 1998b. "Chess for Girls? Feminism and Computer Games." In *From Barbie to Mortal Kombat: Gender and Computer Games*, edited by Justine Cassell and Henry Jenkins, 2–45. Cambridge, MA: MIT Press.

Castells, Manuel. 2001. *The Internet Galaxy: Reflections on the Internet, Business, and Society*. New York: Oxford University Press.

Castells, Manuel. 2008. "The New Public Sphere: Global Civil Society, Communication Networks, and Global Governance." *Annals of the American Academy of Political and Social Science* 616 (1): 78–93.

Castells, Manuel, Mireia Fernandez-Ardevol, Jack Linchuan Qiu, and Araba Sey. 2004. *The Mobile Communication Society: A Cross-Cultural Analysis of Available Evidence on the Social Use of Wireless Communication Technology*. Los Angeles, CA: Annenberg Research Network on International Communication.

Casual Games Association. 2007. *Casual Games Market Report 2007*. http://issuu.com/casualconnect/docs/casualgamesmarketreport-2007/6?e=2336319/1145366.

Cate, Fred H., and Viktor Mayer-Schonberger. 2013. "Notice and Consent in a World of Big Data." *International Data Privacy Law* 3 (2): 67–73.

Cathcart, Robert, and Gary Gumpert. 1985. "The Person-Computer Interaction: A Unique Source." In *Information and Behavior*, vol. 1, 113–124. New Brunswick, NJ: Transaction Books.

Center for Investigative Reporting. 2014. *Ethics Guide*. Accessed August 17. http://cironline.org/ethics-guide.

Chen, Adrien. 2012a. "Remix Everything: Buzzfeed and the Plagiarism Problem." *Gawker*, June 28. http://gawker.com/5922038/remix-everything-buzzfeed-and-the-plagiarism-problem.

Chen, Adrien. 2012b. "Unmasking Reddit's Violentacrez, the Biggest Troll on the Web." *Gawker*, January 15. http://gawker.com/5950981/unmasking-reddits-violentacrez-the-biggest-troll-on-the-web.

Chernaik, Tom, and Sam Ford. 2014. "#ThinkAgain: How Regulator Guidance Can Impact Social Media Marketing." *Journal of Digital & Social Media Marketing* 2 (1): 40–47.

Chess, Shira. 2011. "A 36–24–36 Cerebrum: Productivity, Gender, and Video Game Advertising." *Critical Studies in Media Communication* 28 (3): 230–52. doi:10.1080/1 5295036.2010.515234.

Chess, Shira. 2014. "Youthful White Male Industry Seeks 'Fun'-loving Middle-aged Women for Video Games—No Strings Attached." In *The Routledge Companion to Media and Gender*, edited by Cynthia Carter, Linda Steiner, and Lisa McLaughlin, 168–78. New York: Routledge.

Chess, Shira, and Adrienne Shaw. 2015. "A Conspiracy of Fishes, or, How We Learned to Stop Worrying about GamerGate and Embrace Hegemonic Masculinity." *The Journal of Broadcasting and Electronic Media* 59 (1): 208–20.

Childs, E. C. 2005. "Looking Behind the Stereotypes of the 'Angry Black Woman': An Exploration of Black Women's Responses to Interracial Relationships." *Gender and Society* 19 (4): 544–61.

Chin, Bertha. Forthcoming. "When Hated Characters Talk Back: Twitter, Hate, and the Fan/Celebrity Interaction." In *Dislike, Hate, and Anti-Fandom in the Digital Age*, edited by Melissa Click. New York: New York University Press.

Chodorow, Nancy. 1978. *The Reproduction of Mothering: Psychoanalysis and the Sociology of Gender*. Berkeley: University of California Press.

Choudhury, Santanu, and Jeff Bennett. 2013. "Ford Figo India Ads Lead to Firings." *Wall Street Journal*, March 27. http://online.wsj.com/news/articles/SB100014241278 87324685104578386000459196108.

Chowriwar, Shalaka S., Madhulika S. Mool, Prajyoti P. Sabale, Sneha S.Parpelli, and Nilesh Sambhe. 2014. "Mitigating Denial-of-Service Attacks Using Secure Service Overlay Model." *International Journal of Engineering Trends and Technology* 8 (9): 479–83.

Christians, Clifford G. 2007. "Utilitarianism in Media Ethics and Its Discontents." *Journal of Mass Media Ethics* 22 (2 and 3): 113–31.

Christians, Clifford G., Theodore L. Glasser, Denis McQuail, Kaarle Nordenstreng, and Robert A. White. 2009. *Normative Theories of the Media: Journalism in Democratic Societies*. Urbana, IL: University of Illinois Press.

Cisco Systems. 2012. *Cisco Visual Networking Index: Global Mobile Data Traffic Forecast Update, 2011–2016*. San Jose, CA: Cisco Systems. http://www.cisco.com/en/US/solutions/collateral/ns341/ns525/ns537/ns705/ns827/white_paper_c11-520862.pdf.

Clapp, J. G. 1943. "On Freedom." *The Journal of Philosophy* 40 (4): 85–100.

Clinton, Hilary. 2010. "Remarks on Internet Freedom." *U.S. Department of State*. http://www.state.gov/secretary/20092013clinton/rm/2010/01/135519.html.

CNN iReport. 2013. "iReport Toolkit." *CNN*. http://ireport.cnn.com/toolkit.jspa.

Cobia, Jeffrey. 2009. "The Digital Millennium Copyright Act Takedown Notice Procedure: Misuses, Abuses, and Shortcomings of the Process." *Minnesota Journal of Law, Science, & Technology* 10 (1): 387–411.

Coen, Jessica. 2010. "Commenting on Jezebel: Rules of the Road." *Jezebel*, August 27. Accessed August 8, 2014. http://jezebel.com/5621055/a-friendly-note-on-commenting.

Coen, Jessica. 2012. "Welcome to Kinja, Our New Commenting System." *Jezebel*, June 27. Accessed August 8, 2014. http://jezebel.com/5921598/and-so-it-begins-welcome-to-kinja-our-new-commenting-system.

Cohen, Nicole S. 2008. "The Valorization of Surveillance: Towards a Political Economy of Facebook." *Democratic Communique* 22 (1): 5–21.

Cohen, Stan. 2007. "Downloading Evil." *Index On Censorship* 36 (4): 111–115.

Coleman, Gabriella. 2014. *Hacker, Hoaxer, Whistleblower, Spy: The Many Faces of Anonymous*. London: Verso.

Collins, Jim. 2001. "Level 5 Leadership: The Triumph of Humility and Fierce Resolve." *Harvard Business Review*, January. http://hbr.org/2005/07/level-5-leadership-the-triumph-of-humility-and-fierce-resolve/ar/1.

Collins, Patricia Hill. 2005. *Black Sexual Politics: African Americans, Gender, and the New Racism*. New York and London: Routledge.

Collins, Patricia Hill. 2008. *Black Feminist Thought: Knowledge, Consciousness, and the Politics of Empowerment*. London: Routledge.

Conigliaro, Katie. 2013. "Caitlin Moran and the Sherlock Fandom." *The Fiction Diaries*. http://thefictiondiaries.blogspot.co.uk/2013/12/caitlin-moran-and-sherlock-fandom.html.

Consalvo, Mia. 2008. "Crunched by Passion: Women Game Developers and Workplace Challenges." In *Beyond Barbie and Mortal Kombat: New Perspectives on Gender and Gaming*, edited by Yasmin B. Kafai, Carrie Heeter, Jill Denner, and Jennifer Y. Sun, 177–91. Cambridge, MA: MIT Press.

Consalvo, Mia, and Charles Ess. 2013. *The Handbook of Internet Studies*. Oxford: Wiley-Blackwell.

Constine, Josh. 2014. "Facebook 'Nearby Friends' Will Track Your Location History To Target You With Ads." *TechCrunch*, April 8. Accessed December 1, 2014. http://techcrunch.com/2014/04/18/facebook-location-advertising.

Cope, David. 2005. *Computer Models of Musical Creativity*. Cambridge, MA: MIT Press.

Corporation for Public Broadcasting. 2014. "Public Broadcasting Act of 1967." Sec. 396g. Accessed August 17. http://www.cpb.org/aboutpb/act/PulicBroadcastingAct1967.pdf.

Costine, Josh. 2014. "The Morality of A/B Testing." Accessed August 17, 2014. http://techcrunch.com/2014/06/29/ethics-in-a-data-driven-world.

Couldry, Nick. 2013. "Why Media Ethics Still Matters." In *Global Media Ethics: Problems and Perspectives*, edited by Stephen J. A. Ward, 13–29. Malden, MA: Blackwell.

Courson, Paul, and Matt Smith. 2013. "WikiLeaks Source Manning Gets 35 Years, Will Seek Pardon." *CNN.com*. http://www.cnn.com/2013/08/21/us/bradley-manning sentencing/.

Cox, Kiana. 2013. "Gender and Race as Meaning Systems: Understanding Theoretical, Historical and Institutional Implications of Sexualized Imagery in Rap Music." In *Race, Gender, Class, Media 3.0: Considering Diversity across Audiences, Content, and Producers*, edited by Rebecca Ann Lind, 274–79. Upper Saddle River, NJ: Pearson Education Inc.

Craft, Stephanie, and Charles N. Davis. 2013. *Principles of American Journalism: An Introduction*. New York, NY: Routledge.

Cram, Emily. 2012. "'Angie was Our Sister:' Witnessing the Trans-Formation of Disgust in the Citizenry of Photography." *Quarterly Journal of Speech* 98 (4): 411–38.

Cramer, Benjamin. 2013. "The Two Internet Freedoms: Framing Victimhood for Political Gain." *International Journal of Communication* 7: 1074–92.

Cuneo, Terence. 2014. *Speech and Morality: On the Metaethical Implications of Speaking*. New York: Oxford University Press.

Cunningham, Stuart. 2013. *Hidden Innovation: Policy, Industry and the Creative Sector*. Australia: University of Queensland Press.

Dahlgren, Peter. 2005. "The Internet, Public Spheres, and Political Communication: Dispersion and Deliberation." *Political Communication* 22 (20): 147–62.

Davidson, Amy. 2013. "Obama and Charlie Rose: The NSA's Road to Nowhere." *The New Yorker*. http://www.newyorker.com/news/amy-davidson/obama-and-charlie-rose-the-n-s-a-s-road-to-nowhere.

Davis & Gilbert. 2014. "Contest Entrants' Pins Raise FTC Endorsement Concerns." *Advertising, Marketing, & Promotions Alert*, May. http://www.dglaw.com/images_user/newsalerts/Advertising_Contest_Entrants_Pins_Raise_FTC_Endorsement_Concerns.pdf.

Dean, Howard. 2014. "This Is the Year We Stop the Tea Party's Radical Agenda." To Luis Hestres. September 1, 2014.

Delany, Colin. 2013. "NationBuilder 'Frees' the Voter File?" Accessed August 20, 2014. http://www.epolitics.com/2012/09/13/nationbuilder-frees-the-voter-file.

DeLuca, Kevin Michael, and Jennifer Peeples. 2002. "From Public Sphere to Public Screen: Democracy, Activism, and the 'Violence' of Seattle." *Critical Studies in Media Communication* 19 (2): 125–51.

Delwiche, Aaron, and Jennifer Jacobs Henderson. 2012. "Introduction: What Is Participatory Culture?" In *The Participatory Cultures Handbook*, edited by Aaron Delwiche and Jennifer Jacobs Henderson, 3–9. New York: Routledge.

Denno, Deborah. 1993. "Perspectives on Disclosing Rape Victims Names." *Fordham Law Review* 61 (5): 1113–31.

Desai, Manisha. 2009. *Gender and the Politics of Possibilities: Rethinking Globalization*. Lanhma, MD: Rowman and Littlefield.

DeSantis, Nick. 2013a. "Michigan State U. Reassigns Professor Who Blasted Republicans in Class." *The Chronicle of Higher Education*. http://chronicle.com/blogs/ticker/michigan-state-u-reassigns-professor-who-blasted-republicans-in-class/65591?cid=at&utm_source=at&utm_medium=en.

DeSantis, Nick. 2013b. "Michigan State U. Professor Who Blasted Republicans to Return to Teaching." *The Chronicle of Higher Education*. http://chronicle.com/

blogs/ticker/michigan-state-u-professor-who-blasted-republicans-to-return-to-teaching/69245?cid=at&utm_source=at&utm_medium=en.

Deuze, Mark. 2003. "The Web and Its Journalisms: Considering the Consequences of Different Types of News Media Online." *New Media and Society* 5 (2): 203–30. doi:10.1177/1461444803005002004.

Deuze, Mark, Axel Bruns, and Christoph Neuberger. 2007. "Preparing for an Age of Participatory News." *Journalism Practice* 1 (3): 322–38.

Diaz, Ann-Christine. 2013. "Creatives Sound Off on Scam Ads—And What the Industry Should do About Them." *Advertising Age,* March 28. http://adage.com/article/news/chief-creatives-sound-scam-adsindustry/240606.

Diaz, Sam. 2008. "Apple Says Report of Steve Jobs Heart Attack Is False | ZDNet." *ZDNet.* Accessed August 11, 2014. http://www.zdnet.com/blog/btl/apple-says-report-of-steve-jobs-heart-attack-is-false/10288.

DiBlasio, Natalie. 2013. "Media Torn in the 'He' or 'She' Pronoun Debate." *USA Today,* August 22. http://www.usatoday.com/story/news/nation/2013/08/22/manning-pronoun-he-she/2686449.

DiStaso, Marcia. 2013. "Perceptions of Wikipedia by Public Relations Professionals: A Comparison of 2012 and 2013 Surveys." *Public Relations Journal* 7 (3): 1–23, http://www.prsa.org/intelligence/prjournal/documents/2013_distaso.pdf.

Dixon, Travis. 2013. "He Was a Black Guy: How the News Continues to Create Fear of Blacks." In *Race, Gender, Class, Media 3.0: Considering Diversity across Audiences, Content, and Producers,* edited by Rebecca Ann Lind, 24–30. Upper Saddle River, NJ: Pearson Education Inc.

Dixon, Travis Lemar, and Daniel Linz. 2000. "Overrepresentation and Underrepresentation of African Americans and Latinos as Lawbreakers on Television News." *Journal of Communication* 50 (2): 131–54.

DJNZ, and the action tool development group of the electrohippies collective. 2000. "Occasional Paper no. 1: Client-Side Distributed Denial-of-Service: Valid Campaign Tactic or Terrorist Act?" Original paper is no longer available online, but text is available at http://www.fraw.org.uk/mei/electrohippies/archive/op-01.html.

Donath, Judith S. 1999. "Identity and Deception in the Virtual Community." In *Communities in Cyberspace,* edited by Marc Smith and Peter Kollock, 27–56. New York: Routledge.

Don't Tell Mom We Opened the Xbox One—Walmart TV Commercial. 2014. http://www.youtube.com/watch?v=nM2uM34pg8Yandfeature=youtube_gdata_player.

Douglas, Torin. 2006. "How 7/7 'Democratised' the Media." *BBC News.* Accessed August 11, 2014. http://news.bbc.co.uk/2/hi/uk_news/5142702.stm.

Downey, John, and Natalie Fenton. 2003. "New Media, Counter Publicity and the Public Sphere." *New Media and Society* 5 (2): 185–202.

Dumenco, Simon. 2014. "John Oliver's Hilarious Attack on Native Advertising." *Advertising* Age. August 04. http://adage.com/article/the-media-guy/watch-john-oliver-s-hilarious-attack-native-advertising/294448.

Dusenbery, Maya. 2014. "Jezebel Staff Calls Out Gawker for Refusing to Deal with Their Rape Gif Problem." *Feministing,* August 11, 2014. Accessed August 11, 2013. http://feministing.com/2014/08/11/jezebel-staff-calls-out-gawker-to-refusing-to-deal-with-their-rape-gif-problem.

Dutton, William H. 2013. *The Oxford Handbook of Internet Studies.* Oxford: Oxford University Press.

Dworkin, Gerald. 2010. "Paternalism." In *Stanford Encyclopedia of Philosophy.* Accessed December 5, 2014. http://plato.stanford.edu/entries/paternalism.

Dworkin, Ronald. 1999. *Freedom's Law: The Moral Reading of the American Constitution.* Oxford: Oxford University Press.

Dyer, Richard. 2012. "Stereotyping." In *Media and Cultural Studies Key Works,* edited by Meenakshi G. Durham and Douglas M. Kellner, 275–83. Walden, MA: Wiley-Blackwell.

Edmonds, Rich. 2013. "It's Official: You All Enjoy Playing Games in the Bathroom; Talk Mobile Survey Infographic Reveals All." August 6. http://www.wpcentral.com/talk-mobile-gaming-survey-report-shows-your-responses-cool-infographic.

Edwards, Jan, and Alis Valencia. 2002. "Corporate Personhood and the 'Right' to Harm the Environment." *Peace and Freedom* 62 (3): 10.

Elliott, Deni. 2007. "Getting Mill Right." *Journal of Mass Media Ethics* 22 (2): 100–12.

ESRB.org. 2014a. "About Us." *Esrb.* http://www.esrb.org/about/index.jsp.

ESRB.org. 2014b. "Enforcement." *Esrb.* http://www.esrb.org/ratings/enforcement.jsp.

Ess, Charles. 2010. "The Embodied Self in a Digital Age: Possibilities, Risks, and Prospects for a Pluralistic (Democratic/Liberal) Future?" *Nordicom Information* 32 (2): 105–18.

Ess, Charles. 2013. *Digital Media Ethics,* 2nd ed. Cambridge, UK: Polity Press.

Ess, Charles. 2014. "Selfhood, Moral Agency, and the Good Life in Mediatized Worlds? Perspectives from Medium Theory and Philosophy." In *Mediatization of Communication.* Vol. 21, edited by Knut Lundby, 617–40. Berlin: De Gruyter Mouton.

Ess, Charles. 2015a. "Choose Now! Media, Literacies, Identities, Politics." In *Routledge Handbook of Language and Digital Communication,* edited by A. Georgakopoulou and T. Spilioti, 412–16. Routledge, in press.

Ess, Charles. 2015b. "The Good Life: Selfhood and Virtue Ethics in the Digital Age." In *Communication and the Good Life,* edited by Helen Wang, 17–29. ICA Themebook, 2014. Oxford: Peter Lang.

Ess, Charles and Hallvard Fossheim. 2013. "Personal Data: Changing Selves, Changing Privacy Expectations." In *Digital Enlightenment Forum Yearbook 2013: The Value of Personal Data,* edited by Mireille Hildebrandt, Kieron O'Hara, and Michael Waidner, 40–55. Amsterdam, NL, IOS Press.

Ettema, James S., and Theodore L. Glasser. 1998. *Custodians of Conscience: Investigative Journalism and Public Virtue*. New York, NY: Columbia University Press.

Facebook. 2014. "Advertising on Facebook." *Facebook*. Accessed March 16, 2014. https://www.facebook.com/about/ads/#external.

Facebook Help Center. 2014. "Cookies, Pixels & Similar Technologies." *Facebook*. Accessed December 2, 2014. https://www.facebook.com/help/cookies.

Faircloth, Kelly. 2014. "/R/FacebookCleavage Is Your New Least Favorite Scummy Internet Dump." *Jezebel*. January 15. http://jezebel.com/r-facebookcleavage-is-your-new-least-favorite-scummy-i-1542297739.

Fanlore. 2014. *Kindle Worlds*. http://fanlore.org/wiki/Kindle_Worlds.

Feenberg, Andrew. 1991. *Critical Theory of Technology*. Oxford: Oxford University Press.

Feinberg, Joel. 1971 "Legal Paternalism." *Canadian Journal of Philosophy* 1 (1): 105–24.

Feinberg, Joel. 1984. *The Moral Limits of the Criminal Law*. Oxford: Oxford University Press.

Feinberg, Joel. 1985. *Offense to Others*. Oxford: Oxford University Press.

Feldman, Curt. 2005. "ESRB to Investigate 'San Andreas' Sex Content." *Cnet,* July 8. http://news.cnet.com/esrb-to-investigate-san-andreas-sex-content/2100-1043_3-5780374.html.

Ferguson, Christopher John. 2007. "The Good, the Bad and the Ugly: A Meta-Analytic Review of Positive and Negative Effects of Violent Video Games." *Psychiatric Quarterly* 78 (4): 309–16.

Finlay, Stephen. 2014. *Confusion of Tongues: A Theory of Normativity*. New York: Oxford University Press.

Fisher, Dana R., Joseph Waggle, and Philip Leifeld. 2013. "Where Does Political Polarization Come from? Locating Polarization within the US Climate Change Debate." *American Behavioral Scientist* 57 (1): 70–92.

Fiske, John. 1994. *Introduction to Communication Studies*. New York: Routledge.

Ford, Sam. 2010a. "Does Digital Communication Foster More Ethical Business Behavior?" *Fast Company*, July 28. http://www.fastcompany.com/1675416/does-digital-communication-foster-more-ethical-business-behavior.

Ford, Sam. 2010b. "Could Empathy Teach Marketers to Cease Fire?" *Fast Company*, August 6. http://www.fastcompany.com/1675421/could-empathy-teach-marketers-cease-fire.

Ford, Sam. 2010c. "5 Marketing Lessons from Mr. Rogers." *Fast Company*. September 28. http://www.fastcompany.com/1691558/5-marketing-lessons-mr-rogers.

Ford, Sam. 2011. "Balancing between 'Academy' and 'Industry.'" *Antenna*, August 23. http://blog.commarts.wisc.edu/2011/08/23/balancing-between-academy-and-industry.

Ford, Sam. 2014a. "Marketers Must Make the Ethics of Content Creation a Top Priority." *Advertising Age*, January 15. http://adage.com/article/digitalnext/top-priority-marketers-ethics-content-creation/291029.

Ford, Sam. 2014b. "Listening and Empathizing: Advocating for New Management Logics in Marketing and Corporate Communications." In *Making Media Work: Cultures of Management in the Entertainment Industries*, edited by Derek Johnson, Derek Kompare, and Avi Santo, 275–94.New York, NY: New York University Press.

Ford, Sam. 2014c. "Narrowing the Chasm between PR Professionals and Wikipedia." *Harvard Business Review*, June 10, http://blogs.hbr.org/2014/06/narrowing-the-chasm-between-pr-professionals-and-wikipedia/.

Ford, Sam. 2014d. "Peppercomm's Ford: Our Industry Must Learn Wikipedia Is a Community, Not a Landfill." *PRWeek*, June 13. http://www.prweek.com/article/1298778/peppercomms-ford-industry-learn-wikipedia-community-not-landfill.

Ford, Zack. 2014. "Why Time's Profile of Laverne Cox is a Big Step Forward for Transgender Equality." *Think Progress*, May 29. http://thinkprogress.org/lgbt/2014/05/29/3442571/time-transgender.

Foremski, Tom. 2012. "Report: 51% of Website Traffic is 'Non-human' and Mostly Malicious." *ZDNet*. http://www.zdnet.com/blog/foremski/report-51-of-web-site-traffic-is-non-human-and-mostly-malicious/2201.

Foucault, Michel. 1980. *Power/Knowledge: Selected Interviews and Other Writings, 1972–1977*. Edited by Colin Gordon. New York: Pantheon.

Frankel, Mark S. 1989. "Professional Codes: Why, How, and with What Impact?" *Journal of Business Ethics* 8 (2/3): 109–15. doi: 10.2307/25071878.

French, Peter. 2001. *The Virtues of Vengeance*. Lawrence: University of Kansas Press.

Friedman, Thomas. 2010. "We've Only Got America A." *The New York Times*. http://www.nytimes.com/2010/12/15/opinion/15friedman.html?_r=0.

Fron, Janine, Tracy Fullerton, Jacquelyn Ford Morie, and Celia Pearce. 2007. "The Hegemony of Play." In *Situated Play: Proceedings of DiGRA Conference*, edited by Baba Akira, 309–18. Tokyo, September 24–27. http://ict.usc.edu/pubs/The%20Hegemony%20of%20Play.pdf.

Fullerton, Tracy, Janine Fron, Celia Pearce, and Jacquelyn Ford Morie. 2008. "Getting Girls into the Game: Toward a 'Virtuous Cycle'." In *Beyond Barbie and Mortal Kombat: New Perspectives on Gender and Gaming*, edited by Yasmin B. Kafai, Carrie Heeter, Jill Denner, and Jennifer Y. Sun, 161–76. Cambridge, MA: MIT Press.

Gabbadon, N. 2006. "From Good Times to Bad?: Changing Portrayals of the African American Sitcom Family." Paper presented at the annual meeting of the International Communication Association, Dresden International Congress Centre, Dresden, Germany. Accessed August 20, 2015. http://citation.allacademic.com/meta/p92390_index.html.

Gant, Scott E. 2007. *We're All Journalists Now: The Transformation of the Press and Reshaping of the Law in the Internet Age*. New York, NY: Free Press.

García-Avilés, Jose Alberto. 2010. "'Citizen Journalism' in European Television Websites: Lights and Shadows of User Generated Content." *Observatorio*. Accessed August 11, 2014. http://obs.obercom.pt/index.php/obs/article/viewArticle/360.

Gardner, Eric. 2013. "Octavia Spencer's Tweets at Center of Endorsement Lawsuit." *Hollywood Reporter*, August 28. http://www.hollywoodreporter.com/thr-esq/octavia-spencers-tweets-at-center-616596.

Gaskill, Jake. 2010. "Video Games on Trial: Part Two—California's Arguments." *G4*, October 5. http://g4tv.com/thefeed/blog/post/707915/Video-Games-On-Trial-Part-Two-Californias-Arguments.html.

Gates, Gary. 2011. *How Many People Are Lesbian, Gay, Bisexual, and Transgender?* Los Angeles: The Williams Institute. http://williamsinstitute.law.ucla.edu/wp-content/uploads/Gates-How-Many-People-LGBT-Apr-2011.pdf.

Gee, James Paul. 2007. *What Video Games Have To Teach Us about Learning and Literacy.* Revised and Updated Edition. New York: Macmillan.

Gentile, Douglas A., Craig A. Anderson, Shintaro Yukawa, Nobuko Ihori, Muniba Saleem, Lim Kam Ming, Akiko Shibuya, Albert K. Liau, Angeline Khoo, Brad J. Bushman, L. Rowell Huesmann, and Akira Sakamoto. 2009. "The Effects of Prosocial Video Games on Prosocial Behaviors: International Evidence from Correlational, Longitudinal, and Experimental Studies." *Personality and Social Psychology Bulletin* 35 (6): 752–63.

Georgia Tech. 2013. "Robotic Musicianship Group: Shimon." http://www.gtcmt.gatech.edu/research-projects/shimon.

Gerbner, George, and Larry Gross. 1976. "Living with Television: The Violence Profile." *Journal of Communication* 26 (2): 172–94.

German, Kathleen, and Bruce Drushel, eds. 2011. *The Ethics of Emerging Media: Information, Social Norms, and New Media Technology.* New York: Bloomsbury.

Gerth, Jeff, and T. Christian Miller. 2013. "Use Only as Directed." *ProPublica*, September 20. http://www.propublica.org/article/tylenol-mcneil-fda-use-only-as-directed.

Ghazali, Khadijah Wan Mohd, and Rosilah Hassan. 2011. "Flooding Distributed Denial of Service Attacks—A Review." *Journal of Computer Science* 7 (8): 1218–23.

Ghazali, Suriati, and Azilah Mohamad Nor. 2012. "Media Roles in Male-to-Female Transsexual Identity Formation among University Students in Malaysia." *International Conference on Humanity, History, and Society IPEDR* 34: 184–90.

Gibbard, Allan. 2008. *Reconciling Our Aims: In Search of a Bases for Ethics.* New York: Oxford University Press.

Gillespie, Ryan. 2016. "Normative Reasoning and Moral Argumentation, in Theory and Practice." *Philosophy and Rhetoric.* Accepted Fall 2014.

Gitlin, Todd. 1980. *The Whole World is Watching.* Berkeley: University of California Press.

GLAAD. 2012. *Victims or Villains: Examining Ten Years of Transgender Images on Television.* http://www.glaad.org/publications/victims-or-villains-examining-ten-years-transgender-images-television.

GLAAD. 2014. *Media Reference Guide*, 9th edition. http://www.glaad.org/reference.

Glaser, Barney G., and L. Anselm Strauss. 1967. *The Discovery of Grounded Theory: Strategies for Qualitative Research*. New Brunswick, NJ: Transaction.

Glass, Ira, and Sean Cole. 2013. "505: Use Only as Directed." *This American Life*, WBEZ Chicago Public Media, September 20. Accessed May 20, 2014. http://www.thisamericanlife.org/radio-archives/episode/505/use-only-as-directed.

GlobalPost. 2010. "Blacklisted: The World's Banned Video Games." *Globalpost.com*, December 29. http://www.globalpost.com/dispatch/global/101209/video- games-banned.

Godwin, Mike. 2003. *Cyber Rights: Defending Free Speech in the Digital Age*. Cambridge, MA: MIT Press.

Goldberg, Michelle. 2014. "Feminism's Toxic Twitter Wars." *The Nation*, January 29. Accessed August 8, 2014. http://www.thenation.com/print/article/178140/feminisms-toxic-twitter-wars.

Goldstein, Jessica. 2014. "The Celebrity Photo Hacker's Message to All Women." *Think Progress*, January 15. http://thinkprogress.org/culture/2014/09/02/3477906/celebrity-photo-hacker-message-to-all-women.

Golgowski, Nina. 2012. "High School Teacher Fired for Posting Pictures of His Underage Female Students on 'Creepshot' Website." *The Daily Mail*, January 15. http://www.dailymail.co.uk/news/article-2209611/Creepshot-East-Coweta-teacher-fired-posting-pictures-underage-female-students-Reddit.html.

Gomes, Phil. 2012. "Pillars of Crewe." Corporate Representatives for Ethical Wikipedia Engagement (CREWE) Facebook page. https://www.facebook.com/notes/corporate-representatives-for-ethical-wikipedia-engagement-crewe/pillars-of-crewe/164616033643652.

Gonzalez, Sandra. 2014. "'Teen Wolf' Fans, You Can Stop Scouring Tumblr for Fan Art.'" Accessed November 28, 2014. http://mashable.com/2014/07/21/teen-wolf-mtv-collective.

Goode, Luke. 2009. "Social News, Citizen Journalism and Democracy." *New Media and Society* 11 (8): 1287–1305.

Goodwin, Jeff, James M. Jasper, and Francesca Polletta. 2009. *Passionate Politics: Emotions and Social Movements*: Chicago, IL: University of Chicago Press.

Gorst, Isabel. 2014. "Russian Journalists Attacked While Investigating Solider Burials." *Los Angeles Times*. http://www.latimes.com/world/europe/la-fg-russia-journalists-attacked-20140827-story.html.

Grabianowksi, ed. 2014. "How the ESRB Works." *Howstuffworks.com*. http://electronics.howstuffworks.com/esrb3.htm.

Grant, Jaime M., Lisa A. Mottet, Justin Tanis, Jack Harrison, Jody L. Herman, and Mara Keisling. 2011. *Injustice at Every Turn: A Report of the National Transgender Discrimination Survey*. Washington: National Center for Transgender Equality and National Gay and Lesbian Task Force. http://www.thetaskforce.org/static_html/downloads/reports/reports/ntds_full.pdf.

Green, Shoshanna, Cynthia Jenkins, and Henry Jenkins. 1998. "Normal Female Interest in Men Bonking: Selections from the Terra Nostra Underground and Strange Bedfellows." In *Theorizing Fandom: Fans, Subculture, and Identity*, edited by Cheryl Harris and Alison Alexander, 9–38. Cresskill, NJ: Hampton Press.

Greenberg, Andy. 2012. *This Machine Kills Secrets: How WikiLeakers, Cypherpunks, and Hacktivists Aim to Free the World's Information*. New York: Dutton.

Greenfield, Rebecca. 2013. "How Upworthy Makes Money." Accessed December 20, 2014. http://www.thewire.com/technology/2013/09/how-upworthy-makes-money/69460.

Greenwald, Glenn. 2014. *No Place to Hide: Edward Snowden, The NSA and the U.S. Surveillance State*. New York: Metropolitan Books.

Groshek, Jacob, and Michael Conway. 2012. "The Effectiveness of the Pervasive Method in Ethics Pedagogy: A Longitudinal Study of Journalism and Mass Communication Students." *Journalism: Theory, Practice, and Criticism* 14 (3): 330–47. doi: 10.1177/1464884912454503.

Hacktivismo, and Cult of the Dead Cow. 2001. "The Hacktivismo Declaration." *Hacktivismo.* http://www.hacktivismo.com/public/declarations/en.php.

Haiman, Franklyn S. 1967. "The Rhetoric of the Streets: Some Legal and Ethical Considerations." *Quarterly Journal of Speech* 53: 99–114.

Halberstam, Judith. 2010. "The Pregnant Man." *The Velvet Light Trap* 65. http://muse.jhu.edu/journals/the_velvet_light_trap/v065/65.halberstam.html.

Hall, Emma. 2010. "IPA Report: Ads That Win Awards Are 11 Times More Effective." *Advertising Age,* July 14. http://adage.com/article/global-news/ipa-report-ads-win-awards-11-times-effective/144942.

Hall, J. Storrs. 2001. "Ethics for Machines." *KurzweilAI.net.* http://www.kurzweilai.net/ethics-for-machines.

Hamilton, Carrie. 2009. "Feminist Testimony in the Internet Age: Sex Work, Blogging and the Politics of Witnessing." *Journal of Romance Studies* 9: 86–101.

Hampton, Keith, Lee Rainie, Weixu Lu, Maria Dwyer, Inyoung Shin, and Kristen Purcell. 2014. "Social Media and the 'Spiral of Silence.' " *Pew Research Center,* August 26. http://www.pewinternet.org/2014/08/26/social-media-and-the-spiral-of-silence/.

Hannan, Caleb. 2014. "Dr. V's Magical Putter." *Grantland,* January 15. http://grantland.com/features/a-mysterious-physicist-golf-club-dr-v/.

Haridakis, Paul, and Gary Hanson. 2009. "Social Interaction and Co-viewing with YouTube: Blending Mass Communication Reception and Social Connection." *Journal of Broadcasting and Electronic Media* 53 (2): 317–35.

Harper, Ruth A. 2010. "The Social Media Revolution: Exploring the Impact on Journalism and News Media Organizations." *Student Pulse.* Accessed August 26, 2014. http://www.studentpulse.com/articles/202/the-social-media-revolution-exploring-the-impact-on-journalism-and-news-media-organizations.

Harris-Perry, Melissa V. 2011. *Sister Citizen: Shame, Stereotypes, and Black Women in America*. New Haven, CT: Yale University Press.

Harvie, Jen. 2013. *Fair Play: Art, Performance and Neoliberalism*. London, UK: Palgrave Macmillan.

Hasinoff, Amy. 2012. "Sexting as Media Production: Rethinking Social Media and Sexuality." *New Media & Society* 15 (4): 449–65.

Hatfield, Stefano. 2001. "Scam Entries in Award Contests a Symptom of a Larger Issue." *Advertising Age* 72 (36). http://adage.com/article/viewpoint/scam-entries-award-contests-a-symptom-a-larger-issue/53927.

Hedegaard, Erik. 2012. "All that Chaz." *Rolling Stone* 1148, January 19: 42–45.

Heidegger, Martin. 1977. *The Question Concerning Technology and Other Essays*. Translated by William Lovitt. New York: Harper & Row.

Heider, Don. 2000. *White News: Why Local News Programs Don't Cover People of Color*. Hillsdale, NJ: Lawrence Erlbaum Associates, Inc.

Heller, Corrine. 2014. "Jennifer Lawrence Part of Celebrity Nude Photo Leak, Rep Says 'Authorities Have Been Contacted.'" *EOnline*, January 15. http://www.eonline.com/news/574832/jennifer-lawrence-part-of-celebrity-nude-photo-leak-rep-says-authorities-have-been-contacted.

Herman, John. 2012. "Reddit General Manager Explains Why He Won't Ban Creepy." *BuzzFeedNews*, January 15. http://www.buzzfeed.com/jwherrman/reddit-general-manager-explains-why-he-wont-ban-c#jzqy2r.

Hermida, Alfred, and Neil Thurman. 2008. "A Clash of Cultures: The Integration of User-Generated Content within Professional Journalistic Frameworks at British Newspaper Websites." *Journalism Practice* 2 (3): 343–56. doi:10.1080/17512780802054538.

Herring, Susan C. 1996. *Computer-Mediated Communication: Linguistic, Social and Cross-Cultural Perspectives*. Philadelphia: John Benjamins Publishing Company.

Hickok, Laurens H. 1849. *Rational Psychology: The Subjective Idea and the Objective Law of All Intelligence*. Auburn: Derby, Miller & Company.

Higgins, Eliot. 2014. "Videos and Photographs Claim to Show Civilians Killed by US Led Air Strikes in Syria." *bellingcat.com*. Accessed October 11, 2014. https://www.bellingcat.com/news/mena/2014/09/23/videos-and-photographs-claim-to-show-civilians-killed-by-us-led-air-strikes-in-syria/.

Hills, Matt. 2002. *Fan Cultures*. London: Routledge.

Hills, Matt. 2012. "'Proper Distance' in the Ethical Positioning of Scholar-Fandoms: Between Academics' and Fans' Moral Economies." In *Fan Culture: Theory/Practice*, edited by Katherine Larsen and Lynn Zubernis, 14–37. Newcastle upon Tyne, UK: Cambridge Scholars Publishing.

Hindman, Elizabeth B. 1997. *Rights vs. Responsibilities: The Supreme Court and the Media*. Westport, CT: Greenwood.

Hindman, Elizabeth Blanks, and Ryan J. Thomas. 2014. "When Old and New Media Collide: The Case of WikiLeaks." *New Media and Society* 16 (4): 541–58.

Hirschman, David S. 2008. "So What Do You Do Paul Steiger, Editor-In-Chief, Propublica?" *Media Bistro*, February 13. Accessed May 20, 2014. http://www.mediabistro.com/So-What-Do-You-Do-Paul-Steiger-Editor-in-Chief-ProPublica-a10060.html.

Hoffman, Guy, and Gil Weinberg. 2011. "Interactive Improvisation with a Robotic Marimba Player." *Autonomous Robots* 31 (2–3): 133–53.

Holmes, Anna. 2008. "The Girl's Guide to Commenting on Jezebel: Version 1.2." *Jezebel*, September 22. Accessed August 8, 2014. http://jezebel.com/5053058/the-girls-guide-to-commenting-on-jezebel-version-12.

Holt, Richard. 2004. *Dialogue on the Internet: Language, Civic Identity, and Computer-Mediated Communication*. Westport, CT: Prager Publishers.

Holton, Avery E., Mark Coddington, and Homero Gil de Zúñiga. 2013. "Whose News? Whose Values? Citizen Journalism and Journalistic Values through the Lens of Content Creators and Consumers." *Journalism Practice* 7 (6): 720–37. doi:10.1080/17 512786.2013.766062.

Holtzman, Linda, and Leon Sharpe. 2014. *Media Messages: What Film, Television, and Popular Music Teach Us about Race, Class, Gender, and Sexual Orientation*. New York, NY: Routledge.

Hooks, Bell. 1999. *The Oppositional Gaze: Black Female Spectators, Black Looks: Race and Representation*. London: Turnaround.

Huckabee, Charles. 2013. "Michigan State U. Professor Is Under Fire for Denouncing Republicans in Class." *The Chronicle of Higher Education*. http://chronicle.com/blogs/ticker/michigan-state-professor-is-under-fire-for-denouncing-republicans-in-class/65569.

Hudson, Jr., David L. 2014. "NY High Court says Anti-cyberbullying Law Won't Pass First Amendment Muster." *ABA Journal*, November 1. http://www.abajournal.com/magazine/article/bully_fighting_new_yorks_high_court_says_anti_cyberbullying_law_wont_pass_f.

Internal Revenue Service. 2014. "Charitable Organizations, Exemptions Requirements 501(c)(3) Organizations." IRS Code. Accessed August 11. http://www.irs.gov/Charities-Non-Profits/Charitable-Organizations/Exemption- Requirements-Section-501(c)(3)-Organizations.

Ivory, James D., and Sriram Kalyanaraman. 2007. "The Effects of Technological Advancement and Violent Content in Video Games on Players' Feelings of Presence, Involvement, Physiological Arousal, and Aggression." *Journal of Communication* 57 (3): 532–55.

James, Andrea. 2007. "Don't Tick Off Trans." *The Advocate*, December 18. http://www.advocate.com/news/2007/12/03/don39t-tick-trans?page=full.

James, E. Lincoln, Cornelius B. Pratt, and Tommy V. Smith. 1994. "Advertising Ethics: Practitioner and Student Perspectives." *Journal of Mass Media Ethics* 9 (2): 69–83.

Jansen, Sue Curry. 2007. "Paris is Always More than Paris." In *Theorizing Communication: Reading across Traditions*, edited by Robert T. Craig and Heidi L. Muller, 473–90. Los Angeles, CA: Sage.

Jefferson, Thomas. (1787) 2000. "Amendment I (Speech and Press): Document 8." *The Founders' Constitution*, edited by Phillip Kurland and Ralph Lerner. http://press-pubs.uchicago.edu/founders/documents/amendI_speechs8.html.

Jenkins, Henry. 1992. *Textual Poachers: Television Fans and Participatory Culture*. New York: Routledge.

Jenkins, Henry. 2006. *Convergence Culture: Where Old and New Media Collide*. New York: New York University Press.

Jenkins, Henry. 2011. "Acafandom and Beyond: Week Two, Part One (Henry Jenkins, Erica Rand, and Karen Hellekson)." *Confessions of an Aca-Fan*. Accessed September 13, 2012. http://henryjenkins.org/2011/06/acafandom_and_beyond_week_two.html.

Jenkins, Henry, Sam Ford, and Joshua Green. 2013. *Spreadable Media: Creating Value and Meaning in a Networked Culture*. New York: New York University Press.

Jenkins, Henry, with Ravi Purushotma, Margaret Weigel, Katie Clinton, and Alice J. Robison. 2009. *Confronting the Challenges of Participatory Culture: Media Education for the 21st Century*. Cambridge, MA: MIT Press.

Jewell, K. Sue. 1993. *From Mammy to Miss America and Beyond: Cultural Images and the Shaping of US Social Policy*. London: Routledge.

Jezebel Staff. 2011. "How to Reach Jezebel." Accessed December 10, 2014. http://jezebel.com/5732075/about-jezebel-for-beta.

Johnson, Deborah G. 1985. *Computer Ethics*. Upper Saddle River, NJ: Prentice Hall.

Johnson, Deborah G. 2006. "Computer Systems: Moral Entities but Not Moral Agents." *Ethics and Information Technology* 8: 195–204.

Johnson, Derek. 2007a. "Fan-tagonism: Factions, Institutions, and Constitutive Hegemonies of Fandom." In *Fandom: Identities and Communities in a Mediated World*, edited by Jonathan Gray, Cornel Sandvoss and C. Lee Harrington, 285–300. New York: New York University Press.

Johnson, Derek. 2007b. "Inviting Audiences In: The Spatial Reorganisation of Production and Consumption in 'TVIII.'" *New Review of Film and Television Studies* 5 (1): 61–80.

Johnson, Michelle. 1999. "Of Public Interest: How Courts Handle Rape Victim's Privacy Suits." *Communication Law and Policy* 4 (2): 202–42.

Johnston, Angus. 2014. "Six Questions Every Journalist Should Ask Before Quoting Social Media Posts." *Student Activism*. Accessed July 16, 2014. http://studentactivism.net/2014/03/13/six-questions-every-journalist-should-ask-before-quoting-social-media-posts.

Jones, Bethan. 2014. "Johnlocked: Sherlock, Slash Fiction and the Shaming of Female Fans." *New Left Project.* http://www.newleftproject.org/index.php/site/article_comments/johnlocked_sherlock_slash_fiction_and_the_shaming_of_female_fans.

Jones, Saeed. 2014. "Transgender People are Paying the Price for the Media's Willful Ignorance." *Buzzfeed,* January 19. http://www.buzzfeed.com/saeedjones/transgender-people-are-paying-the-price-for-the-medias-willf.

Jones, Sebastian, and Marcus Stern. 2010. "The New Democrats: The Coalition Parma and Wall Street Love." *ProPublica,* October 25. Accessed November 25, 2014. http://www.propublica.org/article/new-democrat-coalition.

Jones, Steven G. 1998. *Cybersociety 2.0: Revising Computer-Mediated Communication and Community.* London: Sage.

Jordan, Tim. 1999. *Cyberpower: The Culture and Politics of Cyberspace and the Internet.* London: Routledge.

Jordan, Tim. 2002. *Activism!: Direct Action, Hacktivism and the Future of Society.* London: Reaktion.

Jordan, Tim, and Paul A. Taylor. 2004. *Hacktivism and Cyberwars: Rebels With a Cause?* New York: Routledge.

Juris, Jeffrey S. 2005. "The New Digital Media and Activist Networking Within Anti-Corporate Globalization Movements." *The Annals of the American Academy of Political and Social Science* 597 (1): 189–208.

Jurrat, Nadine. 2011. "Mapping Digital Media: Citizen Journalism and the Internet." *Open Society Foundations.* Accessed August 11, 2014. http://www.opensocietyfoundations.org/sites/default/files/mapping-digital-media-citizen-journalism-and-internet-20110712.pdf.

Juul, Jesper. 2010. *A Casual Revolution: Reinventing Video Games and Their Players.* Cambridge, MA: MIT Press.

Juul, Jesper. 2011. *Half-real: Video Games between Real Rules and Fictional Worlds.* Cambridge, MA: MIT Press.

Kafai, Yasmin B., Carrie Heeter, Jill Denner, and Jennifer Y. Sun. 2008. *Beyond Barbie and Mortal Kombat: New Perspectives on Gender and Gaming.* Cambridge, MA: MIT Press.

Kahn, Richard, and Douglas Kellner. 2004. "New Media and Internet Activism: From the 'Battle of Seattle' to Blogging." *New Media & Society* 6 (1): 87–95.

Kaldor, Mary. 2003. *Global Civil Society: An Answer to War.* Malden, MA: Polity.

Kant, Immanuel. (1775–80) 1963. *Lectures on Ethics.* Translated by Louis Infield. New York: Harper Row.

Kant, Immanuel. (1781) 1998. *Critique of Pure Reason.* Translated by Paul Guyer and Allen W. Wood. Cambridge, UK: Cambridge University Press.

Kant, Immanuel. (1785) 1996. "Groundwork for the Metaphysics of Morals." *Practical Philosophy,* translated by Mary J. Gregor. New York: Cambridge University Press.

Kant, Immanuel. (1784) 1991. "An Answer to the Question: 'What is Enlightenment?'" Translated by H. B. Nisbet. In *Kant: Political Writings*, edited by Hans Reiss, 54–61. Cambridge: Cambridge University Press.

Kant, Immanuel. (1785) 1959. *Foundations of the Metaphysics of Morals, and What is Enlightenment?* Translated by Lewis White Beck. New York: Liberal Arts Press.

Kaplan, Andreas M., and Michael Haenlein. 2010. "Users of the World, Unite! The Challenges and Opportunities of Social Media." *Business Horizons* 53 (1): 59–68.

Karpf, David. 2012. *The MoveOn Effect: The Unexpected Transformation of American Political Advocacy*. Kindle edition. New York, NY: Oxford University Press.

Kashner, Sam. 2014. "Both Huntress and Prey." *Vanity Fair*, January 17. http://www.vanityfair.com/vf-hollywood/2014/10/jennifer-lawrence-photo-hacking-privacy.

Kaye, Kate. 2013. "Verizon Uses Phone Data to Connect Dots for NBA, Sponsors | DataWorks—Advertising Age." *Advertising Age DataWorks RSS*, November 8. Accessed April 27, 2014. http://adage.com/article/dataworks/verizon-phone-data-connect-dots-nba-sponsors/245178.

Kaye, Randi. 2010. "How a Cell Phone Picture Led to a Girl's Suicide." *CNN*, January 15. http://www.cnn.com/2010/LIVING/10/07/hope.witsells.story/.

Keating, Cricket. 2005. "Building Coalitional Consciousness." *NWSA Journal* 17 (2): 86–103.

Keller, Bill. 2011. "Dealing With Assange and the WikiLeaks Secrets." *New York Times Magazine*. http://www.nytimes.com/2011/01/30/magazine/30Wikileaks-t.html.

Kerr, Audrey Elisa. 2005. "The Paper Bag Principle: Of the Myth and the Motion of Colorism." *Journal of American Folklore* 118 (469): 271–89.

Kickstarter. 2014. "Livestreaming the 2014 Race for Governor." *The Texas Tribune*. Accessed July 25. https://www.kickstarter.com/projects/texastribune/livestreaming-the-2014-race-for-governor.

Kiel, Fred. 2015. *Return on Character: The Real Reason Leaders and Their Companies Win*. Cambridge, MA: Harvard Business Review Press.

Kirwan, Peter. 2009. "The Rise of Machine-Written Journalism." *Wired.co.uk*. http://www.wired.co.uk/news/archive/2009-12/16/the-rise-of-machine-written-journalism.aspx.

Kiss, Jemima. 2012. "Reddit Blocks Gawker in Row over 'Creepshot' Photos." *The Guardian*, January 15. http://www.theguardian.com/media/2012/oct/12/reddit-blocks-gawker-creepshot-photos.

Klausner, Alexandra. 2014. "Leaked Photos of Olympic Gymnast McKayla Maroney Were Taken When She Was Underage and Are CHILD PORNOGRAPHY, Say Her Attorneys." *Daily Mail*, January 15. http://www.dailymail.co.uk/news/article-2741448/Leaked-photos-Olympic-gymnast-Mckayla.html.

Koch, James V., Robert N. Fenili, and Richard J. Cebula. 2011. "Do Investors Care if Steve Jobs is Healthy?" *Atlantic Economic Journal* 39 (1): 59–70.

Koehler, John O. 1999. *Stasi: The Untold Story of the East German Secret Police.* Boulder, CO: Westview Press.

Kovach, Bill, and Tom Rosenstiel. 2007. *The Elements of Journalism.* New York: Random House.

Kramer, Adam D. I., Jamie E. Guillory, and Jeffrey T. Hancock. 2014. "Experimental Evidence of Massive-Scale Emotional Contagion through Social Networks." *Proceedings of the National Academy of Sciences* 111 (24): 8788–90. doi: 10.1073/pnas.1320040111.

Kranish, Michael. 2014. "Facebook Draws Fire on 'Related Articles' Push." *The Boston Globe,* May 4. http://www.bostonglobe.com/news/nation/2014/05/03/facebook-push-related-articles-users-without-checking-credibility-draws-ire/rPae4M2LlzpVHIJAmfDYNL/story.html.

Krashinsky, Susan. 2013. "Getting Edgy With Ads—and Paying the Price." *The Globe & Mail,* April 29. http://penny2.theglobeandmail.com/servlet/ArticleNews/story/gam/20130429/RBHYUNDAISUICIDEATL.

Kreiss, Daniel. 2012. *Taking Our Country Back: The Crafting of Networked Politics from Howard Dean to Barack Obama.* Kindle edition. New York, NY: Oxford University Press.

Kubey, Robert William, ed. 1997. *Media Literacy in the Information Age: Current Perspectives.* Vol. 6. New Brunswick, NJ: Transaction Publishers.

Kuhn, Thomas S. 1996. *The Structure of Scientific Revolutions.* Chicago: University of Chicago Press.

Kurzweil, Ray. 2005. *The Singularity is Near: When Humans Transcend Biology.* New York: Viking.

Kushner, David. 2014. "Vigilanteville: James McGibney and his Online Army." *Aljazeera America,* October 7. http://america.aljazeera.com/articles/2014/10/7/james-mcgibney-bullyville.html.

Kuykendall, Mae, and Debra Nails. 2013. "Trial by YouTube." *Brain-Mind Magazine* 2 (2): 8–10.

Lajoie, Mark. 1996. "Psychoanalysis and Cyberspace." In *Cultures of the Internet: Virtual Spaces, Real Histories, Living Bodies,* edited by Rob Shields, 154–69. Thousand Oaks, CA: Sage.

Lane, Jill. 2003. "Digital Zapatistas." *TDR: The Drama Review* 47 (2): 129–44.

Lapin, Andrew. 2014. "Texas Tribune Doubles Down on Live Streaming After Success with Wendy Davis Filibuster." *Current.org,* March 11. Accessed May 21, 2014. http://www.current.org/2014/03/texas-tribune-doubles-down-on-live-streaming-after-success-with-wendy-davis-filibuster/.

Larsen, Katherine, and Lynn Zubernis. 2012. "Introduction." In *Fan Culture: Theory/Practice,* edited by Katherine Larsen and Lynn Zubernis, 1–13. Newcastle upon Tyne, UK: Cambridge Scholars Publishing.

Lavidge, Robert J., and Gary A. Steiner. 1961. "A Model for Predictive Measurements of Advertising Effectiveness." *Journal of Marketing* 25 (6): 59–62.

Lazarus, David. 2014. "Verizon Wireless to Expose Customers' Browsing to Advertisers." *The Sydney Morning Herald*, April 26. Accessed April 26, 2014. http://www.smh.com.au/technology/technology-news/verizon-wireless-to-expose-customers-browsing-to-advertisers-20140426-zqzzq.html.

Lecher, Colin. 2014. "Bogus User-Generated CNN Asteroid Apocalypse Article Goes Viral." *Popular Science.* Accessed August 11, 2014. http://www.popsci.com/article/science/bogus-user-generated-cnn-asteroid-apocalypse-article-goes-viral.

Leigh, David, and Luke Harding. 2011. *WikiLeaks: Inside Julian Assange's War on Secrecy.* London: Guardian Books.

Lenhart, Amanda, Sydney Jones, and Alexandra MacGill. 2008. "Adults and Video Games." *Pew Research Internet Project.* http://www.pewinternet.org/2008/12/07/adults-and-video-games/.

Lennick, Doug, and Fred Kiel. 2005. *Moral Intelligence: Enhancing Business Performance and Leadership Success.* Upper Saddle River, NJ: Prentiss-Hall.

Leo, John. 2001. "The Sex-Change Boom." *US News and World Report* 130 (10), March 12. https://groups.yahoo.com/neo/groups/TNUKdigest/conversations/topics/1409.

Lessig, Lawrence. 2006. *Code Version 2.0.* New York, NY: Basic Books.

Levin, Josh. 2014. "Digging Too Deep: Grantland's Exposé of a Trans Con Artist Privileged Fact-Finding over Compassion." *Slate,* January 19. http://www.slate.com/articles/life/culturebox/2014/01/essay_anne_vanderbilt_dr_v_s_magical_putter_grantland_s_expos_of_a_trans.html.

Levy, N. 2004. "Good Character: Too Little, Too Late." *Journal of Mass Media Ethics* 19 (2): 108–18.

Lewis, Anthony. 2007. *Freedom for the Thought That We Hate: A Bibliography of the First Amendment.* New York, NY: Basic Books.

Lewis, Charles. 2007. "The Nonprofit Road." *Columbia Journalism Review,* September 13. Accessed August 18, 2014. http://www.cjr.org/feature/the_nonprofit_road.php?page=all.

Lind, Rebecca Ann, ed. 2013. *Race, Gender, Class, Media 3.0: Considering Diversity across Audiences, Content, and Producers.* Upper Saddle River, NJ: Pearson Education Inc.

Lindlof, Thomas R., and Bryan C. Taylor. 2002. *Qualitative Communication Research Methods.* 2nd ed. Thousand Oaks, CA: Sage.

LiveLeak. 2014. "School Principal Shown Dragging Two Kindergarteners through School's Hallways." *LiveLeak.com.* http://www.liveleak.com/view?i=20b_1393114462.

Livingstone, Sonia, Leslie Haddon, Anke Görzig, and Kjartan Ólafsson. 2011. "Risks and Safety on the Internet: The Perspective of European Children: Full Findings and Policy Implications from the EU Kids Online Survey of 9–16 Year Olds and Their Parents in 25 Countries." *EU Kids Online,* Deliverable D4. London: EU Kids Online

Network. http://www.lse.ac.uk/media%40lse/research/EUKidsOnline/EU%20 Kids%20II%20(2009-11)/EUKidsOnlineIIReports/D4FullFindings.pdf.

Lotan, Gilad, Erhardt Graeff, Mike Ananny, Devin Gaffney, Ian Pearce, and danah boyd. 2011. "The Revolutions Were Tweeted: Information Flows During the 2011 Tunisian and Egyptian Revolutions." *International Journal of Communication* 5: 1375–405.

Lü, Yao-Huai. 2005. "Privacy and Data Privacy Issues in Contemporary China." *Ethics and Information Technology* 7 (1): 7–15.

Lunceford, Brett. 2009a. "Building Hacker Collective Identity One Text Phile at a Time: Reading *Phrack*." *Media History Monographs* 11 (2): 1–26.

Lunceford, Brett. 2009b. "Cyberwar: The Future of War?" In *War and the Media: Essays on News Reporting, Propaganda and Popular Culture*, edited by Paul M. Haridakis, Barbara S. Hugenberg and Stanley T. Wearden, 238–51. Jefferson, NC: McFarland.

Lunceford, Brett. 2011. "The New Pornographers: Legal and Ethical Considerations of Sexting." In *The Ethics of Emerging Media: Information, Social Norms, and New Media Technology*, edited by Bruce E. Dushel and Kathleen German, 99–118. New York, NY: Continuum.

Lunceford, Brett. 2012. "The Rhetoric of the Web: The Rhetoric of the Streets Revisited Again." *Communication Law Review* 12 (1): 40–55.

Lunceford, Brett. 2013. "The Power of Slogans: The Rhetoric of Network Neutrality." In *Legal Issues in Global Contexts: Perspectives on Technical Communication in the Global Age*, edited by Kirk St. Amant and Martine Courant Rife, 27–47. Amityville, NY: Baywood Publishing.

Lustgarten, Abrahm. 2009. "Setting the Record Straight on Hydraulic Fracking." *ProPublica*. January 12. Accessed November 28, 2014. http://www.propublica.org/ article/setting-the-record-straight-on-hydraulic- fracturing-090112.

Lynch, Michael P. 2014. "Privacy and the Pool of Information." *The New York Times*. http://opinionator.blogs.nytimes.com/2014/07/27/privacy-and-the-pool-of-information/.

MacIntyre, Alasdair. 1984. *After Virtue*. 2nd ed. Notre Dame, IN: University of Notre Dame Press.

MacIntyre, Alasdair, and Paul Carus. 1999. *Dependent Rational Animals: Why Human Beings Need the Virtues*. London: Duckworth.

Madison, James. (1822) 2000. "Epilogue: Securing the Republic: Chapter 18, Document 35." *The Founders' Constitution*, edited by Phillip Kurland and Ralph Lerner. http://press-pubs.uchicago.edu/founders/documents/v1ch18s35.html.

Madrigal, Alexis C. 2014. "That Time 2 Bots Were Talking, and Bank of America Butted In." *The Atlantic*. http://www.theatlantic.com/technology/archive/2014/07/that-time-2-bots-were-talking-and-bank-of-america-butted-in/374023/.

Magnanti, Brooke. 2013. "Sherlock, Benedict Cumberbatch and Fanfic: Don't Mess with These Women (and Men)." *The Telegraph*. http://www.telegraph.co.uk/women/

womens-life/10521131/Sherlock-Benedict-Cumberbatch-and-fanfic-dont-mess-with-these-women-and-men.html.

Malik, Om. 2014. "Silicon Valley and Parachute Journalism." *Om Malik*. Accessed August 11, 2014. http://om.co/2014/08/08/east-coast-media-vs-silicon-valley.

Manning, Rita C. 1984. "Corporate Responsibility and Corporate Personhood." *Journal of Business Ethics* 3 (1): 77–84.

Martin, Hugh J. 2000. "Hacktivism: The New Protest Movement?" *Spark-Online* 7.0. http://www.spark-online.com/april00/trends/martin.html.

Marx, Karl. 1977. *Capital: A Critique of Political Economy*. Translated by Ben Fowkes. New York: Vintage Books.

Mastro, Dana E., and Bradley S. Greenberg. 2000. "The Portrayal of Racial Minorities on Prime Time Television." *Journal of Broadcasting and Electronic Media* 44 (4): 690–703.

Mattelart, Armand. 1991. *Advertising International: The Privatization of Public Space*. Translated by Michael Chanan. London: Routledge.

Matthias, Andreas. 2004. "The Responsibility Gap: Ascribing Responsibility for the Actions of Learning Automata." *Ethics and Information Technology* 6: 175–83.

Mayer-Schönberger, Viktor. 2009. *Delete: The Virtue of Forgetting in the Digital Age*. Princeton: Princeton University Press.

Mayer-Schönberger, Viktor, and Kenneth Cukier. 2013. *Big Data: A Revolution That Will Transform How We Live, Work, and Think*. Boston, MA: Houghton Mifflin Harcourt.

McBee, Thomas. 2012. "Trans, but Not Like You Think." *Salon*. August 6. http://www.salon.com/2012/08/07/trans_but_not_like_you_think.

McChesney, Robert. 1997. *Corporate Media and the Threat to Democracy*. New York: Seven Stories Press.

McChesney, Robert. 1999a. *Rich Media, Poor Democracy: Communication Politics in Dubious Times*. Urbana: University of Illinois Press.

McChesney, Robert. 1999b. Introduction to *Profit over People: Neoliberalism and Global Order*. Written by Noam Chomsky, 7–18. New York, NY: Seven Stories Press.

McChesney, Robert. 2012. "Farewell to Journalism? Time for a Rethinking." *Journalism Practice* 6 (5–6): 614–26. doi:10.1080/17512786.2012.683273.

McCormick, Matt. 2001. "Is It Wrong to Play Violent Video Games?" *Ethics and Information Technology* 3 (4): 277–87.

McGeveran, William. 2014 "Big Data and Privacy: Making Ends Meet." *Future of Privacy*. Accessed April 27, 2014. http://www.futureofprivacy.org/wp-content/uploads/Big-Data-and-Privacy-Paper-Collection.pdf.

McGrath, Ben. 2010. "Search and Destroy: Nick Denton's Blog Empire." *The New Yorker*, October 18. Accessed August 8, 2014. http://www.newyorker.com/magazine/2010/10/18/search-and-destroy-2.

McGuire, William J. 1976. "Some Internal Psychological Factors Influencing Consumer Choice." *Journal of Consumer Research* 2 (4): 302–19.

McKenzie, John. 1999. "!nt3rh4ckt!v!ty." *Style* 33 (2): 283–99.

McLuhan, Marshall. 1994. *Understanding Media: The Extensions of Man.* Cambridge, MA: MIT Press.

McQuail, Denis. 2010. *McQuail's Mass Communication Theory.* 6th ed. Thousand Oaks, CA: Sage.

Mehra, Priyanka. 2013. "What Led to the Super Jury's Decision?" *Exchange4Media.com,* April 25. http://www.exchange4media.com/50702_what-led-to-the-super-jurys-decision.html.

Mehra, Priyanka. 2014. "Cannes Juror Speak: Companies Don't Scam & Don't Believe in Scam: Colvyn Harris." *Exchange4Media.com,* June 11. http://www.exchange4media.com/56067_colorredcannes-juror-speak-companies-dont-scam-dont-believe-in-scam-colvyn-harris.html.

Mehra, Vishal. 2013. "Lighten Up! Ford, Others Are Overreacting to Figo Fiasco." *Advertising Age,* April 1. http://adage.com/article/guest-columnists/ford-overreacting-indian-scam-ads/240638.

Mendelson, Scott. 2014. "Jennifer Lawrence Nude Photo Leak Isn't A 'Scandal.' It's A Sex Crime." *Forbes,* January 15. http://www.forbes.com/sites/scottmendelson/2014/09/01/jennifer-lawrence-nude-photo-leak-isnt-a-scandal-its-a-sex-crime.

Meyer, Philip. 2004. *The Vanishing Newspaper.* Columbia: University of Missouri Press.

Meyers, Christopher, Wendy N. Wyatt, Sandra L. Borden, and Edward Wasserman. 2012. "Professionalism, Not Professionals." *Journal of Mass Media Ethics* 27 (3): 189–205. doi:10.1080/08900523.2012.700212.

Mill, John Stuart. 1863. *On Liberty.* Boston, MA: Ticknor and Fields.

Mill, John Stuart. 1907. *Utilitarianism.* 15th ed. London: Longmans, Green, and Co.

Miller, David. 1983. "Constraints on Freedom." *Ethics* 94: 66–86.

Miller, Greg. 2011. "Dead Space 2 Review." *IGN.* http://www.ign.com/articles/2011/01/21/dead-space-2-review.

Milner, R. M. 2009. "Working for the Text: Fan Labor and the New Organization." *International Journal of Cultural Studies* 12 (5): 491–508.

Mitchell, Amy, Mark Jurkowitz, Jesse Holcomb, Jodi Enda, and Monica Anderson. 2013a. "Nonprofit Journalism: A Growing but Fragile Part of the U.S. News System." *Pew Research Journalism Project,* June 10. Accessed August 15, 2014. http://www.journalism.org/2013/06/10/nonprofit-journalism.

Mitchell, Amy, Mark Jurkowitz, Jesse Holcomb, Jodi Enda, and Monica Anderson. 2013b. "Taking Care of Business: A Catch-22." *Pew Research Journalism Project,* June 10. Accessed August 15, 2014. http://www.journalism.org/2013/06/10/nonprofit-journalism.

Mitchell, Amy, Mark Jurkowitz, Jesse Holcomb, Jodi Enda, and Monica Anderson. 2013c. "What Is Financial Health in Nonprofit News?" *Pew Research Journalism Project*, June 10. Accessed August 15, 2014. http://www.journalism.org/2013/06/10/nonprofit-journalism.

MN Editor. 2012. "Reasons Why Black Women Don't Date White Men." *Madame Noire*, January 4. http://madamenoire.com/124921/reasons-why-black-women-dont-date-white-men/.

Mocarski, Richard, Sim Butler, Betsy Emmons, and Rachael Smallworld. 2013. "A Different Kind of Man: Mediated Transgendered Subjectivity, Chaz Bono on *Dancing with the Stars*." *Journal of Communication Inquiry* 37 (3): 249–64.

Montfort, Nick, and Ian Bogost. 2009. *Racing the Beam: The Atari Video Computer System*. Cambridge, MA: MIT Press. http://search.ebscohost.com/login.aspx?direct=trueandscope=siteanddb=nlebkanddb=nlabkandAN=259267.

montycarlo. 2014. Comment on "Working at Vice Media Is Not as Cool as It Seems," by Hamilton Nolan. *Gawker*, May 30. Accessed August 8, 2014. http://gawker.com/working-at-vice-media-is-not-as-cool-as-it-seems-1579711577.

Moon, Dreama G. 2008. "Concepts of 'Culture': Implications for Intercultural Communication Research." In *The Global Intercultural Communication Reader*, edited by Molefi Kete Asante, Yoshitaka Miike, and Jing Yin, 11–26. New York: Routledge.

Moore, James. 2014. "The Trouble with the Trib." *The Huffington Post*, February 18. Accessed August 18, 2014. http://www.huffingtonpost.com/jim-moore/thetrouble-with-the-trib_b_4806251.html.

Moore, Tracy. 2014a. "Sex Spreadsheet Details Wife's Frustration with Husband." *Jezebel*, July 23. Accessed August 8, 2014. http://jezebel.com/sex-spreadsheet-details-wifes-frustration-with-husband-1609734749/all.

Moore, Tracy. 2014b. "Trans Woman Commits Suicide Amid Fear of Outing by Sports Blog." *Jezebel*, January 18. http://jezebel.com/trans-woman-commits-suicide-amid-fear-of-outing-by-spor-1503902916.

Moore, Tracy. 2014c. "The Truth about How Much a Happy Couple Should Have Sex." *Jezebel*, February 27. Accessed August 8, 2014. http://jezebel.com/the-truth-about-how-much-a-happy-couple-should-have-sex-1531835849.

Moravec, Hans. 1988. *Mind Children: The Future of Robot and Human Intelligence*. Cambridge, MA: Harvard University Press.

Morimoto, Lori. 2014a. "Yukata!Batch Goes Global." *On/Off Screen*. Accessed August 15, 2014. http://onoffscreen.wordpress.com/2014/08/15/yukatabatch-goes-global.

Morimoto, Lori. 2014b. Untitled. *Acafanmom*. Accessed August 12, 2014. http://acafanmomarchive.tumblr.com/post/94728128525/penns-woods-said-i-am-sure-you-could-ask-a-few.

Morozov, Evgeny. 2011. *The Net Delusion: The Dark Side of Internet Freedom*. New York: Public Affairs.

Morris, Charles. 2004. "My Old Kentucky Homo: Lincoln and the Politics of QueerPublic Memory." In *Framing Public Memory*, edited by Kendall R. Phillips, 89–114. Tuscaloosa: University of Alabama Press.

Morris, Kevin. 2012. "BlogTV and the Sad, Avoidable Path to Amanda Todd's Suicide." *The Daily Dot*, October 15. http://www.dailydot.com/news/blogtv-amanda-todd-suicide.

Morrissey, Brian. 2012. "Nick Denton: The Banner Ad Era Is Closing." *Digiday*, May 10. Accessed August 8, 2014. http://digiday.com/publishers/nick-denton-the-banner-ad-era-is-closing.

Morrissey, Tracie Egan. 2014. "Girls: Hannah Horvath is a Jezebel Commenter." *Jezebel*, January 27. Accessed August 8, 2014. http://jezebel.com/girls-hannah-horvath-is-a-jezebel-commenter-1509896860/all.

Morton, Patricia. 1991. *Disfigured Images: The Historical Assault on Afro-American Women*. New York: Greenwood Press.

Mowbray, Miranda. 2002. "Ethics for Bots." Paper presented at the 14th International Conference on System Research, Informatics and Cybernetics. Baden-Baden, Germany. July 29 to August 3. http://www.hpl.hp.com/techreports/2002/HPL-2002-48R1.pdf.

Mulkerrins, Jane. 2013. "Jezebel Founder: 'I Wanted To Make Women's Magazine Irrelevant." *The Telegraph*, October 31. Accessed August 8, 2014. http://www.telegraph.co.uk/women/10400095/Jezebel-founder-I-wanted-to-make-womens-magazines-irrelevant.html.

Murphy, Lorraine. 2012a. "Anonymous' #OpAntiBully doxes Teen Twitter Tormentors." *The Daily Dot*, November 23. http://www.dailydot.com/news/opantibully-anonymous-doxes-teen-Twitter-tormentor.

Murphy, Lorraine. 2012b. "Did Anonymous Unmask the Wrong Guy in Its Hunt for the Man Who allegedly drove a Teen to Suicide?" *Slate*, October 17. http://www.slate.com/blogs/future_tense/2012/10/17/amanda_todd_suicide_did_anonymous_dox_the_wrong_guy.html.

Murphy, Lorraine. 2013. "Inside OpAntiBully, the Campaign that avenged Amanda Todd." *The Daily Dot*, July 10. http://www.dailydot.com/news/anonymous-opantibully-interview-amanda-todd.

Murray, Simone. 2004. " 'Celebrating the Story the Way It Is': Cultural Studies, Corporate Media and the Contested Utility of Fandom." *Continuum: Journal of Media & Cultural Studies* 18 (1): 7–25.

Mutter, Alan. 2010. "The Triple Threat to Citizen Journalists." *Reflections of a Newsosaur*. Accessed August 26, 2014. http://newsosaur.blogspot.com/2010/04/triple-threat-to-citizen-journalists.html.

Myskja, Bjørn. 2011. "Trust, Lies, and Virtuality." In *Trust and Virtual Worlds: Contemporary Perspectives*, edited by Charles Ess and May Thorseth, 120–36. New York: Peter Lang.

Nakamura, Lisa. 1995. "Race in/for Cyberspace: Identity Tourism and Racial Passing on the Internet." *Works and Days* 13: 181–93.

Nass, Clifford, and Yongme Moon. 2000. "Machines and Mindlessness: Social Responses to Computers." *Journal of Social Issues* 56 (1): 81–103.

Nass, Clifford, Jonathan Steuer, and Ellen R. Tauber. 1994. "Computers are Social Actors." *CHI '94 Proceedings of the SIGCHI Conference on Human Factors in Computing Systems*, 73–78. Boston: ACM.

National Coalition of Anti-Violence Programs. 2013. "Lesbian, Gay, Bisexual, Transgender, Queer, and HIV-Affected Hate Violence in 2012." http://www.avp.org/storage/documents/ncavp_2012_hvreport_final.pdf.

National Press Club, The. 2008. "Solutions to Traditional Limitations." *National Press Club.* Accessed August 26, 2014. http://press.org/about/journalism-juncture/solutions-traditional-limitations.

Needham, Michael. "What George Soros is Doing . . ." To Luis Hestres. June 16, 2014.

Neely, Sarah. 2012. "Making Bodies Visible: Post-feminism and the Pornographication of Online Identities." In *Trangression 2.0: Media, Culture, and the Politics of a Digital Age*, edited by David J. Gunkel and Ted Gournelos, 101–117. New York, NY: Continuum.

Nelson, Samuel. 2005. *Beyond the First Amendment: The Politics of Free Speech and Pluralism.* Baltimore, MD: John Hopkins University Press.

Nerone, John C., ed. 1995. *Last Rights: Revisiting Four Theories of the Press.* Champaign, IL: University of Illinois Press.

New Organizing Institute. 2014. Accessed August 17, 2014. http://neworganizing.com.

New York Times Co., The. 2004. *Ethical Journalism: A Handbook of Values and Practices for the News and Editorial Departments.* New York: The New York Times Co. http://www.nytco.com/wpcontent/uploads/NYT_Ethical_Journalism_0904-1.pdf.

Newmann, Caryn. 2006. "Outing." *glbtq: An Encyclopedia of Gay, Lesbian, Transgender, and Queer Culture,* December 12. http://www.glbtq.com/social-sciences/outing.html.

Nisbet, Matthew C., and Dietram A. Scheufele. 2013. "The Polarization Paradox: Why Hyperpartisanship Strengthens Conservatism and Undermines Liberalism." *Breakthrough Journal* 3 (1): 55–69.

Nissenbaum, Helen. 2010. *Privacy in Context: Technology, Policy, and the Integrity of Social Life.* Stanford, CA: Stanford University Press.

Nozick, Robert. 1981. *Philosophical Explanations.* Cambridge, MA: Harvard University Press.

O'Donovan, Caroline. 2014. "Q&A: Tarleton Gillespie Says Algorithms May Be New, But Editorial Calculations Aren't." *Nieman Journalism Lab*, July 8. http://www.niemanlab.org/2014/07/qa-tarleton-gillespie-says-algorithms-may-be-new-but-editorial-calculations-arent/.

O'Hagan, Andrew. 2014. "Ghosting." *London Review of Books.* http://www.lrb.co.uk.

O'Sullivan-Gavin, Susan A., and Michelle A. Amazeen. 2016. "The Advertising Industry in the Social Media Age: The Ethical and Legal Implications of Unsanctioned Rogue or 'Scam' Ads." *Journal of Law, Business & Ethics* 22.

Obama, Barak. 2014. "Transcript of President Obama's Jan. 17 Speech on NSA Reforms." *Washington Post,* January 17. Accessed December 2, 2014. http://www.washingtonpost.com/politics/full-text-of-president-obamas-jan-17-speech-on-nsa-reforms/2014/01/17/fa33590a-7f8c-11e3-9556-4a4bf7bcbd84_story.html.

Oliver, Pamela E., and Daniel J. Myers. 1999. "How Events Enter the Public Sphere: Conflict, Location, and Sponsorship in Local Newspaper Coverage of Public Events." *American Journal of Sociology* 105 (1): 38–87.

Osnos, Peter. 2013. "These Journalists Spent Two Years and $750,000 Covering One Story." *The Atlantic,* October 2. Accessed May 20, 2014. http://www.theatlantic.com/national/archive/2013/10/these-journalists-spent- two-years-and-750-000-covering-one-story/280151/.

Outing, Steve. 2005. "The 11 Layers of Citizen Journalism." *Poynter Online.* Accessed August 11, 2014. http://cdn.agilitycms.com/wacc-global/Images/Galleries/RESOURCES/CitizenJournalism/11-Layers-of-Citizen-Journalism-POYNTER2006.pdf.

Overholser, Geneva. 2004. "The Inadequacy of Objectivity as a Touchstone." *Neiman Reports: Neiman Foundation for Journalism at Harvard,* edited by James Geary. Accessed August 22, 2014. http://www.nieman.harvard.edu/reports/article/100725/The-Inadequacy-of-Objectivity-as-a-Touchstone.aspx.

Packard, Laura. 2013. "How To Grow Your List with Effective Online Advocacy." Accessed August 23, 2014. http://powerthruconsulting.com/blog/how-to-grow-your-list-with-advocacy.

Palfrey, John, and Urs Gasser. 2008. *Born Digital: Understanding the First Generation of Digital Natives.* Philadelphia, PA: Basic Books.

Papacharissi, Zizi. 2002. "The Virtual Sphere: The Internet as a Public Sphere." *New Media and Society* 4 (1): 9–27.

Parekh, Rupal. 2013. "Amid Ford Figo Flap, U.K. Awards Show Applauds Scam Ads," *Advertising Age,* March 27. http://adage.com/article/agency-news/amid-ford-figo-flap-u-k-awards-show-applauds-scam-ads/240559.

Parfitt, Ben. 2010. "Switzerland Passes Violent Games Ban." *MCVUK.com,* March 19. http://www.mcvuk.com/news/read/switzerland-passes-violent- games-ban.

Patel, Kunur. 2009. "Cannes: No Ban for Agencies behind Scam Ads." *Advertising Age,* October 14. http://adage.com/article/agency-news/cannes-art-directors-club-issue-scam-ads-guidelines/139683.

Pathak, Shareen. 2014. "This Agency Wikipedia Entry Reads as an Advertisement . . ." *Digiday.* July 22. http://digiday.com/agencies/agencies-editing-wikipedia-entries.

Patten, Tracey Owen. 2006. "Hey Girl, Am I More than My Hair?: African American Women and Their Struggles with Beauty, Body Image and Hair." *NWSA Journal* 18 (2): 24–51.

Patterson, Phillip, and Lee Wilkins. 2013. *Media Ethics: Issues and Cases.* New York, NY: McGraw-Hill.

Patterson, Scott. 2012. *Dark Pools: The Rise of the Machine Traders and the Rigging of the U.S. Stock Market.* New York: Crown Business.

Pegg, David. 2011. "Revealed: The Wikipedia Pages Changed by Bell Pottinger." *The Bureau of Investigative Journalism.* December 7. http://www.thebureauinvestigates. com/2011/12/07/revealed-the-wikipedia-pages-changed-by-bell-pottinger.

Perez, Sarah. 2008. "Steve Jobs Had No Heart Attack . . . and Citizen Journalism Just Failed." *ReadWriteWeb.* Accessed August 11, 2014. http://readwrite.com/2008/10/03/ steve_jobs_had_no_heart_attack_citizen_journalism_failed.

Perez-Pena, Richard. 2007. "Group Plans to Provide Investigative Journalism." *The New York Times,* October 5. Accessed August 17, 2014. http://www.nytimes. com/2007/10/15/business/media/15publica.html?_r=0.

Petronzio, Matt. 2014. "How Much Is the Average Facebook User Worth? [CHART]." *Mashable,* April 24. Accessed April 24, 2014. http://mashable.com/2014/04/24/ facebook-average-worth-chart/?utm_cid=mash-com-fb-main-link.

Petrow, Steven, and Tiq Milan. 2014. "Civilities: Steven Petrow and GLAAD's Tiq Milan on Transgender Etiquette." *The Washington Post,* July 15. http://live.washingtonpost. com/civilities-201400715.html.

Pierce, Olga, and Jeff Larson. 2011. "How Democrats Fooled California's Redistricting Commission." *ProPublica,* December 21. Accessed November 30, 2014. http://www. propublica.org/article/how-democrats-fooled-californias-redistricting- commission.

Pierce, Tess. 2010. "Singing at the Digital Well: Blogs as Cyberfeminist Sites of Resistance." *Feminist Formations* 22 (3): 196–209.

Pilkington, Ed. 2014. "ProPublica's Richard Tofel: 'Our mission is to end abuses of power'." *The Guardian,* January 26. Accessed September 1, 2014. http://www.theguardian.com/ media/2014/jan/26/propublica-richard-tofel- investigative-journalism.

Pollay, Richard W. 1986. "The Distorted Mirror: Reflections on the Unintended Consequences of Advertising." *Journal of Marketing* 50 (2): 18–36.

Polonsky, Michael J., and David S. Waller. 1995. "Does Winning Advertising Awards Pay?: The Australian Experience." *Journal of Advertising Research* 35 (1): 25–36.

Postman, Neil. 1993. *Technopoly: The Surrender of Culture to Technology.* New York: Vintage Books.

Potter, W. James. 2004. *Theory of Media Literacy: A Cognitive Approach.* Thousand Oaks, CA: Sage.

PR News. October 2014. *PR News' Social Media 20/20 Summit.* August 12. http://www. socialmediasummitsf.com/social-media-summit.

Price, Rob. 2014. "There's Child Porn in the Massive Celebrity Nudes Hack." *The Daily Dot,* January 15. http://www.dailydot.com/news/reddit-fappening-celebgate- mckayla-liz-lee-child-porn.

ProPublica Inc. 2013. "Tackling the Toughest Stories, Five Years On." *ProPublica Annual Report.* Accessed May 21, 2013. http://s3.amazonaws.com/propublica/assets/about/propublica_2013report final.pdf.

Public Relations Society of America. n.d. "Industry Ethics Codes." http://www.prsa.org/aboutprsa/ethics/resources/industryethicscodes.

Pugh, Sheenagh. 2005. *The Democratic Genre: Fan Fiction in a Literary Context.* Bridgend: Seren.

Purchese, Robert. 2010. "Germany Retreats from Violent Games Ban." *Eurogamer.net,* May 21. http://www.eurogamer.net/articles/germany-retreats-from- violent-games-ban.

Quinones, Sam. 2013. "Slaying Casts Light on Hollywood's Transgender Prostitutes." *Los Angeles Times,* February 4. http://articles.latimes.com/2013/feb/04/local/la-me-western-bandit-20130204.

Rafalko, Robert J. 1989. "Corporate Punishment: A Proposal." *Journal of Business Ethics* 8 (12): 917–28.

Ramirez, Ximena. 2011. "Sexting Can Lead to Depressive Symptoms and Self Harm." Care2, January 15. http://www.care2.com/causes/study-finds-that-sexting-can-lead-to-depressive-symptoms-and-self-harm.html.

Rand, Ayn. 1957. *Atlas Shrugged.* New York: Penguin.

Rand, Ayn, and Nathaniel Branden. 1964. *The Virtue of Selfishness: A New Concept of Egoism.* New York: Signet Books.

Raszl, Ivan. 2009. "What's Wrong with Advertising Award Shows?" AdsoftheWorld.com. http://adsoftheworld.com/blog/whats_wrong_with_advertising_award_shows.

Ray, Michael L., and Peter H. Webb. 1974. "Three Learning Theory Traditions and Their Application in Marketing." In *Combined Proceedings: American Marketing Association Conference,* edited by Ronald C. Curham, 100–103. Chicago: American Marketing Association.

Ray, Sheri Graner. 2004. *Gender Inclusive Game Design: Expanding the Market.* Independence, KY: Charles River Media. http://site.ebrary.com/id/10061187.

Reeves, Byron, and Clifford Nass. 1996. *The Media Equation: How People Treat Computers, Television, and New Media Like Real People and Places.* Cambridge: Cambridge University Press.

Reilly, Ryan J. 2014. "Eric Holder: DOJ Reviewing Materials on Whether James Clapper Lied to Congress." *Huffington Post.* http://www.huffingtonpost.com/2014/04/08/james-clapper-lied-to-congress_n_5111408.html.

Reporters Committee for Freedom of the Press. 2014. "Diminished Privacy Rights for Public Figure/Official." Accessed July 28. http://www.rcfp.org/federal-foia-appeals-guide/exemption-6/ii-clearly-unwarranted-invasion-personal-privacy/nature-pri-7.

Republication National Committee. 2014. https://www.gop.com/abolish-the-irs/.

Reynolds, Dame Fiona. 2013. "BBC Executive Summary Workplan." *BBC.co.uk.* http://downloads.bbc.co.uk/aboutthebbc/insidethebbc/howwework/reports/pdf/workplan300513.pdf.

Richards, Neil, and Jonathan King. 2014. "Three Paradoxes of Big Data." *Big Data and Privacy: Making Ends Meet.* Accessed April 27, 2014. http://www.futureofprivacy.org/wp-content/uploads/Big-Data-and-Privacy-Paper-Collection.pdf.

Roberts, Chris. 2012. "Identifying and Defining Values in Media Codes of Ethics." *Journal of Mass Media Ethics* 27 (2): 115–29.

Robin, Donald P., and R. Eric Reidenbach. 1987. "Social Responsibility, Ethics, and Marketing Strategy: Closing the Gap Between Concept and Application." *The Journal of Marketing* 51 (1): 44–58.

Robinson, Sue, and Cathy DeShano. 2011. " 'Anyone Can Know': Citizen Journalism and the Interpretive Community of the Mainstream Press." *Journalism* 12 (8): 963–82. doi:10.1177/1464884911415973.

Rodes, C. 2013. "Caitlin Moran is a Bad Feminist (and a Shitty Fan)." *Jezebel.* http://groupthink.jezebel.com/cailtin-moran-is-a-bad-feminist-and-a-shitty-fan-1483881354.

Romano, Aja. 2013. "Why Fans Are Outraged at Sherlock and Watson Reading Sexy Fanfic." *The Daily Dot.* http://www.dailydot.com/news/sherlock-fanfic-caitlin-moran.

Rosen, Jay. 2008. "Afterword: The People Formerly Known as the Audience." In *Participation and Media Production: Critical Reflections on Content Creation*, edited by Nico Carpentier and Benjamin de Cleen, 163–65. Newcastle, UK: Cambridge Scholars Publishing.

Rosenbush, Steve. 2014. "Facebook Ad Surge Reflects Impact of Big Data." *The CIO Report RSS,* January 29. Accessed March 13, 2014. http://blogs.wsj.com/cio/2014/01/29/facebook-ad-surge-reflects-impact-of-big-data.

Ross, Karen. 1996. *Black and White Media: Black Images in Popular Film and Television.* Cambridge, UK: Polity Press.

Rossiter, John R., and Larry Percy. 1985. "Advertising Communication Models." In *Advances in Consumer Research*, edited by Elizabeth C. Hirschman and Morris B. Holbrook 12 (1): 510–24.

Rotunda, Ronald D. 2004. "Current Proposals for Media Accountability in Light of the First Amendment." *Social Philosophy and Policy* 21 (2): 269–309.

Rotzoll, Kim B., and Clifford G. Christians. 1980. "Advertising Agency Practitioners' Perceptions of Ethical Decisions." *Journalism and Mass Communication Quarterly* 57 (3): 425–30.

Ruesch, Jurgen, and Gregory Bateson. 2006. *Communication: The Social Matrix of Psychiatry.* New Brunswick, NJ: Transaction Publishers.

Ruffin, Oxblood. 2000. "Hacktivismo." *Cult of the Dead Cow.* http://w3.cultdeadcow.com/cms/2000/07/hacktivismo.html.

Ruffin, Oxblood. 2004. "Hacktivism, From Here to There." *Cult of the Dead Cow.* http://www.cultdeadcow.com/cDc_files/cDc-0384.

Ruffin, Oxblood, A. Dwarf Named Warren, and Little Marie. 2000–01. "The Hacktivismo FAQ v1.0." *Cult of the Dead Cow.* http://www.cultdeadcow.com/cDc_files/HacktivismoFAQ.

Ryan, Erin Gloria. 2012. "Is a Pervy High School Teacher Posting 'Sexy' Underage Students' Photos on Reddit?" *Jezebel*, January 15. http://jezebel.com/5944669/ is-a-pervy-high-school-teacher-posting-sexy-underage-students-photos-on-reddit?tag=creepshots.

Salen, Katie, and Eric Zimmerman. 2003. *Rules of Play: Game Design Fundamentals*. Cambridge, MA: MIT Press.

Salmon, Felix. 2012. "How Gawker Wants To Monetize Comments." *Columbia Journalism Review*, May 23. Accessed August 8 2014. http://www.cjr.org/the_audit/ how_gawker_wants_to_monetize_c.php.

Salter, Anastasia, and Bridget Blodgett. 2012. "Hypermasculinity and Dickwolves: The Contentious Role of Women in the New Gaming Public." *Journal of Broadcasting and Electronic Media* 56 (3): 401–16. doi:10.1080/08838151. 2012.705199.

Sandoval, Greg. 2008. "Who's to Blame for Spreading Phony Jobs Story?" *CNET*. Accessed August 11, 2014. http://www.cnet.com/news/whos-to-blame-for-spreading-phony-jobs-story.

Sanford, Carol. 2011. *The Responsible Business: Reimagining Sustainability and Success*. San Francisco, CA: Jossey-Bass.

Sanford, Carol. 2014. *The Responsible Entrepreneur: Four Game-Changing Archetypes for Founders, Leaders, and Impact Investors*. San Francisco, CA: Jossey-Bass.

Sanghani, Radhika. 2014. "Women Beware: Your Private Facebook Photos Could Be Uploaded onto a 'Cleavage' Reddit RThread." *The Telegraph*, January 15. http://www. telegraph.co.uk/women/womens-life/10695517/Women-beware-Your-Facebook-photos-could-be-uploaded-onto-a-cleavage-Reddit-thread.html.

Satterthwaite, Ann. 2001. *Going Shopping: Consumer Choices and Community Consequences*. New Haven, CT: Yale University Press.

Savage, Charlie, and Emmarie Huetteman. 2013. "Manning Sentenced to 35 Years for a Pivotal Leak of U.S. Files." *The New York Times*. http://www.nytimes. com/2013/08/22/us/manning-sentenced-for-leaking-government-secrets.html.

Savat, David. 2009. "Introduction." In *Deleuze and New Technology*, edited by Mark Poster and David Savat, 1–11. Edinburgh: Edinburgh University Press.

Scheer, David. 2008. "Teen Is Said to Have Faked Story About Apple's Jobs." *Bloomberg. com*. Accessed August 11, 2014. http://www.bloomberg.com/apps/news?pid=newsar chive&sid=ahAlYCNB4qVo.

Schmidt, Peter. 2014. "Campus Stung by Controversial Video Moves to Ban Recordings in Class." *Chronicle of Higher Education*. http://chronicle.com/article/Campus-Stung-by-Controversial/145595.

Schudson, Michael. 1978. *Discovering the News: A Social History of American Newspapers*. New York: Basic Books.

Schulte, Stephanie. 2011. "Surfing Feminism's Online Wave: The Internet and the Future of Feminism." *Feminist Studies* 37: 727–44.

Schwabach, Aaron. 2011. *Fan Fiction and Copyright: Outsider Works and Intellectual Property*. London: Ashgate.

Schwartau, Winn. 2000. *Cybershock: Surviving Hackers, Phreakers, Identity Thieves, Internet Terrorists and Weapons of Mass Destruction*. New York: Thunder's Mouth Press.

Schweitzer, John C., and J. B. Hester. 1992. "The Importance of Winning Advertising Award Shows." *Southwestern Mass Communication* 7(1): 55–66.

Selby, Jenn. 2014. "Ricky Gervais Backtracks after 'Victim Blaming' Tweet on 4Chan Nude Celebrity Photo Leaks." *The Independent*, January 15. http://www.independent.co.uk/news/people/ricky-gervais-backtracks-after-victim-blaming-tweet-on-4chan-nude-celebrity-photo-leaks-9704497.html.

Selnow, Gary. 2000. "Internet Ethics." In *Political Communication Ethics: An Oxymoron?*, edited by Robert E. Denton, 203–40. Westport, CT: Greenwood Publishing Group.

Shafer, Jack. 2007. "What Do Herbert and Marion Sandler Want?" *Slate*, October 15. Accessed August 17, 2014. http://www.slate.com/articles/news_and_politics/press_box/2007/10/what_ do_herbert_and_marion_sandler_want.html.

Shannon, Claude, and Warren Weaver. 1963. *The Mathematical Theory of Communication*, Urbana, IL: University of Illinois Press.

Sicart, Miguel. 2005. "Game, Player, Ethics: A Virtue Ethics Approach to Computer Games." *International Review of Information Ethics* 4 (12): 13–18.

Sicart, Miguel. 2011. *The Ethics of Computer Games*. Cambridge, MA: MIT Press.

Siddique, Haroon, and Matthew Weaver. 2010. "US Embassy Cables Culprit Should Be Executed, Says Mike Huckabee." *The Guardian*. http://www.theguardian.com/world/2010/dec/01/us-embassy-cables-executed-mike-huckabee.

Siebert, Fred S., Theodore Peterson, and Wilbur Schramm. 1963. *Four Theories of the Press*. Urbana, IL: University of Illinois Press.

Siebler, Kay. 2012. "Transgender Transitions: Sex/Gender Binaries in the Digital Age." *Journal of Gay and Lesbian Mental Health* 16 (1): 74–99.

Sifry, Micah. 2014. *WikiLeaks and the Age of Transparency*. New Haven: Yale University Press.

Signorile, Michelangelo. 2009. *Queer in America: Sex, the Media, and the Closets of Power*. Madison: University of Wisconsin Press.

Singer, Jane, and Ian Ashman. 2009. "'Comment Is Free, but Facts Are Sacred': User-generated Content and Ethical Constructs at the *Guardian*." *Journal of Mass Media Ethics* 24 (1): 3–21.

Skornia, Harry J. 1965. *Television and Society*. New York: McGraw-Hill.

Slavin, Kevin. 2011. "How Algorithms Shape Our World." *TED Talks*. http://www.ted.com/talks/kevin_slavin_how_algorithms_shape_our_world.html.

Smith, Evan. 2013. "Chill, Self-Appointed Integrity Cops." *NeimanLab*, December 18. Accessed December 2, 2014. http://www.niemanlab.org/author/esmith/.

Smythe, Dallas. 2012. "On the Audience Commodity and its Work." In *Media and Cultural Studies: Keyworks (Second Edition)*, edited by Meenakshi Gigi Durham and Douglas Kellner, 185–204. Malden, MA: Blackwell Publishers.

Society of Professional Journalists Code of Ethics. 2014. Accessed August 19, 2014. http://www.spj.org/ethics_code.asp.

Solove, Daniel J. 2004. *The Digital Person: Technology and Privacy in the Information Age*. New York, NY: New York University Press.

Solove, Daniel J. 2007. *The Future of Reputation: Gossip, Rumor, and Privacy on the Internet*. New Haven, CT: Yale University Press.

Solove, Daniel J. 2008. *Understanding Privacy*. Cambridge, MA: Harvard University Press.

Solove, Daniel, J. 2011. *Nothing to Hide: The False Tradeoff Between Privacy and Security*. New Haven, CT: Yale University Press.

Stampler, Laura. 2013. "Unilever Apologizes For Ad Comparing Coming Out To Shooting Dad In The Heart." *Business Insider*, September 3. http://www.businessinsider.com/ad-compares-coming-out-to-shooting-your-dad-in-the-heart-2013-9.

Starbucks Corporation Fiscal 2013 Annual Report. 2013. http://news.starbucks.com/uploads/documents/Starbucks_Fiscal_2013_Annual_Report_-_FINAL.PDF.

Steadman, Ian. 2012. "Anonymous Launches #OpPedoChat, Targets Paedophiles." *Wired*, July 10. http://www.wired.co.uk/news/archive/2012-07/10/anonymous-Targets-paedophiles.

Stein, Louisa. 2011. "On (Not) Hosting the Session that Killed the Term 'Acafan'." *Antenna*. http://blog.commarts.wisc.edu/2011/03/18/on-not-hosting-the-session-that-killed-the-term-acafan/accessed 18 November 2013.

Steiner, Christopher. 2012. *Automate This: How Algorithms Came to Rule the World*. New York: Penguin Group.

Steinmetz, Katy. 2014. "The Transgender Tipping Point." *TIME*, May 29. *www.time.com/135480/transgender-tipping-point*.

Stelter, Brian. 2014. "Buzzfeed Raises Another $50 Million to Fund Expansion." *CNN Money*, August 11. Accessed December 2, 2014. http://money.cnn.com/2014/08/10/media/buzzfeed-funding/index.html.

Stephens, Dionne P., and Layli D. Phillips. 2003. "Freaks, Gold Diggers, Divas, and Dykes: The Sociohistorical Development of Adolescent African American Women's Sexual Scripts." *Sexuality and Culture* 7 (1): 3–49.

Stewart, Hamish. 2001. "Harms, Wrongs, and Set-Backs in Feinberg's Moral Limits of the Criminal Law." *Buffalo Criminal Law* 5 (1): 47–67.

Stone, Alluquère R. 1991. "Will the Real Body Please Stand Up? Boundary Stories About Virtual Culture." In *Cyberspace: First Steps*, 81–118. Cambridge, MA: MIT Press.

Stone, Geoffrey R. 2012. "WikiLeaks and the First Amendment." *Federal Communications Law Journal* 64 (3): 477–91.

Streitfeld, David. 2013. "Google Glass Picks Up Early Signal: Keep Out." *New York Times*, May 6. http://www.nytimes.com/2013/05/07/technology/personaltech/google-glass-picks-up-early-signal-keep-out.html?nl=todaysheadlines.

Stroud, Natalie Jomini. 2010. "Polarization and Partisan Selective Exposure." *Journal of Communication* 60 (3): 556–76.

Stroud, Scott R. 2014. "The Dark Side of the Online Self: A Pragmatist Critique of the Growing Plague of Revenge Porn." *Journal of Mass Media Ethics* 29 (3): 168–83.

Stroud, Scott R., and Danee Pye. 2013. "Kant on Unsocial Sociability and the Ethics of Social Blogging." *New Agendas in Communication: Ethics in Communication Professions*, edited by Minette E. Drumwright, 41–64. New York: Routledge.

Sundén, Jenny. 2003. *Material Virtualities: Approaching Online Textual Embodiment.* New York, NY: Peter Lang.

Sussman, Gerald. 1997. *Communication, Technology, and Politics in the Information Age.* Thousand Oaks, CA: Sage Publications.

Sweeting, Paul. 2005. "Hot Coffee Burns." *Video Business* 25 (30): 14.

Sweney, Mark. 2014. "YouTubers Ads for Oreo Banned for Not Making Clear Purpose of Videos." *The Guardian.* November 26. http://www.theguardian.com/media/2014/nov/26/youtube-ad-oreo-banned-advertising-lick-race.

Tadena, Nathalie. 2014. "FTC's Charges Against Deutsch LA Seen as a Twitter Wake Up Call for Industry." *The Wall Street Journal CMO Today.* November 28. http://blogs.wsj.com/cmo/2014/11/28/ftcs-charges-against-deutsch-la-seen-as-a-twitter-wake-up-call-for-industry.

Takahashi, Dean. 2005. "Ethics of Game Design." *Gamasutra.com.* http://webdocs.cs.ualberta.ca/~games/299/Gamasutra.pdf.

Taube, Aaron. 2013. "10 Ads that Companies Were Forced to Apologize for in 2013." *Business Insider,* December 12. http://www.businessinsider.com/10-ads-that-companies-were-forced-to-apologize-for-in-2013-2013-12.

Taylor, Charles. 1989. *Sources of the Self: The Making of Modern Identity.* Cambridge: Cambridge University Press.

Taylor, T. L. 2006. *Play Between Worlds.* Cambridge, MA: MIT Press.

Tenore, Mallary Jean. 2011. "Journalists Leave Full Time Jobs to Work for Texas Tribune, Embrace Uncertainty." *Poynter.org,* November 3. Accessed August 18, 2014. http://www.poynter.org/latest-news/top-stories/98467/journalists-leave-full-time-jobs-to-work-for-texas-tribune-embrace-uncertainty.

Terranova, Tiziana. 2000. "Free Labor: Producing Culture for the Digital Economy." *Social Text* 18 (2): 33–58. http://muse.jhu.edu/journals/soc/summary/v018/18.2terranova.html.

Texas Tribune, Inc. 2014a. "Code of Ethics." *The Texas Tribune.* Accessed August 18. https://www.texastribune.org/ethics.

Texas Tribune, Inc. 2014b. "Donors and Members." *The Texas Tribune.* Accessed August 18. http://www.texastribune.org/support-us/donors-and-members.

Texas Tribune, Inc. 2014c. "Media Kit." *The Texas Tribune.* Accessed May 25. http://s3.amazonaws.com/static.texastribune.org/media-kit/TheTexasTribune-MediaKit-Jan13.pdf.

Thiel-Stern, Shayla. 2009. "Femininity out of Control on the Internet: A Critical Analysis of Media Representations of Gender, Youth, and MySpace.com in International News Discourses." *Girlhood Studies* 2 (1): 20–39.

Thierer, Adam. 2014. "Privacy in a Post-Regulatory World: Lessons from the Online Safety Debates." *Big Data and Privacy: Making Ends Meet*. Accessed April 27, 2014. http://www.futureofprivacy.org/wp-content/uploads/Big-Data-and-Privacy-Paper-Collection.pdf.

This American Life. n.d. "About Us." *WBEZ Chicago Public Radio*. Accessed July 26, 2014. http://www.thisamericanlife.org/about.

Thomas, Douglas. 2002. *Hacker Culture*. Minneapolis: University of Minnesota Press.

Thomson, Katy. 2014. "Chip Shop Awards." *The Drum*. http://www.thedrum.com/award/chip-shop-awards.

Thorsen, Tor. 2009. "Modern Warfare 2 Massacre 'Not Representative of Overall Experience'—Activision." *Gamespot.com*, October 28. http://www.gamespot.com/xbox360/action/modernwarfare2/news.html?sid=6238331.

Thurer, Shari. 2004. *The Myths of Motherhood: How Culture Reinvents the Good Mother*. New York, NY: Penguin Books.

Tilton, Shane. 2012. *First Year Students in a Foreign Fabric: A Triangulation Study on Facebook as a Method of Coping/Adjustment*. OH: Ohio University.

Traynor, Ian, and Paul Lewis. 2013. "Merkel Compared NSA to Stasi in Heated Encounter with Obama." *The Guardian*. http://www.theguardian.com/world/2013/dec/17/merkel-compares-nsa-stasi-obama.

Truitt, Jos. 2014. "The Media Does Not Have the Power to Decide the Existence of Trans People." *The Guardian*, June 4. http://www.theguardian.com/commentisfree/2014/jun/04/media-trans-people-chicago-sun-times-laverne-cox.

Turkle, Sherry. 1984. *The Second Self*. New York: Simon and Schuster.

Turkle, Sherry. 1995. *Life on the Screen: Identity in the Age of the Age of Internet*. New York: Simon & Schuster.

Vaidhyanathan, Siva. 2011. *The Googlization of Everyting (And Why We Should Worry)*. Los Angeles, CA: University of California Press.

Vallor, Shannon. 2011. "Flourishing on Facebook: Virtue Friendship & New Social Media." *Ethics and Information Technology* 14 (3): 185–99.

Van Aelst, Peter, and Stefaan Walgrave. 2002. "New Media, New Movements? The Role of the Internet in Shaping the Anti-Globalization Movement." *Information Communication & Society* 5 (4): 465–93.

Van den Hoven, Jeroen. 2001. "Privacy and the Varieties of Informational Wrongdoing." In *Readings in CyberEthics*, edited by Richard A. Spinello and Herman T. Tavani, 488–500. Sudbury, MA: Jones and Bartlett Publishers.

Van Dijck, José. 2009. "Users Like You? Theorizing Agency in User-Generated Content." *Media, Culture, and Society* 31 (1): 41–58.

Van Dijk, Teun A. 1987. *Communicating Racism: Ethnic Prejudice in Thought and Talk*. Thousand Oaks, CA: Sage Publications, Inc.

Vivienne, Sonja, and Jean Burgess. 2012. "The Digital Storyteller's Stage: Queer Everyday Activists Negotiating Privacy and Publicness." *Journal of Broadcasting and Electronic Media* 56 (3): 362–77.

Vranica, Suzanne. 2014. "A 'Crisis' in Online Ads: One-Third of Traffic Is Bogus." *Wall Street Journal*, March 23. http://online.wsj.com/articles/SB1000142405270230402630 4579453253860786362.

Wagner, R. Polk. 2003. "Information Wants to Be Free: Intellectual Property and the Mythologies of Control." *Columbia Law Review* 103 (4): 995–1034.

Wahl-Jorgensen, Karin, Andrew Williams, and Claire Wardle. 2010. "Audience Views on User-Generated Content: Exploring the Value of News from the Bottom up." *Northern Lights* 8 (1): 177–94. doi:10.1386/nl.8.177_1.

Walkley, A. J. 2014. "2014 Transgender Violence Statistics Sobering Thus Far." *Huffington Post*, May 12. http://www.huffingtonpost.com/aj-walkley/2014-transgender-violence_b_5298554.html.

Walsh, Michael. 2012. "Teacher Fired after Suggestive Photos of Unsuspecting Female Students Spotted on Reddit's Lurid Creepshots Forum, Investigation Underway." *New York Daily News*, January 15. http://www.nydailynews.com/news/national/teacher-fired-suggestive-photos-unsuspecting-female-students-spotted-reddit-lurid-creepshot-forum-investigation-underway-article-1.1170726.

Walzer, Michael. 1984. *Spheres of Justice: A Defense of Pluralism and Equality*. New York: Basic Books.

Ward, Stephen. 2009. "Researching Ethics." School of Journalism and Mass Communication University of Wisconsin-Madison. Madison: Center for Journalism Ethics. Accessed Aug. 1, 2014. http://www.journalismethics.info/research_ethics/approaches_to_ethics.htm.

Wedeman, Ben. 2014. "Videos Show Brutality of Radical Group ISIS in Syria." *CNN. com*. http://www.cnn.com/2014/02/17/world/meast/syria-isis-leader-videos.

Weiland, Morgan. 2013. "Congress and the Justice Department's Dangerous Attempts to Define 'Journalist' Threaten to Exclude Bloggers." *Electronic Frontier Foundation*. https://www.eff.org/deeplinks/2013/07/congress-and-justice-depts-dangerous-attempts-define-journalist-threaten-exclude.

Wentz, Laurel. 2001. "Ghosts of Cannes." *Advertising Age*, June 11. http://adage.com/article/news/ghosts-cannes/54509.

Wentz, Laurel. 2009. "9/11 Ad for WWF Causes Tsunami of a Crisis for DDB Brazil." *Advertising Age*, September 2. http://adage.com/article/global-news/9-11-ad-wwf-tsunami-a-crisis-ddb-brasil/138775/.

Wentz, Laurel. 2013a. "JWT Entered Sexually Offensive Ford Ads in India's Top Awards Show." *Advertising Age*, March 27. http://adage.com/article/global-news/jwt-entered-sexually-offensive-ford-ads-india-awards-show/240562/.

Wentz, Laurel. 2013b. "Is the Ad-Awards Race Crushing the Client?" *Advertising Age,* April 1. http://adage.com/article/agency-news/ad-awards-race-crushing-client/240640/.

Wentz, Laurel. 2013c. "Publicis Hires Bobby Pawar, Creative Behind Scandalous Ford Figo Ad." *Advertising Age,* May 31. http://adage.com/article/global-news/publicis-hires-bobby-pawar-ford-figo-creative/241817/.

Wentz, Laurel, and Claudia Penteado. 2011. "Fake Kia Ad Gets 5 Brazilian Creatives Banned From 2012 Cannes Festival." *Advertising Age,* July 21. http://adage.com/article/global-news/fake-kia-ad-5-brazilian-creatives-banned-cannes/228855/.

West, Carolyn M. 1995. "Mammy, Sapphire, and Jezebel: Historical Images of Black Women and their Implications for Psychotherapy." *Psychotherapy: Theory, Research, Practice, Training* 32 (3): 455–66.

West, Lindy. 2014. "Teen Girl Raped on Field Trip, Treated Horribly by Seattle High School." *Jezebel,* July 23. Accessed August 8, 2014. http://jezebel.com/teen-girl-raped-on-field-trip-treated-horribly-by-seat-1609763671/all.

Westin, Alan F. 1967. *Privacy and Freedom.* New York: Atheneum.

Wetboek van Strafrecht, article 240a. 2004. http://www.wetboek-online.nl/wet/Wetboek%20van%20Strafrecht/240a.html.

Wheaton, Ken. 2013. "Scam Ads Don't Boost Creativity; They Damage Brands, Hurt Agency Credibility." *Advertising Age,* March 31. http://adage.com/article/ken-wheaton/advertising-scam-ads-damage-brands-hurt-agency-credibility/240639/.

Wiener, Norbert. 1988. *The Human Use of Human Beings: Cybernetics and Society,* Boston, MA: Da Capo Press.

Wilding, Faith. 1998. "Where is the Feminism in Cyberfeminism?" *n.paradoxo* 2: 1–12. http://www.ktpress.co.uk/pdf/vol2_npara_6_13_Wilding.pdf.

Wilkins, Lee, and Clifford G. Christians. 2009. *The Handbook of Mass Media Ethics.* New York, NY: Routledge.

Williamson, Judith. 2005. *Decoding Advertisements: Ideology and Meaning in Advertising.* New York: Marion Boyers Publishers.

Wilson, P. Eddy. 1994. "Corporations, Minors, and Other Innocents—A Reply from R. E. Ewin." *Journal of Business Ethics* 13 (10): 761–74.

Winner, Langdon. 1977. *Autonomous Technology: Technics-out-of-Control as a Theme in Political Thought.* Cambridge, MA: MIT Press.

Winograd, Terry. 1990. "Thinking Machines: Can There Be? Are We?" In *The Foundations of Artificial Intelligence: A Sourcebook,* edited by David Partridge and Yorick Wilks, 167–89. Cambridge: Cambridge University Press.

WOMMA. 2013. "Word of Mouth Marketing Association Guide to Best Practices for Transparency and Disclosure in Digital, Social, & Mobile Marketing." November. http://www.slideshare.net/WOMMAChicago/womma-disclosure-guides-final-bd-approved-11813.

WOMMA. 2014a. "Ethical Word of Mouth Marketing Disclosure Best Practices in Today's Regulatory Environment." January 13. http://www.slideshare.net/WOMMAChicago/womma-ethics-committee-white-paper-2014.

WOMMA. 2014b. "Prioritizing Ethics in Word of Mouth Marketing." Workshop, November 17. http://wommasummit.com/register/pre-summit-legal-ethics-workshop/.

Wood, Jennifer F. 2003. "House Negro Versus Field Negro: The Inscribed Image of Race in Television News Presentations of African-American Identity." In *Say it Loud!*, edited by Robin R. Means Coleman, 95–114. New York: Routledge.

Wray, Stefan. 1999. "On Electronic Civil Disobedience." *Peace Review* 11 (1): 107–11.

Yarbrough, Marilyn, and Crystal Bennett. 1999. "Cassandra and the Sistahs: The Peculiar Treatment of African American Women in the Myth of Women as Liars." *The Journal of Gender, Race, and Justice* 3 (2): 625–57.

Yes Men, The. 2004. *The Yes Men: The True Story of the End of the World Trade Organization.* New York: Disinformation.

Your Mom Hates Dead Space 2. 2011. http://www.youtube.com/watch?v=nKkPFDEiC6 Qandfeature=youtube_gdata_player.

Zagal, José P. 2011. *The Videogame Ethics Reader.* San Diego: Cognella Academic Publishing.

Zelizer, Barbie. 1993. "Journalists as Interpretive Communities." *Critical Studies in Media Communication* 10 (3): 219–37.

Zetter, Kim. 2009. "Parents of Dead Teen Sue School Over Sexting Images." *Wired*, January 15. http://www.wired.com/2009/12/sexting-suit/.

Zubernis, Lynn, and Katherine Larsen. 2012. *Fandom at the Crossroads: Celebration, Shame and Fan/producer Relationships.* Newcastle upon Tyne, UK: Cambridge Scholars.

Notes on Contributors

Michelle A. Amazeen (PhD, Temple University) is an assistant professor of advertising at Rider University in Lawrenceville, New Jersey. She received her MS and BS in Advertising from the University of Illinois at Urbana-Champaign. Michelle's research interests primarily involve advertising, mis/disinformation, and corrections. She has examined the prevalence of inaccuracies in political advertising and how political actors are held accountable for their claims. She has also explored the authenticity of strategic communication efforts in the mediated information environment, including the alignment of corporate social responsibility campaigns with advertising. Her work has appeared in publications such as *Journal of Business Ethics*, *Media, Culture & Society*, and *Social Semiotics*. She has forthcoming articles in *Journalism and Mass Communication Quarterly* and *Journal of Political Marketing*. She recently completed a report on fact-checking for the New America Foundation, a nonpartisan, public policy center in Washington, D.C. and is currently engaged in fact-checking research for the American Press Institute.

Mary Grace Antony is an assistant professor in communication studies at Schreiner University. She received a PhD in communication from the Edward R. Murrow College of Communication at Washington State University. Her research interests include globalization, media, culture, and new media technologies. Her research has appeared in *Journal of Intercultural Communication Research*, *Journal of International and Intercultural Communication*, *Communication Review*, and *New Media & Society*.

Molly Bandonis holds an MA in media and cinema studies from DePaul University. She currently works with Digital Youth Network in Chicago, Illinois, a nonprofit organization that focuses on media literacy research and education. She has written on topics ranging from sexploitation in the media to feminist pedagogical tools and has presented work at the Gender Matters conference and the Pop Culture Association/American Culture Association National Conference.

Lucy Bennett completed her PhD in online fandom at JOMEC, Cardiff University, where she is currently a postdoctoral researcher. Her work on fan cultures appears in journals such as *New Media & Society, Journal of Fandom Studies, Transformative Works and Cultures, Social Semiotics, Continuum, Cinema Journal, Celebrity Studies* and *Participations*. She is the co-founder and co-chair of the *Fan Studies Network*. She is also co-editor, along with Bertha Chin and Bethan Jones, of *Crowdfunding the Future: Media Industries, Ethics and Digital Society* (Peter Lang, 2015).

Tom Bivins, professor & John L. Hulteng Chair in Media Ethics, is author or coauthor of textbooks on mass media ethics, public relations writing, newsletter publication, advertising, and publication design and writing. His professional background includes stints in radio, television, editorial cartooning, and public relations.

Paul Booth is an associate professor at DePaul University. He is the author of *Game Play: Paratextuality in Contemporary Board Games* (Bloomsbury, 2015), *Playing Fans: Negotiating Fandom and Media in the Digital Age* (University of Iowa Press, 2015), *Digital Fandom: New Media Studies* (Peter Lang, 2010), and *Time on TV: Temporal Displacement and Mashup Television* (Peter Lang, 2012). He is the editor of *Fan Phenomena: Doctor Who* (Intellect, 2013). He is currently enjoying a cup of coffee.

Shira Chess is an assistant professor of mass media arts at the University of Georgia in the Grady College of Journalism and Mass Communication. Her research on digital culture, gaming, and gender has been published in several scholarly journals, including the *Journal of Broadcasting and Electronic Media, Critical Studies in Media Communication, Feminist Media Studies,* and *New Media and Society.* Her coauthored book, *Folklore, Horror Stories, and the Slender Man: The Development of an Internet Mythology* was published by Palgrave Pivot (2014).

Bertha Chin is Lecturer of Communication at Swinburne University of Technology. Her work appears in journals such as *Social Semiotics, Journal of Science Fiction Film and Television, Transformative Works and Cultures,* and *Participations.* She is co-editor of *Crowdfunding the Future: Media Industries, Ethics and Digital Society* (2015, Peter Lang), and a special issue on the topic of crowdfunding with *New Media & Society.* She is also board member of the *Fan Studies Network,* and co-director of the World Star Wars Audience Project.

Joe Cutbirth directs the journalism program at Manhattan College and is a fellow at the Manhattan College Center for Ethics. He holds a doctorate in communications from Columbia University, a master's in communication, culture & technology from Georgetown University, and a bachelor's in journalism from the University of Texas at Austin.

Amber Davisson is an Assistant Professor of Communication at Keene State College. She is the author of *Lady Gaga and the Remaking of Celebrity Culture* (McFarland, 2013). Her interdisciplinary scholarship on identity, politics, and digital technology has appeared in such journals as *Rhetoric & Public Affairs*, *Journal of Media & Digital Literacy, Journal of Visual Literacy*, and the *American Communication Journal*.

Charles M. Ess is Professor in Media Studies, Department of Media and Communication, University of Oslo. Ess has received awards for excellence in teaching and scholarship, and held several guest professorships in Europe and Scandinavia (most recently as guest professor, Philosophy Department, University of Vienna, 2013–14). Ess has published extensively in: information and computing Ethics (e.g., *Digital Media Ethics*, 2nd edition, Polity Press, 2013) internet studies (e.g., with Mia Consalvo, *The Handbook of Internet Studies*, Wiley-Blackwell, 2011; with William Dutton, "The Rise of Internet Studies," *New Media and Society* 15 (5), 2013); and internet research ethics (e.g., with Hallvard Fossheim, "Personal Data: Changing Selves, Changing Privacy Expectations," in: M. Hildebrandt, K. O'Hara, M. Waidner, eds., *Digital Enlightenment Forum Yearbook* 2013: *The Value of Personal Data*, 40–55, IOS Amsterdam, 2013). Ess emphasizes cross-cultural approaches to media, communication, and ethics, focusing on virtue ethics and its applications to mediated human lives (e.g., "The Good Life: Selfhood and Virtue Ethics in the Digital Age," in Helen Wang (ed.), *Communication and the Good Life* (ICA Themebook, 2014): Peter Lang, 2015). Ess directs the Centre for Research in Media Innovations (CeRMI—http://www.hf.uio.no/imk/english/research/center/media-innovations/) and edits *The Journal of Media Innovations* (https://www.journals.uio.no/index.php/TJMI/).

Sam Ford is Vice-President of Innovation and Engagement with Fusion, as well as an affiliate with the MIT Program in Comparative Media Studies/Writing and the Popular Culture Studies Program at Western Kentucky University. Previously, he was Director of Audience Engagement at strategic communications and marketing firm Peppercomm—where he conducted the work on which his essay for this book is focused. Sam is coauthor, with Henry Jenkins and Joshua Green, of *Spreadable Media: Creating Value and Meaning in a Network Culture*, and coeditor, with Abigail De Kosnik and C. Lee Harrington, of *The Survival of Soap Opera: Transformations for a New Media Era*. He has written on issues of ethics in marketing and communication for publications like *Harvard Business Review*, *Advertising Age*, and *Fast Company*, among other industry publications. During his time with Peppercomm, he was on the board of directors for the Word of Mouth Marketing Association, where he also served as part of the Ethics Committee.

Ryan Gillespie (PhD, University of Southern California) is a lecturer at the University of California, Los Angeles. His primary areas of study are in ethics (including bioethics and metaethics), religion, and rhetoric, with additional work in media culture, technology, and political economy. His work has been published in *Philosophy & Rhetoric*, *Communication, Culture & Critique*, the *International Journal of Communication*, and the *Journal of Cultural Economy*, as well as in five edited book volumes.

David J. Gunkel is an award-winning educator, scholar and author, specializing in the study of information and communication technology with a focus on ethics. Formally educated in philosophy and media studies, his teaching and research synthesize the hype of high technology with the rigor and insight of contemporary critical analysis. He is the author of over forty scholarly articles, has written five influential books including the award-wining *The Machine Question* (MIT, 2012), lectured and delivered award-winning papers throughout North and South America and Europe, is the managing editor and co-founder of the *International Journal of Žižek Studies* and co-editor of the Indiana University Press series in Digital Game Studies. He currently holds the position of professor in the Department of Communication at Northern Illinois University (United States), and his teaching has been recognized with numerous awards, including NIU's Excellence in Undergraduate Teaching and the prestigious Presidential Teaching Professor.

Luis E. Hestres (PhD, American University) is an assistant professor of communication at the University of Texas at San Antonio, where he teaches courses on digital media production, digital politics and advocacy, and media theory. His research focuses on the intersection of technology, political communication and mobilization, internet freedom, and social change. His work has been published in *New Media & Society*, the *International Journal of Communication*, and *Environmental Politics*, and he has presented at the International Communication Association annual conference and the TPRC conference, among others.

Bethan Jones is a PhD candidate in the Department of Theatre, Film and Television Studies at Aberystwyth University. Her thesis examines the intersections between anti-fandom and fandom, and the role that affect plays in negotiating the boundaries of fannish behavior. Bethan has written on a range of topics relating to gender, fandom, and digital media and has been published in *Participations, Transformative Works and Cultures, Sexualities* and the *Journal of Adaptation in Film and Performance*. She recently coedited a special issue of *New Media & Society* on crowdfunding.

Brett Lunceford (PhD, Pennsylvania State University) is a rhetorician who has been studying hackers and hacktivism for almost ten years, beginning with his dissertation research. And no, although he used to work in the internet industry, he isn't a hacker. He isn't even a script kiddie. His current work focuses on the intersections between the body, sexuality, and technology. He is the author of the book *Naked Politics: Nudity, Political Action, and the Rhetoric of the Body* and more than thirty journal articles and book chapters. His work has appeared in such journals as *Communication Law Review, ETC: A Review of General Semantics, Explorations in Media Ecology, Journal of Contemporary Rhetoric, Media History Monographs, Review of Communication*, and *Theology & Sexuality*. He is the current editor of *the Journal of Contemporary Rhetoric* and serves as vice president-elect of the Media Ecology Association.

Susan A. O'Sullivan-Gavin (JD, Seton Hall University School of Law) is an associate professor of legal studies in the Department of Marketing, Advertising and Legal Studies in the College of Business at Rider University in Lawrenceville, New Jersey. She earned her BA from Seton Hall University and her Juris Doctor from Seton Hall University School of Law. She was previously a faculty associate in the Legal Studies Department at Seton Hall University for fifteen years. Her teaching portfolio includes Social and Legal Environment of Business, Uniform Commercial Code, Corporate Social Responsibility, and Legal and Ethical Issues in Business. Her current research interests and publications include regulation, social media, employment law, and the impact of information technology on course delivery and curriculum design. She is a coauthor of *The Legal Environment of Contemporary Business, 3rd Ed.*

Matthew Pittman is a media studies PhD student in the School of Journalism & Communication at the University of Oregon. His research on social media, television binge-watching, and offline well-being has been published in various journals, and he has presented work at conferences for the MEA, NCA, and ICA. He is a television critic for Reel Spirituality with Fuller Theological Seminary's Brehm Center and has contributed to encyclopedias, books, and manuals on big data and online research. Matthew is also an adjunct professor at Northwest Christian University. He gets much more radical than Tom Bivins and his website is www.matthewpittman.net.

Ryan Rogers is an assistant professor at Marist College. He has earned a BA from the University of Notre Dame, an MA from the S.I. Newhouse School of Public Communications at Syracuse University, and a PhD in mass communication from the University of North Carolina at Chapel Hill. Ryan's professional experiences at media organizations include stints with FOX Sports, ESPN, the NFL Network, and with Warner Brothers on a Harry Potter film.

Scott R. Stroud is an associate professor in the Department of Communication Studies at the University of Texas at Austin. Trained in both the fields of philosophy and communication, his research focuses on pragmatism, the history of rhetoric, and communication ethics. His work on the ethics of revenge pornography has been recognized by awards from the Communication Ethics Division of the National Communication Association and the Moody College of Communication (University of Texas at Austin). He is the author of the books *John Dewey and the Artful Life* (Penn State Press, 2011) and *Kant and the Promise of Rhetoric* (Penn State Press, 2014), as well as *A Practical Guide to Ethics: Living and Leading with Integrity* (with Rita Manning, Westview Press, 2008).

J. J. Sylvia IV is a PhD student in the Communication, Rhetoric, and Digital Media program at North Carolina State University. He also holds an MA in philosophy from The University of Southern Mississippi. His research interests include the philosophy of communication, big data, affirmative critical theory, and digital pedagogy. His research appears in *The Speech & Theatre Association* *of Missouri Journal, Journal of Interdisciplinary Studies in Education*, and the edited collection *Ethical Issues in E-Business: Models and Frameworks* (Business Science Reference, 2010).

Ryan J. Thomas is an assistant professor of Journalism Studies at the Missouri School of Journalism. He received his PhD from the Edward R. Murrow College of Communication at Washington State University. His research on the relationship between journalism and democracy at a time of uncertainty in the journalism field has been published in *Journalism Studies, Journalism Practice, New Media & Society*, and *Digital Journalism*.

Shane Tilton (PhD, Ohio University) is an assistant professor of multimedia journalism at Ohio Northern University. He has spoken more than forty times at a variety of conferences and public forums dealing with issues regarding new media and its social impact. Dr. Tilton was the former chair of the Communication and the Future interest division (National Communication Association) and Two-Year/Small School interest division (Broadcast Education Association). In 2013, Dr. Tilton earned the Kenneth Harwood Outstanding Dissertation Award from the Broadcast Education Association for the best doctoral dissertation in the field of broadcasting and electronic media.

Erin Watley is a PhD candidate in the Communication & Journalism department at the University of New Mexico, where she was a recipient of the Winrock Minority Doctoral Fellowship from 2012 to 2014. The concentration for her program of study is intercultural communication and media studies. Currently, Erin teaches courses on intercultural communication and media history while also working for the UNM Office of Dispute Resolution, Ombuds Services for Faculty. She has also taught public speaking, business communication, and intergroup dialogue. Erin completed her MA in Communication at the University of Illinois, Urbana-Champaign in 2012 where she was a Graduate College fellow from 2010 to 2011. In 2007 she completed her BA at the University of Maryland, College Park, having majored in American Studies and Sociology. The Maryland suburbs of Washington, D.C. are where Erin grew up and the culturally diverse environment played a key role in developing her interest in social issues connected to diversity and identity that are the foundation of her academic pursuits. Erin's research revolves around the improvement of intercultural communication through dialogue, resistant media portrayals, public pedagogy, and social justice.

Susan Wildermuth is an associate professor in the Department of Communication at the University of Wisconsin–Whitewater. She has a master's degree and PhD from the University of Minnesota, Minneapolis with an emphasis in intercultural communication and computer-mediated communication. She received the UWW College of Arts and Communications top awards for both teaching and research. She teaches courses in public speaking, intercultural communication, interpersonal communication, research methods, communication theory, and computer-mediated communication. Her research interests include the scholarship of teaching and learning, intercultural communication and diversity, computer-mediated relationships, and visual communication.

Index